MATTERHORN

The Operational History of the XX Bomber Command

from India and China

1944–1945

MATTERHORN

The Operational History of the XX Bomber Command

from India and China

1944–1945

Terry M. Mays

Schiffer Publishing Ltd

4880 Lower Valley Road • Atglen, PA 19310

Other Schiffer Books by the Author:
Night Hawks and Black Widows: 13th Air Force Night Fighters in the Southand Southwest Pacific • 1943-1945, ISBN: 978-0-7643-3344-6

Other Schiffer Books on Related Subjects:
Chennault's Forgotten Warriors: The Saga of the 308th Bomb Group in China, Carroll Glines, ISBN: 978-0-88740-809-0

Famine, Sword, and Fire: The Liberation of Southwest China in World War II, Daniel Jackson, ISBN: 978-0-7643-4838-9

Library of Congress Control Number: 2016933017

Cover design by Justin Watkinson
Type set in Times New Roman
ISBN: 978-0-7643-5074-0
Printed in China

Published by Schiffer Publishing, Ltd.
4880 Lower Valley Road
Atglen, PA 19310
Phone: (610) 593-1777; Fax: (610) 593-2002
E-mail: Info@schifferbooks.com
Web: www.schifferbooks.com

For My Dad

Senior Master Sgt. Edgar M. Mays (USAF retired)

As an aircraft crew chief, he kept RF-101s in the skies over Cuba during the Cuban Missile Crisis and RF-4 Phantoms in the skies above North Vietnam during the Vietnam War.

Contents

Preface

My interest in World War II bomber operations began as an elementary school student in England, where my father was assigned with the United States Air Force between 1966 and 1969. Every day my school bus utilized a road that passed through the abandoned World War II airfield at Martlesham Heath, which served as the home of the American 356th Fighter Group. I never grew tired of peering at the abandoned hangars, support buildings, and runway. At the age of twelve I discovered the book *Big Friend, Little Friend: The Memoirs of a World War II Fighter Pilot* by Richard Turner. The symbiotic relationship between the bombers and fighters of the Eighth Air Force noted in the title captured my imagination and I became interested in the stories of the bomber crews. As a US Army lieutenant in Germany between 1982 and 1985 with the 228th Signal Company, my unit maintained a communications site and offices within the building in Oberursel, near Frankfurt, where the Germans interrogated newly captured American bomber crews during WWII. Our small offices and store rooms maintained the look of the cells that held American crews in World War II. More than once when at our Oberursel site, I could not help but think about the scared young men—some still in their teens—who found themselves captured and temporarily held in the facility after surviving the downing of their bombers.

As my interest in the men who flew these missions increased over the years, I realized little had been written about the B-29 operations flown from India and China between 1944 and 1945. Books tended to concentrate on the B-29 operations from the Marianas Islands under the XXI Bomber Command and covered the XX Bomber Command missions from India and China in a single chapter—if that. I trust this book corrects this oversight and highlights the achievements of the air and ground crews who conducted operations from India and China and paved the way for the missions originating in the Marianas Islands.

I encountered conflicting information about XX Bomber Command missions and aircraft more than once in published sources while researching this book. In each case, I returned to and cross checked the original World War II documents prepared by not only XX Bomber Command, but also the 40th, 444th, 462nd, and 468th Bomb Groups and their subordinate bomb squadrons. The results and corrections to the conflicts are explained and included within the text of this book. I trust that I caught most if not all of these conflicts and correctly settled them.

There were many challenges researching and preparing this book, and I hope that I succeeded in working through each of them and apologize where I may not have caught something. Many published sources conflict in the spelling of crew member names. Al Schutte, one of my manuscript reviewers, assisted with the identification of the correct spellings and I believe we caught all of them and apologize to the families of any who were missed. Geographical spelling conflicts emerged on more than one occasion during the research process. One example is the town and airfield Cox's Bazar, located today in Bangladesh. XX Bomber Command B-29s frequently utilized Cox's Bazar for refueling and emergency landings. The official name is spelled "Cox's Bazar," although some previously published state it as "Cox's Bazaar."

Photographs within this book are often utilized to identify aircraft participating on a particular mission and not necessarily a crew pictured with it. Although crews were officially and unofficially assigned to individual aircraft, they did not always fly that particular B-29 on every mission. If a B-29 needed additional maintenance, a crew might fly another bomber on a scheduled mission. Sometimes, a crew could be on rest leave and another group would "borrow" their aircraft for a mission. In other cases, a crew, or some of its members, would rotate back to the United States and another crew or individual crew member would be assigned to the B-29 if it remained in the theater. When possible, photographs of bombers with matching crews are included with a particular mission section of the book.

Discussing photographs is a natural lead to another challenge: identifying the names of aircraft. Approximately seventy-five percent of the air crews named their B-29s. Where possible, these names are placed with the aircraft numbers throughout the text. However, it should be noted that the name of a single B-29 could change as crews rotated or planes were lost in combat or due to accidents. I have attempted to identify each named aircraft and reflect any changes during the chronological progression of the book without burdening the reader with the alteration. For example, one will see B-29 #356 of the 468th Bomb Group identified first as *Georgia Peach* and later as *Lassie* without noting the name change. The month of a name change might be known, but not the specific day; thus, a B-29 could fly under one name and participate days later in another mission under a different name.

It is important to note that the XX Bomber Command numbered each operational mission in the chronological order it was flown—until February 1945. It should be noted that the XX Bomber Command altered the mission number sequencing from the chronological dates between February 27, 1945, and March 17, 1945. Thus, readers will notice Mission #38 is followed by Mission #40; the XX Bomber Command flew the latter mission immediately after the former. I placed a note in the text to remind readers of the change in sequencing, since this book is organized chronologically rather than by mission number sequencing for ease in tracing the operational history of XX Bomber Command and its bomber groups.

TERRY M. MAYS
Charleston, South Carolina

Acknowledgments

I am indebted to many individuals for their assistance while preparing this book; hopefully those whom I inadvertently forget to mention will forgive me. This book is a product of not only considerable research at the Air University Library and Air Force Historical Research Agency, but also the collective memories of XX Bomber Command veterans with whom I either had the pleasure of chatting or exchanging emails and phone calls. I am indebted to many other XX Bomber Command veterans who wrote about their experiences in personal diaries or newsletters published by veteran associations and their families who shared these narratives and photos.

Special thanks go to three Bomb Group Association Presidents—Al Shutte (468th BG), Nate Hicks (40th BG), Bill Howe (444th BG)—for their support behind this project. Unfortunately, Nate Hicks passed away before the completion of the book and I would like to extend condolences to his family. Nate was very supportive of the book and how its availability would be an asset for future generations wanting to know more about XX Bomber Command operations from India and China.

Thanks are also due to the following XX Bomber Command veterans and family members, as well as others who have assisted the project in some way: Harry Changnon, Al Lukas, Ira Matthews, Jack Millar, John Misterly, Steve Kelleher, Howe family, Wilkins family, Robert Schumacher, Halbert Hewitt, Calvin Brown, Lee family, Lou Jones, Wood family, Kamp family, Calvin family, Wotipka family, Albert family, Daly family, Willis family, Seith family, John Bailey, Urban family, Briggs family, Fountain Brown, Caudle family, Crocoll family, Brusco family, Barnes family, Decker family, Mackey family, Hodgdon family, Burke family, Balkinaa family, Claypool family, Bozzuto family, Kulicka family, Gardner family, Taylor family, Franks family, Conley family, Hilyard family, Albert family, Mahli family, Ray Archer, Seith family, Slonina family, Clendenen family, Lundquist family, Macer family, Schaal family, Buzza family, Wemple family, Mahli family, Coppola family, Watkins family, Poplaski family, Fearsad family, Barg family, Houghdahl family, Franckling family, Vocovsky family, Brooks family, Seith family, Corey family, Read Vaughn, Betty Gracie, Ray Archer, Pat Miller, Sparky Corradina, Evans family, Kenney family, Nancy Bessler, Bob Rich, Smith family, Don Stockett, and Charles Harper.

The librarians and inter-library loan staff at the Citadel's Daniel Library provided much appreciated assistance. Smiles and special thanks go to Merida and South Lincoln Bakery for their morale-building support during the research and writing stages of this project.

Al Schutte and Brad Guglielmino reviewed the original draft manuscript of this book for clarity and I appreciate their assistance. Al was also very helpful with double checking the names of people and aircraft.

Chapter 1

Establishing a Strategic Bombing Campaign in the China, Burma, India (CBI) Theater

With its baptism of fire, the Superfortress was fast on its way to becoming a legend among Japanese fighter pilots. Stories quickly spread through the Japanese airfields concerning the airplane that was being described as a "stupendous giant" or a "monstrous bull."

— Gen. Curtis LeMay

Capt. Hideo Miyabe, leader of the 2nd *Chutai* (Squadron) of the Japanese 64th *Sentai* (Air Combat Group), scanned the skies as he flew along the border between China and India on April 26, 1944.[1] He led eleven other Japanese aviators flying Nakajima Ki-43 Oscar fighters in a combined operation with the 204th *Sentai*. Both units flew Oscars from bases in Burma. The single-engine Oscar proved to be one of the best Japanese fighters of World War II. The plane could achieve 329 mph and fly approximately 1,095 miles. Pilots in the aircraft downed more Allied fighters than any other Japanese plane during the war. Those assigned to the 64th *Sentai* admired Miyabe, who not only established rigorous standards for training, but also demonstrated an often rare nurturing for his subordinates. Miyabe graduated from officer school in 1939 and rose to become the 2nd *Chutai* leader for the 64th *Sentai* in February 1943. Others later noted Miyabe as a modest man who rarely discussed his aerial exploits and awards, including the coveted *Bukosho*, one of Japan's highest awards for distinguished military valor.

As the twelve Japanese aircraft patrolled along the border, one of the fighter pilots noticed a massive silhouette 2,000 feet above and in the distance from the Oscars. This was the first encounter between the Boeing B-29 Superfortress and the Japanese military. Six of the Oscars led by Miyabe broke formation and climbed to the altitude of the B-29. Three fighters flew along each side out of gun range of the B-29 for ten minutes as the Japanese pilots studied this new opponent. The Japanese knew the B-29s were in the theater so the encounter could not have been a total surprise, yet actually seeing such a huge aircraft must have been daunting for the Japanese pilots. Miyabe assembled the six aircraft into a semi-circular formation for a coordinated group assault on the B-29. The first Japanese pilot attacked from the right rear and below the bomber. He flew to within 400 yards of the plane with guns blazing before breaking the attack. At least eight rounds struck the B-29, holing the pressurized fuselage and wounding side gunner Sgt. Walter Gilonski. The bomber's gunners attempted to return fire, but combat inexperience resulted in the mishandling of the weapons systems; three of the four upper guns and the machine guns in the tail jammed, while failure to wind the spring loading mechanism resulted in the loss of the cannon in the B-29's tail. Maj. Charles Hansen, flying B-29 #330 of the 468th Bomb Group (BG), continued to turn his bomber, providing the best angles for his working machine guns to defend the aircraft. At the same time he pushed the B-29 to gain altitude and possibly lose the Japanese fighters. Two more Oscars made passes from below the American bomber but somehow missed the lumbering giant. A fourth fighter discovered the B-29 could fight back; tail gunner Sgt. Harold Lanahan managed to clear his twin machine guns and opened fire as the fourth fighter approached. He later reported the Oscar trailed black smoke as it turned and dived away from the B-29.

Low on fuel, the six Japanese pilots broke contact with the B-29 as Hansen climbed to an altitude they could not reach. The B-29 landed with Lanahan claiming a "probable" kill of the Japanese fighter. Despite the claim, all twelve Japanese pilots safely returned to their base, with Miyabe

The Boeing B-29 Superfortress. The B-29's defensive armament included four .50-caliber remote-controlled machine gun turrets and a gun position in the rear of the bomber with .50-caliber machine guns and a 20mm cannon in the early versions of the bomber. (*US Air Force*)

Japanese Nakajima Ki-43 Oscar. Capt. Hideo Miyabe commanded a force of twelve Oscars that engaged the B-29 flown by Maj. Charles Hansen of the 468th BG over the Hump on April 26, 1944. This encounter was the first combat between the B-29 and Japanese fighters. (*Lukas*)

The pre-production YB-29. This model carried a "cheek" machine gun position below and behind the cockpit, as well as a ball turret on the bottom of the aircraft that is not visible in this photograph. Boeing built fourteen YB-29s. (*US Air Force*)

reporting he knocked out an engine and destroyed the Superfortress.[2] In 1988, Gen. Curtis LeMay—XX Bomber Command (BC) leader from August 1944 to January 1945—considered the encounter in hindsight and wrote, "The response was disappointing—no doubt to both sides."[3] Miyabe later assumed command of the 64th *Sentai*, received the *Bukosho* on June 10, 1945, and survived the war with at least twelve aerial victories. Hansen and eleven others perished on August 20, 1944, when #330 struck a mountain ten miles east of their forward base in China returning from the second raid over Yawata, Japan.[4]

The Consolidated B-32 Dominator. The B-32 carried Wright R-3350 engines, the same power plant utilized by the B-29. The army settled on the Boeing design for its very heavy bomber requirement, but permitted limited production of the Consolidated airplane as a backup in the event the former encountered problems. (*US Air Force*)

The B-29 Program

America's B-29 program emerged from a bomber competition issued in 1940 by the US Army. As war enveloped Europe and Asia, the army requested American aircraft manufacturers for bomber designs that could carry 2,000 pounds of bombs at 400 mph for a distance of 5,000+ miles. Boeing, Consolidated, Douglas, and Lockheed proposed initial designs, with Boeing and Consolidated actually producing test aircraft for the Very Long Range (VLR) program. The army ordered two prototypes of the Boeing design, identified as the XB-29, in August 1940. Consolidated built what became known as the XB-32 based on an army request the following month.

Another view of the Consolidated B-32 Dominator. Approximately 116 Consolidated B-32 Dominators eventually rolled off the assembly line and a few made it to the Pacific Theater by mid-1945. Note the B-32 mounted a twin machine gun turret in the nose of the aircraft, unlike the B-29. (*US Air Force*)

Consolidated originally based the XB-32 very heavy bomber design on its B-24 Liberator with twin vertical stabilizers. The company switched to a single vertical stabilizer with the production of the third experimental aircraft. The XB-32 carried Wright R-3350 engines, the same power plant utilized by the XB-29. The army settled on the Boeing design for its very heavy bomber requirement, but permitted limited production of the Consolidated airplane as a backup in the event the former encountered problems. Approximately 116 Consolidated B-32 Dominator bombers eventually rolled off the assembly line and a few made it to the Pacific Theater by mid-1945.[5]

Boeing's design benefited from the company's development of the highly rated B-17 Flying Fortress during the 1930s. The army ordered a third XB-29 test model and then contracted with Boeing for fourteen additional test aircraft and 250 production planes in May 1941, before the plane made its maiden flight. Brig. Gen. Kenneth B. Wolfe of Materiel Command referred to the contract as a "$3 billion gamble."[6] Wolfe eventually developed the final plan for Operation Matterhorn (the bombing of Japan by B-29s staging through China) and led the bombers to India as

Col. Lewis Parker (far left), commander of the 40th Bomb Group, and Gen. Kenneth Wolfe (in the round hat in the center), commander of the 58th Bomb Wing prior to leading the XX Bomber Command, inspect personnel undergoing B-29 training in Kansas. (*Pratt County Historical Society*)

The Wright R-3350 radial engine utilized in the B-29. Early design problems and weather conditions of the China-Burma-India Theater led to many engine failures and crashes before the issues were solved. (*US Air Force*)

the first commander of XX BC. Thus, Wolfe oversaw Operation Matterhorn from development of the B-29 to preparation of the bombing plans, and finally to India and China for its first combat operations.[7]

In June 1941—the month following the 250-plane order—Boeing began construction of a new aircraft plant for the B-29 in Wichita, Kansas; production of the B-17 consumed the work areas of existing Boeing production facilities, forcing the company to seek the new location. The army also adopted the Wright R-3350 engine for the B-29 during the same month. The R-3350 18-cylinder, air-cooled engine with supercharger delivered up to 2,200 horsepower. The 74,500 pound bomber needed all 2,200 horsepower from each of the four engines to become airborne with a 2,000 pound bomb load while carrying an eleven-man crew and their associated weapons, gear, and equipment. The R-3350 engines proved to be very troublesome due to overheating, resulting in the aborting of many B-29s on combat missions with the XX BC. Many others crashed as a result of engine failure and these issues will be discussed throughout this book.

By the end of February 1942, the Army placed orders for 1,600 B-29 bombers, negating any thought of producing the bomber at one plant in Wichita. Boeing would oversee the production at its own plant, as well as the work of three sub-contractors: General Motors's Fisher Division made sub-assemblies; North American Aviation produced fuselage sections and assembled the bomber in Kansas City, Missouri; and Bell Aircraft Corporation performed the same mission as North American and assembled B-29s in Marietta, Georgia. Assembly lines operated by Boeing in Renton, Washington, and Martin in Omaha, Nebraska, opened later in the war.[8]

The B-29 Superfortress generally carried a crew of eleven men, including a pilot, co-pilot, navigator, bombardier, fight engineer, radar operator, radio operator, top gunner, left gunner, right gunner, and tail gunner. The addition of the radar operator gave the plane one more crew member than the B-17 or B-24. The first five crew members in the list flew in the forward pressurized compartment. Pressurization of the B-29 presented its crew the advantage of not having to wear oxygen equipment under normal conditions, compared to the men flying in other bombers who generally wore problematic oxygen masks above 10,000 feet. The bombardier rode in the nose of the plane in front of the pilot and co-pilot. He assumed responsibility for all aspects of the bomb load, including verifying the shackling of the ordnance in the two bomb bays and inspecting their fuses before take-off on each mission. The forward area of the cockpit presented the bombardier with an impressive view and his bomb sight rested immediately behind the front plexiglass on the nose of the aircraft. When bombing visually, the bombardier assumed control of the aircraft through his Norden bomb sight minutes before arriving at the target release point. After "bombs away," he also assumed responsibility for the strike camera that snapped photographs showing where

Assembly of the forward pressurized compartment of the B-29 by Boeing in Seattle, Washington. This compartment housed the pilot, co-pilot, bombardier, navigator, radio operator, and flight engineer. (*US Air Force*)

Assembly of B-29 engine nacelles by Martin employees in Omaha, Nebraska. (*US Air Force*)

B-29 assembly line. (*US Air Force*)

B-29s at the Boeing assembly facility in Wichita, Kansas, in 1945. Note the late-production upper turrets with four machine guns; early production models carried two guns in each turret. (*US Air Force*)

the munitions fell in relation to the aiming point. During aerial combat with Japanese fighters, the bombardier could assume control of the upper and lower forward gun turrets to defend the B-29. This scenario occurred frequently due to the tendency for approximately half of all Japanese fighter attacks to emerge from the front of the bombers. The pilot and co-pilot commanded the aircraft from seats behind and slightly elevated above the bombardier's station in the nose. The pilot sat on the left side of the bomber and the co-pilot—a fully trained pilot—on the right from the perspective of looking toward the nose from the tail. The co-pilot assisted the pilot in all aspects of flight, relieved him for periods during long missions, and stood ready to assume command of the B-29 if the pilot became incapacitated.

The cockpit of a B-29. The bombardier sat in the nose of the aircraft, just in front of the pilot and co-pilot. (*US Air Force*)

The navigator, radio operator, and flight engineer sat behind the pilot and co-pilot. The flight engineer was not only a commissioned officer, but sometimes pilot trained. The level of technical and flight training of the flight engineer varied, and as the war progressed the Army Air Force introduced non-commissioned officers to the B-29 flight engineer program. The flight engineer monitored the mechanical functions of the bomber throughout a mission, including throttle control and fuel usage and transfer between tanks. The flight engineer on B-17s and B-24s was a non-commissioned officer who doubled as the top turret gunner. The navigator also rode in the forward pressurized compartment behind the pilot and co-pilot. He tracked the movement of the aircraft at a small desk with a collection of maps, charts, and navigation aids. The navigator performed the crucial task of informing the pilot of the plane's precise location, where to turn to follow the briefed flight path, and when to expect arrival at home base or the Initial Point, at which the bomber began its final run to a target. His calculations aided not only the pilot, but also the flight engineer, as the latter maintained vigil on the fuel supply. The radio operator—a non-commissioned officer—oversaw all air-to-ground, air-to-air, and internal intercom communications for the crew, as well as the onboard equipment associated with the SCS-51 Instrument Landing System. The SCS-51 emitted a ground-based signal in cooperation with marker beacons, permitting the radio operator to monitor the location of the bomber in relation to the optimum glide path for landing during poor weather conditions or at night.

The right gunner of a B-29. The B-29's defensive system featured remotely controlled gun turrets. Gunners could pass operation of the weapons to other gunners and the bombardier, depending on the threat. The guns were operated via the remote sighting mechanism. (*US Air Force*)

Entrance to the rear pressurized compartment in the B-29. Note the bunks for crew rest on the left. These were removed later. (*US Air Force*)

A pressurized tunnel ran from the forward compartment along the top of the bomb bay area and into an aft pressurized compartment where the radar operator and top, left, and right gunners stationed themselves. The top gunner, riding in an elevated seat nicknamed the "barber chair," served as the senior individual operating the Central Fire Control (CFC) system. Boeing and the military experimented with a variety of defensive guns on the B-29, settling on an electronic system that included two top and two bottom turrets, each holding two .50-caliber machine guns (later models of the B-29 increased the number to four guns per turret). The gunners, including the bombardier in the forward compartment, remotely controlled the weapons from their stations based on the direction of pending fighter threats. The aft compartment also housed the left and right gunners, each manning a position on one side of the aircraft. The gunners peered though plexiglass blisters, operated the guns from a movable sight that controlled the firing direction of the turrets, and could pass control of the weapons to each other, as well to the bombardier in the forward compartment. The top gunner provided the primary coordination for allowing individual gunners and the bombardier to assume control of the turrets. The plane boasted a computer that automatically calculated gun corrections for the speed of the attacking fighter, as well as the bomber, altitude, temperature, and distance to the target. The B-29 certainly earned its nickname—the Superfortress. The radar operator, with his array of electronic equipment, also sat in the aft compartment. He served as an alternate navigator and bombardier with the APQ-13 "Mickey" radar system. The APQ-13—quite primitive by modern standards—provided a rough outline of terrain features, including bodies of water and urban areas, and required considerable training to tune and operate the equipment, as well as interpret the scope "picture." During thick cloud cover, the radar operator could supplement the navigator's calculations by interpreting the radar returns from the terrain below the bomber. "Interpreting" is utilized rather than another word because the radar operator often required considerable experience to understand the signal picture on the scope. The clearest returns were coastal areas, where it could be much easier to distinguish the contrasts between ground and water. The radar operator could also be called upon to guide the B-29 to the bomb release point during darkness or heavy cloud cover. Dropping the ordnance by this method could be a more calculated guess than precision placement. The tail held a third but isolated pressurized compartment for the final crew member. The tail gunner's armament included twin .50-caliber machine guns and a 20 mm cannon on the early B-29 models. His only contact with the rest of the crew was via the intercom during pressurized flights. More details on each crew position on the B-29 will emerge as this study turns to reviewing the operational missions of the XX BC from India and China between 1944 and 1945.

Establishing the B-29 Strategic Bombing Campaign for the CBI

Chinese Nationalist leader Chiang Kai-shek dispatched his aviation adviser, retired American army officer Claire Chennault, and Chinese Gen. Pang-Tsu Mow to the United States in November 1940. Chennault's mission included lobbying for American air support and supplies to help the Chinese in their war with Japan. President Franklin D. Roosevelt and others displayed enthusiasm for providing the Chinese with American bombers for the purpose of attacking Japan; however, the Japanese home islands were immune from most land-based aircraft. Unoccupied areas of eastern China lay close enough for bombers like the B-17 to reach Japanese home soil, but challenges, including training Chinese crews, supplying the aircraft, and problems with such long-range missions would have made operations

Chiang Kai-shek (left) and Gen. Claire Chennault (right) stand on either side of Madame Chiang Kai-shek. Chiang dispatched Chennault, his personal advisor, to lobby President Franklin D. Roosevelt for American-built bombers. He maintained persistent demands for greater American air involvement in China. (*Franklin D. Roosevelt Museum*)

Curtiss P-40 Warhawk fighters. This was taken after the United States entered World War II. In December, the United States opted to provide Chiang Kai-shek with 100 Curtiss P-40 Warhawks rather than the bombers he requested. (*US Air Force*)

difficult, if not impossible. The lack of sufficient numbers of the new B-17 bomber to arm both the American and Chinese military added to the problems. In December, the United States opted to provide Chiang with 100 Curtiss P-40 Warhawk fighters rather than bombers and offered to send Gen. Henry "Hap" Arnold to China to discuss American aid. These initial discussions demonstrate the administration believed taking the air war to the Japanese to be an important strategy. Chennault initiated the recruitment of 300 Americans to fly and maintain the P-40s as civilians contracted by the Chinese government. The unit led by Chennault as the American Volunteer Group (AVG) is better known as the Flying Tigers and electrified American newspaper readers as their exploits emerged from China.[9] The Flying Tigers officially evolved into the American Army Air Force 23rd Fighter Group in 1942.

Despite the desire to provide more assistance to China in 1942, American and British discussions centered on a "Germany first" policy for ending the war. Although limited American manpower and materiel resources arrived in Asia during the year, the Allies checked Japanese expansion to the south in New Guinea and the Solomon Islands by the fall of 1942. However, reversals continued in the China-Burma-India (CBI) Theater as Allied forces withdrew from Burma to India. Many of the Chinese forces fighting in Burma retreated into China, with at least half of the men dying before reaching their destination.[10]

The Japanese commenced an April 1942 offensive in China as retribution for the local population's assistance to the Doolittle Raiders and to deny the Allies access to airfields in the eastern part of the country. The United States realized it needed to do something to assist the Chinese to keep them in the war and help stabilize the CBI Theater.

Two theories prevailed for countering Japanese gains in the CBI Theater. American Gen. Joseph ("Vinegar Joe") Stilwell served as the overall American commander in the CBI, as well as the senior liaison with Chiang. In this capacity Stilwell coordinated the American supplies to China. Stilwell, fluent in Chinese, viewed Chiang with suspicion and believed he preferred to preserve his manpower and supplies for a future fight against communist guerrilla leader Mao Tse Tung, rather than aggressively prosecute the war against Japan. Stilwell often clashed with Chiang and continually requested the United States place greater pressure on the Chinese leader to support ground operations in Burma and a re-training of the Chinese army. His plan called for a massive re-training of Chinese troops before conducting extensive operations against the Japanese. Chiang disagreed with the idea out of concern the Americans might actually establish a well-trained Chinese army that would operate as an independent force outside his authority as he faced not only Japan, but also Mao.[11]

Chiang Kai-shek (left) and Gen. Joseph Stillwell (right) stand on either side of Madame Chiang Kai-shek. Stilwell served as the overall American commander in the CBI, as well as senior liaison with Chiang. Stilwell often clashed with Chiang over the strategy to employ against the Japanese in China. (*Franklin D. Roosevelt Museum*)

British Prime Minister Winston Churchill and President Franklin D. Roosevelt at the Casablanca Conference in January 1943. The two leaders discussed a strategic air campaign directed at Japan from bases in India. Army Chief of Staff Gen. George C. Marshall advised that Japanese industries lay vulnerable to aerial bombardment. (*US Army*)

The second theory can be attributed to Gen. Claire Chennault, now the commander of American air units in China. Chennault believed the United States should provide more aircraft and supplies for increased air operations against the Japanese in China. Chiang agreed with Chennault that China could be held through air power and limited Chinese ground operations as opposed to Stilwell's desire to re-train Chinese soldiers for a land campaign.

The conflicting views of Stilwell and Chennault presented the United States government with polar opposite theories for the CBI area of operations. President Roosevelt noted the merits and challenges in both plans, resulting in an authorization of each in a modified form at the Casablanca Conference in January 1943. Chiang's opposition to Stilwell's ideas for re-training much of his army hindered the complete adoption of the ground war concept, while logistical difficulties negated a massive build-up of American air power in China. Roosevelt and Churchill, while promoting a "Germany first" strategy, agreed to a campaign to re-capture Burma from the Japanese. A successful campaign in northern Burma could re-open the land routes to China and increase the flow of supplies from India. The two leaders also discussed a strategic air campaign directed at Japan from bases in India. Army Chief of Staff Gen. George C. Marshall advised that Japanese industries lay vulnerable to aerial bombardment. Destroying these industries would severely hinder the Japanese war effort as the Allies continued their operations in the Southwest Pacific and contemplated new offensives in the central Pacific and Burma. Marshall reminded those in attendance that an air campaign in the CBI Theater would strain the logistics chain into and through the area, requiring bombers stage through China from bases in India, rather than being permanently maintained in the former.[12] Roosevelt supported the plan, knowing that he must provide assistance to keep Chiang active in the war effort and maintain Chinese morale. He also ordered Gen. Arnold to personally visit China to discuss these issues with Chinese and American officials. At this time, the president and others were considering increasing the 14th Air Force under Chennault with B-17 or B-24 bombers; altering this plan to operations under a separate air force emerged later. Historians have written that the first discussions for employing the B-29 or B-32 in air operations from China occurred at the Quadrant Conference in August 1943. The American and British Combined Chiefs of Staff (CCS) actually introduced this idea at the January 1943 Casablanca Conference, although it did not become a definite part of the strategic bombing plan until August at the Quadrant Conference.[13]

Prime Minister Winston Churchill joined President Roosevelt for the Trident Conference—also known as the Washington Conference—in May 1943. The Allied leaders reconfirmed the "Germany first" policy, but directed their attention to shifting military assets to the war against Japan once Berlin fell. Roosevelt and Churchill affirmed they must seek ways to stabilize the situation in the CBI area and keep the Chinese in the fight, including increasing supplies for China that would have to be flown over the Himalaya Mountains (nicknamed the Hump) from India due to the loss of road access through Burma and continuing with the plans made in Casablanca four months earlier.

The two leaders met again in Quebec, Canada, in August 1943, for the Quadrant Conference. This meeting resulted in major decisions related to an aerial campaign against Japan. Gen. Arnold presented a bombing plan developed by Gen. Wolfe. The document, titled "Air Plan for the Defeat of Japan," called for deploying the new B-29—not B-17 or B-24 bombers—in central China. The Army Air Force could convert existing aircraft models into transport versions to increase the flow of supplies needed by the bombers across the Hump from India. The document described initiating air raids against Japanese industrial targets beginning in 1944 and optimistically declared that 780 B-29s flying five missions each month could force a Japanese surrender in six months.

Gen. Henry "Hap" Arnold after his promotion to five-star general. Arnold, the commanding general of the Army Air Forces, assumed personal command of the 20th Air Force and placed the first combat B-29s into the XX BC under his organization to keep them independent of theater commanders. (*US Air Force*)

Gen. Stilwell asked to review the plan and recommended a modification to reflect the Casablanca discussions of staging the bombers through China from bases in India. This would reduce the amount of supplies needing to be ferried across the Hump and reflected the probability of a Japanese offensive in central China to capture bomber capable airfields. American officials approved this final plan under code name Operation Matterhorn. On November 10, 1943, Roosevelt requested permission for the establishment of American bomber bases in India and Indian government assistance in their construction and logistical requirements. The same day, Roosevelt wired Chiang and requested the construction of five airfields in the area around Chengtu, northwest of Chungking, capable of handling the B-29 bomber by March 1944.

On March 23, 1943, Gen. "Hap" Arnold, Commanding Gen. of the Army Air Forces, tasked the Committee of Analysis (COA, a body comprising military and civilian personnel established in December 1942 to review strategic bombing targets) to develop recommendations for the strategic bombing of Japan. The COA members prepared a document that noted destroying the strategic economic assets of Japan included not only bombing the Japanese islands, but also specific facilities in Japanese-held territories, as well as the sea and air routes that linked the two areas. The body presented their research and recommendations in a document to Gen. Arnold on November 11, 1943, immediately prior to the Cairo (Sextant) Conference. The document listed six industries but did not organize them in priority: (1) merchant shipping, (2) the steel industry (via the coke ovens), (3) urban industrial areas, (4) aircraft plants, (5) anti-friction bearing industry (ball bearings), and (6) the electronics industry. In discussions, the COA members believed the steel industry should be the most important strategic bombing priority against Japan due to the concentration of the coke ovens in a small number of locations in the home islands, Manchuria, and Korea.

Chinese leader Chiang Kai-shek, President Franklin D. Roosevelt, and British Prime Minister Winston Churchill at the Cairo Conference in November 1943. The three reviewed plans to construct B-29 airfields in India and China and commence bombing operations against Japan. Roosevelt promised Chiang to begin combat operations by March 1944. (*US Army*)

Soviet Premier Joseph Stalin, President Franklin D. Roosevelt, and British Prime Minister Winston Churchill at the Tehran Conference in November/December 1943. Roosevelt presented a letter to Stalin requesting access to base four-engine bombers in his country once the Soviet Union entered the war against Japan. The Soviet leader waited months to respond. (*Franklin D. Roosevelt Museum*)

Debates continued into 1944, and many senior military personnel believed the best utilization of the B-29s would be from bases in Australia to attack Japanese shipping and harbor facilities rather than China until better situated airfields could be constructed following the capture of the Marianas Islands. However, the president remained committed to placing B-29s in Chengtu, China, as a show of support for Chiang Kai-shek. The main coke oven facilities lay within range of B-29s operating from China, helping prompt declaring this industry the most important strategic bombing priority on the COA list. The COA report received some criticism for not listing the petroleum industry in the six priorities; this was corrected when the decision was made to also stage the India-based bombers through Ceylon (Sri Lanka) for strikes against the Japanese-controlled petroleum refineries in the Netherlands East Indies (Indonesia).

Roosevelt, Churchill, and Chiang met November 22-26, 1943, at the Cairo (Sextant) Conference to discuss the war and postwar strategy in Asia. Premier Joseph Stalin of the Soviet Union declined an invitation, since he signed a non-aggression pact with Japan and a meeting with Chiang could prove troublesome for his relations with Tokyo. He met Roosevelt and Churchill days later in Teheran (also known as the Eureka Conference) without Chiang. In Cairo, Roosevelt, Churchill, and Chiang reviewed plans to construct airfields in India and China and commence bombing operations against Japan. Roosevelt promised Chiang to begin combat operations by March 1944. In Teheran, Roosevelt presented a letter to Stalin requesting access to base four-engine bombers in the Soviet Union when Moscow entered the war against Japan. The Soviet leader waited months to respond. Delays in discussions, the Soviet entry in the war after the commencement of the B-29 campaign from Saipan and Tinian, and the first atomic bombing of Japan made the idea unnecessary.[14]

Assembling a Team of All-Stars for the 58th BW

The Army Air Force established the 58th BW under the command of Gen. Wolfe on June 1, 1943, and added four bomb groups: the 40th, 444th, 462nd, and 468th. Gen. Arnold not only assigned Gen. Wolfe to lead the organization, but also moved experienced bomber commanders and other prominent officers into the organization. Gen. Wolfe was probably the military officer most familiar with the B-29 and its components, having overseen the project for years. While not a former combat commander, he held

Left: Gen. Kenneth Wolfe, the first commander of the 58th BW and XX BC. (*US Air Force*)

Right: Gen. Laverne "Blondie" Saunders followed Gen. Leonard Harmon as 58th BW commander in March 1944 and assumed temporary command of the XX BC from July to August 1944, until the arrival of Gen. Curtis LeMay. Saunders commanded the 11th BG in Hawaii during the Japanese attack on Pearl Harbor. (*US Air Force*)

numerous engineering and development related positions in the United States and Philippine Islands; these, along with liaison responsibilities with the Lockheed and Douglas aircraft plants, made him an ideal candidate for overseeing the establishment of the 58th BW and its training in the new B-29 aircraft. Wolfe assumed command of the newly formed XX BC in November 1943.

To protect the B-29s from theater commanders who wanted to divert them to tactical targets rather than their planned utilization against Japanese strategic targets, including the steel, aircraft manufacturing, and petroleum industries, Arnold formed the XX Air Force with himself as nominal commander. Wolfe served as his XX BC operational commander. The 58th BW functioned as the sole combat wing under the XX BC while assigned to the CBI Theater. Essentially, the XX BC assumed most of the 58th BW's duties due to the single wing organization underneath the command. In this work, the four groups are referred to as flying for the XX BC, rather than the 58th BW, upon arriving in India and conducting combat operations in the CBI Theater due to this reality. The command re-activated the 58th BW, which then assumed a more traditional role as a wing, overseeing the four B-29 Groups in January 1945. At that point in time, the Army Air Force (through the XX Air Force) prepared to transfer the XX BC and the 58th BW to different locations in the Pacific, where the latter would reorganize under the XXI BC in the Marianas Islands.

Gen. Laverne "Blondie" Saunders—former commander of the 11th BG—arrived in 1943 to serve with Wolfe. Saunders later followed Gen. Leonard Harman as 58th BW commander in March 1944, and assumed temporary command of the XX BC from July to August 1944, until the arrival of Gen. Curtis LeMay to replace Wolfe. Saunders commanded the 11th BG in Hawaii during the Japanese attack on Pearl Harbor. He managed to put a B-17 into the air in search of the Japanese carrier fleet, but the bomber could not locate the enemy vessels. During the struggle for Guadalcanal, Saunders commanded the 11th BG, flying from Espititu Santo, in the New Hebrides islands, where his crews frequently staged through Guadalcanal as they supported the Solomon Islands campaign.

Saunders received the Navy Cross on November 18, 1942, for his actions during a B-17 attack on Japanese shipping in Tonolei Harbor. The group commander flew as an observer on a B-17F piloted by Maj. Allen Sewart. The B-17s scored numerous hits on the Japanese vessels and turned for home as enemy fighters began swarming them. The fighters made head-on attacks against many of the bombers, including the one carrying Saunders. Machine gun fire smashed into the nose of the B-17, wounding the bombardier, pilot, and co-pilot, who received a stomach injury. Saunders dragged the co-pilot from his seat and sat beside the pilot. Another burst of machine gun fire struck the cockpit and Maj. Sewart slumped with at least one bullet in his chest. Saunders assumed control of the bomber from the co-pilot's seat as the Japanese fighters continued their runs against the plane. The fighters knocked out both engines on the left wing, which then ignited. Saunders remembered: "I leveled the plane as best I could and tried to get Sewart's body out of the pilot's seat where the trim tabs were located, but Sewart was jammed in and the shifting weight as I moved caused the plane to lurch. I jumped back in the co-pilot's seat and leveled the ship again."[15]

The defensive guns of the B-17 began failing in the midst of the battle; the crew lost the ball turret, upper turret, a side, and the two .30-caliber nose guns to malfunctions. Saunders piloted the crippled B-17 into a cloud bank, attempting to lose the Japanese fighters. Although concealed, the plane continued to lose altitude. The crew prepared themselves in the radio compartment as Saunders guided the heavy bomber near New Georgia Island. The bomber struck the water, breaking into two pieces and resulting in Saunders striking his head on the cockpit windshield.

Boeing B-17Fs. Col. Laverne Saunders received the Navy Cross following a 1942 B-17F attack on Japanese shipping in Tonolei Harbor. Saunders, an observer on the mission, assumed control of the bomber after Japanese fighters wounded the pilot and co-pilot. He eluded the fighters and ditched the bomber. (*US Air Force*)

The navigator and Saunders pulled the wounded co-pilot out and exited the cockpit as the rest of the crew escaped from the radio compartment. The co-pilot died before the two rafts reached shore on Baga Island.

Another B-17 pilot observed the crash and circled the area until the men below were out of the water. He then dropped a few supplies and departed to report their position. An Australian coast watcher on Vella Lavella Island also watched the crash and helped arrange their rescue the next day. The action presented Saunders with a first-hand view of Japanese fighter capabilities, as well as the strengths and weaknesses of the armor plating (or lack thereof) and defensive armament of the B-17 in 1942. These experiences would serve him well as future commander of the 58th BW.[16] There is something comforting when one knows the person sending you into combat has been there himself.

Left: Post-war photo of Col. Richard Carmichael, who assumed command of the 462nd BG. Carmichael flew one of the B-17s that landed during the Japanese attack on Pearl Harbor and personally led the first American B-17 raid against the Japanese base at Rabaul. (*US Air Force*)

Right: Postwar photo of Col. Alfred Kalberer, who received the Silver Star for his actions in the June 1942 raid on the Romanian oil refinery at Ploesti by thirteen American B-24s. Kalberer commanded the 462nd BG after August 1944. (*US Air Force*)

Col. Leonard Harman talking with a B-29 crew in India. Harman commanded the 58th BW until April 1944, when he assumed command of the 40th BG until August 1944. (*US Air Force*)

Col. Richard H. Carmichael—former commander of the 19th BG—joined Wolfe to oversee training and assume command of the 462nd BG. Carmichael flew one of the B-17s that landed during the Japanese attack on Pearl Harbor. His 19th BG fought as the only B-17 group in the Southwest Pacific in early 1942, as American forces battled to hold the Philippine Islands and the surviving air power withdrew to Australia. Carmichael led the first American B-17 raid against the Japanese base at Rabaul on February 22-23, 1942. The 19th BG planned the raid to include nine operable B-17s, but only five planes hit the target due to mechanical problems, bad weather, and a ground collision involving two of the bombers. Poor weather and steam from a volcano reduced visibility and the ability to accurately assess any damage. Later reports indicated the bombers sank one Japanese transport and damaged another vessel. As the B-17s withdrew from Rabaul, Japanese Mitsubishi A6M Zero fighters rose to challenge them. Four of the B-17s made it back to Port Moresby and then Australia. The B-17 piloted by Carmichael landed with two wounded gunners.[17] While the raid produced moderate damage, Carmichael provided a morale boost for Allied forces fighting a losing defensive war since December. Carmichael commanded the 462nd BG until August 20, 1944, when he was shot down on mission #7 to Yawata, Japan. The Japanese held him until August 1945 as a Prisoner of War (POW). Col. Alfred Kalberer replaced Carmichael and led the group until the end of the war.

Col. Leonard F. Harman served as Wolfe's deputy and then assumed command of the 58th BW when his boss became XX BC commander in November 1943. In April 1944, Harman moved to the 40th BG and led not only this group, but also all of the B-29s on the XX BC's first combat mission (Bangkok), as well as the first mission to Japan. Harman, like Wolfe, had worked with B-29 production issues since the inception of the bomber. He presented the initial Materiel Division briefing to the presidents of Martin and Boeing aircraft companies on the requirements for a new VLR bomber, resulting in the latter's development of a design known as Model 294—the forerunner of the B-29. Harman also flew as the co-pilot on the B-17B that set a new class speed record for aerial flight between Seattle and New York in 1939. Harman's predecessors included Col. Lewis R. Parker, who led the 40th BG from July 1943 to February 1944. Parker's past experience included assignments to bomber squadrons in the 1930s and engineering positions, giving him both operational and technical expertise. He joined the Eighth Air Force in Great Britain on temporary duty to obtain combat experience with bombers. Parker bailed out of a stricken bomber on his second mission and ended the war as a prisoner. In February 1944, Col. Louis E. Coira replaced Parker as 40th BG commander until Harman moved into the position in April 1944. Col. William Blanchard commanded the 40th BG from August 1944

Col. Lewis Parker served as commander of the 40th BG from July 1943 to February 1944. While on temporary duty to obtain combat experience with the Eighth Air Force before his group deployed to India, Parker bailed out of a stricken bomber and ended the war as a German prisoner. (*Pratt County Historical Society*)

Postwar photo of Col. Louis Coira, who served as the 40th BG commander between February 1944 and April 1944, when Col. Leonard Harman assumed the reins of the group. (*US Air Force*)

Postwar photo of Col. William Blanchard, who commanded the 40th BG between August 1944 and February 1945. (*US Air Force*)

until mid-February 1945, when he departed India to become the operations officer of the XXI BC in the Marianas Islands. Col. Henry Sullivan moved into the position and commanded the group through the rest of the war.

Col. Alva Harvey—former commander of the 25th BG (B-17) in 1941 and a veteran of the first American bombing raid over Berlin—arrived to command the 444th BG. He led the group until April 1945. Col. Howard Engler—a former Boeing P-12 bi-plane pilot with the 43rd Pursuit Squadron in the 1930s—received the 468th BG and commanded the group until August 1944, when Col. Ted Faulkner moved into the position. Col. James Edmundson replaced Faulkner in November 1944, after the latter went down with a B-29 during a raid on Singapore. Edmundson commanded the group until the end of the war.

Establishment and Training of the 58th BW

The first combat B-29 rolled out of the Wichita assembly plant in July 1943. Original plans called for B-29s to begin deploying to India in January 1944. In October 1943, Gen. Arnold informed an irritated President Roosevelt that the arrival date would have to slip to March or April 1944, due to production delays. The president dispatched a scathing letter to Gen. Marshall, expressing his displeasure at the news and reminding the chief of staff that American promises to Chiang were not being upheld. Roosevelt revised the operational dates in his November 1943 cable to Chiang and during a face-to-face meeting in Cairo the same month. Arnold requested the Joint Chiefs of Staff make the B-29 America's top priority for aircraft production, diverting materiel from other aircraft. The chiefs in turn tasked the Joint Aircraft Committee to review the issue. The committee reported that problems in the production process and not materiel shortages plagued the delivery of B-29s.

Gen. Arnold established the XX BC and assigned Gen. Wolfe to lead the organization. The first operational B-29s would form the four bomber groups under the 58th BW, with a second wing (the 73rd BW) slotted for formation after its predecessor deployed to the CBI Theater. Plans changed later and the 73rd BW joined the XXI Bomber Command in the Pacific. The army tapped Wolfe's deputy Gen. Leonard Harman to lead the 58th BW. Arnold and Harman established their headquarters at Smoky Hill Army Airfield near Salina, Kansas, and discovered a chaotic situation. The lack of ready B-29s forced crews to often train in other aircraft, leading to delays in their certification on the new bomber. Lt. John Misterly, a

Left: Col. Alva Harvey, former commander of the 25th BG (B-17) in 1941 and a veteran of the first American bombing raid over Berlin, served as the commander of the 444th BG between August 1944 and April 1945. (*US Air Force*)

Right: Col. Ted Faulkner commanded the 468th BG between August 1944 and November 1944. The 468th BG lost Faulkner when he and his B-29 crew went down during a mission to Singapore. (*Schutte*)

Col. James Edmundson commanded the 468th BG from November 1944 to March 1946. Edmundson received the Purple Heart for a wound he got during the Japanese attack on Pearl Harbor. In early 1942, he was credited with destroying one of the first Japanese submarines sunk during the war. (*US Air Force via Shutte*)

navigator with the 444th BG, commented that he flew his first training mission for the group in a Martin B-26 Marauder two-engine bomber. While disappointed it was not a B-29, Misterly at least expressed pleasure at flying in a combat rather than a training aircraft.[18]

Engine failure during training missions or flights to haul spare parts to the 58th BW seemed to be prevalent for the air crews. Cpl. B. Vic Dison Jr., a 40th BG tail gunner, made an emergency B-29 landing in Wichita, Kansas, where the entire crew remained confined to their hotel rooms due to not having dress uniforms to wear. Dison remarked that the crew learned from this lesson and began carrying dress uniforms on all future training missions in case they were hampered again by engine trouble.[19]

Misterly of the 444th BG and eight other crewmen bailed out of a B-29 with an engine trailing smoke and flames. The crew flew a grueling training mission, during which they simulated bombing runs on Salt Lake City, Los Angeles, and El Paso. After completing the final simulated attack, the crew turned toward the northeast and home. As the crew began relaxing, the flight engineer noticed abnormal readings on his board and called for the left side gunner to check engine #2. The anxious reply indicated smoke and flames trailing the engine. The pilot, Lt. Bart

Capt. Cornelius Meyer and his crew with a Boeing B-17 Flying Fortress in 1943, prior to deployment of the 58th BW as the operational wing under the XX BC. Personnel were frequently forced to train on the B-17 due to a shortage of B-29s. (*Pratt County Historical Museum*)

Crews undergoing B-29 training in Kansas. (*Pratt County Historical Society*)

Ellis, attempted to smother the flames with the engine's fire extinguisher. After two failures he ordered Misterly to gather the rest of the crew into the aft cabin and prepare to bail out. The co-pilot remained in the cockpit to assist efforts to extinguish the fire and safely land the bomber. The pilot did not want to take chances with the other crew members on board; he called Misterly on the intercom and ordered him to get everyone out of the airplane. The men began jumping until only Misterly and the radar operator, Orville Dudley—nicknamed "Roundy" due to his build—remained. Misterly picked up, "[Dudley] turned and looked at me; he was scared shitless. I put my boot in his back and gave him a hell of a push. He flew out into space and I heard him yelling for a split second."[20]

Misterly followed Dudley out of the plane. A strong gust of wind caught the chute after he landed. After popping the quick release, Misterly fell backwards and landed flat on a cactus. Spines painfully pierced his body and any movement made it worse. He lay there for over three hours before a rescue team found him. They cut him from the cactus, placed him face first on a litter, and transported him to the Biggs Army Airfield hospital, where a doctor required two hours to remove all of the deeply embedded spines and stitch the wounds. The other crew members parachuted without injuries. Ellis managed to extinguish the engine fire by diving the B-29 and safely landed the aircraft.[21]

Crews learned to have fun despite the rigors of training. Cpl. Dison mentioned a training mission in a B-17 during which the co-pilot tried to have fun at his expense:

> [We were on] another mission in a B-17 with the two newest members of the crew on their first ever airplane flight when an incident occurred. I had been in the cockpit for a while and headed for the rear of the plane. As I proceeded through the bomb bay, I decided to use the relief tube (the closest thing to a toilet on a B-17). This was noted by Dave Webster [right gunner] who was now in the cockpit area. He advised Walt Pytko [co-pilot] who was flying the plane. Walt put the plane into a series of dives, turns, and climbs. Being wedged between the bomb racks, I had no trouble. After finishing my "business," I proceeded to the rear of the plane. Just outside the radio room, I had to step over the radio operator's [Cpl. Marv Fears] regurgitated lunch at the entrance to the gunners' compartment. Here I saw our newest crew members ready to vacate the plane. They were sure something was wrong with the plane after Walt's maneuvering. One crewman had pulled his ripcord and his parachute was lying the length of the gunnery compartment floor.[22]

B-29 production, as well as the construction of airfields in India and China, remained behind schedule. Arnold, Wolfe, Harman, and many others struggled to untangle the B-29 production process and oversee construction of the airfields in India and China. In late December, Gen. Arnold ordered Wolfe to travel to the CBI Theater and personally invigorate the airfield construction process. Arnold's October 1943 promise to President Roosevelt that he could have bombers in the CBI Theater in time for March 1944 operations began slipping upon the realization Boeing and its sub-contractors could not deliver as originally promised. By mid-January 1944, the 58th BW did not have any combat-ready B-29 bombers. Problems lay at all levels of B-29 production. In February, Arnold personally traveled to Bell Aircraft's B-29 facility in Marietta, Georgia. Following discussions with plant personnel, Arnold ordered 58th BW technicians to the facility to assist its work and requested that Bell move some of its own personnel to Marietta from other plants.

Many refer to the period of March 1944 to April 1944 as the "Battle of Kansas." On 1 March 1944, Arnold informed Wolfe that he expected the first combat-ready B-29s and crews to depart for India on March 10. Arnold flew to Kansas on March 9 to be on hand as the first B-29s headed

Lt. Col. Louis Coira (second from left), commander of the 40th BG, inspecting personnel of the 45th Bomb Squadron in Kansas during October 1943. (*Pratt County Historical Society*)

Gen. Hap Arnold during his inspection tour at Pratt Army Air Field, Pratt, Kansas. His visit resulted in the "Battle of Kansas" to increase the delivery and preparation of B-29s for deployment to India. (*Pratt County Historical Museum*)

for India, but disappointment prevailed, as he found that not even one B-29 stood combat ready for departure to the CBI Theater. Arnold fumed as he ordered an overnight report on the exact readiness status of every B-29 at the airfield. The next day, Arnold appointed Gen. Bennet Meyers as his personal representative to oversee B-29 readiness and ordered top priority status to the bomber over all other programs for whatever was needed to get 150 of them airborne to India by mid-April. Arnold wrote in his memoirs:

> I told Meyers he had to get those airplanes out on time, and the crews must be ready to go with them. He must take every plane in turn, make a list of shortages, then get in touch with every factory in the United States that was involved, and insure that the parts were sent to the base by airplane. He was to send special airplanes for the parts, if necessary, so they could be installed on the B-29s with the least possible delay.[23]

Parts and technicians began flowing to Kansas from all areas of the country. Military and civilian technicians battled fatigue, snow, and each other as they worked around the clock under the oversight of Meyers to meet Arnold's deadline. The first combat-ready B-29 launched on March 26 and the rest of the combat ready aircraft were airborne to India by April 15. XX BC and the 58th BW won the "Battle for Kansas."

Deployment of the 58th Bomb Wing

Air crews began departing for India in March 1944. Each crew flew the same route through Presque Isle (Maine) and then on to Gander Lake (Newfoundland, Canada), Marrakech (Morocco), Cairo (Egypt), and Karachi (then India; now Pakistan), with a final destination at a group airfield near Calcutta (India). Crews deploying after the initial 150 planes in April often flew through Brazil to West Africa and then across the African continent and the Middle East to India. Rescue vessels plied the oceans along the water routes in case a plane went down. 40th BG aircraft carried not only the eleven-man crew and their personal baggage, but also a spare engine, bomb bay fuel tanks, spare parts, and emergency repair kits.

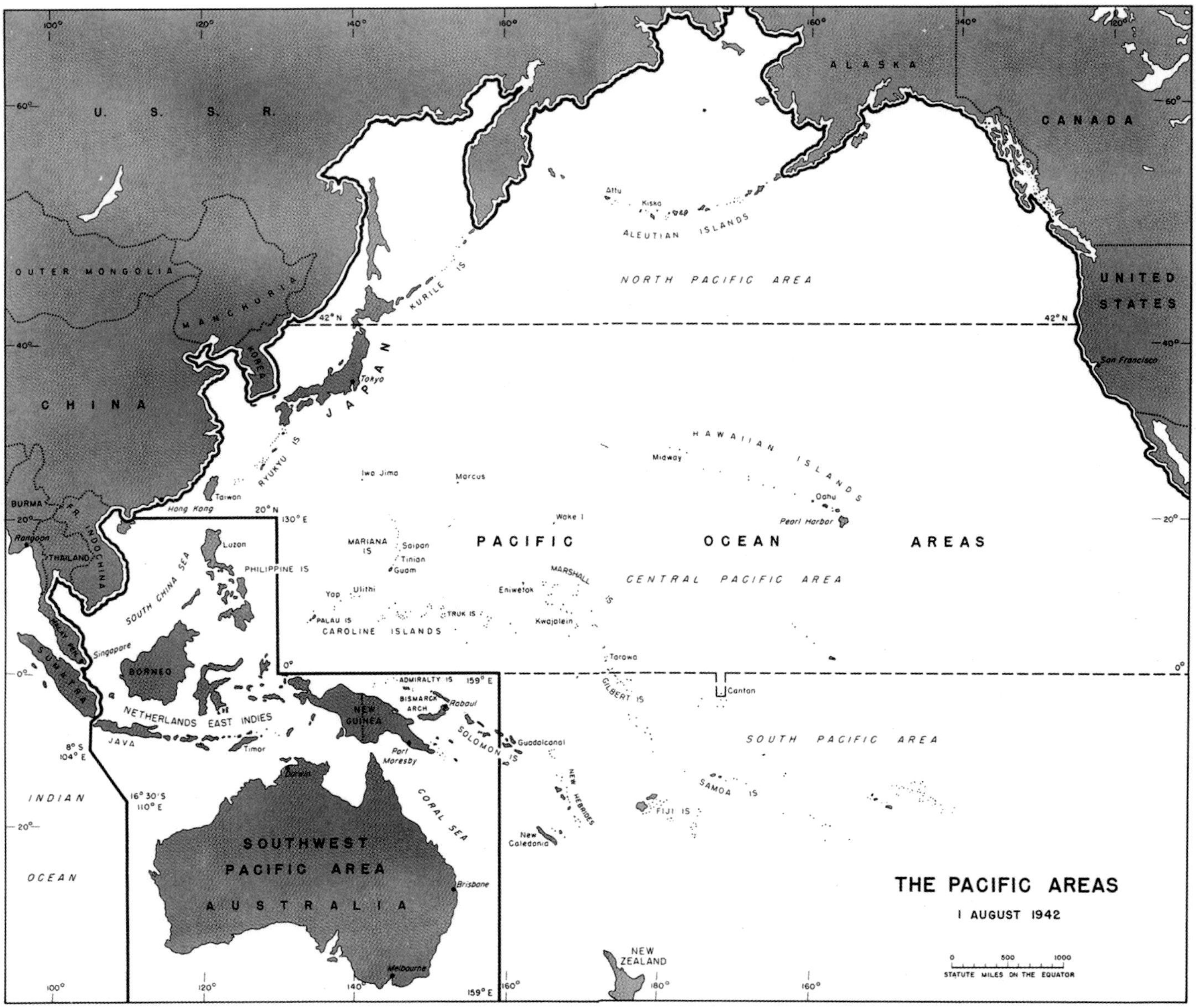

Map of the Pacific Area showing theater command boundaries. The China-Burma-India Theater—the destination of the XX BC—lay west of the Pacific Ocean Area and the Southwest Pacific Area. (*US Army*)

The group briefed the crews on only the first leg of the flight to Maine.[24] Crews still did not know their final destination and many speculated a departure from the country in Maine meant it would be England. The second B-29 to depart Kansas did fly to England, where it was openly photographed and shown to dignitaries to establish some confusion among the Axis powers as to the destination of the wing. A planned "leak" of information at the same time indicated the B-29 could not perform as designed and would now serve as an armed transport plane in Asia. The Japanese were not fooled by the deception attempt.[25]

The first plane to develop trouble along the route made an emergency landing in Maine. Once ground crews arrived and repaired an engine the plane continued to Newfoundland, where many crews waited in a snowstorm for clearance to depart as other crews were already crossing Africa. Capt. James Pattillo of the 468th BG approached his landing in Maine and encountered a strong cross wind that nearly put him into a snowbank. The pilot aborted the landing and returned for a second and successful attempt. When Pattillo landed in Newfoundland the next day, he witnessed B-29s sitting along snowdrifts while crews and mechanics repaired engines.[26] The new power plants continued to plague the bombers throughout their travels to India and beyond. Capt. Pattillo departed Newfoundland in the late afternoon for the long night flight to Morocco. During the night a dancing fire appeared along the edges of the propellers and along the cockpit frame. The frightened crew imagined the worst scenario and questioned the pilot about the fire on the engines. Pattillo explained the phenomena known as "Saint Elmo's Fire"—a harmless electrical discharge experienced by mariners and air crews.[27]

Lt. Misterly and his crew were among the many riding out the storm in Newfoundland when they heard of the first crash of a B-29 deploying to India. The B-29, destined for Cairo from Marrakech, crashed on take-off. Misterly and others absorbed whatever news they could acquire about the accident. Fortunately, all crew members survived the crash, which was later blamed on pilot error.[28] Lt. Yates Smith, a bombardier with the 468th BG, flew with his crew on the air route from Newfoundland to Morocco and witnessed this first crash as the plane attempted to depart for Cairo:

> While there, a B-29 did take-off for Cairo, Egypt. It appeared the pilot wanted to give a performance about the take-off ability of the B-29. He took off with no flaps. About half-way down the runway, he must have found his problem, and called to the Co-pilot to give him some flaps. The flaps started to come down, and they continued to come down until he had full flaps. He only attained about 50 feet of altitude. The plane began to settle, and bellied in an olive grove. The plane caught on fire, and all the crew escaped. It was rumored the crew returned to the states for further training.[29]

Capt. Pattillo encountered engine issues as he departed the airfield in Morocco. The red line temperature for the engines began at 290 degrees. The flight engineer's instrument panel indicated the temperature of all four engines between 310 and 340 degrees as the B-29 struggled to gain altitude before reaching the Atlas Mountains. Pattillo ordered the flight engineer to close the cowl flaps, which provided ventilation for the engines but also resulted in the drag that slowed the speed and climb of the lumbering bomber. The instruments indicated rising engine temperatures, but the plane began gaining altitude. The pilot then asked the flight engineer to crack the cowl flaps to then permit limited cooling of the engines. The B-29 cleared the mountains and the crew settled in for the flight to Egypt.[30]

When Lt. Smith and his crew arrived in Cairo, the navigator for the aircraft purchased several bottles of perfume and placed them in his B-4 personal bag. The crew stored all of their baggage in the bomb bay, rather than the pressurized compartments. Smith mused the perfume corks blew en route to Karachi, forcing the navigator to air his clothes for months. "He never did get rid of the powerful aroma."[31] Misterly arrived the day before his twentieth birthday in anticipation of celebrating by seeing the pyramids, sphinx, and other historical sites of Egypt. Disappointment replaced excitement upon hearing all aircraft needed to immediately continue to Karachi the next morning. As a birthday present, pilot Bart Ellis risked a reprimand and circled the pyramids for Misterly after lifting off from the airfield.[32]

Engine problems continued to plague the B-29s. Maj. Jack Millar, a pilot with the 468th BG, remained grounded for two weeks in Cairo while maintenance personnel replaced all four engines.[33] The 58th BW lost another B-29 at Cairo and Yates Smith witnessed its crash:

> As the departure time from Cairo was at night, we witnessed a sight at the Cairo airport I will not forget. One of the B-29 crews was departing. They had gotten about ½ hour out from Cairo, and developed engine trouble. The pilot returned to Cairo, and was attempting a night heavy weight landing on a strange field...He "landed" about 30 feet above the runway...When the plane did hit the runway, it drove the landing gear up through the wings. The plane skidded several thousand feet on the runway with a brilliant display of sparks. When it finally did come to a rest, the entire crew came running out of the plane. The plane burst into flame, and was a total loss. There was some 50 caliber ammunition in some of the gun turrets. This exploded, and sent shells in all directions. Some of the ammo went through the vertical stabilizer of our plane parked in the infield. This held us up until these were repaired. We had battle damage, and we had not even flown any combat![34]

The 58th lost a second bomber in Cairo. Maj. Benton W. O'Neal of the 40th BG, piloting #249, crashed on landing as the nose gear collapsed. An investigation indicated the nose gear was weakened due to improper towing at another location; all crewmen survived the accident.[35] From Cairo, deploying B-29 crews flew across the Middle East to Karachi. The 58th BW lost two more B-29s in Karachi. A 468th BW B-29 crashed prior to Smith and his crew landing:

Douglas C-47 Skytrain over the Egyptian pyramids. Many of the 58th BW personnel mentioned seeing the pyramids as the highlight of their flights from the United States to India. (*US Air Force*)

> We arrived at Karachi, India, in a terrible sand storm. Major Blackmore's plane (42-6357) was due to land in front of us. We were all running low on fuel. There were no electronic approach systems available as there are today. Everyone was having difficulty finding the runway. Blackmore's plane crashed just before we landed. His plane slid on the ground, and into a British barracks killing some of the soldiers inside.[36]

Maj. Ernest Blackmore and four of his crew also died in the accident. Smith and his crew remained in Karachi five days while an investigation reviewed why the bombers were arriving so low on fuel. The excessive burning of fuel in the arriving B-29s from Cairo resulted from a difference in British and American coding systems. The British coded 90-octane fuel with the color blue and the Americans marked 100-octane fuel with the same color. The B-29s were fueled with 90-octane rather than 100-octane fuel. The lower octane forced the crews to utilize higher power settings to maintain engine temperature, which in turn burned more fuel.

An example of a Liberty Ship. Most 58th BW ground personnel sailed on Liberty Ships as they deployed from the United States. (*US Navy*)

40th BG personnel at the Casablanca, Morocco, tent city during their travels to India. (*Kulicka via 40th BG*)

Misterly's B-29 arrived in Karachi and the crew rested before beginning the final stage of the journey. Following a rack of ribs and wine prepared in a Karachi cafe for the entire crew, Misterly departed for Calcutta and then the B-29 airfield at Charra—also known as "Hell's Half Acre."

Many of the ground crew members and spare air crews traveled by ship to India. Some sailed by a Pacific Ocean route via Australia, while others crossed the Atlantic Ocean and the Mediterranean Sea before passing through the Suez Canal and completing the journey to India across the Indian Ocean. Morton Roth of the 1st Bombardment Maintenance Squadron's dispensary section (40th BG) sailed by the latter route. The personnel of his squadron sailed on the Liberty ship *Abraham Lincoln* from Newport News, Virginia. Roth remembered a couple hundred men packed into one large compartment for living space with cots suspended from poles "six deep." The cot held a man and all of his equipment, as storage areas did not exist. The vessel sailed on February 13, 1944, based on an original planned departure of the group aircraft in mid-March. The men aboard the vessel faced a savage storm soon after sailing, with Roth declaring, "I went to sleep with one hand on the pole from fear of falling." The sailors manning the vessel and the passengers ate separate meals. Roth lamented eating "K" and "C" rations for six days during another storm and a monotony of powdered eggs, stew, and cold sandwiches when the weather calmed. The Navy personnel enjoyed better rations or "three hearty meals" as Roth noted. "One day two of them became ill and we treated them in the ship's hospital. They brought us food from the galley whenever possible to show their appreciation."[37] The *Abraham Lincoln* docked in Oran, Morocco, where the passengers spent a week in a temporary camp awaiting their next vessel. A pass into Oran proved to be the highlight of the layover:

> After issue of a doughboy kit, we rode off in trucks. The first thing we did was visit the immense Red Cross [building]. I ate a few sandwiches and went to a movie. The night dwindled away with me propped up on a bar stool, guzzling cognac and beer that tasted like urine. In a mild stupor, I met the truck to take us back to camp.[38]

Ed Vickery of the 40th BG also sailed from Newport News on the *Abraham Lincoln*. Vickery remembered the sailors doing their best to frighten the army personnel on board their vessel, "The crew on the *Lincoln* wasn't much help; they were always telling stories of how many ships were torpedoed on the last crossing or how lousy the ships were being built and how many just fell apart in the rough seas."[38]

Lt. George Steinman of the 40th BG's 3rd Bomb Maintenance Squadron departed Virginia on February 12, 1944, aboard the *Caleb Strong*. Steinman experienced the same storms encountered by the vessel carrying Roth and Vickery.

The journey of Roth and Vickery continued on the converted liner *Champollion* from Oran to Naples, Italy. Despite the change of vessels the food did not improve. Vickery painfully declared, "The food was pitiful, more than once I saw worms in my food. I practically lived on bread, butter, and marmalade for the whole trip. I haven't used

The Liberty Ship *Abraham Lincoln*. Many of the 58th BW ground personnel crossed the Atlantic Ocean from Newport News, Virginia, to Oran, Morocco, aboard this vessel. (*US Navy*)

Many 40th BG ground personnel sailed on the *Wharton* from the United States. (*Changnon via 40th BG*)

marmalade once since I got out of the service—I had enough for a lifetime on that trip."[39]

All three men awakened on board their ships in Italy as German aircraft attacked Naples harbor, where many transport and combat vessels lay at anchor. Steinman wrote in his diary:

> The city and harbor are in ruins; ships sunk all over the harbor, which is well filled with all types of Allied vessels. We will spend the night here. We awakened at 0130 by bombs and gunfire. We went into the halls [of the vessel] as the bombs rocked the ship. The air raid lasted 45 minutes and then I went back to bed. I was scared![40]

Following further stops in Egypt and Aden, the vessels carrying the initial personnel assigned to the 58th BW arrived in India.

Some air crew members deployed utilizing a combination of air and sea vessels. Lt. Willard Holderby, a 468th BG navigator, sailed from Newport News on March 18, 1944, after a long train ride from Kansas. Holderby's experiences on the *Butner* contrasted greatly with that of Roth. The navigator sailed on a large transport carrying an estimated 5,000 men compared to Roth's voyage on a Liberty ship converted to a troop carrier. Holderby commented that he enjoyed good food, including roasted turkey; cokes and candy at the bar in the lounge; and even a piano in another lounge. From Casablanca, Morocco, Holderby boarded an Air Transportation Command (ATC) Douglas C-54 Skymaster for a flight to India via Libya, Egypt, and Iran. In Tripoli, Libya, Holderby enjoyed talking with British veterans of the North Africa campaign and commented that destroyed vehicles could be seen from the air stretching from Tripoli to nearly Cairo. A disappointed Holderby did not have time to visit the pyramids while in Egypt and marveled at the geography of the Middle East as he flew to Iran. The airfield in Iran served as an exchange point for American military aid to the Soviet Union. Holderby saw between 50 and 100 Bell P-39 Airacobra fighters sitting on the airfield with newly painted red star insignias for the Soviet Union. A ten-hour flight from Abadan, Iran, brought Holderby to Karachi. Following a brief layover in Karachi, the plane continued to Kharagpur, arriving on April 11, 1944.[41]

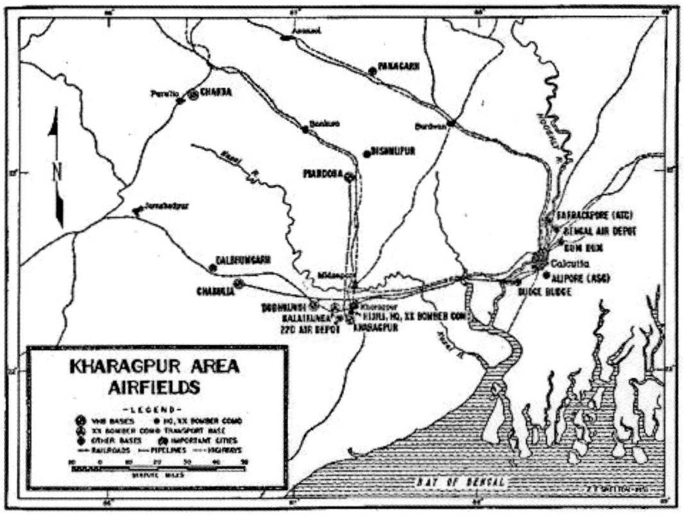

Map showing XX BC B-29 bases around Kharagpur, India. (*US Air Force*)

Gen. Kenneth Wolfe, commander of XX BC, greets Col. Leonard Harman and the first B-29 crew to arrive in India. (*US Air Force*)

Arrival in India

The Allies lengthened the runways at four airfields in India for the XX BC. Each Group operated from its own base: Chakulia (40th BG); Charra and then Dudhkundi (444th BG); Piardoba (462nd BG); and Kharagpur (468th BG). The XX BC established a fifth field at Kalaikunda as a transport base. Everyone complained about the extreme heat, humidity, and dusty conditions prevalent to the area. The bases—originally built by the British—included newly extended runways for the B-29s and few amenities for the air and ground crews, who initially lived in tents. Buildings of local construction for quarters and offices soon replaced the tents. Crews found themselves living in "basha"-style buildings constructed with bamboo and plaster walls, thatched roofs, and hard earth or concrete floors. Prefabricated Nissen and "basha"-style huts served as administrative offices. Some groups even received ex-Italian prefabricated huts from Eritrea, complete with bullet holes from the British campaign in that region.[42]

Establishing the main group bases in India accomplished two goals: keep the B-29s as far away as possible from Japanese bombing and strafing attacks and reduce the amount of supplies needing transport across the Hump. The American bases lay west of Calcutta, which was at the current limit of Japanese aircraft ranges from their air bases. The Chinese were completing the forward staging bases in western China as the bombers arrived in India. The plan for bombing Japan included shuttling fuel and other supplies across the Hump for storage at the forward bases. The day before a raid on Japan or Manchuria (and later other eastern destinations, such as Formosa), the B-29s would fly across the Hump. After refueling and checking maintenance in China the planes launched for their raid. The B-29s returned to the forward air bases for refueling, maintenance, and off-loading any crew members needing immediate medical attention and then flew back across the Hump to India as soon as possible. The plan may seem sound on paper, yet in reality, the XX BC probably faced the greatest logistical challenges of the American bomber campaign against the Axis powers.

Col. Harman flew the first B-29 (#331 *Gone With The Wind*) to arrive at the XX BC bases in India and landed on April 2. Others soon followed on the 11,500-mile journey from Kansas to the bomber fields west of Calcutta. Thirty-two B-29s arrived in India by April 15 and 130 planes by May 8. The XX BC deployed 150 B-29s to India, resulting in a total loss of five bombers along the route and another four damaged due to mishaps.[43] Japanese intelligence sources pinpointed which Indian airfields the Allies prepared for the B-29 groups. Holderby wrote that his duties as one of the earliest arriving crewmen included digging slit trenches in response to Japanese radio threats of bombing the airfield in mid-April.[44]

Misterly distinctly remembered the realization of living among another culture halfway around the world from his native California: "We had to get used to the weird sounds of the night in India. The combination of jackal's calls with native drums was anything but soothing...the

An Indian snake charmer with a cobra. (*Moore via 40th BG*)

The first B-29 to cross the Himalaya Mountains to China. Gen. Laverne Saunders arrived in this aircraft and his "one star" can be seen in the Plexiglass at the bottom of the forward compartment. Gen. Claire Chennault (eighth person from the right) is in the dark military uniform. (*US Air Force*)

more fortunate had lanterns and insect repellent and could brave the bugs for a game of cards. No one ventured forth without both."[45]

Capt. Pattillo remembered settling into his basha hut after an exhausting flight into their new base. As he lay in his rope bed, a rustling noise in the thatch ceiling drew his attention. A quick glance pinpointed an eighteen-inch lizard chasing something in the thatch. Suddenly, a nine-inch centipede dropped from the ceiling onto the ground. One of the crewmen chased it with a shovel and ended its slithering movement toward the door. Warnings about cobras went unheeded until one of the squadron commanders encountered one in his hut. From that point, everyone carried a flashlight whenever moving from bed at night.[46]

Lt. Robert Schumacher, a flight engineer with the 444th BG, received a special welcome committee that greeted his crew after landing in India:

> We flew from Karachi to our base [in India] and landed in the afternoon. After unloading personal items and getting set up for the night, several of us gathered under a huge tree. Someone had brought a gas lantern and after it was lit, it was hung on a large branch. The lantern illuminated a large circle. Among the personal items were several cases of beer. Warm beer beats no beer so everyone was commenting on our "home" when a very large snake entered the circle of light. One of the guys nearest the snake tossed an empty beer can at it. The snake, large king cobra, coiled and displayed its hood. Needless to say, the area was evacuated in record time![47]

Forward Bases in China

Gen. Saunders flew the first Boeing B-29 Superfortress to enter China, crossing the 23,000-foot Himalaya Mountains from India on April 24, 1944. Gen. Chennault led the welcoming party, including 75,000 Chinese laborers cheering the arriving bomber. Capt. William O'Malley—the navigator aboard Saunders's B-29—described this first flight into China with excitement. "And there was China! A most amazing landscape of thousands of cultivated rice paddies. For the first time in my life I had the feeling of being in a different world...Thousands of coolies lined each side of the runway...Everywhere the Chinese would smile and yell 'Ding Hao,' meaning 'very best.'"[48]

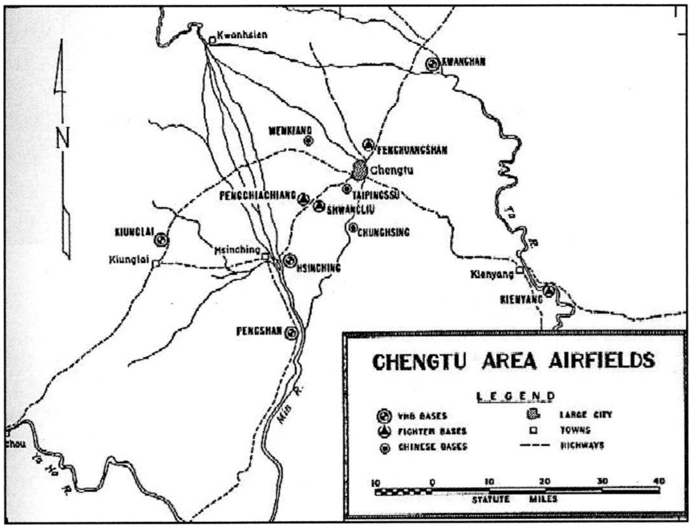

A map showing XX BC airfields around the Chinese town of Chengtu: Hsinching (code named A-1 for the 40th BG), Kiunglai (code named A-5 for the 462nd BG), Kwanghan (code named A-3 for the 444th BG), and Pengshan (code named A-7 for the 468th BG). (*US Air Force*)

Housing conditions for one group of Chinese who constructed XX BC airfields in China. (*US Air Force*)

A mixture of homemade concrete known as "slurry" topped the rocks and was then flattened with giant rollers pulled by huge gangs of men and women during the construction of XX BC runways in China. (*US Air Force*)

On April 26, two more of the massive bombers crossed the Hump carrying gasoline for storage in China. One of these planes, flown by Maj. Charles Hansen, was the B-29 probed by Japanese Capt. Hideo Miyabe and his fellow Oscar fighter pilots.

American engineers surveyed the area around Chengtu, in western China, after Chiang Kai-shek agreed to President Roosevelt's plan to stage B-29s through the country for raids on Japan. The engineers recommended five sites for B-29 bases and all were approved by the Chinese on December 16, 1943. Further discussions resulted in the selection of Hsinching (code-named A-1 for the 40th BG), Kiunglai (code-named A-5 for the 462nd BG), Kwanghan (code-named A-3 for the 444th BG), and Pengshan (code-named A-7 for the 468th BG). The plan also included three fighter bases and several outlying fighter strips for the 312th Fighter Wing (FW) to defend the bomber fields. Gen. Stilwell requested the extensions of runways at several existing B-24 bases for utilization by B-29s. However, the Japanese *Ichi-Go* campaign forced changes in this plan.

Americans planned the airfields and supervised Chinese engineers in the project. Massive labor substituted for heavy construction machinery. The negotiations and frustrations associated with American funding of the construction is worthy of a book itself. An estimated 400,000+ drafted and contracted laborers toiled on all of the airfield projects beginning in late January 1944, and the tremendous efforts of the Chinese in building the airfields are well documented. The Chinese workers literally built the runways by hand. They carried rocks from rivers and streams in baskets, buckets, and wheelbarrows and laid them for the runway foundation. They laid and fitted large stones by hand at the foundation and placed rocks of decreasing size as they moved upward. Laborers utilized small hand-held hammers to break rocks.

An estimated 400,000+ drafted and contracted laborers toiled on all of the airfield projects beginning in late January 1944. Note those working with hoes and hauling rocks and other material in baskets. (*US Air Force*)

Chinese workers moving rocks for runway construction. Upon completion, each bomber field boasted an 8,500-foot runway of rocks and slurry that stood six feet above the rice paddies still in the area. (*US Air Force*)

One of the XX BC airfields in China. Note the mountains the pilots had to contend with when landing or taking off during day as well as night. Many planes went down in the mountains surrounding the airfields. (*40th BG*)

A mixture of homemade concrete known as "slurry" topped the rocks and was then flattened with giant rollers pulled by huge gangs of men and women.[49] Upon completion, each bomber field boasted an 8,500-foot runway of rocks and slurry that stood six feet above the rice paddies still in the area.

The human cost of the project is not as well documented as the results of the work. The Chinese appropriated many local rice paddies, often paying the owners less than the true value of the land. They conscripted most of the labor, paying wages so small that families often had to help feed those working on the airfields. Yet despite the hardships, the Chinese laborers accomplished a project that one would find difficult to duplicate in other societies.

With the B-29s at their rear bases in India, the XX BC turned to the logistical needs for preparing the forward bases in China for operations against Japan beginning in June 1944. Transporting fuel and supplies required for each mission from China as well as just maintaining the forward bases proved to be a monumental task for the crews of the XX BC and the ATC. Flying the Hump proved to be as stressful as combat missions and just as dangerous. A review of these flights—later credited as combat missions for tour durations—will be covered in chapter 3.

Chinese laborers break rocks for runway construction with hand-held hammers. Note the long pipe in the mouth of the man on the right and the two Curtiss P-40 Warhawks in the background. (*US Air Force*)

B-29 #825 of the 462nd BG crashed in Kunglai, China, on May 7, 1944, after crossing the Hump from India. (*US Air Force*)

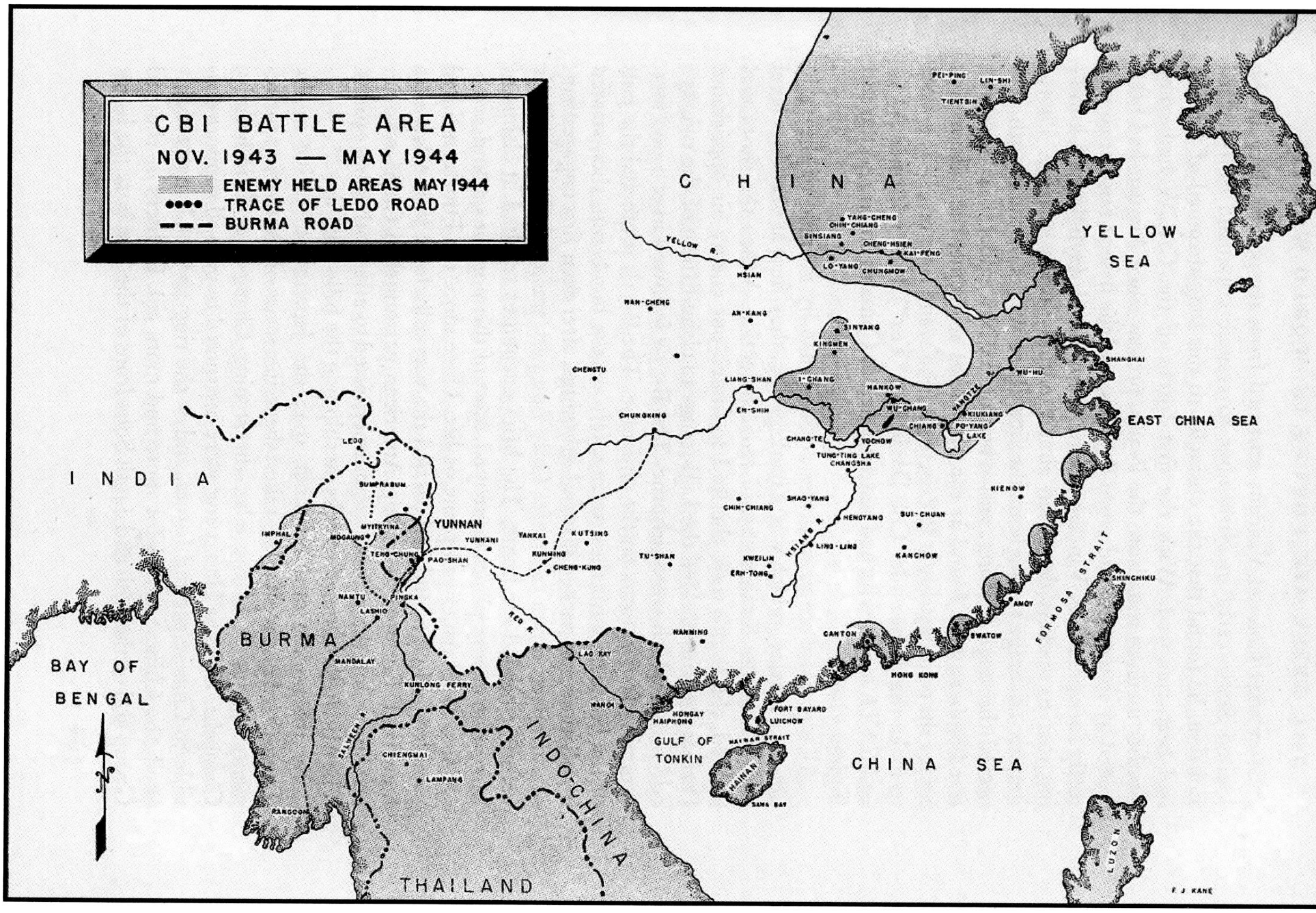

A map of the China-Burma-India (CBI) Theater at the time of the arrival of the XX BC. (*US Air Force*)

In early June 1944, the XX BC conducted its first combat operation—a mission intended to provide crews with combat experience before bombing Japan. Flying from India to conserve the precious fuel stocks in China, the raid resulted in the total loss of five B-29s and the deaths of 15 crewmen. Coupled with three more combat missions in June and July, crashes along the Hump, and an accident, the XX BC began August 1944 with the loss of twenty-six B-29s (two repairable). One-hundred-thirty B-29s arrived in India from the United States by May 8, 1944. In the six weeks of mid-June through July 1944, the XX BC lost 20% of the B-29 force present in India on May 8. Many more would be lost before the separation and final transfer of the XX BC and the 58th BW from India and China in March 1945.

Chapter 2

June 1944: The First Missions

Frankly, we were all pretty scared.

— Lt. Frank Noble (40th BG),
Yawata Raid

In late spring 1944, Allied forces made slow but steady progress against the Japanese except in China, where the Japanese opened Operation *Ichi-Go* in April. In May, British and Indian forces checked a March 1944 Japanese incursion into the area around Imphal, India, forcing them to withdraw into Burma in July. During the spring, Allied forces seized the important airfield at Myitkyina, Burma; established final control over the Admiralty Islands near New Guinea; and landed troops at Biak, New Guinea, as well as Mindanao in the Philippines. Tense fighting continued in Burma as the Allies pushed to seize the town of Myitkyina and drive south.

The Japanese offensive Operation *Ichi-Go* resulted from the Japanese desire to capture airfields in Hunan province and seize a railway corridor between northern China and Indo-China. American aircraft operating from the Hunan fields supported Chinese forces and attacked Japanese shipping along the east coast of China. Japan calculated the United States would deploy B-29s to China and these eastern bases, placing them in easy range of the Japanese home islands. The capture of the airfields would force long-range American bombers to remain in western China, where they would face a more difficult journey to Japan if they attacked at all from that location. Japan assigned over 510,000 soldiers to the huge offensive that continued until December 1944.[1] Operation *Ichi-Go* did not have a major impact on B-29 operations since plans were already in place to stage the bombers through the Chengtu area of western China.

Considerable pressure sat on the shoulders of Gen. Kenneth Wolfe to launch the XX Bomber Command (BC) into combat operations. Hump flights hauling gasoline and other supplies across the Himalaya Mountains to the forward bases in China continued in preparation for the first raid on Japan. The B-29s could not fly to Japan without sufficient fuel stockpiled in China and the movement of this precious commodity proved to be painfully slow and difficult. At the same time, the crews did not hold sufficient operational training experience for a mission to Japan. Wolfe signed a field order on May 17 for a night raid on May 27 within Southeast Asia for the bomber crews to obtain combat experience before attacking the Japanese home islands. A night raid would reduce the effectiveness of the Japanese fighter and anti-aircraft artillery defenses while allowing the crews to place live ordnance over a target. Gen. Arnold vetoed this field order and directed Wolfe to continue bomber training for another week and then dispatch the crews on a daylight raid so they could practice the type of precision mission the United States envisioned against Japanese strategic targets. In response, the B-29 crews practiced formation flying and conducted bombing missions to a range on Halliday Island.

On May 26—exactly one month after Maj. Hansen's encounter with Japanese fighters over the Hump—XX BC directed the 462nd Bomb Group (BG) to dispatch four B-29s across the most southern Hump route to tempt an engagement with the Japanese. The Group record notes,

Gen. Laverne Saunders flew in the first B-29 to arrive in China. Saunders (far left) is talking with two American fighter pilots. Their Curtiss P-40 Warhawks are in the background. (*58th BW*)

Map showing the targets bombed or mined by the XX BC during 1944 and 1945, after launching from bases in India and Ceylon. (*US Air Force*)

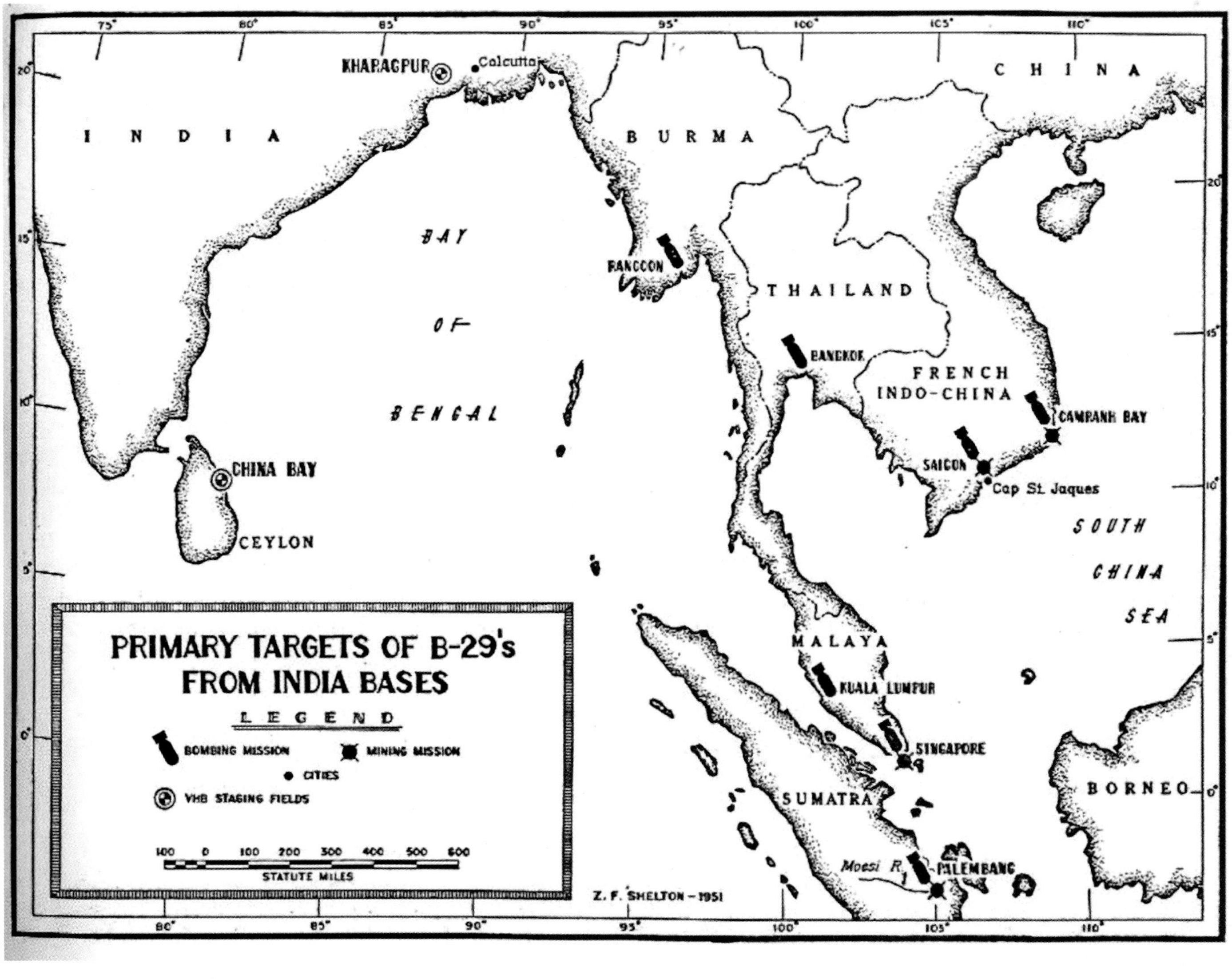

Indians constructing a taxi strip for the 40th BG at the Chakulia airfield. (*US Air Force*)

Runway construction in Chakulia, India. (*US Air Force*)

"The purpose of the flight was primarily to invite Japanese fighter interception and test the fire power and defensive capabilities of the B-29 in a four-ship formation."[2] The group launched the four bombers and one returned early due to an engine problem. A group of Japanese fighters spotted the B-29s near Myitkyina, in northern Burma. However, they chose to fly parallel to the bomber formation and as the group record relates, "...the Japanese seemed content to observe the B-29s from a distance without making an attempt at actual interception."[3]

40th BG briefing for Mission #1 to Bangkok, Thailand. (*Wood via 40th BG*)

Mission #1: Bangkok, June 5, 1944

Gen. Wolfe earmarked the Makasan railway workshops in Bangkok as the primary target for the first B-29 combat mission. The lack of sufficient flying time and training in B-29s in Kansas, as well as limited time to prepare for combat after arriving in India, meant crews needed a mission to hone their skills before tackling a mission over China to Japan. Bangkok offered an important target that could be flown from India without deleting precious supplies of fuel being stockpiled in China for the first raid on Japan. Intelligence sources also indicated fighter and anti-aircraft resistance should be lighter than over Japan. The secondary targets in case one or more bombers could not locate or bomb the primary were the Malagon rail yards in Rangoon for the 40th BG and 444th BG and the Central Railroad station also in Rangoon for the 462nd BG and 468th BG. Based on Gen. Arnold's directions to Gen. Wolfe, this would be a daylight raid.

Briefing for Mission #1. (*US Air Force*)

Another view of crews attending the briefing prior to Mission #1. (*US Air Force*)

The primary target in Bangkok included the only heavy locomotive and railway car repair shop along the Burma-Thailand railroad network. In March 1944, Japanese troops crossed into India from Burma. The Japanese actions were not part of a strategic offensive, but actually a move to forestall an anticipated Allied offensive into Burma from India and cut the railway carrying military supplies. Japanese forces advanced quickly onto the plain near Imphal, forcing the Allies to withdraw orderly and form a defensive perimeter around the city. Counterattacks north of Imphal managed to slowly force the Japanese back to the Burmese border. In early June, fighting continued on Indian soil and most Japanese supplies and troops destined for Burma traveled by railway from Bangkok due to the hazard of Allied attacks along the water route from Singapore. A successful B-29 attack on the Makasan railway workshops in Bangkok, Thailand, could reduce the number of rolling stock capable of carrying supplies to the Japanese troops fighting in eastern India, as well as those combating the Allies in Burma near Myitkina.

Bomb loads for the Bangkok mission included 500-pound general purpose high explosives and M18 incendiary clusters designed to break into smaller bomblets and ignite multiple fires. The groups fused the general purpose (high explosive) bombs to allow penetration of the workshops before exploding. The XX BC wanted to test the new M18 incendiaries and the primary target provided this opportunity. Many of the buildings and freight cars were constructed from wood and a small oil processing facility was in the area, offering a highly flammable target for the incendiary munitions. The first three bomb groups over the target carried the general purpose weapons while the final group held the incendiaries.

The XX BC earmarked 112 aircraft and ninety-eight launched for the first B-29 combat raid: 40th BG (twenty-six planes), 444th BG (twenty-six planes), 462nd BG (twenty planes), and the 468th BG (twenty-six planes). Thirteen of the airborne planes aborted: twelve due to mechanical problems and #229 of the 468th BG failed to locate its formation in the foul weather. One B-29 crashed on take-off. Those planes failing to even take-off suffered primarily from ignition and supercharger regulator trouble. Oil leaks dominated the list of problems for B-29s aborting the mission and returning to India, which also included failures in oil coolers and distributor seal leakage. Failures of the fuel transfer system proved especially troublesome. Many aircraft returned from the raid with nearly exhausted fuel tanks and two ditched as a result of failed fuel transfer pumps. Mechanical conditions were not the only problems faced by the crews of this first XX BC mission; the mission launched as a tropical cyclone roared across the Bay of Bengal. The foul weather resulted in B-29 crews joining the formations of other groups rather than their own, planes bombing individually and not in a formation, and one plane aborting after not being able to locate its formation.

The B-29 that crashed on take-off belonged to the 40th BG. Maj. John Keller piloted B-29 #318 as it rolled down

Engine maintenance on a 40th BG B-29, probably in India, judging by the clothing choice of the mechanic. XX BC maintenance personnel faced many challenges related to weather, logistics, and an aircraft rushed to combat. (*40th BG*)

#298 *Katie* of the 40th BG undergoing an engine change. Malfunctioning engines proved to be a major concern during the early months of the XX BC campaign from India and China. (*40th BG*)

the runway. Midway on the take-off roll, Keller lifted the nose wheel from the ground and held it in the air, causing the tail skid to hit the runway several times. The plane lifted from the runway and appeared to be flying normally. The left wing dropped but the pilot leveled it. The wing then dropped again and the plane lost altitude and struck the ground in a fireball. Ten crew members and one observer died in the crash. The co-pilot survived, although seriously injured, and reported that engine #2 on the left wing lost power during the take-off, causing the crash.[4]

Maj. John Millar, pilot of the 468th BG's #356 *Georgia Peach*, aborted the mission due to failing engines. Several hundred miles over the Bay of Bengal, two of *Georgia Peach*'s four engines suddenly shut down; Millar tried to restart them but failed. The plane began losing altitude, forcing Millar to reverse course and head back to India. The crew jettisoned the bomb load, ammunition, and extra equipment in an attempt to slow the steady loss of altitude. Millar managed to keep his ship aloft as they reached the coast of India and offered his men their only two options: abandon *Georgia Peach* and parachute into the jungle and swamps below or ride the plane in for a forced landing. The crew opted to ride with Millar.

Millar reached his Indian base barely above treetop level and approached for an emergency landing. By now, *Georgia Peach* flew on one engine and she would lose that last power plant while landing. Millar chose to delay lowering his landing gear to reduce the altitude loss caused by the extra drag. He knew if he waited too long the plane would settle on the landing gear before it was fully extended and would end up bellying across the runway. Millar gave it his best estimate and lowered the gear just prior to touchdown. Left gunner Sgt. Lyle Dickinson later stated that as he watched through his blister window, the landing gear fully extended with only one foot of clearance above the runway.[5]

Ground crew of the 40th BG's #281 *Heavenly Body*. Ground crews performed near miracles to keep B-29s operational and have been highly praised by the air crews during and after the war. (*Kamp via 40th BG*)

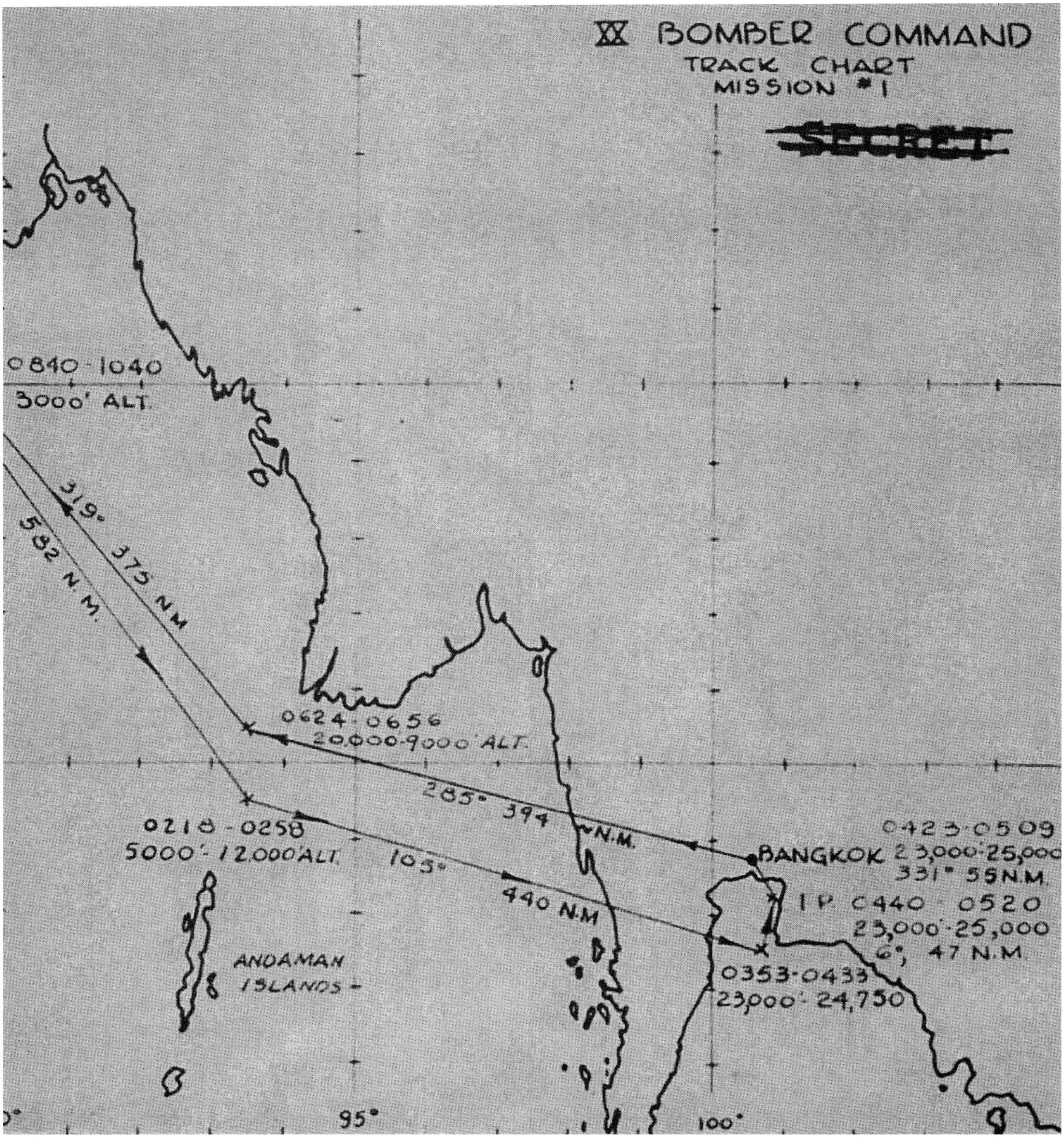

XX BC utilized this chart to brief pilots and navigators on the routes to and from Bangkok, Thailand, during Mission #1. The bombers flew toward the southeast off the coast of Burma until reaching a point south of Bangkok, where they conducted a 90° turn to the north to reach the Initial Point (IP). From the IP, the bombers turned slightly to the northwest on the bomb run before retiring back to the Bay of Bengal and returning to India. (*US Air Force*)

The 40th BG's #344 *Princess Patsy* takes off during Mission #1 to Bangkok, Thailand. (*40th BG*)

Maj. John Keller (front row, far left) and his crew from the 40th BG's #318. The B-29 crashed after taking off for Mission #1. The co-pilot (Lt. Burton Elsner, second from left in the front row) was the only survivor. (*40th BG*)

The 40th BG's #310 (later named *Hump Happy Jr.*) takes off from India during Mission #1. (*40th BG*)

Maintenance cleaning for the forward upper turret guns on the 40th BG's #342 *Sister Sue*. After a May 1944 test of the plane's defensive armament, gunner Cal Brown related, "I pulled the trigger and lowered my sight and swung to the left and put three rounds in [our] number 1 engine." (*Calvin via 40th BG*)

The central fire control gunner's position at the top of the B-29, where he maintained a vigil looking from an upper blister. He is holding onto a remote-controlled gun sight. (*US Air Force*)

Another 40th BG B-29 suffered damage from its own guns during the mission. To understand how this could happen, one can turn to a similar incident with #342 *Sister Sue*—another 40th BG B-29—over India two months earlier. *Sister Sue* required an engine change after arriving in India. The crew tested the new engine after its replacement and the pilot, Capt. Ernest Turner, requested the crew to check their gun systems while airborne. The electrical control of the turrets could be passed between crew members based on who had the best view of an attacking fighter. The bombardier assumed the primary lead operating the forward upper gun turret unless on the final bomb run. Crew member Cal Brown, central fire control (CFC) senior gunner, reported that bombardier Lt. Tom Sample powered his system to fire the upper turret:

> The gun sight in the nose was pointed forward as were the guns in a stowed position. After the system was powered up, Sample closed the action switch on his gun sight, the guns harmonized with his sight and he pulled the trigger, nothin happened. He said "Brown these guns won't fire, what's the problem?" I said "give the turret to me and I'll see if they will fire from my gun sight." Sample turned his control off and I turned mine on and I had control of the turret. My gun sight was pointed at about 10 o'clock high. When I closed my action switch, the guns harmonized with my sight, I pulled the trigger and they worked fine. I told Sample to try again from his sight. It was still pointed forward so the guns harmonized with his sight and would not fire. I told him to give the turret back to me. I closed my action switch, the guns harmonized with my sight, I pulled the trigger and lowered my sight and swung to the left and put three rounds in number 1 engine. One round went though the prop blade. Capt. Turner said "CEASE FIRE, CEASE FIRE." Oil came streaming up and over the wing and the prop was feathered and we came down and landed.[6]

Upon landing, Col. Walter Lucas met the plane and asked which crew member held responsibility for central defensive fire control. Brown indicated he was the man and Lucas demanded to know what happened. Brown explained he did not know but intended to discover the problem. A check of the forward gun turret revealed the problem:

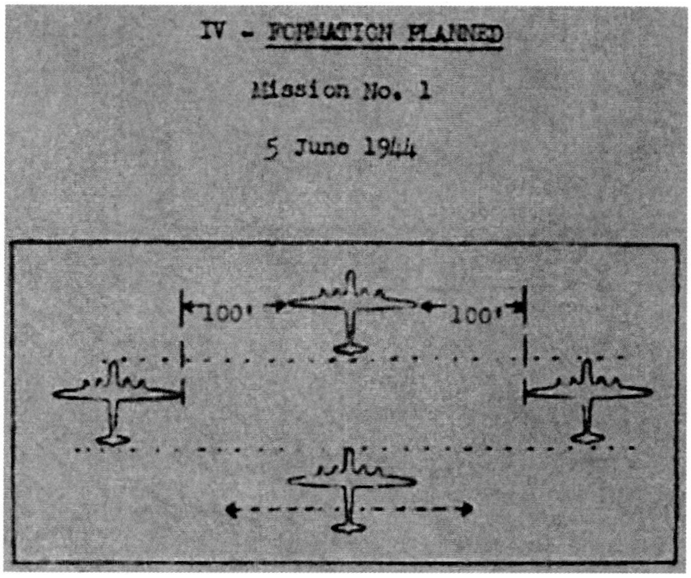

The positioning of B-29s to establish a four-plane formation for Mission #1. This diagram accompanied the XX BC's pre-mission briefing documents. (*US Air Force*)

> We tore into the turret and found the fire interrupter, which we called a "gallon bucket," which was a sleeve with raised cams mounted on it to resemble the outline of the plane. Whenever the guns were pointed at any part of the plane, micro switches would ride up into these cams and cut the firing circuit to the guns. In our upper forward turret this sleeve was installed backwards at the factory. Meaning that when Sample tried to fire forward, the tail was out in front of the plane. Had the guns been pointed aft, he could have shot the tail off. I reported this to Colonel Lucas. All the planes in the Group were grounded and we heard that there were three planes that had the same problem.[7]

A similar issue re-occurred to the 40th BG B-29 during the Bangkok mission and fortunately, the malfunctioning turret did not cause enough damage to bring down the bomber.

Seventy-seven B-29s bombed the Makasan railway workshops in Bangkok through heavy to complete cloud cover, forcing most of the planes to drop by radar. Several aircraft flew more than one bomb run, trying to pinpoint the workshops through the clouds. Seven aircraft arrived at Bangkok, but were not able to bomb for various reasons. Bomb wing and group records do not indicate the specific reasons for the failure to bomb the target, but maintenance documents annotate at least six B-29s suffered bomb bay related mechanical problems. One example is B-29 #332 *Belle of Baltimore* of the 462nd BG, which failed to drop its bombs due to a faulty release mechanism. The crew managed to correct the problem and drop their bomb load near Tavoy, Burma, with unobserved results due to overcast skies. Another 462nd BG B-29 dropped its ordnance prior to completing the bomb run. B-29 #248 *Green Dragon*, flown by Capt. R. Steen, lost an engine as it turned into the final bomb run, forcing the pilot to feather it. Japanese fighters spotted the crippled bomber and attacked from the 3 o'clock position. The bombardier jettisoned the bomb load and the pilot took evasive action into the clouds to avoid the fighters.[8]

Reconnaissance photographs taken during and after the mission indicated little damage to the railway workshops in Bangkok: an estimated 18 bombs fell within the target area with 14 causing damage to buildings, rolling stock, and track. Several civilian buildings outside the target area suffered destruction or damage during the attack. Photographs of the target area did not show any damage to the railway workshops from incendiaries, but other photographs seemed to show they possibly hit a Japanese barracks area.

Anti-aircraft fire over Bangkok proved to be meager and inaccurate, with only one B-29 receiving a single minor flak hole in its rudder. The Japanese tended to fire in patterns of 20□30 bursts lasting two to three seconds. Although the bursts were at correct altitudes, they were often approximately 500 yards to the right of the bombers. Due to the heavy clouds that day, the Japanese may have been employing radar-directed guns as well as utilizing fighters as spotters. One B-29 crew reported seeing a lone Japanese fighter at their altitude but beyond gun range as several bursts of anti-aircraft fire erupted close to the bomber. The B-29s employed a standard defensive tactic, changing altitude as soon as they released their bombs over the target.

Japanese fighter opposition proved to be light, and it has been speculated that the appearance of the B-29s over Bangkok caught everyone on the ground by surprise despite indications they had been warned of their approach. The XX BC mission report summarizes the fighter resistance over Bangkok:

Post-mission reconnaissance photograph utilized to produce the damage analysis after Mission #1. (*US Air Force*)

> Opposition by enemy fighters was negligible, consisting of nine enemy aircraft making a total of twelve passes over the target area at altitudes from 20,000 to 25,000 feet. Evidence exists that the Japanese air raid warning nets had been alerted; yet there was no attempt at interception before the general target was reached. Despite the fact that the first B-29 reached the target at 0422Z, the first definite attack did not materialize until 0452Z. The last attack was made at 0532Z, 30 minutes before the last B-29 left the target.[9]

The few seemingly half-hearted aerial engagements were the first since the probing of the B-29 piloted by Maj. Charles Hansen over the Hump in April 1944. B-29 gunners were awarded a total of one "probable" fighter destroyed and two "damaged" fighters. Officially crediting bomber gunners proved to be a difficult task throughout the war. Gunners submitted their claims during the intelligence debriefing following each mission. The intelligence personnel reviewed the debriefings of each man to develop a clearer picture of the aerial combat and sort out how many enemy fighters were downed by the gunners. The military reported bomber and fighter gunnery scores in terms of three categories: "destroyed," "probable," and "damaged." "Damaged" indicates the gunner placed rounds into the attacking fighter but did not cause enough damage to indicate it crashed as a result of the engagement. The category "probable" means a gunner more than likely destroyed the fighter but crash confirmation is lacking. Proof that would verify a "probable" kill and give the gunner official credit could include a second witness to the event, evidence of a crash site, or clear indication of destruction, such as an aerial explosion of the fighter. Fighter attacks against bombers tended to be over enemy territory at high altitudes, negating locating a crash site. Claims tended to be inflated for many reasons. The fog of war resulted in confusing and fast aerial attacks as fighters streaked toward and away from the bomber formations. Smoke or contrails from a fighter often led to destruction claims, even though the fighter might have sustained minor or even no damage. Often a fighter spinning toward the earth and on fire would be claimed by multiple gunners who had fired upon it. The April 1944 attack on Maj. Hansen's B-29 is a good example of this confusion. The B-29 tail gunner reported watching a Japanese Oscar trailing smoke and diving toward the ground. Following the intelligence debriefing he was awarded a "probable" kill of the fighter. After the war, Capt. Hideo Miyabe, the Japanese commander on the mission, noted that all of his fighters returned safely. In turn, Miyabe claimed and received credit for downing Hansen, who actually landed safely with only eight bullet holes in the fuselage but carrying a wounded gunner.

B-29 crews reported fighter attacks over Bangkok were varied and executed with little or no planning of how to attack the Superfortress. Many Japanese aircraft flew beyond gun range and never attacked the bombers. Post-mission intelligence personnel estimated from the collection of debriefings that nine fighters attacked the B-29s, including four Nakajima Ki-43 Oscars, two Nakajima Ki-44 Tojos, one Kawasaki Ki-61 Tony, one Kawasaki Ki-45 Nick, and one unidentified aircraft. The lack of determined attacks could have resulted from an underestimation of the B-29's speed and/or a desire by the Japanese aviators to observe the bombers on a mission to gather more information for future engagements.

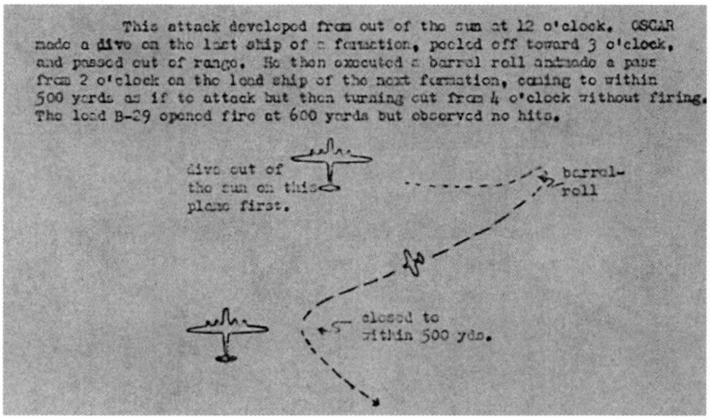

XX BC produced this diagram and description of a Japanese fighter attack against B-29s from a post-mission intelligence debriefing of crew members. The incident occurred during Mission #1. (*US Air Force*)

468th BG B-29s returning to India following Mission #1. (*US Air Force*)

In one brief engagement, an Oscar fighter approached a B-29 in a Split-S maneuver from the 10 o'clock position above the bomber (referred to as 10 o'clock high). The bombardier in the upper forward turret and the senior gunner in the upper aft turret opened fire when the Oscar approached within 1,000 yards of the bomber. The fighter broke off the attack at 500 yards and turned toward the 5 o'clock position, where the tail gunner opened fire with a short burst; the crew observed tracers striking the Oscar's belly and tail. The Japanese plane continued its withdrawal without presenting any indication the hits altered its flight.[10]

Another Oscar approached a B-29 formation of four bombers from a high frontal dive and flew alongside them out of gun range. The fighter then turned toward one of the bombers for a level attack at the 3 o'clock position. The upper and lower aft turrets commenced firing at 600 yards and the Oscar broke away and dove without returning fire. The gunners aboard the bomber reported tracers appeared to hit the Oscar as it broke its attack, but they could not see any damage.[11]

A third Oscar made what is perhaps the most elaborate attack against the B-29s; the Japanese pilot demonstrated he was probably a veteran and had engaged bombers in earlier battles. He dove out of the sun at the 12 o'clock position on a formation of four B-29s. He fired upon the last bomber in the formation and peeled off toward the 3 o'clock position. The Japanese pilot made a barrel roll and attacked the lead B-29 in the next formation from the 2 o'clock position. He approached within 500 yards of the bomber and then turned toward the 4 o'clock position and departed the area without firing. The second B-29 opened fire on the Oscar but the gunners did not observe any hits. It is not known whether the Oscar pilot experienced problems with his guns or was testing the response of the B-29 gunners.[12]

The XX BC lost four B-29s returning from Bangkok: two 40th BG bombers ditched in the Bay of Bengal; one 444th BG B-29 crashed in China; and a 462nd plane made a crash landing in India. Capt. John N. Sanders, piloting #282 of the 40th BG, ditched due to a lack of fuel. Sanders flew the mission without testing the B-29's fuel transfer system after take-off from India. The fuel system pump performed well during a test on the ground prior to the mission and according to the group report, "its previous excellent air operation was taken for granted."[13] After completing the bomb run and turning towards home Sanders initiated a transfer of fuel. When the pump failed, Sanders asked his navigator to plot a return course to the nearest Allied airfield at Cox's Bazar in India (currently Bangladesh), near the border with Burma. Upon arrival, the navigator indicated he was not sure of the plane's exact location and the field they spotted could be held by the Japanese. Rather than risk landing and handing a new B-29 to the Japanese, the pilot opted to continue farther to Chittagong, India. The fuel tanks emptied fourteen miles short of Chittagong, forcing the crew to ditch approximately 1½ miles off shore. Sanders made an impressive landing, but both pressurized compartments began filling with water as soon as the plane settled.

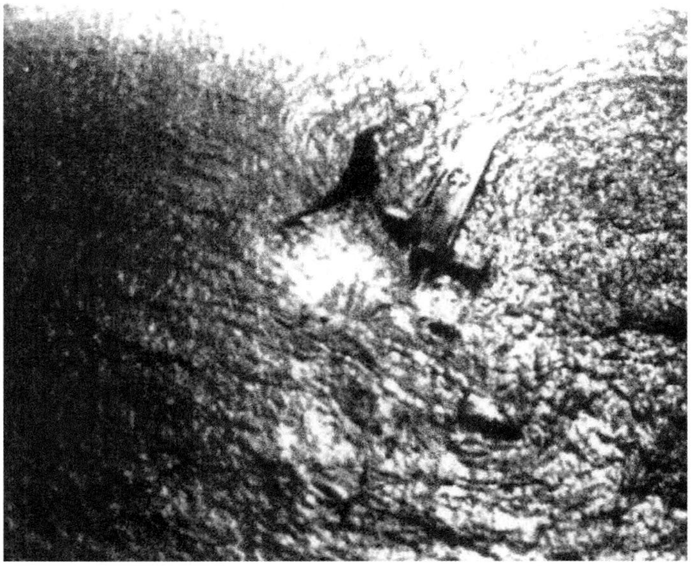

#242 of the 40th BG is floating in the Bay of Bengal after the crew ditched on the return from Mission #1. Incredibly, the B-29 remained afloat and beached itself the day after the crash. (*US Air Force*)

Sanders checked the others in the forward compartment and then climbed through the pilot's window onto the top of the fuselage. He looked toward the rear hatch behind the radar compartment and noticed it was not open. The pilot ran along the top of the aircraft to the hatch and managed to pry it open. An inflated life raft blocked the exit and had to be cut free of the aircraft. He then pulled Sgt. J. J. Drenk (senior gunner) from the B-29 but could not see other crew members. Looking toward the forward area, Sanders saw Lts. W. C. Burrows (co-pilot) and C. H. Moore (flight engineer) attempting to open the top gun sight blister and remove Sgt. D. H. Capshaw (right gunner) from the wreck. Capshaw sustained a hip injury in the crash and struggled with pain as his crew members tugged to pull him free of the aircraft. Two Royal Air Force Supermarine Spitfires circled to pinpoint the B-29's position and guide a rescue vessel. A total of six men made it into two life rafts to await a British Air Sea Rescue launch that arrived forty-five minutes later. As the crew boarded the launch one of the Spitfires buzzed the B-29, alerting the others to the appearance of Lt. W. E. Eckelman (bombardier) at a blister opening. Although the bombardier flew in the forward section with the command crew members, his ditching station was the aft gunner and radar compartment. Sanders and Moore returned to the bomber via a small dinghy. They entered the B-29 and began chopping their way through the aft compartment with axes in search of any other survivors. Finding none, they returned to the launch with Eckelman.

The bombardier later informed debriefers the rear pressurized door opened on impact and the compartment flooded. He remembered Lt. Solomon Fishman calling for others to follow him. At this point Eckelman reported all of the crew members in the aft had survived the crash. Eckelman had a difficult time getting past the overturned cots and the armor plated door and passed out. He regained consciousness and heard the sound of the Spitfire flying above the bomber. According to the crash report:

> He [Eckelman] was tangled in control cables and the smell of gas was very strong, burning his nostrils, eyes, and skin and making breathing difficult. He pulled out his gun and fired 2 shots through the fuselage to attract attention, after which the gun jammed and he lost his clip with the remaining 5 shells in the water when he tried to fix it in the darkness. He then realized that he was caught between the armor plate doors and the cots but was finally able to work himself loose. He turned and was able to see that the top blister was off. Finally, he managed to open the armor plate and get past it into the gunners' compartment and out the blister hole...[14]

The bomber remained afloat and beached itself the next day. Sanders returned to the plane on June 7 with representatives of the XX BC and 40th BG to remove classified material, assess the damage, and search for missing crewmen. The four missing crew members were seen alive by Eckelman before he passed out, but they were never found. A number of escape-related modifications to B-29s evolved from analyzing this crash. The ditching report praised Sanders for his judgment to ensure the B-29 did not fall into Japanese hands when the crew did not know which side held the airfield at Cox's Bazar. At the same time, the report noted the crew should have known this information and stressed that front line details should be emphasized in greater detail prior to future missions.[15]

A second 40th BG B-29 (#304) ditched in the Bay of Bengal due to a faulty fuel transfer system. The pilot, Maj. Alex Zamry, checked the transfer pump en route to the target and it proved operative. After bombing the target Zamry checked the pump again. During each check, the pilot did not transfer more than a small amount of fuel due to his desire to maintain the plane's center of gravity. Zamry attempted to transfer fuel when the gauges for each engine averaged 350 to 400 gallons. The pump failed and the flight engineer conducted several procedures to correct the problem. The crew began dumping fuel in

Maj. Alex Zamry (center, bottom row) and his crew of the 40th BG's #304 ditched in the Bay of Bengal due to a faulty fuel transfer system while returning from Mission #1 to Bangkok. Zamry did not survive the crash. (*40th BG*)

First Lt. Ashley Briggs, co-pilot of the 40th BG's #304, shakes the hand of the village chief who helped him and the other crew members when they ditched returning from Mission #1 to Bangkok. (*Wotipka via 40th BG*)

preparation for an emergency landing when all attempts at transfer proved unsuccessful.

The B-29 landed well, but ocean swells quickly covered the nose and its forward compartment. The Identification Friend or Foe (IFF) device contained an explosive device designed to detonate upon a crash to ensure this highly sensitive equipment did not fall into Japanese hands. When the IFF device detonated, it is believed it ignited the remaining fuel on board the aircraft, resulting in a large explosion.[16] Sgt. Wayne Wiseman, the left gunner, declared:

> Upon hitting the water, we were blown out of the ship, all except Lieutenant Briggs [Ashley Briggs, co-pilot] and Lieutenant Phalon [Joseph Phalon, flight engineer] who escaped through a window, and it seemed it shot me under the water like a bullet for I could feel the water pressure on my chest...After coming up and going down for the third or fourth time, I finally got my Mae West to inflate and could see some of the other fellows around. It seemed as if Lieutenant Beal [Jesse Beal, radar operator] and I were further away from the ship than the others and I saw Lieutenant Briggs and Lieutenant Phalon finally get the rubber life rafts out of the top of the ship.[17]

The plane carried the standard crew of eleven plus one observer. All aboard escaped from the B-29 and survived the explosion except Zamry and Sgt. Joseph Harvey, the radio operator. Wiseman continued to find himself pushed farther from the aircraft and the others by the powerful swells. The gunner and Beal, who had a broken arm and leg, hollered for the other crew members in life rafts to pick them up, but they could not see them because of the swells. Some of those in the rafts had broken bones and others were vomiting blood. Wiseman called out throughout the night in a vain attempt to be found. A wave brought Wiseman and Beal together and they struggled to survive the night, vomiting from sea water, fighting the swells for air, and combating a rain squall:

Five 40th BG crew members of #304 pose with the village chief who aided them following their ditching on the return leg of Mission #1. First row (l-r): Joe Phalon, Gil Bleyl, "The Chief," and Jim Evans. Back row (l-r): Barney Wotipka and Ashley Briggs. (*Wotipka via 40th BG*)

The Chief who, along with other villagers, rescued the crew of #304. (*Wotipka via 40th BG*)

> We kept on floating and wondering just when we would run into one of those sharks, for we knew they were there. We kept fighting the waves and the crabs that would pinch us with a terrific pinch. I had more trouble with them for my clothes were torn...It seemed now he [Beal] was even delirious at times. We weathered that squall much the same as we did the other, by going as long as we could and then turning around to get a little air. That was the longest and most dreadful night I have ever spent or hope to spend in my life.[18]

The next afternoon, the two men spotted a small boat. Although it could be a Japanese craft, the pair struggled toward it to find their crew members, who had tied the two rafts together. Those on the rafts hauled Wiseman and Beal on board and gave them the little fresh water still in the emergency bottles. Although land could be seen, it took hours to reach due to the tides and each life raft beached on a different small island. People living nearby spotted one of the groups and returned to rescue all of the men. The crew members traveled by small boat to a local village, where they were fed and cared for until a plane spotted a mirror waved by Lt. Barney Woptika, the bombardier.[19] The village chief visited the 40th BG after the incident, receiving a hero's welcome from the surviving crew members.

The 444th BG lost a B-29 after the bombing of Bangkok. Capt. Booth G. Malone, piloting B-29 #361, experienced a fuel shortage due to engine trouble and diverted his aircraft to the American airfield at Kunming, China. The crew expended their remaining fuel over Yu-Chi (nearly sixty miles short of Kunming), forcing them to bail out. The Chinese aided the crew and helped them reach the airfield for evacuation back to India. All of the crew survived except one of the gunners, Staff Sgt. Alfred Oren.[20] The fourth XX BC loss on the return from Bangkok involved the 462nd BG's #336, which crash landed at Dum Dum airfield, near Calcutta, due to fuel shortage. Engine #4 cut out due to lack of fuel as the plane landed, resulting in a loss of control and a total washout of the bomber. All of the crew members survived.[21]

Placing the Bangkok raid into perspective and going strictly by the calendar, Rome fell to Allied military units the same day as the first B-29 combat mission in Asia. The next day, American, British, and Canadian forces landed in Normandy, France, commencing the ground campaign against Germany through France while demands mounted for Wolfe to launch the first B-29 strike on the Japanese home islands.

Mission #2: Yawata, June 15-16, 1944

The XX BC and each group reviewed the lessons learned from the first B-29 mission and continued hauling fuel and supplies across the Hump to China in preparation for the first Superfortress raid on Japan. Although Wolfe mounted the June 5 attack on Bangkok, the highest levels of the United States government wanted the morale boost of a strike against Japan itself. Gen. Hap Arnold—officially the XX Air Force commander, as well as the entire Army Air Force—contacted Wolfe the day after the Bangkok raid and urgently informed him the chiefs of staff needed an immediate raid on the Japanese home islands in support of the Chinese who were in retreat in eastern China due to the *Ichi-Go* offensive. The raid would also support an "important operation" in the Pacific (the invasion of Saipan). Not only would the bombing boost Chinese morale, but the raid combined with the Saipan invasion would serve as a major victory in the eyes of the American public. Wolfe replied he could place fifty B-29s over a Japanese target by June 15 and fifty-five bombers if delayed to June 20. Arnold countered and informed Wolfe to have seventy planes over Japan on June 15. It was important for American political and military leaders to launch the first B-29 attack on the Japanese home islands the same day as the invasion of Saipan. Wolfe placed tight fuel restrictions on the 312th Fighter Wing (FW), protecting his forward bases and pushing as much fuel forward from India as operationally possible.

B-29 #336 of the 462nd BG. The group lost #336 when it crash-landed in Dum Dum, India, due to fuel shortage on the return flight of Mission #1. (*US Air Force*)

The 40th BG's #254 *Hump Happy Pappy*. (*US Air Force*)

XX Air Force and XX BC selected the Imperial Iron and Steel Works at Yawata, on the island of Kyushu, as the primary target in accordance with the strategic bombing priorities outlined in the November 1943 Committee of Analysis document. Imperial produced an estimated 24% of Japan's steel output. Analysts indicated damage to the three coke ovens would have the greatest impact on reducing steel production; B-29 crews were briefed to utilize the largest coke oven as the main aiming point for their bomb loads. Laoayo Harbor, through which phosphates, coking coal, and manganese flowed from China destined for Japan served as the secondary target.

Yawata lay 3,200 miles from the B-29 bases in China. Flying the B-29s in a combat formation for such a distance would place additional strain on the crews. In response, Gen. Arnold concurred with a request to conduct the mission at night, with crews flying and bombing individually by radar, rather than in formation. The plan called for two pathfinder B-29s to depart before the other planes. The earliest arriving bombers would hit the target from 8,000 to 10,000 feet. Subsequent bombers would increase the altitude to 14,000 to 18,000 feet based on the theory Yawata should be sufficiently illuminated by the bombs of the first crews over the target.

Air crews continued hauling fuel and supplies across the Hump immediately after the Bangkok mission in preparation for the first raid on Japan. The 468th BG lost two B-29s within three days after Bangkok. On June 7, Maj. James Pattillo and his crew crashed crossing the Hump on a return flight from China. Pattillo flew nearly 200 miles in #271 *Hellin' Helen* with a runaway propeller that he could not feather before crashing.[22] On June 8, Lt. Leslie

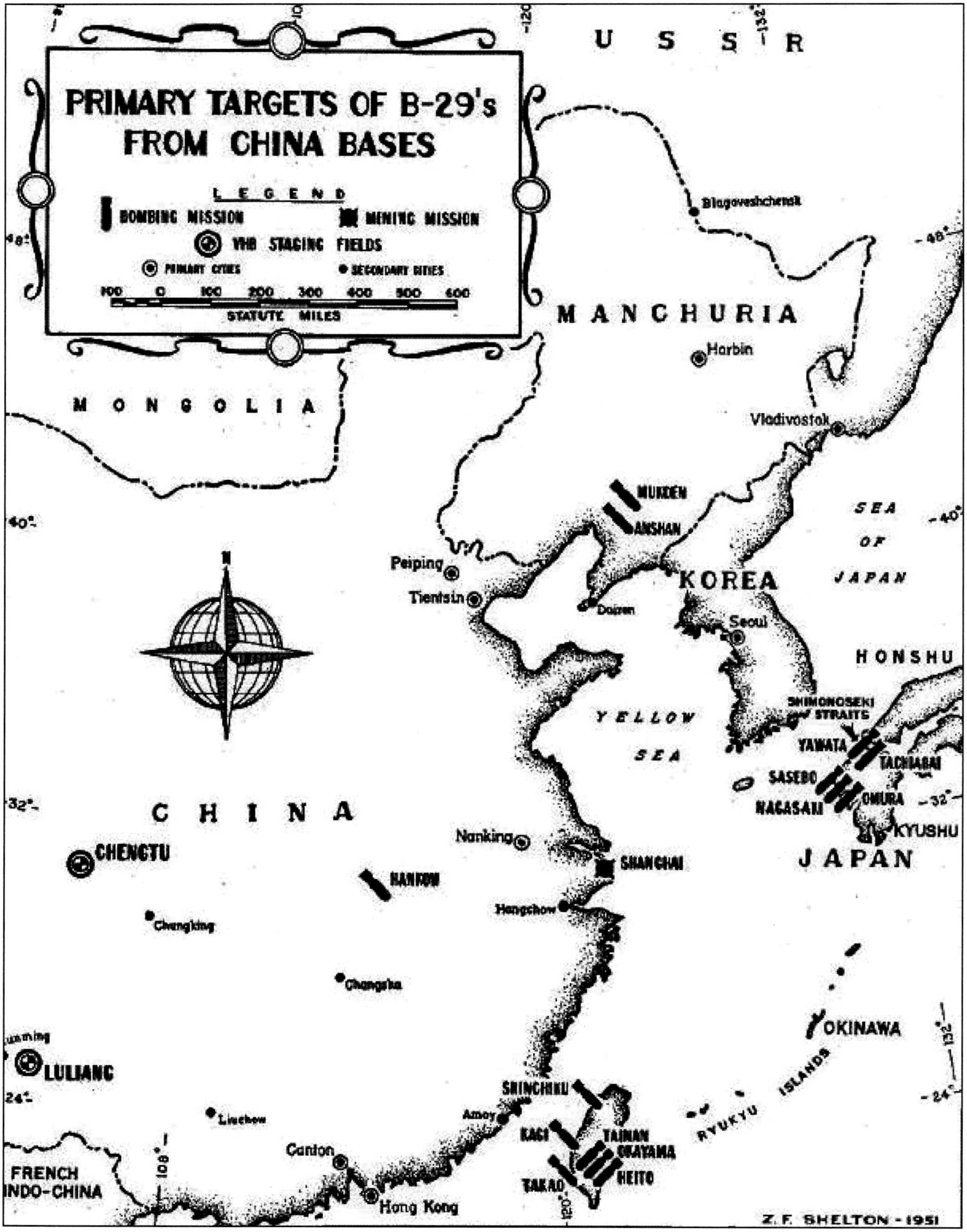

The targets bombed or mined by the XX BC during 1944 and 1945, after launching from the forward bases in China. (*US Air Force*)

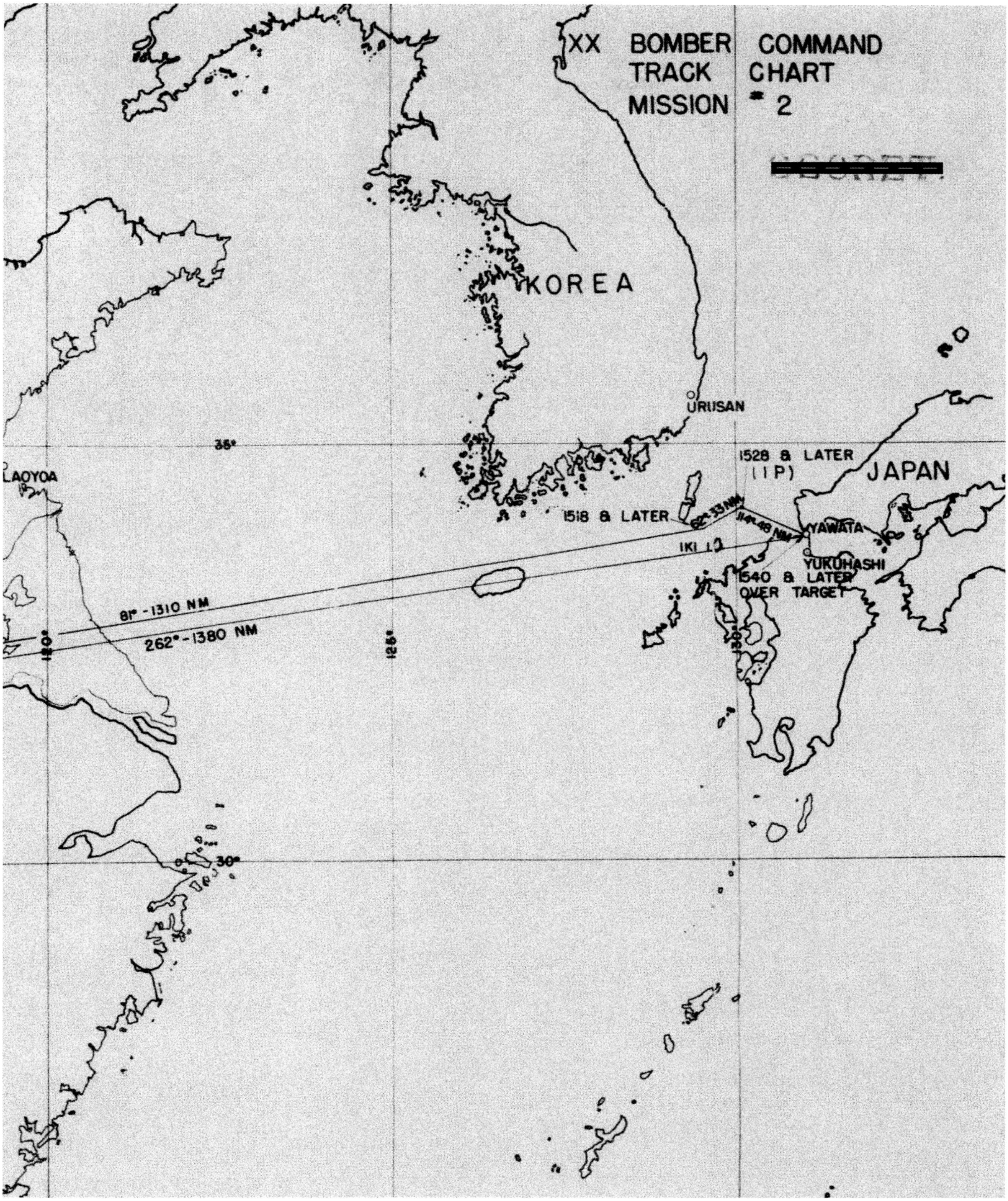

XX BC pilots and navigators were briefed on the route to and from Yawata for Mission #2 utilizing this map. This particular section shows the routes between the Chinese coast on the left and Japan on the right. The Korean peninsula is clearly visible at the top. (*US Air Force*)

B-29 mechanics utilizing an engine hoist. (*Albert via 40th BG*)

Maintenance personnel of the 40th BG gather for a group photo with #831 *Queenie*. Maintenance crews worked long hours with personnel shortages in lousy weather to prepare the B-29s for Mission #2 to Yawata, Japan. (*40th BG*)

Sloan and his crew disappeared in #314 over the Himalaya mountains. A month later, they returned on foot to Chengtu.

Maintenance crews again worked long hours with personnel shortages in lousy weather to prepare the B-29s. The 9th Bombardment Maintenance Squadron suffered a throat infection epidemic that hospitalized twelve mechanics and further complicated this critical period.[21] Sgt. David McConnell of the 468th BG became the group's first fatal casualty when a 500-pound bomb fell on him while loading a B-29 on June 14 for the Hump flight to the forward base in China. An investigation determined the bomb release mechanism failed and the group buried him the next day with military honors.[22] Ordnance personnel loaded eight 500-pound bombs into each B-29 as air crews prepared for the first stage across the Hump to China.

The first of seven B-29s lost on Mission #2 to Yawata crashed attempting to cross the Hump to the forward base in China. Capt. Marvin Stockett, pilot of #261 *Stockett's Rocket* of the 40th BG, disappeared somewhere over the mountain range. The 40th BG declared the crew missing after a diligent search of all auxiliary airfields where they might have landed in an emergency. The eleven crew members and one passenger were never found.

Ground crews in China checked the arriving B-29s and topped off their fuel tanks in anticipation of the pending mission. The crew of the 468th BG's #356 *Georgia Peach*, still smarting over their aborted mission to Thailand, prepared to make up for the lost opportunity by being among the first B-29s to drop a payload on Japan. Crew members were issued parachutes with special jungle kits, as well as Mae West life jackets, flak suits, "pointee-talkee" Chinese phrase books, and survival kits containing fishhooks, first-aid equipment, and other items.

Mission briefings occurred in China rather than India for security reasons. Thus, crews flew from India to China knowing they were preparing for a mission the next day but did not know the destination. Jerry Noble, a 40th BG flight engineer, commented that "you could have knocked us over with a feather" upon learning the bombers were bound for Japan. The lack of clear intelligence about Japanese defenses in the vicinity of Yawata left crews guessing as to what they would encounter in the night skies over the target. Noble stated, "They said maybe you'll run into fighter planes and maybe you'll run into flak. Nothing definite, so we really didn't know what to

The 468th BG's #229 in India. Capt. Richard Hughes, pilot of B-29 #229, crashed at the end of the runway while attempting to take off for Yawata, Japan, during Mission #2. (*US Air Force*)

expect."[25] Sgt. Robert Hall, the central fire control gunner on the 40th BG Bill Hunter crew, offered more details of the briefing:

> Inside the briefing room, there was a big sheet of brown paper over the maps at the front of the room. Someone told us to look at the persons on our left and right, and if we did not know them, raise a hand. Security precautions. After everyone was identified, they uncovered the map, and there was an audible gasp—a piece of yarn marked the course, eastward across China, across the Yellow Sea, to Japan. So this was what we had been training for. The time had come. I felt worried, but more about whether the plane could make it there and back than about enemy action.[26]

Sixty-eight B-29s launched the afternoon of June 15, 1944. Gen. Laverne Saunders and Col. Howard Engler flew on #274 *Lady Hamilton* with Capt. Herman Sancken of the 468th BG. Eleven journalists and photographers accompanied other aircraft to report on the first American bomber attack on Japan since the Doolittle raid in 1942.

Capt. Richard Hughes, pilot of B-29 #229 of the 468th BG, crashed at the end of the runway while attempting to take off for Yawata. Capt. John Hechinger, 793rd Bomb Squadron historical officer, wrote, "As the ship was immediately enveloped in flames, ammunition cooked off and the bombs exploded. It was most certainly a miracle that every member of his [Capt. Hughes] crew got out safely with only minor scratches and burns and shock."[27]

Hechinger commended Capt. "Doc" Mitchell, who immediately raced to the scene in an ambulance as the plane burned and exploded. Mitchell emerged from the chaos with the crew "covered with mud and drenched from head to foot from lying in the rice paddies [as the ammunition and bombs exploded on board the B-29]."[28] A second B-29 (#220, launched to conduct post-mission photographic reconnaissance) crashed on take-off from Chengtu after the main force departed. All eleven crewmen died.

Four bombers aborted and returned to Chengtu with mechanical issues. One of these B-29s developed engine trouble approximately two hours out and returned to the base. Reports indicated the crew members of the crippled plane openly wept and cursed at the missed opportunity to be among the first to strike Japan in a B-29. The frustrated pilot reportedly exclaimed "Damn the engines! Damn the engines!"[29]

The planes launched late in the day to reach their target at night. The darkness and poor weather prevented formation flying so the bombers headed for Yawata in loose groups. Millar seemed pleased with the poor weather. "We ducked into the soup clouds and stayed there to prevent enemy fighters from attacking us," he said. "It provided excellent cover." Japanese fighters scrambled to intercept the B-29s but were not able to catch the giant bombers. "I could see some of their planes taking off, but I knew that we were much faster than they were, and by the time they got up to our altitude, we would be long gone," explained Millar. Daylight faded before the planes departed Chinese airspace. The men donned their Mae West vests as the bombers approached the East China Sea.[30]

Navigation was difficult during the leg across the sea. Lt. Edward Kwasniewski, Millar's navigator, managed to make a couple star shots through breaks in the clouds. However, a strong shift in the wind caused *Georgia Peach* to drift north toward the Korean Peninsula. Japanese naval vessels detected the American bombers and opened fire with anti-aircraft guns. "All of a sudden," Millar remembered, "the clouds on the left side of our plane lit up and we felt concussions .... I saw the first shot and called the tail gunner. About that time a dozen more shots came and all missed us. The reception was too hot and uncomfortable."[31]

The wreckage of the 40th BG's #220, tasked to fly a reconnaissance mission to assess damage after Mission #2. The B-29 crashed on take-off from Chengtu after the main force departed. All eleven crewmen died in the crash. (*US Air Force*)

Steve Krupinski and his crew pose with a Boeing B-17 Flying Fortress prior to deploying to India with the 40th BG. Krupinski flew #220 when it crashed on take off for reconnaissance duty behind the main force for Mission #2. (*US Air Force*)

40th BG radar officer Ferris Albers reminisced about facing the approaching darkness as the planes few eastward to Japan:

> After takeoff, the few hours of daylight left provided us with our first glimpses of the part of China between our base and the coast. We soon left the fertile fields and terraced hills of Szechwan and flew in the direction taken by the great Yangtze. As the sun set, I remember one of the gunners striking up the song, "How I hate to see that evening sun go down." We all knew what he meant and were thinking it would be a long time until the sun rose again, and we would still be flying, we hoped.[32]

The radar operator on each B-29 served two functions for the crew: navigation and a means to bomb the target when obscured by clouds, smoke, or darkness. B-29s carried the AN/APQ-13 ground scanning radar system. The radar sets of the period were limited in range and their ability to project outlines of terrain. They worked best when over water because the sets could more easily distinguish and display shore lines and vessels against the flat background of an ocean or lake. Lt. Albers served as the radar operator on Bill Hunter's crew and commented on the AN/APQ-13 as utilized on the Yawata mission:

> On the radar set in this plane, I had almost a 50-mile range, which was very good at the time. In the early part of the trip, radar was not of much use because the terrain was mostly mountains. In fact maps were not of much use either because they weren't accurate. A few hours later we entered a region of lower land and large lakes. The water and land contrasts were much better places for the operation of the kind of radar we carried. Still we found it not too useful since the water in the lakes and rivers of this area varied in level some 30 feet in different seasons, which changed the shapes of the shorelines.[33]

The AN/APQ-13 assisted the crews spotting naval vessels. 468th BG navigator Edward Kwasniewski asked his pilot, Maj. Jack Millar, to look at the radar screen in the cockpit. Several blips indicated the presence of Japanese naval vessels below them. Although the Japanese knew large planes were flying overhead, cloud cover hindered visual identification. Kwasniewski called for a new course heading and the pilot obliged.

Maj. Jack Millar and #356 *Georgia Peach* of the 468th BG. During Mission #2 to Yawata, Japan, several searchlights discovered #356 *Georgia Peach* as it approached the target and anti-aircraft guns hurled a barrage at the illuminated B-29. Bright bursts lit the night sky behind and below the bomber. (*Millar*)

Radar operator Sgt. W. J. Yoder on #276 *Black Magic* of the 40th BG taken during Mission #17 to Omura, Japan. (*Schutte via 40th BG*)

The 468th BG's #279 *Postville Express*—the first B-29 to bomb Japan. Gen. Laverne "Blondie" Saunders flew onboard #279 when the XX BC bombed Yawata during Mission #2. (*Schutte via 468th BG*)

The 468th BG's #279 *Postville Express* and her crew members. (*US Air Force*)

As the B-29 crews approached the Initial Point (IP) for the bomb run, those not already wearing a parachute, flak vest, helmet, and Mae West quickly donned them in preparation for the Japanese response to their presence. Flight engineer Jerry Noble of the 40th BG probably spoke for every man on the mission when he stated, "Frankly, we were all pretty scared. We didn't know what to expect, and I think we were all expecting hell to break loose any minute."[34]

Gen. Saunders, as the senior commander on the raid, dropped his bombs at 11:38 p.m. and directed his radio operator to send the signal "Betty, Betty, Betty," indicating the first bombs were falling on Japan. Col. James Garcia, the chief intelligence officer, selected his wife's name as the pre-arranged signal. The XX BC crews encountered flak, fighters, and searchlights over Yawata. As *Georgia Peach* of the 468th BG neared Yawata at approximately midnight, Millar could see the entire city was well lighted, indicating they had caught the Japanese by surprise. Almost as soon as the crew began congratulating themselves on catching the defenders unaware the city went black, indicating the Japanese knew the bombers were approaching. Bombardiers found the target not only under black-out conditions, but also covered by haze and a defensive smoke screen.

Flak could be a terrifying experience for air crews. During the day, exploding flak in the distance often projected an innocent appearance of black cotton balls. Up close and in greater numbers they turned more sinister, as the bombers flew through a maze of smoky remnants hanging around them. Flak exploding near an aircraft could rock the plane and send shards of hot metal through the fuselage, wings, and engines. At night, the terror increased as the flak exploded suddenly near a bomber with a blinding flash. Tracers from Japanese night fighter aircraft added to the eerie scenes above a target at night. Ferris Albers, a 40th BG bombardier, remembered the shock of Japanese night defenses when first encountered over Yawata. "Sitting in the nose of the plane with such a terrific view was scary. The tracer shells fired at us reached far above us...I just knew we were going to fly into one or into a burst of flak."[35]

Japanese anti-aircraft gun development and production lagged behind those of Germany; the 75 mm Type 88 anti-aircraft gun developed in 1928 remained the primary weapon against bombers for the duration of the war. It fired a shell that could reach 23,500 feet, yet reportedly lacked accuracy above 16,000 feet. Although the Japanese produced an updated version of this gun, only sixty-five of them emerged from factories. They did employ a larger 120 mm gun, but produced only 154 of them and they could not cover all of Japan. The Japanese were also behind the Allies and Germans in the development of fire control and radar equipment to direct their guns.[36]

The 462nd BG's #329 *Ding Hao*. A flak fragment struck #329, flown by Maj. A. Smith, tearing off its tail light and nearly wounding tail gunner Staff Sgt. E. Lancey during Mission #2 to Yawata. (*US Air Force*)

The crews encountered heavy anti-aircraft flak over four locations, including Yawata, Iki Island, Okino Island, and Koko, Korea. Over Yawata flak tended toward meager to moderate but inaccurate. Returning crews noted the Japanese delivered their heaviest flak concentrations against bombers caught in the beams of ground searchlights. They believed some Japanese aircraft performed "spotter" duties, reporting the altitude of the bombers in the vicinity of gun batteries. Flak from guns at the other three locations also proved to be meager and inaccurate.

Automatic weapons fire targeted the B-29s over five locations, including near Nanking and west of Hwanglo, China.

Flak did strike six bombers over Yawata that night and one round of anti-aircraft fire found Lt. Ellis of the 444th BG. The damage proved to be minor and the B-29 continued its mission. Navigator Lt. Misterly remarked, "As we turned off our target we dove to 5,000 feet in an attempt to avoid further attacks by the Japanese flak batteries and soon passed out of their range."[37] A flak fragment struck Maj. A. Smith's B-29 (#329 *Ding Hao* of the 462nd BG), tearing off its tail light and nearly wounding tail gunner Staff Sgt. E. Lancey. Another 462nd BG B-29 (#312 *Mysterious Mistress*), flown by Capt. S. Jones, also returned with flak holes. Lt. Robert Schumacher, a flight engineer with the 444th BG, explained the Yawata flak from his perspective riding in the rear section of the B-29's forward compartment, "The flight engineer did not have good visibility outside of the airplane. I spent the war riding backwards, staring at a huge instrument panel and outside I could see #3 and #4 engines...I didn't personally see any of the fighters over Yawata from my viewpoint but could see and hear the anti-aircraft shells exploding."[38]

The Japanese employed searchlights in cooperation with their anti-aircraft batteries. The powerful beams could locate a bomber and provide ground gunners or night fighters an opportunity to determine the altitude and direction to bring down the huge aircraft. The Japanese employed their searchlights and worked feverishly to locate the American bombers as they approached Yawata. Maj. Jack Millar, piloting the 468th BG's *Georgia Peach*, slipped on special dark glasses despite the night sky. If a Japanese searchlight illuminated his cockpit, the glasses would reduce its blinding effect. Several searchlights discovered *Georgia Peach* as it approached the target and anti-aircraft guns hurled a barrage at the illuminated B-29. Bright bursts lit the night sky behind and below the bomber. The Japanese were having difficulty estimating the altitude and speed of the Americans flying over their homeland and many crews reported moderate but normally inaccurate flak that night. "Everyone was very tense but stuck to his station," Millar later wrote to his parents. Bombers on either side of *Georgia Peach* appeared boxed in by the searchlights that, when combined with anti-aircraft bursts, reminded the pilot of a July Fourth celebration.[39] Searchlights found William Hunter's 40th BG B-29 over Yawata. Radar operator Ferris Albers wrote, "Although we were familiar with searchlights, we had never encountered one in flight. The Japs caught us with one, and I remember the eerie feeling. I think it almost blinded us, and I recall the tail gunner declaring over intercom that he couldn't see anything. I think Hunter did a little evasive action to get us out of the terrific glare."[40]

YANK reporter Sgt. Stoumen mentioned the searchlights in his August 1944 magazine story: "The searchlights were brighter now, but their dangerous pointing fingers were diffused through the undercast of clouds. The tail gunner, S/SGT [Staff Sgt.] F. G. Hodgen, said our tail was caught several times by lights. Apparently we were not seen through the clouds, and the lights moved on."[41]

The searchlights presented Tillman Durdin of the *New York Times* with his first view of aerial warfare as he flew with Maj. Robinson Billings and his crew:

> Far off to our right, perhaps still thirty miles away, faint searchlights sawed away at an acute angle in the mists. There was a mass of lights and at their base drifted a yellow dull haze of fires...Billings lost altitude steeply, for we were one of the ships assigned to make a low run. Searchlight cones brightened. There seemed to be scores of them. We could see the ground flashes of ack-ack now and processions of tracers arching into the sky.[42]

Japanese searchlights also pinpointed the crew of Lt. Col. Robert Sullivan and his crew. Clay Gowran of the *Chicago Daily Tribune* flew on the Yawata mission with the Sullivan crew. He stood between the pilot and co-pilot during the bomb run, watching the searchlights seeking targets:

> Suddenly our plexiglass nose glowed as a light caught us. Immediately five others pinned us, then the guns opened up. Unable to deviate from the bombing run, we had to sit there and take it. Ahead I saw at least a dozen heavy guns flashing. Red tracers flicked by. The sharp crack of shells bursting around us smacked our eardrums and the ship quivered and tossed in the turmoil of the barrage. With a shower of sparks and flame, something hit us.[43]

The damage proved minor and the B-29 returned safely to Chengtu. The Japanese relieved the local anti-aircraft gun commander and transferred him to Manchuria after the Yawata raid.[44]

Although the initial mission after action reported Japanese aircraft opposing the force as "weak and ineffectual," night fighters proved to be the most dangerous defensive obstacle over Yawata that June night. The intelligence briefing noted night fighters could be awaiting the bombers, and crews remained tensely alert as they neared Yawata. Although flak damaged six bombers, night fighters scored one confirmed kill of a B-29 over the target. The Japanese 4th *Sentai* employed the Kawasaki Ki-45 Nick for air defense in the Yawata area. The two-engine fighter reached speeds of 336 mph and climbed to a maximum altitude of 32,800 feet. The 4th *Sentai* converted eight of the Nicks to night defense by June 15, 1944: six carried 20 mm and 13 mm guns, while the other two planes mounted 37 mm cannon. Although only fifteen pilots held night fighter qualification, twenty-four Nicks (most lacking night fighter armament conversions) launched to meet the XX BC B-29s approaching Yawata.[45] Three of the night fighters employed a standard Japanese ruse by turning their landing lights on and off to attract the attention of the bomber crews while another fighter approached from the opposite direction, counting on not being noticed by the distracted Americans. Pilot Jack Millar encountered a Japanese night fighter after closing his bomb bay doors; the cockpit crew flinched as a Japanese fighter suddenly appeared, its guns spitting flames in the darkness. The enemy plane passed over the B-29's nose and disappeared into the night without damaging the bomber. Sgt. Ignacio Vaccaro, a tail gunner on another Superfortress, landed after the mission and found two unexploded 20 mm shells from a Japanese fighter piercing the back of his seat-pack parachute.

Robinson Billings's crew briefly battled a night fighter over Yawata. Reporter Tillman Durdin wrote in his dispatch, "'There's a fighter right on our wing'" shouted a gunner. Billings looked, too, and chimed in, 'He's got a light right in my eyes. Shoot the _____!' I heard our guns sputter. The fighter, which seemed to be a two-engine job, peeled off and snapped out his lights."[46]

Sgt. Stoumen, the army correspondent with *YANK* magazine, wrote that throughout his plane's flight engine #3 periodically spewed sparks for some unknown reason. This did not seem to degrade the engine's performance so the crew continued on the mission. As the bomber approached Yawata the chief gunner screamed, "Tracers! They are coming right past the ship!" The crew frantically searched the sky for the Japanese night fighter firing the tracers until someone called on the intercom to say it was just engine #3 shooting sparks into the night sky. The entire crew broke into a chorus of laughter that eased the tension.[47]

Many accounts of the Yawata raid repeat early army reports that state one bomber fell to anti-aircraft guns over the city that night, but post-war reviews of records indicate the bomber (#230 *Limber Dugan* of the 468th BG) fell to the night fighter guns of Warrant Officer Sadamitsu Kimura. American post-mission reports correctly note the B-29 lay in the beam of a searchlight when it began to burn and fall to the ground; crews and intelligence personnel at the group and wing level assumed flak struck the bomber. As *Limber Dugan* flew trapped in the spotlight the illumination attracted Kimura, flying a Ki-45 Nick. Kimura approached from below the plane, firing his guns until "Everything became white because of the reflected light off the big fuselage of the enemy plane. I started to fire, and I could tell that I hit it. The nose came down slowly and it started to spin. I saw one piece of the fin come off."[48]

The fog of war tended to impact the claims of Japanese fighter pilots as it did with bomber gunner claims against Japanese aircraft in later raids. Returning Japanese fighters claimed to have brought down seven B-29s and damaged another six bombers over Yawata that night. In reality, one B-29 fell to their guns.[49] A second B-29 (the 462nd BG's #287) returned with bullet holes from fighters in its fuselage. The next day, an official Japanese radio statement monitored by the United Press altered the claims of the Japanese fighter pilots to six total aircraft destroyed over Yawata, two of them B-29s.[50] One has to wonder what other aircraft they thought they encountered in the night skies. American gunners did not file any claims against Japanese fighters, but the 4th *Sentai* reported one of its fighters returned with minor damage from a gunner on board one of the bombers.[51]

A journalist in Yawata witnessed the attack and presented a Japanese view of the raid:

> Now all the city is black. Suddenly in the north we heard the sound of enemy planes...Minute by minute the noise approached. At this moment there was a shot, like a skyrocket, into the air...I could clearly see the figures of the enemy planes. At once anti-aircraft began to shoot. The guns shouted like lightning. But the hateful enemy planes flew on.[52]

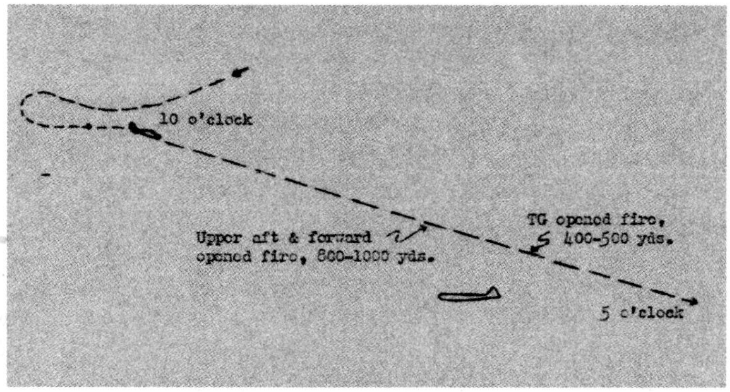

The post-mission debriefing of crews resulted in this drawing illustrating the pattern flown by a Japanese pilot who attacked one of the B-29s. (*US Air Force*)

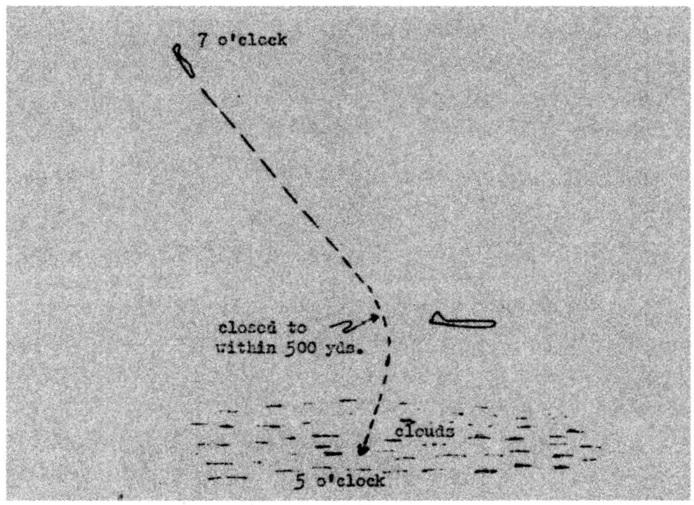

Another drawing developed from the post-Mission #2 debriefing of a B-29 crew. The XX BC produced this drawing to review Japanese fighter tactics. (*US Air Force*)

Mechanical, human, and environmental challenges played havoc on the B-29 crews, who were not only under-trained in their primary aircraft before deploying, but were also flying bombers rushed into combat before many of the problems that plagued most new planes could be solved. Added to these issues were a thirteen-hour mission to the Japanese home islands and back to China after crossing the Hump the previous day, high winds that interfered with navigation to Yawata, the visual impairments of a night raid, and Japanese air defenses.

Japanese intelligence sources in China reported the launch of the mission earlier in the day and their radar facilities tracked the incoming B-29s; the high value target of Yawata was prepared for its first air raid. Each B-29 crew arrived to find the area under black-out conditions that interfered with the bombardiers' ability to locate and hit the target. Under ideal conditions, the bomber needed to fly a straight line from the IP to the target for the bombardier to locate and bring the plane across the center of the area, as proven by future XX BC Commander Curtis LeMay while assigned to the Eighth Air Force in Europe. Many of the B-29s flying from the IP to the target area conducted evasive maneuvers to avoid Japanese defenses. These changes in a straight flight path from the IP added to the complication of accurately locating the target and its aiming point in the dark.

William Hunter's 40th BG crew provided a glimpse into the "perfect storm" that struck many of the B-29 crews on their first mission to bomb Yawata. Navigator Leonard Jellis guided Hunter to the IP after an incredible six-hour flight across China and the open sea. Working closely with radar operator Ferris Albers, Noble battled high winds that toyed with his predicted path of the B-29 and cloudy skies that limited star shots to verify his position

Right gunner Staff Sgt. Charles Bacon at his position aboard the 40th BG's #281 *20th Century Unlimited.* The gunner is utilizing binoculars as he looks through the blister on the side of the aircraft during a daylight raid. (*Schutte via 40th BG*)

plots. Hunter flew the stressful Hump carrying a full load of fuel and bombs, only to land, refuel, get a brief night's sleep, and then fly six hours to the Japanese home islands at night. At the IP, Hunter released the B-29 to bombardier Frank McKinney for the final run over the target. Flight engineer Jerry Noble kept his eyes glued to the panel, watching for any changes in engine performance and concerned about being located by searchlights that would bring attention to the bomber by flak batteries:

We turned into the target run, and as soon as we got to the mainland, searchlights started hunting for us. None of them could get us, though, because [bombardier] Mac (Frank McKinney) was doing some pretty good evasive action. We were at 14,000 feet true altitude. There was a little flak, but most of it was below and behind us. Bombs were away at 2230, and we peeled off and got the hell out of there.[53]

This photo illustrates the secondary role of the bombardier as a gunner. First Lt. Charles Biehle is aboard the 40th BG's #276 *Black Magic*, looking through his gun sight during Mission #17, a daylight raid on Omura, Japan. (*Schutte via 40th BG*)

The final bomb run from the IP to the target actually proved to be more complicated and problematic for the crew. McKinney assumed control of the B-29 at the IP. The darkened city prevented the bombardier from obtaining a clear view of the upcoming target, so he requested Albers as radar operator to utilize his equipment and locate the area of the steel facility and drop the bombs. Albers quickly discovered his task would be challenging; the AN/APQ-13 radar set operated properly only when the bomber flew straight and level. Maneuvering the aircraft interfered with the set's ability to receive signal returns and interpret them on the scope for Albers, who guided the plane toward the target area:

To Mac, sitting out in the unprotected glass nose, the scene must have been really impressive. He began doing evasive action, i.e, putting the ship into twisting turns in an attempt to disturb the aim of the ground guns. Of course, during each turn my scope became useless, and soon Mac was making a new turn as quick as he came out of an old one. When he called back to ask where the target was, I told him he'd have to level out before I could see, so for a moment we leveled out, but again went into wild turns. Somewhat confused by these unexpected difficulties, I was not as vehement as I should have been about leveling out. Mac and I had not worked together enough for an understanding of each other's tasks, and he did not realize that he was fouling me up with his turns, and my remonstrance on the bomb run had little effect. Then, too, our great speed left little time for fine adjustments. We were all in a state of high excitement. An enemy was shooting at us for the first time in our lives, and the performance

> of our technical tasks had never presented so many difficulties...But soon I was uncomfortably aware that things were not going well. I knew about how long the run to the target should have taken, and we did not level out until it was just about gone. When we did, we were naturally quite badly off course. As something resembling the target area passed beneath us, I hit my bomb release switch, and I cried, "Bombs away" to my own and everyone else's great relief. Hunter immediately took over manual control of the ship, and we turned sharply about to the left to get out of the flak area.[54]

Maj. J. Lancaster of the 462nd BG, flying B-29 #312 *Mysterious Mistress*, salvoed one of his bomb bay fuel tanks and his bomb load over Yawata.[55] The Japanese may have found Lancaster's discarded fuel tank after the raid; a Radio Tokyo broadcast on June 19 claimed a discovered B-29 fuel tank as evidence of a downed aircraft from the raid, rather than a tank that had been jettisoned:

> Clear cut evidence that one of the enemy planes that was shot down by defense units over Northern Kyushu on 16 June was a B-29 Superfortress has been revealed in two vivid photographs appearing in this morning's Asahi Shimbun, radioed from Noji. The first photograph shows a member of the Army-Navy Technical Staff inspecting the tank of the ill-fated B-29 while the other photo shows the inscription on the tank, proving beyond any doubt that it was a B-29.[56]

As the 468th BG's Millar crew approached the IP, navigator Edward Kwasniewski provided his pilot with a new course heading, setting up the bomb run to target the Imperial Iron and Steel Works. The bombardier opened the bomb bay doors and initiated the bomb run. "My knees were beating against the control column," Millar later recalled. Millar noticed a flash on his instrument panel indicating the release of the bombs at the same time he heard the bombardier shout, "Bombs away!" The pilot initiated a banking maneuver and set a course for China. The gunners called on the intercom to report they could see bombs striking the ground. After traveling some distance from the target Millar recalled, "I did turn the plane around so the crew could get a good look at the fires that had been set at Yawata."[57]

Seven bombers hit secondary targets and six dumped their bombs and returned early because of mechanical issues; Maj. L. Mackall's B-29, #332 *Belle of Baltimore* of the 462nd BG, is an example of the former. Mackall's plane developed radar problems en route, forcing the pilot to divert to the secondary target, the docks at Laoyao, on the Chinese coast. Mackall later claimed the bombs he dropped "flashed with such intensity that the cockpit was alight."[58] Another crew also bombed Laoyao, while five bombed other targets of opportunity.

Returning crews delivered optimistic initial reports of the bombing. Post-strike photos showed the bombing results at Yawata were quite poor. Only one bomb fell on an Imperial Steel Works building—the power house. Additional damage could be seen at the Kokura Arsenal and other business, industrial, and civilian areas. The Japanese falsely claimed the bombers hit a school, killing 500 children. This claim was made more absurd by the fact the B-29s struck around midnight, when children are not attending school. The Japanese did admit to a damaged rail line.[59]

Crews still faced another six hours in the air over China. The tail gunner on William Hunter's 40th BG crew requested the pilot descend and depressurize the aircraft after leaving the target so he could come out of his confined compartment in the rear of the aircraft. Hunter relates the tail gunner had a very special reason:

> Seems as though he had forgotten to take his "emergency can" aboard prior to takeoff. When one has to go—one has to—even if this is a real important mission—first over Japan since Doolittle...Being the resourceful man that he was, he used his flak helmet in the emergency. When searchlights started beaming, flak flying, he was reminded to put his helmet on. Oops! He forgot. Only [his] pride was hurt. Crew welcomed him up front like a skunk at a picnic.[60]

Millar recalled the clouds dissipated over the East China Sea as the planes approached China. Intelligence personnel briefed crews that if it became necessary to ditch, an American submarine would be on station to retrieve survivors, but Millar observed that "finding [a submarine] at midnight in the ocean would be quite a challenge." Nearing China before dawn, the crews became more alert to possible attack by Japanese fighters. "The skies were clearing over the sea, and I knew we'd still be over enemy territory when daylight came," Millar recalled. They again encountered clouds over China, and Millar maneuvered his plane into the cloud banks. The Japanese did not attempt to intercept the bombers during their return home.[61]

The 40th BG airfield in Hsinching (A-1), China. (*Daly via 40th BG*)

Crew members distributed rations during this leg of the journey. Stoumen reported every man on his bomber received a large can of grapefruit juice and a chicken sandwich made with bread that was "too thick." Dessert consisted of chewing gum and cigarettes.[62] Robinson Billings's crew feasted on pineapple juice and Spam sandwiches.[63] Having been aloft for more than nine hours, the bomber crews were now dealing with fatigue. Millar stated, "We had to fight ourselves to stay awake as the predawn set in."[64] But the observers could afford a nap and Stoumen took the opportunity to lie down, using a parachute as a pillow. Others were not so fortunate; the engineer and navigator on Stoumen's B-29 consumed benzedrine tablets earlier in the flight to combat fatigue and ensure the bomber safely reached Chengtu.[65]

The return flight from the target proved to be more dangerous for the XX BC crews than actually bombing Yawata; three bombers did not return after departing the target area. The 468th BG initially listed two B-29s as MIA, and the Chinese found both crashed into mountains north of Chengtu—one only 100 miles away—during the return flight. In July, searchers found the wreckage of #231, piloted by Maj. Kenneth Akins, and determined the crew flew into the side of a mountain 100 miles north of Chengtu without any survivors. The second B-29 (#826, flown by Lt. Robert Pilchard) crashed into a mountain 200 miles north of Chengtu. The Chinese buried both crews.[63] Robert Schenkel, a *Newsweek* correspondent, died in one of the crashes.

A third B-29 made an emergency landing in China. Harry Zinder of *Time* and *Life* magazines flew with the crew of Capt. Robert Root of the 444th BG. The pilot landed his bomber (#293) on an emergency grass airfield near Neihsiang. Chinese soldiers witnessed the landing and approached to offer assistance; they promised to secure gasoline, tools, and prepare the air strip for the bomber to depart, but Japanese aircraft spotted the downed bomber before any repair work could begin. Zinder wired his editor:

> Then we heard the buzz of two Japanese fighters. They peeled off and splattered bullets across the wings and through the fuselage and kicked up little spurts of grass and mud along the ditch in which we lay. Nine Japanese fighters and six bombers next appeared overhead and when the fighters were through strafing, the bombers came in leisurely as though it were target practice... They must have known this was one of the bombers that raided their homeland and they were determined to kill anything in it or around it.[66]

The 40th BG's William Hunter and his crew were the first to arrive in Chengtu after the long return flight across China. Hunter pushed his B-29 approximately 20 mph faster than other crews to Yawata and back, landing ahead of schedule. According to radar operator Ferris Albers:

> I had crawled through the tunnel to be in front for landing. As we piled out, we were greeted by just one man—our squadron operations officer—who was only partly dressed, as he rushed from sound sleep when the tower notified him we were landing. We got back an hour earlier than the next ship and nearly two hours ahead of some. Our speed had proved to be our own undoing since the base was fully awake by the time the second ship back arrived, and someone took motion pictures of generals greeting that crew.[67]

Jack Millar remembered being hustled away for debriefing immediately upon landing at 8:30 a.m. and was fed egg sandwiches and coffee in the debriefing room. Following the debriefing sessions crew members darted for the mess hall and then to bed. The next day, Millar received a personal radio greeting from none other than Tokyo Rose. As proof of effective Japanese intelligence gathering, Tokyo Rose read the names of several American officers on the Yawata raid, including Millar, and warned them of their fate if they ever attempted to attack the Japanese homeland again. Millar found it humorous that while

The 40th BG's #288, which they converted into a photographic reconnaissance aircraft. Note the removal of the lower front gun turret as part of the conversion. (*40th BG*)

Chinese consume their lunch while working on a XX BC airfield near Chengtu. (*Changnon via 40th BG*).

Chinese crushing rocks with a hand-pulled roller during XX BC airfield construction near Chengtu. (*US Air Force*)

Tokyo Rose bragged of Col. Jim Edmundson's death during the Yawata raid, Edmundson was standing beside him.[68] The radio broadcast named six colonels and lieutenant colonels supposedly on board a single B-29 downed over Yawata. Beyond the absurdity of having six high ranking officers on one plane, all six men were safely in China.[69]

Lt. Misterly offered a mission summary that adequately described the rigors of bombing Japan in few words, "The mission to Japan was one of the most demanding and tiring missions anyone was asked to accomplish during World War II. Each segment was an ordeal, crossing the Hump twice, flying across the great expanse of China twice, and bombing a well defended target."[70]

The XX BC did not have time to rest; demands for a second raid on Japan flowed from the United States immediately after the Yawata raid. Returning bombers from China had to "borrow" 15,000 gallons of fuel from the 312th FW just to get home to India. Restocking the Chengtu airfields and launching a new mission would prove difficult, dangerous, and cost Gen. Wolfe his job.

Chapter 3

July 1944: A Return to Japan and the First Raid to Manchuria

The Sasebo Mission was further evidence that we needed a great deal more training.

— Lt. John Misterly (444th BG)

The American and Japanese fleets clashed in the Battle of the Philippines Sea—also known as the "Great Marianas Turkey Shoot"—four days after the June 15 Yawata raid. The Japanese sortied to challenge the American naval force gathered for the invasion of Saipan and upcoming landings on Tinian and Guam. American naval pilots sank three Japanese aircraft carriers and damaged an additional three while destroying between 550 and 650 naval and land-based aircraft. American losses totaled one damaged battleship and the loss of 123 aircraft. The battle signaled the effective end of Japanese carrier-based aviation as a serious threat to the American Navy and helped ensure American success in capturing Saipan and Tinian and liberating Guam.

The United States announced in July it had secured Saipan, although small pockets of Japanese resistance persisted until September. In October, the first B-29 of the XXI Bomber Command (BC) landed on Saipan, from where bombing operations would begin against targets in Truk Lagoon, the Marianas Islands, and the Japanese home islands the same month. On July 21, American forces landed on Guam and then invaded Tinian on July 24. Tinian would also serve as a B-29 base in the coming months.

Two days after the Yawata mission, Gen. Hap Arnold informed Gen. Kenneth Wolfe he needed XX BC back in the air to conduct a second raid on Japan, as well as strikes against the Japanese steel industry in Manchuria and the petroleum industry in the Dutch East Indies. The latter two operations were identified as worthy strategic targets in the early planning phases of Operation Matterhorn. The Yawata mission depleted fuel supplies to a mere 5,000 gallons at Chengtu and the operations to Japan and Manchuria demanded re-stocking fuel in China. Wolfe informed his superior that if Air Transport Command (ATC) could allocate 1,500 tons of fuel to supplement that carried by his B-29s he could launch a large-scale mission to Manchuria by August 20, with a much smaller operation bound for Japan or an attack on the Dutch East Indies prior to that date. At the same time, he noted airfields in Ceylon were required to stage the petroleum raid in the Dutch East Indies and the runway lengthening projects at these Royal Air Force bases on the island were ongoing.

The cautious estimates of Wolfe did not satisfy Arnold, who on June 27 demanded a small (fifteen plane) night raid on Japan before July 10, followed by a minimum 100-plane attack on Manchuria before July 30 and a fifty-plane strike against Palembang upon completion of the airfield lengthening on Ceylon. In reply, Wolfe offered a counter plan that reduced the number of B-29s earmarked for Manchuria by half. Arnold received Wolfe's message on July 1 and relieved him of command on July 4.[1]

Although Arnold relieved Wolfe, he recognized the latter's tremendous technical experience in the development of the B-29 and willingness to assume the challenging lead in overseeing the first combat operations of the bomber under harsh logistical conditions, despite never holding a combat command in his career. Rather than simply shifting Wolfe to another brigadier general position, Arnold opted to promote and assign him as the new commanding general for materiel command, where his prior engineering and combat experience could prove

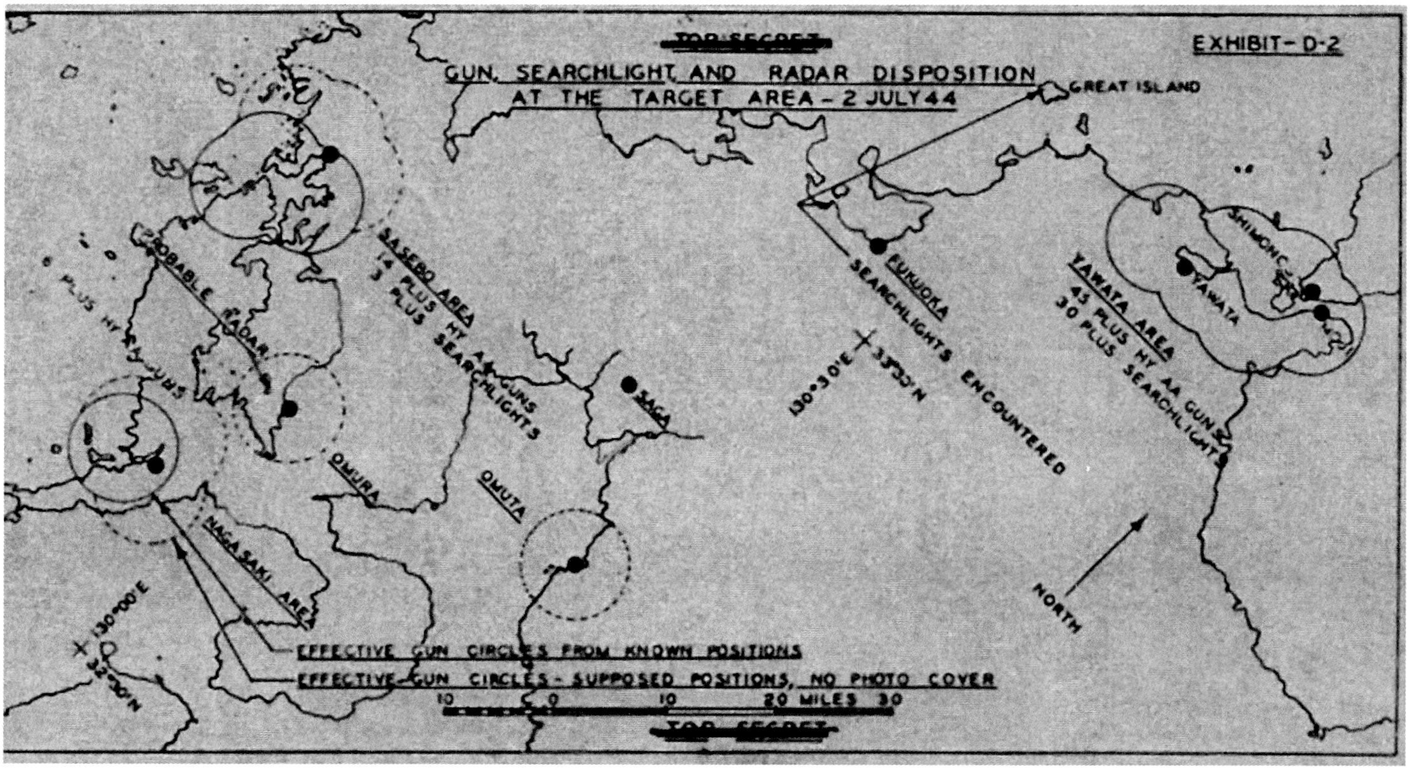

XX BC Intelligence map marking the range of Japanese anti-aircraft guns, radar, and searchlights around target areas on Kyushu Island. XX BC bombers targeted locations on Kyushu during Mission #3. (*US Air Force*)

The 40th BG's #281 *20th Century Unlimited*. Although unit records are not clear, it appears #281 underwent a name change to *Heavenly Body*. Japanese fighters shot down #281 *Heavenly Body* in October 1944. (*40th BG*)

useful to the Army Air Force. Col. LaVerne Saunders, commander of the 58th Bomb Wing (BW), assumed temporary command until the arrival of the new XX BC Commander, Gen. Curtis LeMay.

Mission #3: Sasebo, July 7–8, 1944

Pressure for a return to Japan continued as XX BC made slow progress rebuilding fuel stocks in China. American government and military leaders wanted to have a psychological edge on the Japanese, who had to be wondering if the United States could continue to send bombers over their homeland at regular intervals or if the June attack on Yawata was an infrequent affair. All four groups identified bombers for participation in Mission #3 and its five primary targets on Kyushu Island. The mission called for a night strike against all of the targets, including the Sasebo Naval Base (eighteen bombers), the Akunoura Engine Works at Nagasaki (three bombers), the Omura Aircraft plant (two bombers), the Imperial Iron and Steel Works at Yawata (one bomber), and the Imperial Iron and Steel Works at Tobata (one bomber). A planned strike on Japan with only twenty-five bombers and two photo-reconnaissance B-29s demonstrated the critical impact of the fuel stockpiles in China. It also meant the equivalent of 203 B-29 Hump missions would be required to prepare

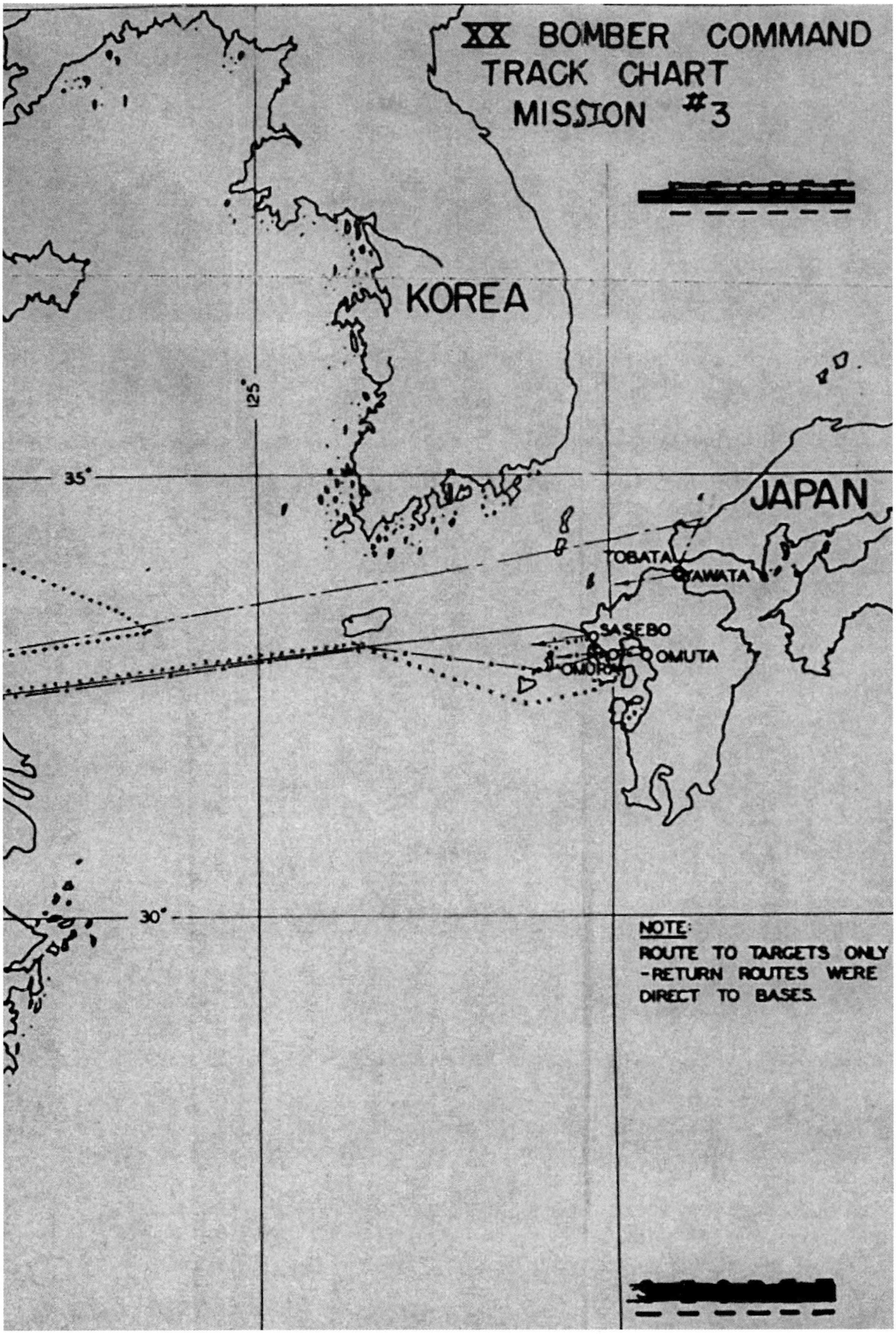

XX BC tracking chart showing the routes to and from the five targets of Mission #3. The B-29s approached from China (left side) and bombed targets on Kyushu (right side). (*US Air Force*)

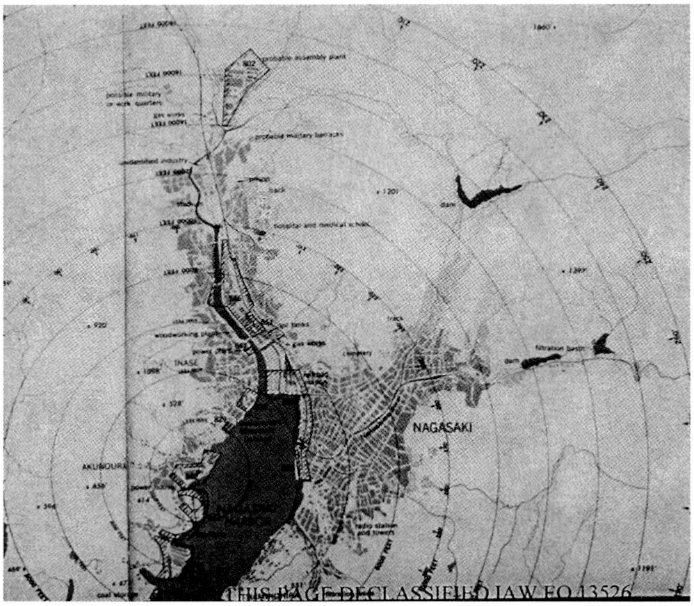

XX BC planning map for the three B-29s designated to bomb the Akunoura Engine Works in Nagasaki during Mission #3. The release point over the target is the center of the smallest circle on the map on the left side of Nagasaki Harbor. (*US Air Force*)

this small force for a flight to Japan. At the same time, the mission would cut into the efforts to stockpile the equivalent of 700 B-29 Hump flights required to move the fuel needed for a 100-plane raid on Manchuria. This study recognizes that ATC carried up to half of the XX BC's fuel supplies to Chengtu, except during June and July, when it hauled approximately one-quarter of the total. Stating the requirements in "B-29 Hump flights" helps establish the immensity of this airlift task.

Planners identified the Laoyao port facilities in China as the secondary target, with the docks and storage areas in Hankow, China, as the target of last resort. The mission also established a special photo reconnaissance operation consisting of two aircraft over the Miike Dyestuffs (a chemical plant) in Omura. Sasebo, the main primary target, served as Japan's third largest naval base. The facility also constructed up to 2% of Japan's military vessels and 12% of the country's maritime engines. The Sasebo Naval Base contained drydocks and American intelligence noted that some Japanese vessels damaged in the recent naval engagements in the Marianas Islands (Battle of the Philippines Sea in June) could be there for repair. The Akunoura Engine Works assembled maritime engines for naval vessels and supported an adjacent construction and repair operation. Earlier photo reconnaissance noted an expansion project at the newly constructed Omura Aircraft plant; assigning two bombers to strike the plant could delay the opening of the new expansion areas. B-29s targeted the Imperial Iron and Steel Works at Yawata during the first raid on Japan and planned to return with one bomber during Mission #3. The facility produced more steel than any other Japanese plant. The Imperial Iron and Steel Works at Tobata, earmarked for a single B-29, supported the steel producing operations at Yawata. The Japanese utilized the secondary and target of last resort for transloading military equipment and supplies destined for their forces fighting in China. The destruction of any supplies in these cities could hamper Japanese military operations.

Returning to Japan for Mission #3 served four purposes: first, it would demonstrate to the Japanese that the United States could and would continue to bomb the home islands despite obvious logistical challenges; second, the United States wanted to harass Japanese military and industrial facilities. At best would be the destruction or reduced output capacity for these facilities and at worst the raid would serve to possibly shake Japanese morale as American bombers flew across their home islands. Third, the raid would gather additional intelligence about Japanese facilities on the island and test their defenses. Fourth was another raid on Japan would benefit American and Chinese morale.

Most of the B-29s carried eight 500-pound general purpose bombs filled with high explosives as well as at least two photo-flash bombs. The latter "flashed" at a height of 4,000 feet after being dropped, allowing night photographs to record the effectiveness of the bombing run. To place twenty-seven aircraft over Japan, the XX BC launched twenty-eight bombers from India and twenty-six eventually arrived at forward bases in China. Two (#297 and #348 *Bengal Lancer* of the 40th BG) returned to India due to mechanical problems and two (#237 *Sir Trofrepus* of the 40th BG and #315 *Deacon's Disciples* of the 444th BG) landed en route to the forward bases. Both of the latter joined the other twenty-four B-29s the next day. The arrival of the bombers at Chengtu was not a surprise to the Japanese, who continued to gather intelligence related to the take-offs and landings of B-29s in China and tracked their missions with radar. Twenty-one of the B-29s in China were designated for the mission and eighteen became airborne, with #290 *Wempy's Blitzburger* and #308 *Feather Merchant* of the 40th BG and #390 *Gallopin Goose* of the 468th BG not able to get off the field. B-29

The 444th BG's #323 *Eileen*, which was reconfigured as a tanker, crashed during a flight across the Hump on June 26, 1944. All crew members perished. (*444th BG*)

#351 from the 40th BG returned early due to an exhaust collector ring failure, leaving only seventeen planes from an originally planned twenty-five bombers (not counting the two photo reconnaissance designated aircraft) heading toward Japan.[2]

A total of eleven aircraft bombed the Sasebo Naval Base from altitudes varying between 15,000 and 19,000 feet. An effective blackout, as well as a thick undercast of clouds, prevented crews from visually bombing the target and forced them to rely on radar. A twelfth plane designated to hit Saesbo experienced radar problems and dropped its bomb load approximately fifteen miles north of Sasebo on an undetermined target. The conditions over both locations resulted in crews not being able to view the results of their bombing, nor take photo-flash pictures. The closest intelligence to a post-strike assessment involved two tail gunners reporting they saw secondary flashes from the vicinity of the naval base as the bombers cleared the area.

The bomber over the Omura Aircraft Plant reported the same conditions and results. Poor to no visibility forced the crews to bomb utilizing radar that produced images of varying clarity, often requiring intense interpretation. Scope pictures of islands and shore lines were more effective for navigation and bombing because the land features contrasted well with water in the returned radar images. However, pinpointing a precise location utilizing the radar image proved challenging, with operators relying on as much chance as technical skill at times. Lt. Ferris Albers of the 40th BG reflected on the delicate temperament of the B-29 radar set:

> In those days turning on the Q-13 was quite a complicated process that consumed several minutes and demanded critical adjustments. Even with all the required hocus-pocus, we were seldom certain of the results. Sometimes the moving line on the scope would when turned on, fail to be in synchronization with the turning of the antenna, and indications would jump around on the scope, and the small gears in the rear of the scope would grind and clash with a violence which threatened such delicate machinery.[3]

Although the night sky was clear over the Imperial Iron and Steel Works, the lone bomber crew over this target reported a thick haze above the ground that obstructed their view. The crew did note seeing several fires after depositing their bomb load, including a single 500-pound incendiary cluster. The 462nd BG's #346 *Man O' War*, piloted by Lt. Col. John Gregg, struck the secondary target after shutting down an engine following a fire; they claimed their bombs struck the dock area, although official results could not be determined. Gen. LeMay presented the Distinguished Flying Cross to Gregg for his successful efforts in pressing to the secondary target despite the loss of an engine. Two 462nd BG planes (#213 *Liberty Belle* and #329 *Ding Hao*) flew to the target of last resort due to fuel transfer problems. One of these bombers miscalculated its position and timing, resulting in bombs dropping approximately twenty miles from Hankow. The results of the other bomber were undetermined.

Crews reported Japanese flak over Sasebo as meager and inaccurate, with the bursts below and to the right of the bombers. The B-29s drew flak from other locations along their route, including Hirado Island, where they noted the bursts were to the left or right of the bombers but at the correct altitude. Some crews witnessed automatic weapons fire aimed at them, even though they were normally beyond the range of such weapons. The Japanese employed searchlights over Sasebo, Nanking, Hankow, and other areas, although none pinpointed a bomber. Eight Japanese fighters intercepted three of the B-29s over China during the return flight. The fighter pilots did not display aggressive tactics and flew as though they were still not sure how to tackle the lumbering bombers. The fighters (seven Nakajima Ki-43 Oscars and one Kawasaki Ki-61 Tony) made a total of ten attacks on the bombers. The most aggressive pilot—flying an Oscar—approached a B-29 from 11 o'clock high and broke away at 150 yards. Another Oscar attacking from the same position turned at 300 yards, with the bomber's gunners claiming they damaged it. One B-29 (the 462nd BG's #287) sustained minor damage from a Tony; the Japanese pilot attacked #287 from 11 o'clock at a very high rate of speed and commenced firing at 800 yards. The bombardier attempted to return fire from the upper forward guns but was not able to due to failure of the central fire control gunner to throw the switch allowing him to assume control of the turret. In response, the bomber pilot initiated evasive action by slipping to the right and turning into the attack. The fighter pilot pulled away from his attack at 400 yards and rolled to the right after leaving the bomber with holes in a crankcase, causing the engine to smoke, but the B-29 pilot did not need to feather the propeller and the bomber returned safely.[4]

The 40th BG's #914, offering an excellent view of the tail gunner's position. The tail gunner flew in his own small pressurized compartment. (*40th BG*)

Capt. Parsons, a 468th BG pilot, made an emergency landing at Liangchan, China, on the return flight from Japan. Parsons, flying #264 *O'Reilly's Daughter*, experienced engine trouble and a fuel shortage. The pilot also feathered an engine due to an oil issue. After refueling and checking the plane at Liangchan the crew continued to Chengtu and landed safely.[5]

Capt. Parsons of the 468th BG made an emergency landing with #264 *O'Reilly's Daughter* in Liangchan, China, on the return flight from Mission #3 to Sasebo, Japan. After refueling, the crew continued to Chengtu. Here the Chinese military is refueling the B-29 by hand from small cans. (*Schutte via 468th BG*)

Mission #4: Anshan, July 29, 1944

In late June, XX Air Force directed Bomber Command to fly a minimum 100-plane mission against the steel targets in Anshan, Manchuria, sometime between July 20 and 30, 1945. The slow process of staging fuel coupled with aircraft mechanical issues and recent operational and accidental bomber losses hampered the ability to meet this demand. XX BC informed its headquarters that it could mount the raid but not with 100 planes, as there were only 127 B-29s in the theater. They promised to do their best to put every available aircraft into the air to Manchuria. Their plan called for a longer period for aircraft maintenance in the rear area, an earlier cessation of Hump cargo flights to prepare those planes for a combat mission, increased time to move the bombers from India to China, and a more lengthy period for the B-29s to remain on the ground in Chengtu prior to the mission. The command received permission to begin flying the bombers forward up to five days prior to D-Day, which was originally set for July 30; this would permit aircraft with mechanical problems to return to India for repairs and then continue to China. B-29s arriving in China needing maintenance would have extra time for its completion before the mission. Providing for additional maintenance time in India and China permitted the greatest number of available aircraft for the Anshan operation, but considerable risk lay in this plan, since the B-29s remained on the ground for up to five days where Japanese spies could observe them and help guide Japanese bombers assigned to sow as much destruction among them as possible.

Preparations for the upcoming mission to Anshan, Manchuria, illustrates not only the engine problems faced by many crews whether they flew the Hump or an operational bombing run, but also the incredible skill and determination displayed by maintenance crews to keep the bombers in flying condition. Crashes on take-off by XX BC aircraft during previous missions led to a change in procedures. If a plane experienced a problem during or immediately after take-off, the crew would now salvo the bombs and forward bomb bay tank prior to a crash landing to minimize the possibility of a fire and/or exploding bombs. The 40th BG launched planes on July 26 en route to A-1 in China for the upcoming Anshan mission; all planes arrived safely. The next day, the 40th BG dispatched eight planes and three experienced problems, with two making emergency returns to India and one crashing with fatalities. One B-29 crew noticed oil leaking from the bottom of engine #1's nacelle approximately twenty-five minutes after lifting off the ground. The leak drained so much oil from the engine that it had to be feathered and the crew returned and managed a safe landing. An inspection of the engine revealed that someone did not properly secure the oil sump plug; the ground crew replaced the plug and filled the oil tank. As the B-29 taxied to the runway the plane experienced a magneto problem with engine #3. The crew again returned the bomber for repairs, ending that day's flying.[6]

A second 40th BG bomber crew made it as far as Imphal when they spotted a fire in engine #1. They immediately feathered the propeller and dropped their bombs (not armed for explosion) and returned to the field, where they safely landed. Maintenance crews discovered a fuel hose clamp had not been properly attached. The clamp slipped off during flight, permitting fuel to spill onto the hot engine and start a fire that burned holes in the top cowling. Fortunately, no one was injured in either of these two incidents.[7]

The Chinese military refueling #264 *O'Reilly's Daughter* by hand at Liangchan. (*Schutte via 468th BG*)

A third view of #264 *O'Reilly's Daughter* being refueled by the Chinese military. The Chinese are pouring gasoline from drums into small cans via funnels and then hauling the cans up the ladder to the top of the wing, where they are poured into the fuel tanks. (*Schutte via 468th BG*)

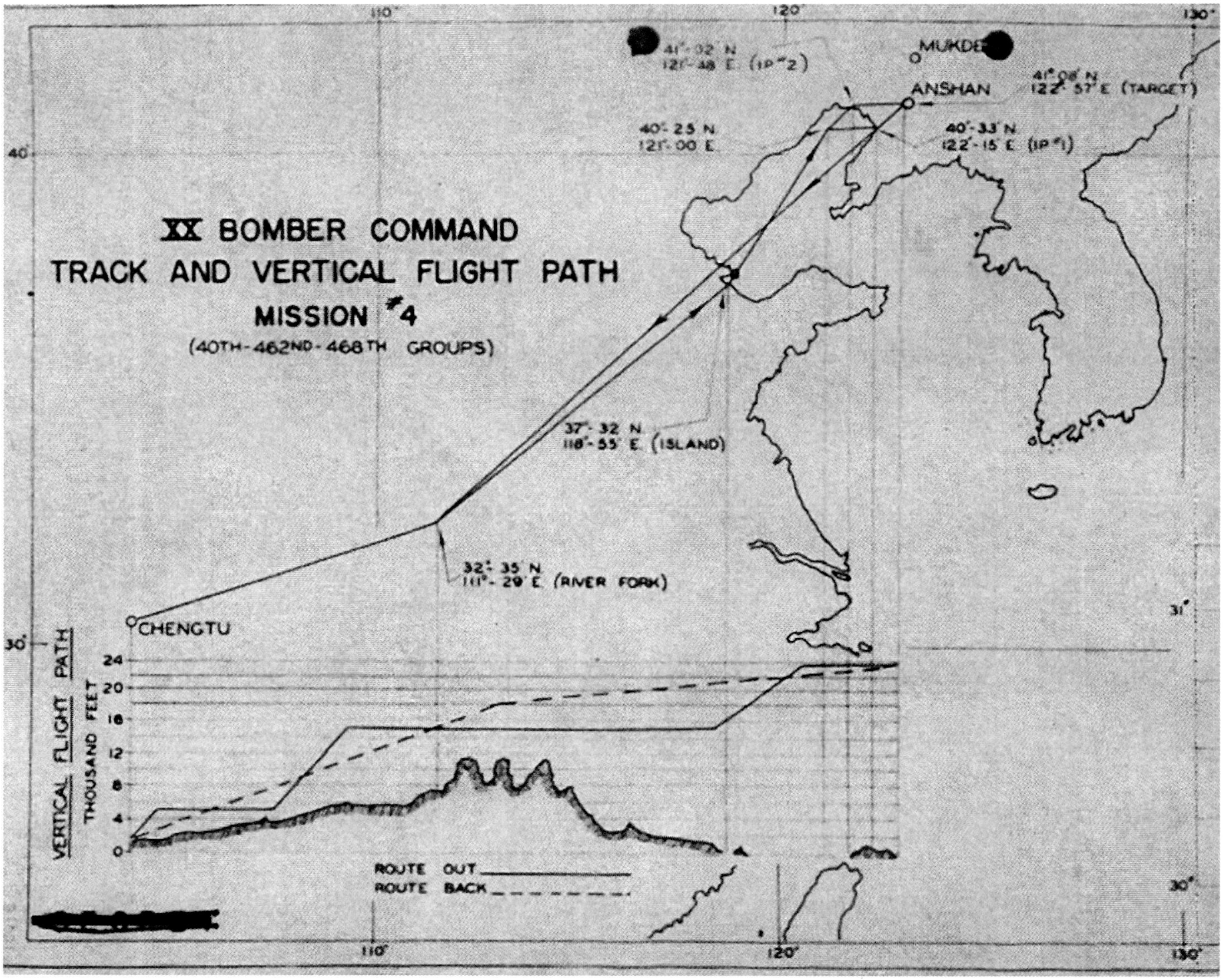

XX BC tracking chart showing the B-29 route from the Chengtu area in western China to Anshan, Manchuria, and return during Mission #4. (*US Air Force*)

The third 40th BG crew did not make a safe return to Chakulia. B-29 #291, piloted by Capt. Alvin Hills, climbed for approximately ten minutes after take-off when the flight engineer, Flight Officer Irvin Gaver, noticed a high temperature on engine #2. Gaver recommended Hills level the plane to cool the engine. After another ten minutes, the co-pilot, 1st Lt. William Houston, called out a fire in engine #3. Hills feathered the engine and told Gaver to shut off the fuel and switch on the fire extinguisher. The engine continued to burn as Hills initiated a turn to return the plane to Chakulia; the problems with engine #2 continued to increase. Hills ordered bombardier 2nd Lt. Roger DiLollo to salvo the bombs and forward fuel tank in preparation for an emergency landing. Engines #1 and #4 also began showing signs of problems. As the engines cut out, Hills dropped the nose of the aircraft to gain speed for an emergency landing. The bomber cleared the cloud cover at a mere 100 feet as the pilot made a desperate search for a landing location. He spotted a clear area of earth and put the plane down in a belly landing. Hills reported after the incident:

> Normal contact was made with the ground at about the radar section, and an explosion occurred on the right side. We slid along the ground for quite a distance and then came to a sudden stop. By this time the entire cabin of the plane was filled with flame. I proceeded through the pilot's window to safety. I then helped Lieutenant Houston, the co-pilot, out to the bank of a creek, away from the flames. Lieutenant DiLollo was dazed and was walking around in front and to the left of the front.[8]

Nine of the thirteen personnel on board died in the crash, including Gaver, Houston, and DiLollo; the latter two died in the hospital. Houston succumbed to his injuries later the day of the crash and DiLollo held on until August 1.

One 462nd BG B-29 flew the Anshan raid as a tribute to the near miracles performed by personnel of the 10th Bombardment Maintenance Squadron. A Boeing Aircraft Corporation field representative condemned an engine nacelle on the bomber that was damaged in a fire. Maintenance crews removed a nacelle from another plane and completed all of their work the day before the scheduled departure to China for the Anshan mission. The air crew made a test flight of the repaired B-29 at 7 p.m. and promptly struck a bird, tearing a large hole in the leading edge of a wing. After the pilot returned the bomber to the airfield, the maintenance crews commenced the non-stop repair of the plane, ensuring it could participate in the upcoming raid. Everyone worked through the night and into the next afternoon, completing the work at 2 p.m. The air crew then flew the B-29 to the forward base in China that afternoon and departed the next morning for Anshan thanks to the crew chief and his personnel, who reportedly worked thirty-three hours without sleep finishing the nacelle work and then repairing the wing damage.[9]

The crew of the 40th BG's #306 *Pampered Lady* returned early from Mission #4 after losing oil in engine #1. (*40th BG*)

XX BC adjusted the schedule and set July 29 for Mission #4 to bomb the Showa Steel works at Anshan, Manchuria, a Japanese "puppet state" in northeast China. Manchuria (Manchukuo) was an area in northeast China seized by Japan in 1931. The port facilities at Chinwangtao, China, were the secondary target, with the tertiary target located at the port of Taku. Planners identified the railroad yard at Chenghsien as the target of last resort. The Showa Steel works ranked first in the Japanese empire for metallurgical coke production, second in pig iron, and third in steel production. The port at Chinwangtao exported up to 5,600,000 metric tons of coking coal from Manchuria to Japan. At any one time seven or eight vessels lay in the harbor, awaiting their loading of coking coal. The loss of these vessels and the destruction of the harbor facilities with stored coking coal could have a major impact on Japanese industry. Non-coking coal departed Manchuria via the port of Taku. Other commodities transloaded onto vessels in Taku included iron, cotton, pig iron, and salt. The rail lines passing through the yards at Chenghsien served as an important transportation alternative to the Yantze River. Destruction of the yards and rail cars stopped there would impede the Japanese utilization of the rail line between Peking and Hankow.[10]

Intelligence analysts calculated the daylight raid could encounter heavy Japanese resistance. Plans outlined the utilization of four-plane diamond formations with aircraft 100 feet apart and level with each other for mutual protection against Japanese fighters. Tight formations—a proven strategy by the Eighth Air Force in Europe—permitted gunners on multiple bombers to mass their fire and defend each other. Formation flying also provided an opportunity for coordinated bombing patterns. Gen. LeMay introduced more aircraft to formations and added the concept of a "lead" crew for each after his arrival. Aircraft not able to join a formation of at least three planes before entering enemy territory would bomb the target of last resort and return. Formations reduced to less than three B-29s after entering enemy territory should attempt to join another formation. If not able to do so, they should bomb the nearest designated target and return to base. Rain soaked the field where the 444th BG bombers waited and the resulting conditions forced a delay in their participation in the operation.

The 40th BG lost #351, piloted by Capt. Murr Skousen, when it crashed with two engines on fire after take-off during Mission #4 to Anshan. (*40th BG*)

Loading machine gun ammunition on #348 *Bengal Lancer* of the 40th BG prior to a mission. During Mission #4, the crew in this aircraft dropped their ordnance on the target of last resort—the railroad yard in Chenghsien, China. (*40th BG*)

Seventy-nine B-29s from the other three groups sat in the forward areas and all but seven managed to become airborne for Mission #4. The 40th BG lost #351, piloted by Capt. Murr Skousen, when it crashed with two engines on fire after take-off. Eleven aircraft from the 40th BG, 462nd BG, and 468th BG did not bomb the primary target: one of these B-29s (#312 *Mysterious Mistress* from the 462nd BG) bombed the secondary target; two (#348 *Bengal Lancer* of the 40th BG and the 468th BG's #284 *The Challenger*) dropped their ordnance on the target of last resort; four (#237 *Sir Trofrepus* of the 40th BG and the 462nd BG's #359 *Missouri Queen*, #360, and #287) bombed targets of opportunity; three jettisoned their loads; one returned with its load; and one crashed. The targets of opportunity were a rail line (#237 *Sir Trofrepus*), an airfield (#359), and railroad bridges (#360 and #287). Six planes encountered bombing problems over the primary target: four reported bomb rack malfunctions and two crews noted personnel errors that resulted in premature release of ordnance. Aircraft #294 *Monsoon* of the 40th BG placed four bombs on the primary before encountering a problem with the other four. The crew cleared the problem and dropped their remaining four bombs on the target of last resort. B-29 #301 faced a similar issue after releasing four bombs. The crew later jettisoned the other four bombs before landing. The personnel errors occurred in the 468th BG: aircraft #356 *Georgia Peach* released all eight bombs twelve to fifteen miles from the primary

The 40th BG's #294 *Monsoon* placed four bombs on the primary before encountering a problem with the other four during Mission #4 to Anshan, Manchuria. The crew cleared the problem and dropped the remaining four bombs on the target of last resort. (*40th BG*)

The 468th BG's #442 *Power Play* as seen from another B-29. During Mission #4 to Anshan, the bombardier in #422 *Power Play* realized lead bomber #356 *Georgia Peach* released its bomb load too early, so he held four bombs and dropped them over the primary target. (*Schutte via 468th BG*)

target, while B-29 #442 *Power Play* released four bombs upon seeing #356 *Georgia Peach* drop its load. The bombardier realized the error and managed to hold the other four bombs and dropped them over the primary target.[11]

A 40th BG B-29 (#466 *Able Fox*) failed to drop its ordnance on the primary target due to rack problems. The pilot flew his crew to the secondary target and the issue persisted. As the crew worked to clear the problem the pilot diverted to the tertiary target, only to experience a third failure to release bombs. The frustrated crew managed to hand-jettison the bombs before returning to base. Another problem over the primary target quickly developed when one of the planes in the first formation successfully hit a by-products installation close to the aiming point, sending smoke across the latter and obscuring the aim of subsequent bomber formations.[12]

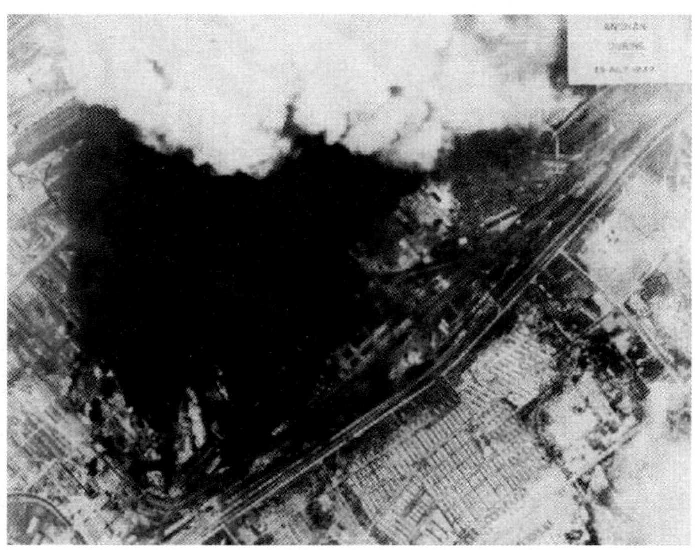

Smoke rising from the Showa Steel works in Anshan, Manchuria, during Mission #4. (*US Air Force*)

B-29 #312, piloted by Capt. Arthur Till of the 462nd BG, bombed the secondary target due to a mechanical issue. The resulting engine outage and fuel shortage forced the crew to land at Ankang on the return flight. Maintenance personnel worked diligently to replace the engine while the Japanese attempted to destroy the bomber on the ground. The air battles above the stricken B-29 resulted in the loss of a Japanese Kawasaki Ki-48 Lily bomber. The B-29 finally became airborne again and returned on August 3.[13]

Japanese anti-aircraft fire ranged from meager and inaccurate to intense and accurate. Most of the flak over Anshan consisted of intermittent patterns of twenty to thirty bursts. The B-29 crews spotted a lone aircraft shadowing their formations and probably transmitting altitude data to the Japanese gunners below. The bombers received meager and inaccurate flak over Chenghsien, but encountered none over Taku and Chinwangtao. The Japanese also fired meager and inaccurate flak from other locations along the bomber formation route. Five bombers returned with minor flak damage, including #474 of the 462nd BG (hole in the left side of the stabilizer) and the 468th BG's #408 *Ready Teddy* (five inch rip in the rudder), #397 *Million Dollar Baby* (hole in the right side of the stabilizer), #253 *Windy City* (four holes in the nose wheel door), and #272 *Miss Shorty* (three inch cut in a propeller). The Japanese did not employ smoke screens at any of the targets, but they did have ten to thirty barrage balloons at Taku.

The 462nd BG lost #256 *Ramp Tramp*, piloted by Capt. Howard Jarrell, when the crew diverted to Vladivostok in the Soviet Union after flak damaged engine #3. The flight engineer reduced power and estimated the B-29 could remain aloft up to four hours; within that time the crew would need to crash land or bail out over Japanese occupied territory in China. With Vladivostok only two hours away, Jarrell made the decision to enter Soviet air space, rather than risk going down in Japanese held territory. Although the Soviet Union remained neutral in the war between the Allies and Japan until August 1945, the crew did not take any chances and hand-shredded their classified documents, placing the pieces into the forward tire well. Soviet fighters intercepted the B-29 and fired across its nose, forcing the bomber to land at a small grass airfield. Jarrell lowered the landing gear and in the process the small pieces of shredded paper scattered across the countryside. The B-29 pilot cut his engines upon touching down and the plane raced across the grass airstrip, finally coming to rest at the far end. Soviet military personnel shoved the crew from the bomber and initiated an interrogation to determine the specifications of the bomber, the American inventory of B-29s, and the "secret weapon" they dropped prior to landing. The confused crew finally realized the Soviets were referring to the small pieces of shredded paper raining across the countryside after the landing gear dropped. The Americans refused to answer questions and asked to speak to the American consul. They remained interred within the Soviet Union for seven months before being permitted to "escape" into Iran with the crews of three other B-29s that diverted to the country. The Soviets retained all four B-29s (three landed and one crashed) that entered their air space prior to their declaration of war on Japan and reverse engineered them to produce the Tupolev Tu-4 Bull bomber, a nearly exact copy of the B-29 Superfortress. Gen. LeMay commented after the war:

> ...the Tu-4 was outwardly identical to a B-29 down to the apparently faithful copies of Wright Cyclone engines. Those bootlegged Cyclones were in fact, so faithful to the originals that the Soviets had many of the same technical problems that the USAAF faced with the originals in the early B-29 program...If imitation really is the sincerest form of flattery, then the bootlegged Tu-4 was among the highest tributes that would be paid to the Superfortress in the postwar years.[14]

Fighters added another element to the Japanese anti-aircraft defenses over Manchuria; forty-four Japanese pilots attacked eighteen of the B-29s on Mission #4. Sixty percent of the attacks occurred during a thirty-two minute period over Anshan; 11% were over Chenghsien and the remaining 29% were along the flight route. Japanese fighters did not challenge the bombers over Taku. Two B-29s sustained minor damage from fighters while the gunners aboard the bombers filed claims for three probables (one Tony; one Mitsubishi A6M Hamp—a variation of the Zeke—and one Nakajima Ki-44 Tojo) and four damaged (two Mitsubishi A6M Zekes and two Oscars). The first tail gunner to file a claim for damaging a Japanese fighter by utilizing a 20 mm cannon occurred on this operation. The gunner reported he damaged an Oscar through the dual use of the machine guns and 20 mm cannon mounted in the bomber's tail. The majority of fighter attacks originated from the right and rear of the bombers (between 2 and 7 o'clock). The Japanese pilots proved to be aggressive and flew well as coordinated teams. As related in the post-mission analysis:

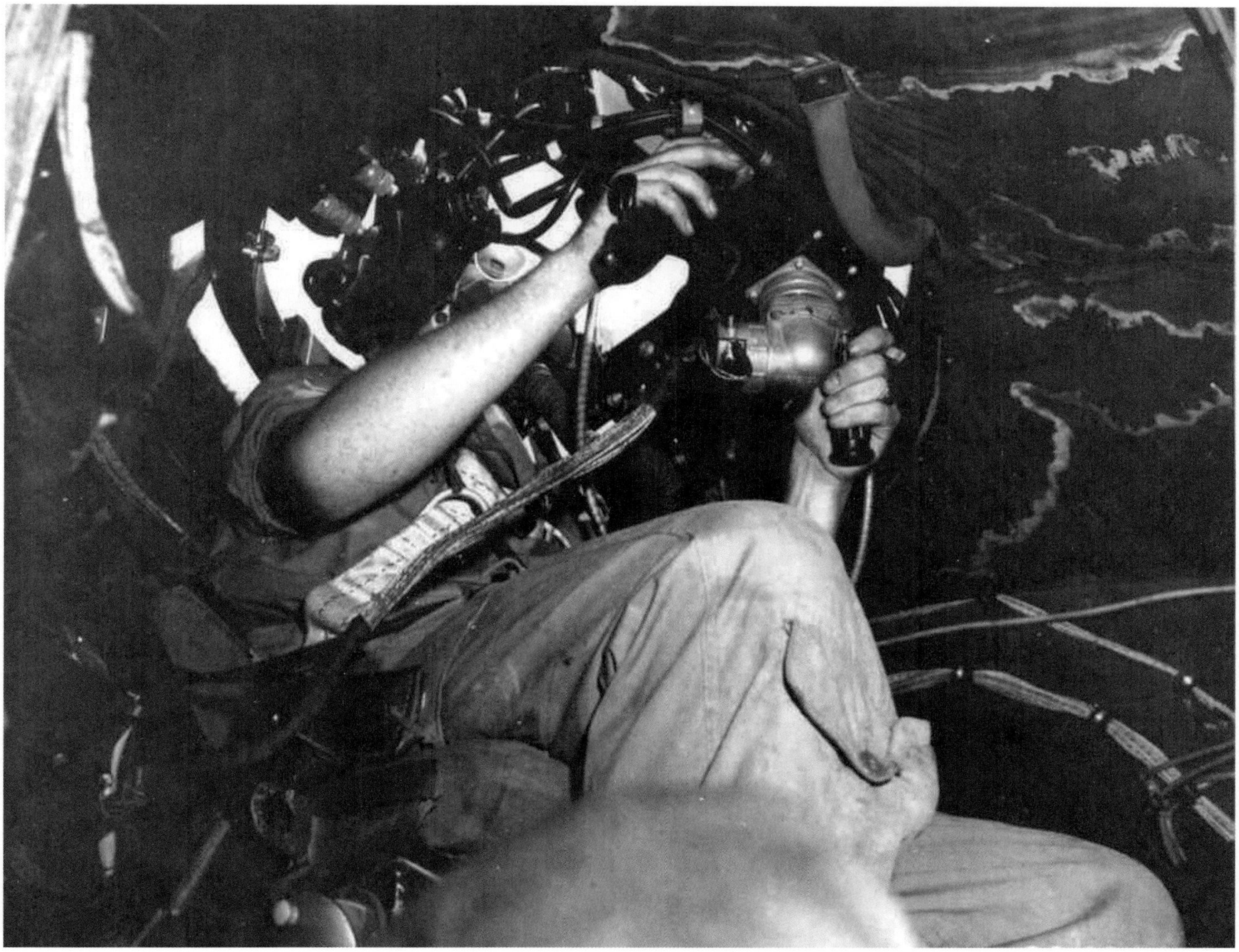

Central fire control (CFC) gunner Sgt. Thomas Clark aboard #281 *20th Century Unlimited* of the 40th BG. The CFC gunner served as the crew's senior gunner and manned the upper blister. Crew members frequently referred to this seat as the "barber's chair." (*Schutte via 40th BG*)

Four Tojos relied on the familiar Jap trick in which one fighter performed slow rolls and other aerobactics while the other three made a series of passes at the B-29. A new type of coordinated attack was made by two Zekes. Once came in at 7 o'clock high and the other at 4 o'clock level. As they approached, the B-29 opened fire on the diving Zeke at 800 yards and on the other at 900 yards. The latter immediately broke away with a roll and a dive, but the Zeke at 7 o'clock high closed to 500 yards, made a half-roll to the right, and ended with a dive. No fire was observed from either of the enemy aircraft.[15]

The 40th BG's #344 *Princess Patsy* returned with several bullet holes from Japanese fighters during Mission #4. (*40th BG*)

It is interesting to note that gunners expended 23,900 rounds test firing their weapons but only 1,230 rounds defending their bombers. Two 40th BG B-29s sustained minor fighter damage: a Japanese fighter punctured a fuel tank and ruptured a hydraulic line on aircraft #466 *Able Fox*, while #344 *Princess Patsy* flew home with several bullet holes.[16]

An American Curtiss P-40 Warhawk flown by the Dutch and captured by the Japanese. A P-40 Warhawk with Chinese-American Composite Air Wing (CACW) insignia, but apparently captured and flown by the Japanese, engaged the B-29s in cooperation with Japanese aircraft during Mission #4. (*Lukas*)

A 468th BG bomber crashed due to a combination of factors, including mechanical problems and Japanese flak and fighters. B-29 #274 *Lady Hamilton*, piloted by Capt. Robert Mills, developed trouble with engine #2 approximately forty miles south of Chenghsien. The problem slowed the B-29, which dropped out of its four-ship formation. Mills diverted to the target of last resort to drop his bomb load and return to base, but anti-aircraft fire over the target struck the bomber, adding minor damage to the existing problem. At nearly the same time five enemy fighter pilots smelled blood and jumped the wounded B-29, knocking out engines #3 and #4. Mills ordered his crew to bail out as he struggled to maintain altitude. Mills never left the crippled bomber, but eight of his crew did jump and were retrieved by Chinese guerrillas who assisted them to return to Chengtu after a month-long journey.[17] The Japanese planes downing Mills and his crew included three Tonys, one Tojo, and one American-built Curtiss P-40 Warhawk with the markings of the Chinese-American Composite Wing (CACW).

> The CACW was a combined unit of Chinese and American pilots assigned to the 14th Air Force flying P-40s, North American P-51 Mustangs, and North American B-25 Mitchell bombers in 1944. The CACW included the original Flying Tigers, who had transferred from Chinese to United States service in 1942. The Japanese captured several P-40s during the early years of WWII and repaired more than one to flying condition.

B-29 crews on Mission #4 did not report any attempts by the Japanese to masquerade as an Allied fighter pilot to maneuver closer to the bombers before attacking. The Japanese pilot flying the P-40 clearly and openly cooperated with the other fighters attacking B-29 #274 *Lady Hamilton*.

Reconnaissance aircraft returned with photographs indicating the attack on Anshan caused light damage to the target. Direct hits knocked out two of the sixteen coke oven batteries that would require one year to repair and return to full operational capacity. Including damage to a third coke oven battery and a blast furnace, the raid reduced the capacity of the plant by approximately 20%.

Improved weather conditions finally permitted twenty-four of the 444th BG's planes to take off and fly to the group's newly designated primary target at Taku later the same day. Of these, three (#212, #462 *Princess Eileen II*, and #262 *Round Trip Ticket*) bombed the target of last resort at Chenghsien and five returned early due to mechanical issues. Although listed in the official records as bombing the primary target, #300 actually dropped only one bomb due to a malfunction and later released the rest of its load on an unspecified target of opportunity. The Superfortresses did not encounter any Japanese opposition during the mission. The bombing results at Taku Harbor included damage to two large *godowns* (warehouses) and associated wharfs, as well as a direct hit on a 150-200 foot collier vessel and the near miss of a second ship. Bombs cut rail lines and sidings and destroyed several buildings at the Yung Li Alkali Pant.[18]

Gen. Arnold continued to believe that high altitude daylight precision raids against strategic targets remained the best use of B-29s. While the bombing results at Anshan and Taku were not spectacular, the bombers were hitting the targets and scoring more damage against the facilities than against plants during the two night raids to Japan. Most crew members preferred the safety of night raids, but they were not placing ordnance on the targets. In September, Gen. Curtis LeMay also adopted this strategy as XX BC commander and directed an increase in daylight raids with larger formations similar to the missions he led in Europe.

Flying the Hump

40th BG crewman George Lowry referred to the Hump as "rocks in the clouds" when remembering his flights across the Himalaya Mountains between India and China. A corner of the Himalaya Mountains stretched between the XX BC bases in northeast India and the wing's forward airfields in northwest China. Flying between one of the group bases in India and its forward airfield in China covered approximately 1,200 miles and lasted between 5 and 5½ hours...in good weather. B-29s bound for Japan and later Manchuria, Formosa, and eastern China could not reach their targets by launching from India. Basing the bombers in India added a measure of safety because the bases near Calcutta were just beyond fighter range from Japanese bases in Burma, while the forward airfields in northwest China near Chengtu were within range of Japanese bombers stationed in occupied areas of that country. Missions to Japan, Manchuria, Formosa, and eastern China required the B-29s fly from India to northwest China, where they refueled and performed maintenance

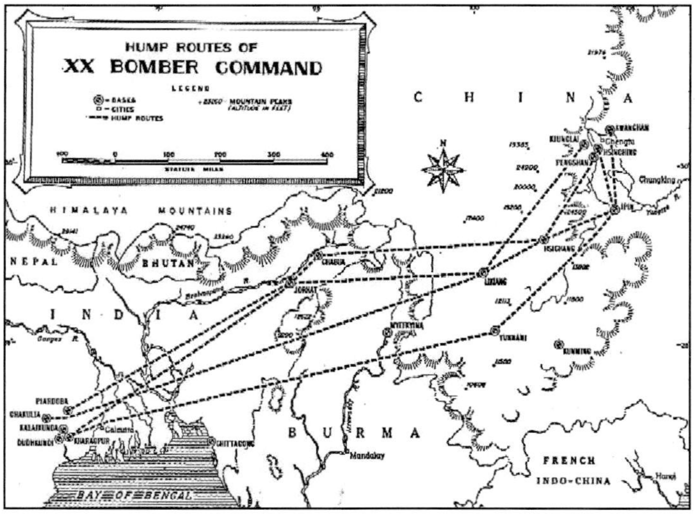

The four primary routes across the Hump from India to China. The most northerly routes flew across higher mountains; the most southerly routes presented a greater chance of interception by Japanese fighters. (*US Air Force*)

checks before launching again for their targets. Returning from the targets, the bombers landed in northwest China to refuel and receive any required maintenance before flying back across the Hump to India. Aircraft of the XX BC and Air Transportation Command (ATC) hauled fuel supplies across the Hump to build the stockpiles required for missions.[19]

The original Operation Matterhorn plans called for the B-29s to haul their own supplies across the Hump for stockpiling in China due to the 1942 loss of the Burma Road, which permitted ground movement of supplies from Burma to China. In mid-1944, the Allies were still constructing the Ledo Road from India across northern Burma and into China as a means to haul supplies to Chiang Kai-shek. The Allied offensive in the area around Myitkyina proved important for securing that area of Burma for the passage of the Ledo Road (also known as the Stilwell Road). The first convoy to utilize the full length of the Ledo Road arrived in China in February 1945—after the XX BC had ceased to launch missions from Chengtu, except for two small aerial mining operations to the Yangtze River. Starting in April 1944, the bombers were not able to ferry the estimated tonnage listed in the original plans due to extreme environmental conditions, mechanical problems with the new B-29 and its engines, and the strain it placed on units. Gen. LeMay recognized the challenges behind flying supplies across the Hump for stockpiling. "We were flying seven trips over the Himalayas with every B-29, off-loading as much gas as we could to still get back to India. On the eighth trip across the Hump to Chengtu, we would finally take a load of bombs and fly a bombing mission against the Japanese."[20]

Gen. LeMay's comments illustrate the challenge—every seventy-five plane B-29 mission launched from Chengtu required 525 B-29 supply flights across the Hump! Tonnage did increase between May (the first full month of Hump flights) and September, as more B-29s flew fuel to China and each group converted select bombers into gas haulers. The latter aircraft flew without armament except tail guns and carried a reduced crew and extra internal fuel tanks. These planes could haul more than twice the amount of fuel as a standard B-29 with extra tanks. ATC provided limited cargo space for fuel destined to Chengtu, but any tonnage destined for the XX BC meant less tonnage heading to Gen. Chiang Kai-shek and the 14th Air Force in China, continually sparking political discourse over supplies. Except for June and July, the ATC hauled approximately the same amount of XX BC fuel as XX BC B-29s and a limited number of Curtiss C-46 Commandos crossing the Hump. Between May and September, monthly Hump tonnage increased from 1,950 tons to 4,581 tons.

Getting fuel across the Hump proved to be one of the greatest challenges of Operation Matterhorn. Pilots faced a combination of environmental issues over the Himalaya Mountains coupled with aircraft mechanical problems and hostile terrain if parachuting or crashing along the route. Weather above the Hump could be absolutely clear, delivering air crews an unprecedented and spectacular view of the mountains below them. At other times, the weather changed quickly to present crews with harrowing wind conditions and limited to zero visibility. Low cloud cover frequently hid mountain peaks, adding to the many obstacles facing pilots. The crews referred to the routes as the "aluminum trail" due to the long string of crashed bomber and transport aircraft strewn across the mountains between India and China. Some aircraft simply disappeared, never to be heard from or found again in these conditions.

The intense storms over the Hump baffled pilots, as their planes were violently tossed and became lost in the blinding conditions. One ATC Douglas C-54 Skymaster transport aircraft remained aloft an incredible fifteen hours during a storm thanks to the ingenuity of two engineers aboard the plane:

Higher peaks of the Hump in winter from over 20,000 feet. (*Willis via 40th BG*)

Another view of a snow-covered peak of the Hump. (*Changnon via 40th BG*)

> The pilot, Capt. Frederick M. Mills, and the co-pilot, 1st Lt. William W. Wetzel, used every flying trick they knew to come out of the storm. The engineers, Sgt. F. A. Kliembriel and Pvt. William D. Carter, watched the ship's instruments - saw her gauges indicate a critically low fuel reserve. Realizing that if the gasoline in the cargo compartment could be transferred to the tanks, the C-54 could be kept aloft almost indefinitely, the engineers cast around for a means of accomplishing this. They found a piece of hose in the rear of the plane. Shoving one end of the hose into one of the gasoline barrels and the other into the fuselage tank, they pumped barrel after barrel of gasoline to replenish the constantly-decreasing reserve. By the time her gear touched a familiar airstrip in China, 20 barrels of gasoline had been pumped from the C-54's cargo compartment to the power plants.[21]

The XX BC B-29 aircrews faced the same hazards as the ATC crews, but often credited the latter for their stamina while facing the rigors of the cross-Himalaya missions. The bomber crews flew in pressurized aircraft, which helped mitigate, but not eliminate, the weather conditions in the skies above the mountains. George Lowery of the 40th BG remarked after the war, "We talk and we listen to those Air Transport crews in and out of the [flight] pattern, hauling gasoline in drums. What a disagreeable time they must have. No heat, no oxygen. Can't even climb up safely above the mountains. And those fellows have to come down in here on instruments all the time!"[22]

Douglas C-54 Skymaster began operating across the Hump in October 1944. It could not fly the most northerly route due to its altitude limitations, but had sufficient range to fly directly from Calcutta, India, to bases in China. (*US Air Force*)

Willard Holderby, a navigator with the 468th BG, encountered sharp wind changes during a June 1944 flight across the Hump:

The Himalaya Mountains. Note the leading edge of the horizontal stabilizer on the right side of the photograph. (*40th BG*)

Clouds often obscured the mountain peaks of the Himalayas. (*40th BG*)

> On the second flight of June 16th [1944], we encountered a terrific thunderstorm. It seemed it would tear the plane to bits. [Fuel] Tanks were broken loose in the rear and a huge hole was cut in the floor. The climb indicator once showed us to be climbing at the rate of 4,000 feet a minute, while both the Pilot and Co-pilot had the stick all the way forward. We were all thankful to land in one piece at our forward base in China.[23]

Wind gusts could fluctuate between 100 and 200 mph within the Himalaya Mountain range, completely flipping aircraft on more than one occasion. 1st Lt. Thomas Sykes of the ATC survived one of these terrifying flips caused by excessive winds:

> With our airspeed going from 300 to 400 m.p.h., the rate of climb went up to 4,000 feet a minute and suddenly we were on our back. While hanging in my safety belt and with the dirt from the floor falling all around, I realized that it would be impossible to bail out. The co-pilot and I fought the controls until we finally righted the ship at 21,000. We had made a complete 180-degree turn and were headed in the direction from which we had come. We had been in the air quite long and decided that our destination must be closer than the point of departure. We turned and bucked our way through the storm and made it.[24]

At least one B-29 also found itself inverted as the air currents tossed the aircraft into a backwards loop. On August 19, Ernest Turner of the 40th BG was piloting a B-29 returning from China when he encountered severe winds near Imphal, India. Turner and his crew descended from 18,000 feet and broke through the clouds at 15,000 feet. A stratus layer of clouds lay ahead of the aircraft and Turner entered it on instruments. At just above 10,000 feet, Turner flew into a cumulus thunderhead that placed the bomber into "up and down" drafts of air. Turner needed his co-pilot, William Johnson, to help control the B-29 as the drafts rocked the plane with turbulence. Turner later wrote:

> We went through four very severe ascents and descents; on the fourth ascent the plane started an uncontrollable climb. We couldn't read any of the instruments as the dials were all spinning crazily, but I could see that the nose oil pressure dropped to 0-5 lbs. At the start of this climb, the engines were running at 1800 RPM and were pulling 23 inches. The plane climbed vertically, was flipped over on its back, and then slid off on the left wing. After flipping over on the left wing, the plane went into a dive. My head was leaning against the armor glass due to the angle of dive. Dust settling back on the floor got into my eyes. Being strapped in had helped in regaining control of the plane as it rolled out of the loop. We finally brought the plane out of the dive at approximately 3,000 feet with engine operation normal. The first indicated airspeed which had been readable was 380 mph; this dropped to 320 mph at the end of the dive.[25]

#303 *Typhoon McGoon III* over the Hump during the summer of 1944. (*Seith via 40th BG*)

Navigator Robert Mullin was not strapped into his seat as the B-29 hit the thunderhead. His memories present an incredible portrait of the turmoil within the forward section of the huge bomber as she flipped within the storm:

> The first tremendous down draft threw me clear out of my seat onto the floor. As I struggled to get up, the aircraft was caught in a violent vertical current that tossed us upward. The only thing for me to hold on to was the leg of my navigator's table. (Remember, our early airplanes had a two gun upper forward turret and the navigator's table had a leg). I wound my legs around the leg of the table and just held on. I glanced up toward the nose and could see the Bombardier, Thomas E. Sample, bouncing around like a football. I could see our Radioman, "Pop" Gardner, was worse off than I. Having no table leg to hang on to, he was flat on his back and, with both hands, was warding off a fire extinguisher that had broken loose from its fastenings. It was suspended in mid-air and was slowly spinning around as the airplane went through its violent gyrations.[26]

Co-pilot William Johnson added another perspective from the cockpit:

> As the plane went inverted, our engines stopped. Having never heard of a B-29 in this position, I expected the wings to snap off. They didn't! Our next thought was to avert a spin and restart the engines. We pulled back on the control column to get the nose down to regain flying speed and used rudder control to stop the spin tendency. We finally brought the plane out of the dive by using the trim tab control only, because the two of us did not have strength enough to pull the control column back. The air speed indicator passed the red line, and we were pulling too many G's to even rise from our seats. The plane was brought down to 500 feet to avoid turbulence. We flew all the way back to Chakulia at this altitude to stay below the overcast. To a man, we kissed the ground when we landed and gave thanks to our Maker on this day.[27]

Gunners Earl Rogers and Theodore Urban were belted into their seats and rode out the flip, but central fire control gunner Calvin Brown sat unsecured in his chair as the B-29 approached the storm:

> I was riding the barber chair and watching the top of the airplane and maybe dozing off now and then. I could see a huge cloud ahead of us which didn't look any different from many we had flown through in the past. We flew into it and it wasn't long until I saw lightning jumping all over the airplane, from tail to wingtips to nose to every part of the plane. I was fully awake by then. All of a sudden, I was pushed down into the barber chair so hard I couldn't move. The next thing I knew, I was out of my chair trying to get into my chute while floating in mid-air along with everything else in the gunner's compartment. Then I hit the floor and couldn't move. The next sensation was floating in mid-air again and hitting the top of the plane and my gun sight then down to the floor again. I know what it feels like to be weightless.[28]

The engine problems that plagued the early B-29 program did not abate over the Hump; many crews found themselves flying in the inhospitable skies over the Himalaya Mountains when an engine decided to cease functioning. Maj. James Pattillo of the 468th BG found himself in this predicament on June 7, while hauling cargo across the Hump in B-29 #271. One of the engines on the left wing developed a runaway propeller. Pattillo attempted to shut down the engine and feather the propeller, which would allow it to turn freely in the wind and not place drag upon the aircraft and possibly tear the engine from its mountings on the wing. The pilot worked to feather the propeller for 200 miles without success as the bomber slowed due to the excessive drag. Drainage of oil during this attempt compelled problems as Pattillo requested a position fix from the navigator. Thick cloud cover, changes in speed

A view of the Himalaya Mountains—"the Hump." (*40th BG*)

as the pilot applied emergency power to the other three engines, and the loss of 7,000 feet altitude left navigator Lt. Richard Cournoyer unsure of the plane's precise location within the mountain range. Pattillo later noted the plane continued to sink "into what appeared to be mountains" and ordered the crew to abandon the aircraft. The eleven-man crew began bailing out from the bomber as Pattillo fought to maintain a steady flight path to help the men come down together. As the crew members broke through the clouds in their parachute descents they could see a river below them. The pilot released the controls, leaving the aircraft after the last man jumped. The B-29 immediately turned itself toward the dead engine in a sharp left turn. Pattillo bailed out from the aircraft and later reported watching the plane as he descended. The bomber "went into a diving turn to the left, air speed then started building up." The airspeed increased to the point that the plane actually began climbing again. "...[A]fter climbing slightly it started into a second dive and kept this up until it hit the ground." Cournoyer commented later that the bomber passed so close to him that his parachute momentarily deflated. The plane crashed near Loshan, in China's Sichuan Province.[29]

Rescue parties found nine of the crew members within five days of the crash. Right gunner Sgt. Eric Tidy drowned after landing in the river; even a good swimmer could become entangled in cords or not be able to release their parachute upon hitting the water. His body floated downstream and was found a week after the crash. Search parties never found the eleventh crew member, co-pilot Lt. Geoffrey Matthews.

Many crashes over the Himalaya Mountains remain a mystery due to the loss of the entire crew: B-29 #238 of the 468th BG is one of these many examples. The 468th BG converted the bomber to a tanker to haul fuel across the Hump for staging in China. Capt. Eddie Winkler piloted the aircraft—a veteran of eighteen Hump missions—across the Himalaya Mountains on October 1. Weather conditions were poor and the plane never arrived in China. A search eventually discovered the crash site on Omei Mountain, but no one will ever know the specifics of what happened that day.[30]

XX BC B-29s were adorned with three types of symbols: each "bomb" represents the completion of a bombing mission; a camel indicates a supply trip across the Hump; and the Japanese flag below the camels notes the crew received credit for the destruction of one Japanese fighter. (*40th BG*)

A 40th BG B-29 flying across the Hump during the summer of 1944. (*40th BG*)

Consolidated C-87 Liberator Express, the cargo version of a B-24 Liberator bomber, flew the Hump in support of the XX BC and other American units in China. (*US Air Force*)

Capt. Winkler bailed out from another B-29 he piloted just five weeks prior to this incident. His bomber developed a runaway propeller on a return cargo flight from China on August 25. He and the other six crew members bailed out of the doomed aircraft and were safely recovered. No one survived the crash in October. The military declared all eight crew members and two passengers dead after the incident.[31] A search team recovered the identifiable remains of five men. The military transferred their bodies from China for reburial in the United States in 1949. The exact circumstances behind the October crash will never be known. While the military did locate remains at this crash site, bodies were unrecoverable in many losses, as planes struck mountains at high altitude in remote areas. In many instances, the location of the crash could never be determined.

Many incredible XX BC survival stories developed over the months as downed crewmen emerged from the mountains days and weeks after being declared missing. The first great tale of survival involved a 468th BG crew led by Lt. Leslie J. Sloan. The pilot and his crew delivered a load of fuel to China on June 6. The return trip that day began well, with clear weather and inspiring views of the mountains towering around them. Suddenly, the B-29 shook violently, indicating a blown engine cylinder. Sloan attempted to feather the propeller on the damaged engine, but it refused to turn freely and instead reversed itself. One of the crewmen yelled "fire" over the intercom and bright flames trailed the engine as Sloan hit the fire extinguisher switch. The fire extinguisher failed to smother the fire and the drag from the propeller took its toll as the bomber began to lose altitude in the mountainous area.

Sloan ordered the crew to bail out at 22,000 feet; everyone except one gunner departed. Three crew members experienced parachute problems during the descent. Flight engineer Lt. Robert Casey exited through the nose-wheel opening. He wore a spare parachute on this mission as his regular gear underwent checking and repacking. Casey pulled the cord on his chute, only to find it refused to budge. The cord was designed to open the top of the pack and permit the silk parachute to unfurl and open in the wind. The flight engineer continued to yank on the cord as panic gripped him. With a mighty two-handed tug, the cord loosened and the parachute emerged from the pack. He made a hard but safe landing on rocky terrain before collapsing his chute and initiating a search for the other crewmen. Tail gunner Sgt. John Moore squeezed himself from the rear gunner's compartment and jumped with his chest parachute. Moore's parachute pack also refused to open when he tugged on the cord. In desperation, the gunner manually ripped open the top of the pack as he tumbled toward the ground. The chute finally opened, breaking his descent. Gunner Sgt. Virgil Bailey experienced torn panels in his parachute. Although he dropped much faster than the other men, he survived the landing without injuries.

An armed party of Yi people (often referred to as the LoLo) approached Casey soon after his landing and motioned for him to surrender his pistol. By the end of

The 468th BG's #242 *Esso Express* shown in the United States. The 468th BG converted this B-29 to a special tanker that could haul more fuel over the Hump than a regular Superfortress. (*US Air Force*)

the next day the Yi had located all of the crewmen and gathered them in a village. The men noted the Yi were shorter and stockier than Chinese people around the forward B-29 bases. They wore heavy goat hair cloaks in the cold mountainous climate while the Americans were in short sleeves and light pants, having expected to land in warm Indian weather. The Yi placed the Americans in the local chief's thatch and mud hut and boiled a goat that smelled so foul that none of the survivors would attempt to eat it. Hunger persuaded the men to indulge in the goat, now mixed with chicken, the next day.

Attitudes toward the stranded Americans improved when the chief observed the kindness exhibited by the men to his son, who had a crippled arm. The Yi finally allowed them to depart over two weeks later. The Americans and their guides carried a plate of raw opium—a gift from the chief to pay their way through other tribal areas. Someone stole the opium two days later and their guides frequently changed until they reached an area of walled villages. The inhabitants treated the American crew well and led them to the home of a retired Chinese army general who fed them and ensured they arrived safely at a trading post. An Englishman at the post procured a boat for the crews and sent them downstream to an Army Air Force weather station, from where they flew to Chengtu. The twenty-eight-day odyssey emerged as the first of many great XX BC survival tales.[32]

Capt. Jay Woodruff was piloting #326 of the 40th BG on a gasoline cargo run across the Hump to China when an engine began spewing oil. Woodruff guided the crippled bomber to an emergency field where Chinese workers would not move off the runway. Tragically, nine of the workers were killed instantly. (*40th BG*)

Even forced landings at emergency fields during Hump flights could result in long periods on the ground. Capt. Jay Woodruff piloted B-29 #326 of the 40th BG on a gasoline cargo run across the Hump to China on June 19, when an engine began displaying signs of trouble. The engine lost power and spewed oil, prompting Woodruff to shut it down and feather the propeller. The plane began losing altitude at approximately 200 feet per minute over the highest terrain along the Hump. Bombardier Joe Buckowitz salvoed the lower bomb bay fuel tanks to reduce the weight of the aircraft and he experienced difficulty closing the bomb bay doors. When they finally closed, the B-29 had dropped from 23,000 to 18,000 feet. The radio compass proved inoperable and the radio operator called a ground station for directions. Meanwhile, navigator Tom Brennan saw through the clouds and made a visual identification of the plane's position.

As the pilot debated whether to continue the flight or make an emergency landing another engine began smoking and losing oil. This new development settled the question and Woodruff banked the crippled aircraft toward an emergency field near Hsichang. Co-pilot Bill Clay ordered the crew into crash positions and assisted Woodruff as he prepared to put the lumbering bomber onto what a map labeled as a "rubble paved" runway. Woodruff remembered the landing, as it turned disastrous for Chinese laborers on the ground:

> Trees and buildings just off the end of the runway necessitated considerable altitude at the point of approach. When we made contact with the ground, the field remaining was so obviously short that I applied full brakes. The main wheels locked and we skidded on the soft turf until we reached the pavement at the end. The pavement turned out to be just the foundation of a runway, composed only of very large stones. Chinese workers were laboring at the end of the runway and they made no effort to get out of the way as the plane came at them. Tragically, nine were killed instantly by our propellers.[33]

The massive bomber struck a small ditch and then rough stones lay just beyond it. Woodruff continued:

> [the B-29] folded and we skidded only a few feet farther on main gear and nose. The nose was "ground off." The engineer and pilot's compartments were completely wrecked. Bill Clay and I got out of the pilot's compartment with considerable difficulty, extracting ourselves from the wreckage of controls, seats, etc. We were uninjured except for scratches and bruises. The rest of the crew likewise was uninjured. The plane from the rear of the radio compartment to the tail looked to be intact. The props were ruined and there was some damage to flaps from flying stones.[34]

Tail gunner Hank Pisterzi found himself inside the elevated rear compartment: "When the plane came to rest in the ditch at the end of the runway, the nose was crushed but the tail was undamaged and up in the air and I was in it. The tail gunner's position is normally about two stories in the air. When the plane ended up I had to extricate myself from the tail gunner's position which was then about three stories above ground."[35] An American sergeant greeted Woodruff and his crew after they extracted themselves from the bomber; he led a four-man weather detachment based at the field. Within thirty minutes a Chinese general named Chang du Lon arrived with a bad attitude toward the crew following the deaths of the laborers and the wrecking of his airfield. Woodruff explained the situation through the general's interpreter. When Gen. Chang realized the plane came down for an emergency landing, the local laborers would not clear the runway, and the crew had bombed Japan four days earlier (Yawata on June 15) his mood changed. Days of parties for the crew followed.

Capt. Jay Woodruff and his crew with Chinese military and civilian personnel after their rescue following an emergency landing during a Hump crossing. (*40th BG*)

A Douglas C-47 Skytrain of the Chinese National Aviation Corporation crossing the Hump. (*Lukas*)

The 40th BG decided to salvage the bomber and fly it back to India. A crew of seventeen mechanical and engineering specialists arrived by aircraft from India to assist the crew in replacing all four engines and propellers, repairing minor structural damage, and even adding a new nose section. While the Americans tackled the task of repairing the aircraft, they were also drafted to assist with the recovery of other downed American airmen. Art Reibe, a maintenance specialist, remembered:

> In addition to our duty to attempt to salvage the plane, we were to be on the lookout for any other downed airmen. On two occasions, we were awakened in the night. We were loaded onto a Chinese truck. The truck had no fuel tank, just a 55-gallon drum on its rear bed. A dipper full of some sort of alcohol was passed forward to a Chinese soldier riding the front fender. In turn, he slowly metered it into the exposed carburetor. Much of the alcohol never made it to the engine being short stopped by the troops. Soon we were all drunk. The hairpin curves of this road were a first class nightmare. While the Chinese intelligence notified us twice, only one crew came in while we were in Hsichang. This crew had lost several members and most were badly hurt. Within a day they were flown out.[36]

A C-46 Commando periodically arrived at the emergency field to ferry tools, supplies, C-rations, and PX supplies, such as cigarettes. A local Chinese cook mixed the C-rations with locally procured corn and eggs and the men noted he produced marvelous dishes. A delay in a supply flight resulted in the crews running out of cigarettes and Art Reibe volunteered along with another American to catch a Chinese C-47 flight across the Hump to acquire a fresh supply of tobacco, but the men did not realize the ordeal they would face for a few cigarettes:

> George Lundquist and I caught a CNAC [Chinese National Aviation Corporation] C-47 and flew across the Hump in it to Chabua, a base in the upper Assam valley. The plane had seen better days. It was full of holes. It was wired up Toonerville Trolley style. It had no parachutes and only one walk-around oxygen bottle which was traded off between the pilot and radio operator. George and I were turning blue from the cold and lack of oxygen by the time we got to India. The next day the Chinese went back over the Hump to Kunming where the Red Cross let us sign out for two cartons of cigarettes. Getting to Haichang from Kunming took some doing. We were assigned to another CNAC plane but missed it. It crashed shortly after take-off. We caught another plane which took us to Kweilin in eastern China. With the base surrounded by the Japanese on three sides, we nevertheless touched down long enough to unload and load cargo and refuel. Then it was off to Chungking and then to Hsinching (A-1). Neither George nor I know how we eventually got back to Hsichang but it was at least a week later. All for two cartons of cigarettes.[37]

Curtiss C-46 Commando. Air Transportation Command (ATC) and XX BC crews flew supplies across the Hump in the C-46. (*US Air Force*)

Another view of the Curtiss C-46 Commando. The C-46 could carry twice the payload of a C-47 and proved to be quite adept at facing the adverse weather conditions of the Hump. (*US Air Force*)

Curtiss C-46 Commando crossing the Hump. Initial problems with the aircraft were solved and the plane continued to fly with small airlines serving remote areas of Africa and the Arctic into the twenty-first century. (*US Air Force*)

The inability to load pieces of a nose section onto a C-46 cargo aircraft brought the project to a halt. The Americans, with Chinese assistance, pulled the wreck away from the runway, gave the approximately 8,000 gallons of gasoline to the Chinese army, and allowed them to strip the plane. B-29 #326 never made it back across the Hump.

Lt. Bart Ellis of the 444th BG flew a bomber delayed en route to the forward bases for staging prior to the July mission to Sasebo. He departed India with his crew on July 4 to haul cargo across the Hump in preparation for the mission. The sound of a loud bang and the lurching of the B-29 alerted the crew to a potentially serious engine problem. Flight engineer Lt. Walt Smith called on the intercom to the aft compartment and asked for a gunner to observe the engines on the right wing. Sgt. Ron Ellis reported, "There's a lot of black smoke trailing number three." The flight engineer called for the pilot to feather engine #3 as navigator Lt. John Misterly replotted the crew's position and the time it would take to reach Chengtu on three engines. After a nervous interlude another engine failed. "Then we heard still another blast and this time the plane shook as if given a push sideways," exclaimed Misterly. The radio operator placed a MAYDAY call and Ellis ordered the cargo dropped to reduce weight in the plane and help keep her airborne over the mountains. A

Cockpit of the Curtiss C-46 Commando. (*US Air Force*)

second B-29 caught up to the Ellis crew due to the plane's reduced speed. The crew of the arriving B-29 radioed they would slow down and fly above the stricken bomber. While there was little they could do beyond showing their presence and confirming a bail out position if necessary, the second crew provided the valuable service of just being there in a time of need. Misterly felt confident the crew would be able to make their airfield in China as the plane began clearing the highest peaks. The radio operator called the control tower and requested they prepare for an emergency landing. Misterly remembered the safe landing with considerable relief:

The landing was accomplished with expertise. Bart had to be the best pilot in the entire USAAF, I had said it before and I said it again. We taxied in with the red and yellow [emergency] vehicles following, a mother hen being escorted by her chicks...Comments made about the loss of the two engines were not too complimentary. Looking at it another way, the other two got us here and that was the bottom line.[38]

Curtiss C-46 Commando assembly line. The Curtiss-Wright Corporation constructed approximately 3,180 C-46s during World War II. (*US Air Force*)

Interior of a Curtiss C-46 Commando. The folding seats demonstrate the plane's utilization for both cargo and personnel during World War II. Note the load master's chair at the forward end of the cargo area. (*US Air Force*)

1st Lt. Robert Spellman and his crew pose with a Boeing B-17 Flying Fortress prior to their deployment to India. Spellman (back row, center) and his 444th BG crew perished while attempting to cross the Hump in B-29 #309 *Miss Carriage* on September 2, 1944. (444th BG)

The Douglas C-47 Skytrain. Douglas built over 10,000 of these rugged planes during its production history and they saw extensive service across the Hump. (*US Air Force*)

An American Red Cross center in China. (*40th BG*)

American cemetery in China. (*40th BG*)

Panic and ignorance of survival skills could quickly kill downed air crews. While some crews parachuted onto mountainous terrain, others jumped from crippled aircraft into thick jungle vegetation. The forests of northern Burma were teeming with mosquitoes, leeches, snakes, mites, spiders, flies, and red ants. The ants are a half-inch long and live in trees, where they construct nests from leaves. Many veterans remember these vicious ants with jaws that drew blood when they clamped down on flesh. Gen. William H. Tunner, the commander of ATC, recorded one horrible incident in his memoirs involving a downed air crewman. A C-46 crew bailed out along the southern Hump route and landed in the jungle. The pilot and co-pilot made it out of the jungle safely after a week. A search party set out to locate the radio operator, who did not emerge from the jungle. A "sickening odor" led the team to the body of the missing crewman. According to Tunner, the rescuers were able to reconstruct what happened. The young man came down safely into the trees and became stuck in his harness, hanging five feet from the ground. He apparently attempted to free himself and lost his balance, resulting in hanging upside down by his leg. His head and hands were on the ground, where Burmese red ants found and began biting him. Tunner wrote, "He frantically brushed away the undergrowth as far as he could reach. By this time the boy must have been in a panic. A vine covered tree trunk was within easy reach. He could have climbed it with his hands and gotten himself in position to extricate his leg, but he made no effort to do so."[39]

The radio man apparently utilized his pistol to shoot at the harness strap that held his leg. He fired until only a quarter inch of the strap still held him, but only one bullet remained in his weapon. Tunner concluded the account by writing, "The pain and horror of the ants swarming over him became too much to endure. The boy used his last bullet on himself."[40]

Chapter 4

August 1944: The Longest Mission

The flak was heavy and after leaving the target area the fighter planes went to work.

— Lt. Robert Schumacher (444th BG)
(interview with the author on the August Yawata mission)

The United States secured the island of Tinian, in the Marianas, on August 1, 1944, and Guam nine days later. With the capture of Saipan in July, the three islands provided locations for American bases, including the establishment in the fall of new B-29 fields under the XXI Bomber Command (BC). Myitkyina, in northern Burma, fell to Allied forces on August 3, clearing the way for the Ledo Road to pass near the town as it wound from India to China following its completion at the end of the year. From Myitkyina, Allied soldiers pushed southward toward Rangoon. By the end of August, the last Japanese troops still battling British and Indian soldiers near Imphal, India, were retreating back into Burma.

In India, Gen. Curtis LeMay arrived at the end of August to assume command of XX BC and oversee B-29 operations launched from the China-Burma-India Theater. LeMay replaced Gen. LaVerne Saunders, who held temporary command after the relief of Gen. Kenneth Wolfe in July. As Saunders awaited LeMay's arrival, he prepared to launch the longest B-29 raid in the China-Burma-India Theater.

Mission #5: Palembang, August 10–11, 1944

The decision to bomb the Pladjoe petroleum refinery at Palembang, on the island of Sumatra in the Netherlands East Indies, occurred before the first B-29s departed the United States. Japan acquired 78% of its aviation gasoline and 22% of its fuel oil from this single refinery. Military and civilian authorities viewed the crippling of the Pladjoe refinery as an important strategic military objective and discussed a possible aerial attack by the new Superfortress during the November 1943 Cairo Conference. Arnold and Saunders disagreed on many aspects of the mission, including time and the method of attack, as well as the number of aircraft committed to the raid. The final agreement between the two commanders set the number of attacking B-29s at fifty planes conducting a night raid utilizing their radar systems. The bombers would need to stage through Ceylon, located at the tip of the Indian peninsula, due to the extreme range of the target from the B-29 bases in India. The availability of only one Royal Air Force (RAF) airfield on Ceylon (located at China Bay) contributed to the need to limit the number of bombers assigned to the raid. The original plans requested the runway extensions of four (later revised to two) RAF bases, but this was changed again to one field. Although Arnold called for 112 aircraft to strike Palembang, Saunders countered he could only stage fifty B-29s at the one RAF base with sufficient runway length for the large planes. All fifty aircraft would fly from India and stage through Ceylon for the attack against the refinery on Sumatra.

The mission actually consisted of two separate objectives: bombing the refinery and mining the Moesi River. Vessels carrying fuel and oil from the refinery sailed the Moesi River; a successful mining of the river could sink vessels and block the channel. The secondary target for this mission was identified as the Pangkalan Brandan Refinery in the Netherlands East Indies, which produced 16.3% of Japan's aviation fuel. Briefers marked the Indarun Cement

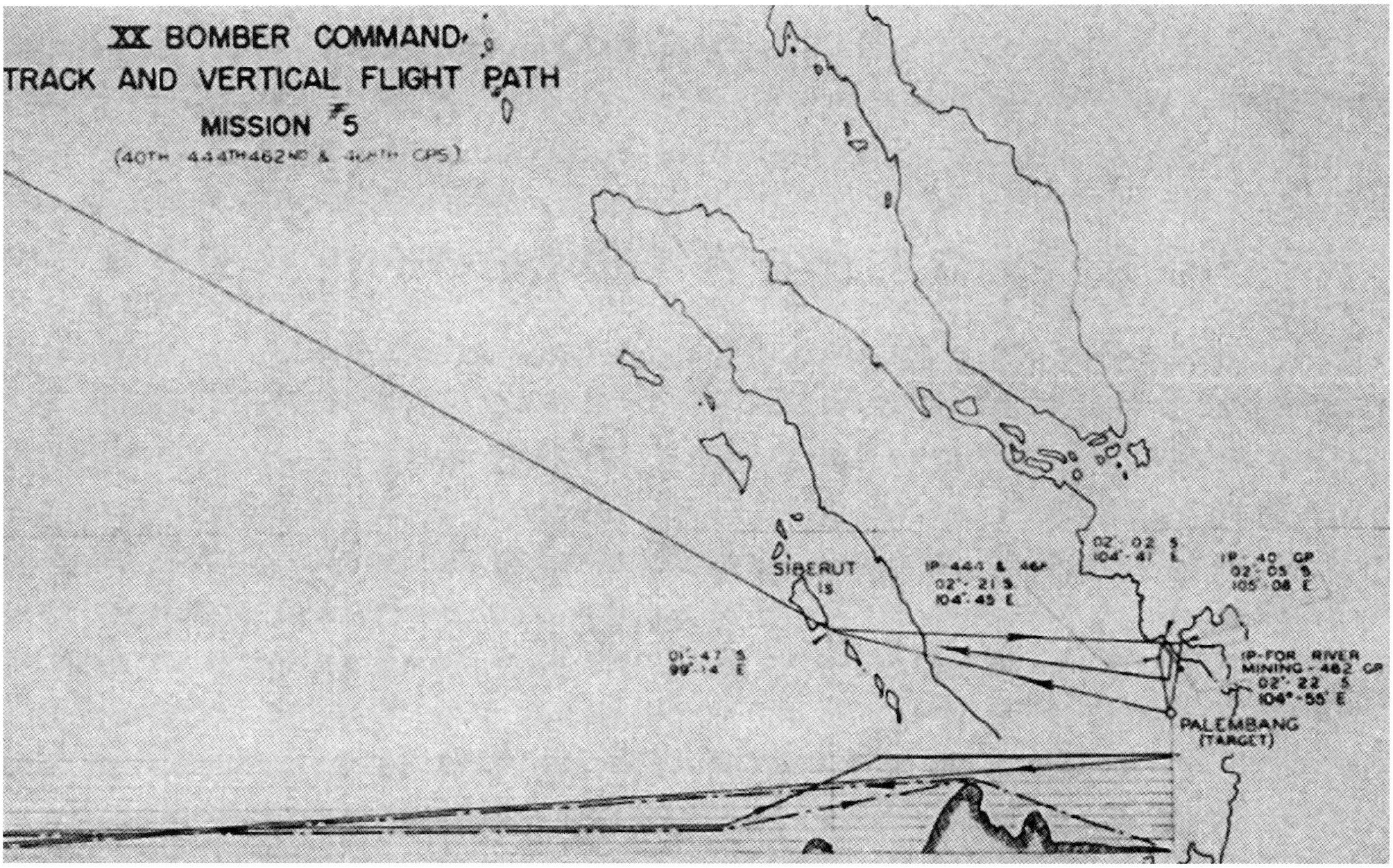

XX BC tracking chart showing the B-29s' routes across the Bay of Bengal (left side) and then passing over the island of Sumatra to the Pladjoe refinery and return. (*US Air Force*)

Plant in the Netherlands East Indies as the target of last resort. The plant produced 200,000 tons of cement annually and supplied the Japanese military with all of its cement for fortification construction in the area. The XX BC also conducted a simultaneous diversionary attack on Nagasaki, Japan, referred to in official records and this book as Mission #6. The main purpose behind the small raid on Nagasaki involved demonstrating to the Japanese that B-29s could strike simultaneous targets across Japanese held territory.[1]

Planners earmarked fourteen B-29s of the 462nd BG for the mining mission to the Moesi River, while the other groups targeted the refinery. 462nd BG Commander Col. Richard Carmichael personally led his bombers on the mining mission. The bombers bound for the refinery flew with general purpose and incendiary weapons, while the 462nd B-29s held AN-MK 26 aerial mines. These 1,000-pound mines carried parachutes and were dropped from aircraft over a waterway. The mines could arm themselves immediately or sink and wait for arming by a self-contained timer. The latter allowed the mines to become active over varying lengths of time in the hopes of lulling the Japanese into thinking a particular area was clear of mines. Although this was the first B-29 mining mission, the XX BC would carry out several more through March 1945. The most common problem the command encountered with the AN-MK 26 mines centered on defective parachutes; many mines were carried to the target and dropped, only to have the parachutes fail and the ordnance miss their assigned areas, or even explode upon hitting the water.[2]

The runway extension at China Bay placed a B-29 over water as soon as it lifted and cleared the end of the field; fifty-four B-29s made perilous take-offs from Ceylon. Each bomber carried the absolute maximum load of ordnance and fuel due to the extreme distance—the longest mission flown by B-29s from the China-Burma-India Theater. Maj. Thomas Vaucher of the 462nd BG flew with his crew to mine the Moesi River and managed to become airborne with four struggling engines and a prayer. As

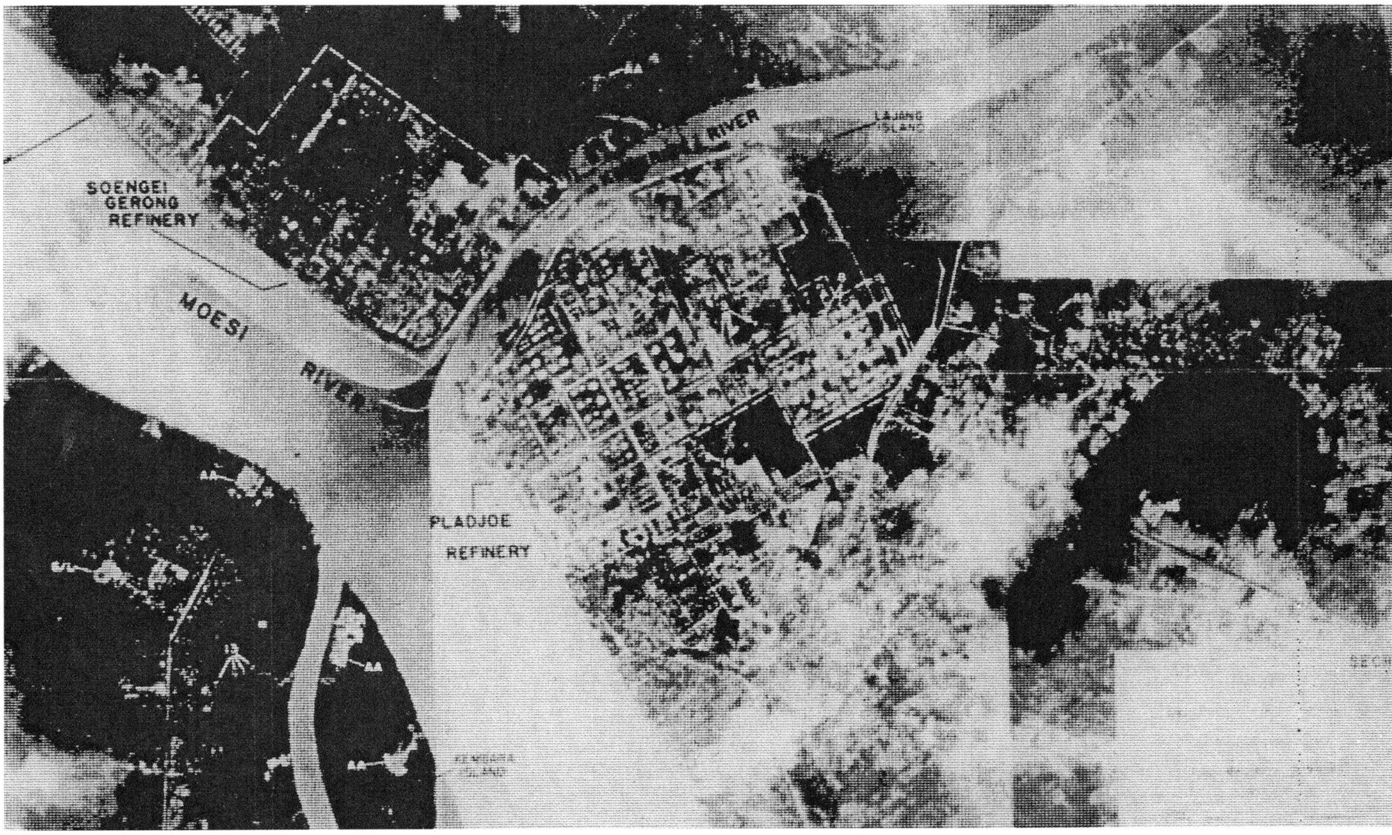

Aerial reconnaissance photograph of the Pladjoe refinery, the primary target of Mission #5 to Palembang, on the island of Sumatra in the Netherlands East Indies. (*US Air Force*)

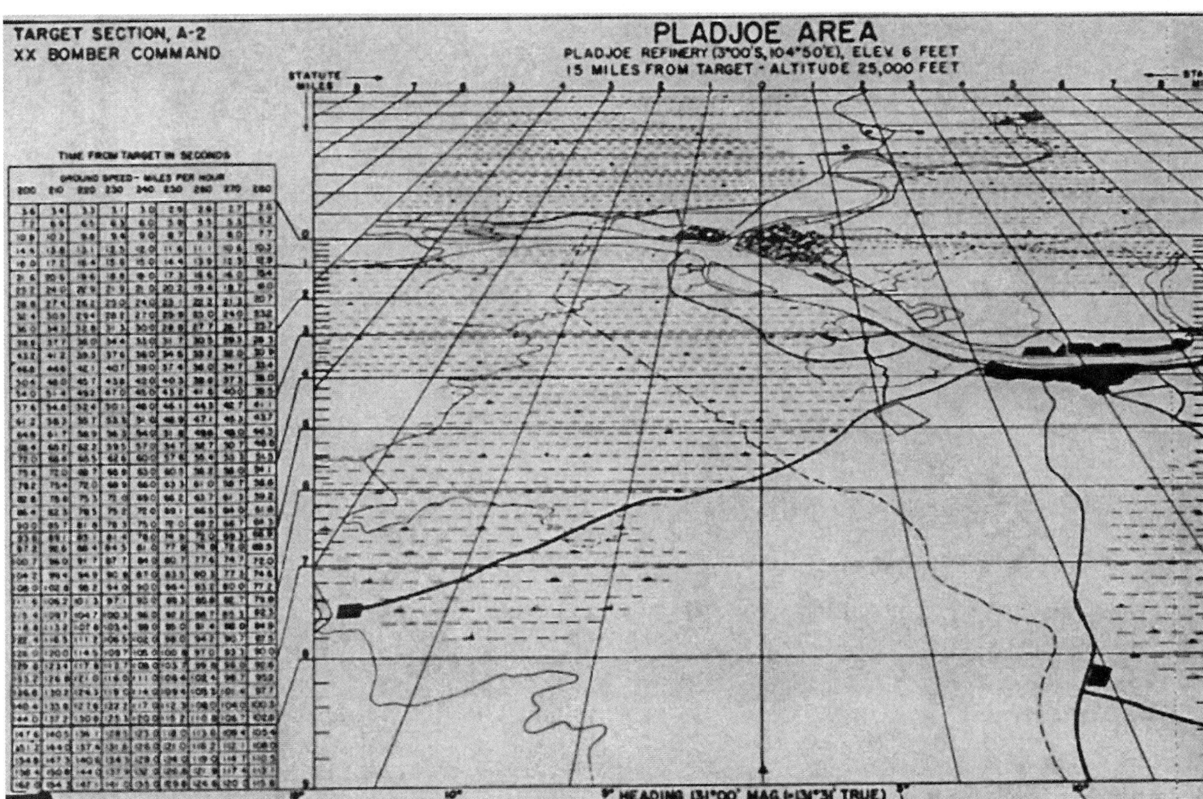

XX BC drawing illustrating how the Pladjoe refinery would look when approached at 25,000 feet from a distance of fifteen miles. With Mission #5 set as a night attack, radar operators needed to be able to match the contrasting water and land on this chart to the returns they would see on their scopes. (*US Air Force*)

B-29s staged through a Royal Air Force (RAF) airfield in Ceylon prior to commencing Mission #5 to Palembang. (*Bailey via 40th BG*)

the B-29 slipped down the runway with the heaviest load ever attempted on the bomber, Vaucher noticed the plane did not seem to gain any lift. He quickly reached the point at which he could not abort the takeoff and kept pulling to lift off the runway. Vaucher noted later he glanced from his cockpit and noticed the small flags that indicated wind direction. Rather than flying against his direction, the flags unfurled in the opposite direction, indicating the B-29 did not have a headwind to assist producing lift under the wings.

A second view of XX BC B-29s prior to launching Mission #5 to Palembang from an RAF base in Ceylon. (*Bailey via 40th BG*)

The runway ended at the ocean and Vaucher mentally prepared for the lumbering bomber to splash into the water. Rather than plunge into the ocean, the Superfortress became airborne just above the waves and continued at that height for approximately three miles. The plane would not gain even a few feet of altitude. Navigator Lt. Michael Egan stood near the pilot, reached out and touched the latter's shoulder, and exclaimed softly, "God be with you." A small island appeared directly in the path of the B-29 and the crew realized they would crash onto it if they did not gain altitude. Any attempt to turn the aircraft at such an extreme low altitude would place a wing tip into the ocean and bring down the big bird in a twisting crash. The bomber approached the island with alarming speed when it suddenly began to lift above the waves. The B-29 continued to gain altitude as it passed safely over the island and rose to join the other planes heading for Sumatra. Vaucher noted he learned years later the bomber benefited from a form of lift caused by the compression of air between the wings and ground beneath it. Vaucher and his crew survived the incident and now headed south at an average altitude of 1,000 feet to lay mines in the Moesi River.

Eight B-29s returned to Ceylon due to mechanical difficulties; an additional six bombers did not bomb the primary target due to diminishing fuel reserves. Three of these planes could not locate the target and turned back to Ceylon due to fuel concerns; one of these B-29s bombed a target of opportunity. Three other planes bombed the secondary target when they calculated they did not have sufficient fuel to reach the refinery area and return. A seventh plane returned early due to a combination of mechanical problems and bad weather. Maj. Vaucher and his crew nearly turned around due to fuel concerns. Flight engineer William Boyer alerted Vaucher to a fuel consumption problem as the B-29 neared two hours of Sumatra. By Boyer's calculations, the bomber would not have sufficient fuel to lay the mines and return safely to Ceylon. The stressful take-off and flight resulted in a severe headache for the pilot and this news served to only increase the pain. Following a short nap in the small crew bunk in the aft compartment, Vaucher reviewed Boyer's calculations and discovered an error to the embarrassment of the flight engineer and his own relief. Vaucher and his crew continued toward the Moesi River.[3]

Thirty-nine B-29s reached the primary target, with thirty-one bombing the Pladjoe Refinery and eight laying mines in the Moesi River. Mission troubles continued as the bombers approached the refinery; a 40th BG B-29 assigned to drop illumination flares over the refinery to guide other bombers was one of the planes that did not reach Sumatra. Crews arriving late in the bomber stream reported the refinery lay under excellent blackout conditions and a thick undercast of clouds, making the loss of the illumination flares even more troublesome for accurate night bombing. The bombers dropped 104 500-pound general purpose and seventeen incendiary clusters on the refinery during the three-hour period it took for bombers to reach the target. The crews could not see the results of the bombing, but did note several fires. The 462nd BG birds laid sixteen mines in the Moesi River. The three 40th BG planes dropping their ordnance on the secondary target refinery reported thick undercast and were not able to observe results. One 468th BG B-29 struck the Djambi Airfield as a target of opportunity due to lack of fuel. Despite poor visibility, the crew reported the bombs exploded across the runway.[4]

Maj. Vaucher flew one of the 462nd BG B-29s that mined the Moesi River. The pilot increased his altitude to 12,000 feet to clear the mountains along the northern and western edges of Sumatra and threaded the plane through at least one mountain pass to conserve precious fuel. Palembang and the Moesi River lay in the southern quarter of the long island situated along a north-south axis. Vaucher brought the ship down to 1,500 feet and broke free of the clouds that plagued the other bombers over the refinery to see the mouth of the river. The pilot banked the aircraft from the mouth and flew up the river at 500 feet. The river navigation lights appeared as briefed earlier to the 462nd BG crews by a Dutch captain. Vaucher dodged a vessel in the river and continued as orange tracers from a machine gun lit the sky. The bombardier placed the mines according to plan and the pilot gained altitude and turned for the return flight to Ceylon.[5]

Maj. John Misterly, a navigator with the 444th BG, flew with his crew against the Pladjoe refinery. Misterly remembered approaching the target at night and seeing it "lit up like Broadway."[6] The navigator surmised the Japanese did not expect such a long-range bombing mission against the refinery. The 444th BG B-29s approached the refinery in trail and at altitudes between 10,000 and 17,000 feet. This strategy meant the bombers flew single file over the target but at staggered altitudes to avoid aerial collisions and force the Japanese anti-aircraft gunners to keep adjusting the range of their weapons. Late arrivals contended with blackout conditions. The bombers at higher altitudes avoided many of the lower caliber anti-aircraft defenses, but also expended more fuel than planes at lower altitudes.[7]

The Japanese defenses engaged the Superfortresses as they approached the target; crews reported meager and inaccurate anti-aircraft fire in the vicinity of the refinery. While inaccurate, the Japanese engaged the bombers with heavy to intense flak at other locations along the route.

The Japanese also employed ground-to-air rockets and automatic weapons fire at eight locations along the route and at the refinery. Misterly noted, "The smaller caliber automatic weapons fired tracers resembling fireworks. The red balls floated past and exploded impairing our night vision. It was terrifying because we were aware any one of the streaks could mean the end. They were not fireworks."[8]

Despite all of the ordnance hurled skyward by the Japanese, none of the B-29s sustained damage from anti-aircraft fire. Japanese aircraft conducted twenty-six single or coordinated attacks against the B-29s. Post-mission intelligence analysis estimated the crews spotted up to thirty-seven fighters, although nearly all were identified as single or dual engine aircraft due to poor night visibility. A disproportionate percentage of the fighter attacks occurred against the mine laying B-29s due to their low altitude and slower speeds over the Moesi River. Crews reported two well coordinated although ineffective multiple fighter attacks during the mission:

> Six enemy fighters attacked one B-29 in train and in rapid succession from 1 o'clock low, opened fire at 1,000 yards, closed to about 300 yards, performed wing-overs, and exited the area at 4 o'clock high. Gunnery was poor but the execution of the attack was excellent.
>
> The other coordinated attack was made by two fighters, one of which entered high at 1 o'clock, opened fire at 600 yards, and went out at 7 o'clock low. Seconds later, another fighter attacked from 1 o'clock high, dived under the B-29, and broke to 7 o'clock low after opening fire.[9]

Nervous gunners aboard the Superfortress occasionally fired their weapons into the dark of night, thinking they were being stalked by Japanese fighters on the flight back to Ceylon. Vaucher cautioned his gunners to hold their fire, as they were more likely shooting at nothing or even other B-29s making their escape across the night sky. Nerves settled over time and the crew rested as their pilot followed his navigator's directions back to Ceylon. The flight engineer broke the peaceful silence by calling out a fire in engine #3; the crew feathered the propeller and hit the fire extinguisher switch. Although the fire retardant worked, the plane now flew on three engines. (Fuel consumption actually increased with three rather than four working engines due to the strain on the power plants to keep the plane aloft.) Vaucher decreased fuel mixture levels to conserve as much of it as possible.

As the plane approached the position of a British cruiser stationed as a rescue and recovery vessel, Vaucher made the decision to keep flying rather than ditch and await recovery; the fuel gauges still indicated the lumbering bomber could reach Ceylon. The pilot surmised that if they ditched, going down closer to Ceylon was preferable to the open ocean, where they would have to wait for the British to locate them. As the plane approached Ceylon, Boyer continued to manipulate the fuel system as individual engines died from lack of gas and had to be restarted. Vaucher safely set the B-29 down and the crew waited for the delivery of a new engine to continue their journey back to India.[10]

Capt. Ira Matthews of the 40th BG returned to China Bay on two engines:

> [A]s our plane neared the coast of Sumatra we began to lose oil through a leak in #4 engine's oil cooler. The Flight Engineer [Louis Grace] estimated that we would have to shut down the engine and feather its propeller soon after we bombed the target. According to his aircraft performance charts, our plane could not reach China Bay on three engines from Sumatra. If we bombed the target, we would be forced to ditch our plane in the Indian Ocean. I had to make a decision. We could salvo our bombs into the ocean and return to the airfield, or bomb the target with the prospect of having to ditch our plane before reaching China Bay. I carefully considered these options while weighing them against the fact that the oil refinery was producing most of Japan's aviation fuel. I made a decision that would place us in a life-threatening situation: I elected to attack the target. All 10 crew members supported me without hesitation. We wanted to help destroy the target regardless of the risk involved.[11]

Matthews and his crew continued flying toward the refinery and deposited their bomb load on the target. The pilot turned his B-29 and navigator Herbert Hirschfeld set a course for Ceylon. Matthews continued the narration:

Capt. Ira Matthews (far left, back row) and the crew of the 40th BG's #579 *Eddie Allen*. Matthews returned on two engines from Mission #5. (*US Air Force*)

> Realizing that there was no hope of reaching China Bay on three engines at our current gross weight, we decided to jettison every removable object not required to safely fly the plane. Once we were beyond enemy fighter aircraft range, the gunners fired all ammunition. Then the Bombardier [Charles Biehle], Radio Operator [Fred Thompson], and Radar Operator [Stanley Sienkiewicz] helped to jettison the bomb racks, gun sights, gun computers, armor plate, bulletproof glass, cabin pressure regulators, bomb bay fuel tanks, and the bomb sight and its stabilizer...Other than a few seat cushions and seat belts (items useful during a ditching or crash landing) the compartment was bare from the bomb bay bulkhead to the aft bulkhead. Even the padded green upholstery was gone. The compartment looked like a new fuselage section sitting on the Boeing Wichita production line.[12]

The crew opted to keep flying toward Ceylon and passed the position of the British cruiser serving as the outer layer of a rescue team awaiting any B-29s in trouble after bombing the refinery. They then flew past a British destroyer waiting to assist bombers between the cruiser and shore and finally declined the assistance of a Dutch Consolidated PBY Catalina flying boat patrolling between the destroyer and Ceylon. Two hundred miles from China Bay the oil pressure in engine #1 dropped and the engine died. Matthews continued his descent toward the RAF base on two engines and prepared his lightened bomber for a landing at China Bay:

B-29s buzz an airfield in China. (*40th BG*)

> Since we had jettisoned our parachutes, everyone took his ditching/crash landing position. The RAF tower operator was so excited that he could hardly talk to me. Our Commanding Gen. was in the tower with him, which added to his excitement and to ours. Everything was in order. We were cleared for a straight-in approach and landing. When the runway came into view, we were virtually lined up for a landing. We continued to descend through 6,000 feet, and I held off lowering the gear and extending the flaps until I was sure we would make the runway. Then we literally floated to an extremely soft landing at a touchdown speed of less than 70 miles per hour—30 miles per hour below a normal landing speed. When we turned onto the first taxiway, the nose wheel strut was fully extended due to our light gross weight. It felt like we were taxiing up a steep incline. Suddenly, both engines stopped running. Their booster pumps had become uncovered when the remaining fuel flowed to the rear of the tanks. Later, our Flight Engineer and a Boeing Service Engineer drained the fuel, and found 140 gallons.[13]

A 444th BG B-29 (#420 flown by Capt. Furchner) ditched ninety miles from Ceylon. One gunner (Robert J. Carl) died in the crash and the Royal Navy picked up the survivors. The raid produced minor damage to the refinery, but the XX BC later learned that three Japanese vessels sank and three were damaged after striking mines laid in the Moesi River. These actions delayed but did not halt the shipment of petroleum from the refinery.[14]

An interesting postscript involves Capt. Matthews, who brought home his B-29 on two engines and stripped of everything the crew could hurl overboard. The 40th BG converted his B-29 to a gasoline tanker to haul fuel from India to China due to the stripped condition of the bomber at the end of the mission. For many years Matthews faced bureaucratic questioning about the equipment his crew threw into the sea to save his B-29:

> We were soon to become well versed in the art of military paper work. The XX Bomber Command Staff did not believe that we threw our parachutes, pistols, and flak vests overboard. One officer accused us of lying about the .50 caliber machine guns. He insisted that the guns could not be removed in flight. When he came to Chakulia [40th BG home base in India] and looked at the plane, he quickly changed his mind. Letters were still being written about our mission when my crew finished its combat tour and returned to the States six months later in February 1945. I was stationed at Maxwell Field, Montgomery, Alabama, long after World War II, when I received the last letter concerning the pistols having been jettisoned over the Indian Ocean.[15]

Mission #6: Nagasaki, August 10–11, 1944

The XX BC flew Mission #6 to Nagasaki the same night as Mission #5 to Palembang. Each bomb group contributed aircraft to this mission, as well as Mission #5. The XX BC utilized the small stock of fuel in China for a simultaneous mission over Japan and the opportunity to puzzle the Japanese about the strategic capabilities of the B-29s based in India. Palembang represented the first mission flown directly from India since Mission #1 to Bangkok. Thus, the XX BC demonstrated it could simultaneously hit two targets in different corners of the Pacific Theater, even though flying with reduced numbers of B-29s. The official mission report noted, "The psychological effect of following up the full-scale attack delivered against Anshan, Manchuria [Mission #4], on 29 July with not only a heavy raid against Sumatra thousands of miles to the south but also with a simultaneous attack against the Japanese homeland over 3,000 miles from Palembang was a prime consideration in the planning."[16]

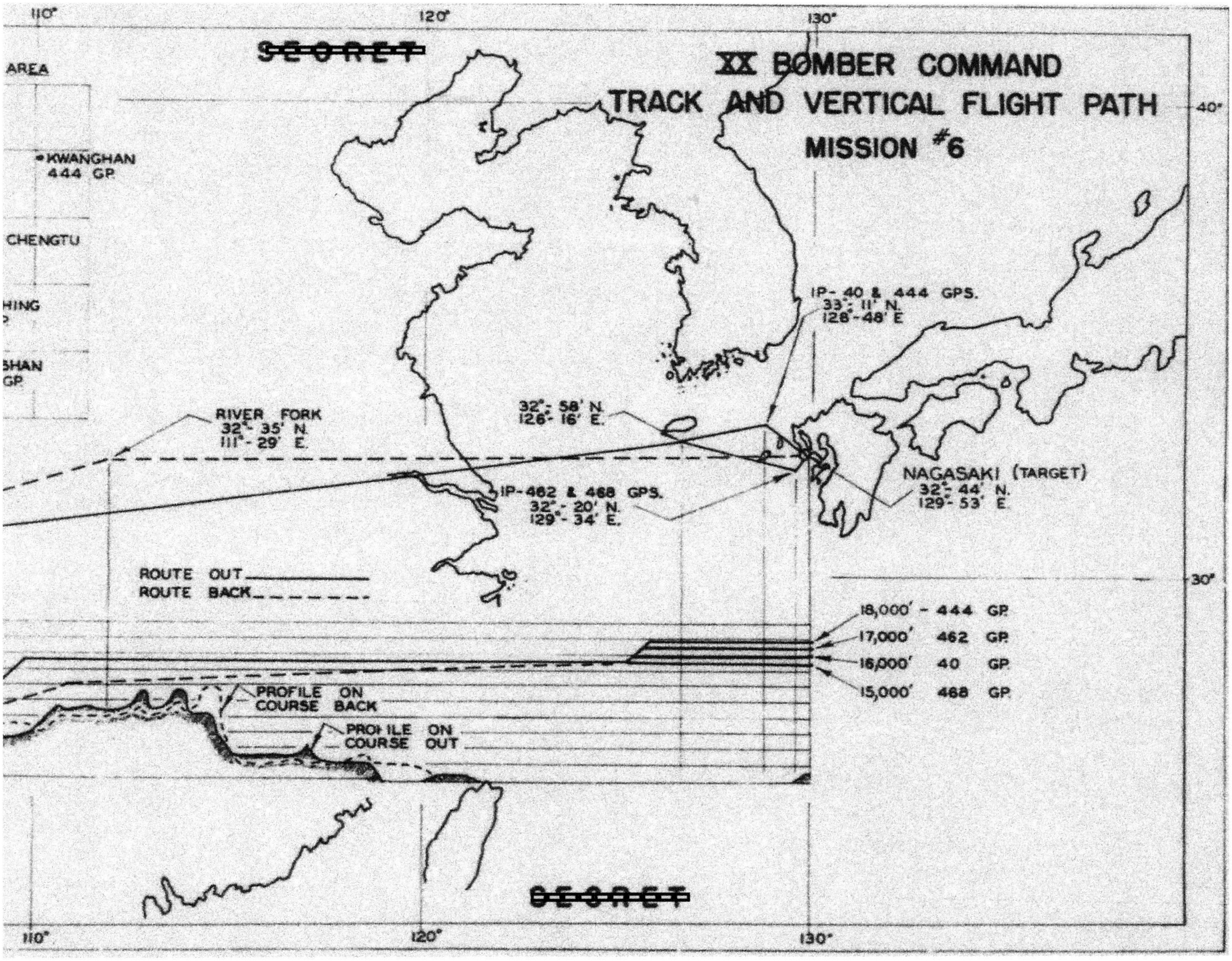

XX BC briefing map for pilots and navigators showing the routes to and from Nagasaki (Mission #6) from eastern China. The solid line shows the route to Nagasaki and the dashed line is the return route. (*US Air Force*)

Chinese moving drums of aviation fuel for XX BC B-29s. (*Kerstner via 40th BG*)

Temporary fuel drum storage at the flight line in China. Note the B-29 in the background. (*US Air Force*)

#319 *Himalaya Hussy* aborted Mission #6 to Nakasaki, Japan, and returned home due to weather and radar difficulties. (*Urbanic via 40th BG*)

During Mission #6 to Nagasaki, Japan, the 40th BG's #298 *Katie* aborted and returned to its base in China due to an oil leak in engine #2. (*40th BG*)

Urban areas of Nagasaki were the primary target for the night incendiary raid. The field order listed the Point Island storage area in Shanghai, China, as the secondary target and the Hankow docks and storage area as the target of last resort. Mission #6 was the first B-29 firebombing operation of a Japanese city in WWII. Nagasaki was one of Japan's greatest shipbuilding cities and served as the home for a steel and munitions plant, military barracks, and storage areas; firebombing the city could ignite widespread destruction across all of these military and military support areas. Any damage to the secondary and target of last resort could destroy military equipment and disrupt the supply chain for Japanese troops operating in China. Gen. Arnold and the XX Air Force initially disapproved Shanghai as the secondary target and requested another target in Japan, but XX BC staff noted the secondary target needed to be along the bomber route that would generally have a different weather pattern than the primary target in case of a last minute rerouting of the entire mission or individual bombers experiencing mechanical difficulties. Each plane carried an ordnance mix consisting of thirteen M-18 incendiary clusters and three M-26 fragmentation clusters.[17]

Thirty-three B-29s launched from India for the forward movement across the Himalaya Mountains to China. One bomber (#237 *Sir Trofepus* of the 40th BG) returned due to maintenance problems and one (#452 of the 444th BG) caught fire while still over India, forcing the crew to bail out. Twenty-nine of the thirty-one B-29s in China took off for the mission to Nagasaki, including bombers from all four Groups: the 40th BG (7 B-29s); 444th BG (7 B-29s); 462nd BG (8 B-29s); and the 468th BG (7 B-29s). Two aircraft returned early: the 40th BG's #298 *Katie* (oil leak in engine #2) and #319 *Himalaya Hussy* (also the 40th BG, due to weather and radar difficulties).

Twenty-six of the bombers dropped their loads on the primary target and three struck targets of opportunity. Crews encountered poor visibility due to blackout conditions and thick clouds over Nagasaki that grew denser between the arrival of the first bomber and the departure of the last B-29 nearly two hours later. Fires were visible after the passage of the bombers, but crews could not pinpoint their exact locations. One B-29 (the 462nd BG's #444 *Humpin' Honey*) bombed Sasebo; one crew (#389 *Party Girl* of the 468th BG) dropped its ordnance on the port town of Yingshan, China, thinking they were over Hankow; and the third (#243 *Roger the Lodger* of the 468th BG) released its ordnance on a light at an unknown position after becoming lost due to radar problems. The crew navigated by the moon and estimated their target lay approximately one hour's flying distance from Nagasaki. The poor visibility at Nagasaki prevented photo reconnaissance from determining any damage inflicted by the raid. Although the crews witnessed fires, no one knew how much damage they actually delivered to the Japanese city. Later reconnaissance determined the raid imposed minimal if any damage to military and industrial areas.[18]

Japanese anti-aircraft fire along the route and over Nagasaki was meager and generally inaccurate. Some crews witnessed

A 40th BG B-29. (*Bailey via 40th BG*)

The 40th BG's #319 *Himalaya Hussy* crossing the Hump between India and China. (*40th BG*)

a lone Japanese aircraft flying parallel to their courses that could have been reporting speed, altitude, and direction of the bombers, but anti-aircraft bursts remained inaccurate. Some ground batteries accurately fired at a passing group's altitude but not at the precise position of the bombers. Ground and naval units also utilized automatic weapons fire against the bombers but results were inaccurate, although the rate could be quite intense, as reported by the B-29 crews. At least four locations across Kyushu Island employed multiple searchlights, seeking to pinpoint the bombers. Although at least one bomber crew noted beams moved across their wings, none of the aircraft were located and fixed by the roaming searchlights. One pilot felt threatened by the closeness of the beams and initiated evasive maneuvering action.

The few Japanese aircraft in the skies that night targeted only three bombers. Other crews witnessed tracer rounds and in one case an exploding phosphorous bomb, but did not see any fighters actually targeting them. The first kill credited to a B-29 tail gunner firing the 20 mm gun on a bomber mission (Tech Sgt. H. C. Edwards) occurred during this mission:

> Described as a low-wing single-engine fighter, the enemy plane attacked from 7 o'clock high and opened fire at 600 yards, at which time, the B-29 tail gunner returned fire; the fighter appeared to explode in the air and later was observed burning on the ground. The attack took place after "bombs away" 3 miles south of the primary target at 1542Z.[19]

A second Japanese fighter approached another B-29 five minutes prior to the Initial Point and passed within 200 yards of the bomber's nose. The fighter did not commence firing and the bomber crew also did not fire. The third Japanese fighter, a twin engine Kawasaki Ki-45 Nick, jumped a B-29 (#389 *Party Girl* of the 468th BG) near Hankow, China, after it mistakenly bombed Yingshan:

> ...the Nick attacked at 1426Z, just after the aircraft had evaded searchlights at Hankow; the attack came from 11 o'clock low and closed to only 1,000 yards after the B-29 opened fire at 1,500 yards with the lower forward turret. The enemy plane went out at 9 o'clock without returning fire. The Nick's landing lights were turned on and presented a sharply defined, though distant, target.[20]

Two B-29s went down due to fuel exhaustion, although one plane would be re-fueled and flown back to its forward base nearly two weeks later. Stanley Brown, flying #359 *Missouri Queen* of the 462nd BG, landed near the front lines in China after becoming lost and running low on fuel. The plane bogged itself in the mud of the small Allied airfield. Later reports indicated a Japanese fighter damaged two of the plane's engines during the return flight, but this was not known at the time the XX BC prepared the official post-mission report. The American 312th Fighter Wing dispatched aircraft to fly cover for the B-29 stranded on the ground while the crew awaited

Gen. Laverne "Blondie" Saunders (front row, center) with other members of the 58th BW staff in the summer of 1944 in India. (*Changnon via 40th BG*)

Personnel from the 25th Squadron (40th BG) pose with #374 *Tabooma II* in India. (*40th BG*)

#263 and other 40th BG B-29s at A-1 in China during the summer of 1944. (*40th BG*)

parts and mechanics arriving by transport aircraft. During the period required to repair the bomber, the American fighters shot down three Japanese planes attempting to interrupt the process. The mechanics and crew members stripped the bomber of all unnecessary equipment and jacked the plane out of the mud. They and the Chinese laid 4,500 rail ties to fill soft spots in the runway and four crew members flew the B-29 from the field on August 23.[21]

The 468th BG lost #243 *Roger the Lodger*, the bomber that released its load on an unknown light as a target of opportunity. The crew experienced a fuel shortage on the return flight, forcing them to bail out. All returned safely and the lack of fuel was attributed to the fact the crew reported their "target" lay approximately one hour from Nagasaki, requiring the bomber to remain aloft up to two hours longer than originally planned.[22]

It should be noted that most published sources state the 444th BG's #419 (serial number 42-63419) crashed on this mission due to icing; the 444th BG actually lost this B-29 on November 11, 1944. At some point a typo or administrative error may have altered the date to August 11 from the actual November 11 and this has been duplicated by others. (A review of this aircraft loss can be found in the chapter detailing Mission #16 on November 11.)

Mission #7: Yawata, August 20, 1944

Mission #7 directed the XX BC's groups to stage through China for a return to the Imperial Iron and Steel Works at Yawata, Japan. Planners called for another night raid against the facility that served as one of the two largest producers of steel in the Japanese empire. The secondary target was the port and shipping facilities at Laoyao, China, and the railroad yards at Kaifeng, China, were the target of last resort. As with Mission #2, the coke plants at the Imperial Iron and Steel Works would be the aiming point for the B-29s. The Japanese recently established Laoyao as a new port for the export of coking coal for their steel producing plants. Destruction of the port could eliminate supplies of coking coal stored there in warehouses or being loaded onto ships and disrupt the supply of this critical element. The Kaifeng railroad yard supported the rail line running from Laoyao into the interior of China. Successful bombing of the yard could destroy Japanese military supplies and obstruct their flow to front line forces.[23]

XX BC staff questioned the 20th Air Force directive to hit Yawata with incendiary bombs at night. With two of the previous six missions targeting Yawata, the Japanese must have been aware the iron and steel works in the city were a priority for American strategic bombing efforts and they would certainly be working to upgrade anti-aircraft defenses around the area. XX Air Force received a reply from India requesting a daylight raid with general purpose munitions to increase the chances of the destruction of the coke ovens before the Japanese could establish a greater density of anti-aircraft guns in the area. Incendiary bombing of the coke ovens would not accomplish the type of destruction required for the mission and were more effective on tightly packed building complexes and urban areas. In addition, incendiary munitions would result in smoke that could easily obscure the target area, as experienced on earlier missions. A daylight raid flown by B-29s in formation might be able to accomplish what night raids by the groups flying over the target as individual planes had not been able to achieve while taking advantage of the few anti-aircraft defenses at the present time. Changing the directives would pose a number of risks, as discussed in the mission report:

> It was realized that this proposed mission would probably result in increased losses due to the fact that: (A) the aircraft would be over Japan proper during daylight and would therefore be exposed to a heavier concentration of anti-aircraft and fighters, and (B) the flight back would, of necessity, require night navigation, finally terminating with the accomplishment of a night landing. It was also realized that in the event weather conditions at the target should make radar bombing necessary, the results would probably be less than be expected from a night incendiary attack on the urban area.[24]

XX Air Force granted permission for the change on August 5. The B-29s would fly in four-ship diamond formations and carry general purpose munitions. The plans changed the day of the mission to hit Yawata with a daylight and night force; such a tactic could easily throw the Japanese off balance as to the precise target of the second wave, even though their early warning networks would track the bombers. The decision resulted from an accident with a 462nd BG B-29 and a large number of mechanical problems in China rather than a calculated plan to confuse Japanese defenses

The XX BC initially assembled its B-29s at the forward bases in China. Three bombers returned to bases in India after take-off due to mechanical difficulties; two landed en route with mechanical trouble; and one (the 40th BG's #425 *"B" Sweet*) crashed during the movement. The pilot, Capt. William Schaal, reported a routine flight until reaching a point approximately seventy miles from the group's forward base in China. Engine #4 began throwing oil and attempts to feather the propeller failed. The engine continued to increase in speed, resulting in a dangerous vibration that threatened to sheer it from the wing and send pieces of metal across the rest of the plane. Lt. Col. H. Sullivan, 40th BG deputy commander and a passenger on the B-29, advised Schaal of the problem and ordered

Crew of the 40th BG's #425 *"B" Sweet* after they bailed out over the Hump prior to Mission #7. Chinese peasants gathered the crew and escorted them to a Chinese Catholic priest, who assisted them reaching the group airfield. (*Briggs via 40th BG*)

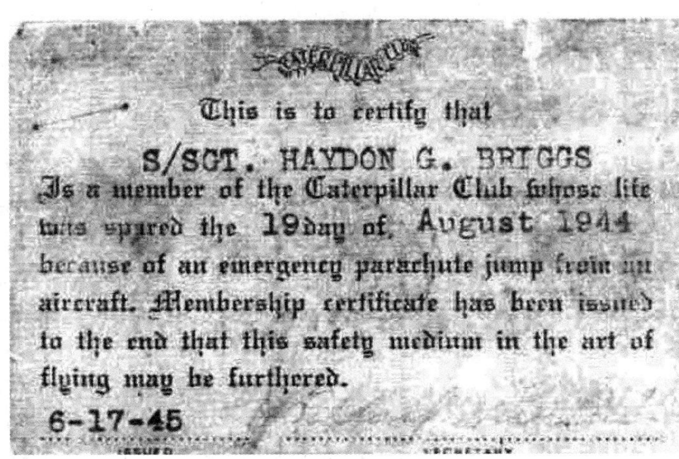

Caterpillar Club

This is to certify that
S/SGT. HAYDON G. BRIGGS
Is a member of the Caterpillar Club whose life was spared the 19 day of August 1944 because of an emergency parachute jump from an aircraft. Membership certificate has been issued to the end that this safety medium in the art of flying may be furthered.
6-17-45

The Caterpillar Club Card of Staff Sgt. Haydon Briggs, one of the crew members who bailed out from the 40th BG's #425 *"B" Sweet* over the Hump prior to Mission #7. (*Briggs via 40th BG*)

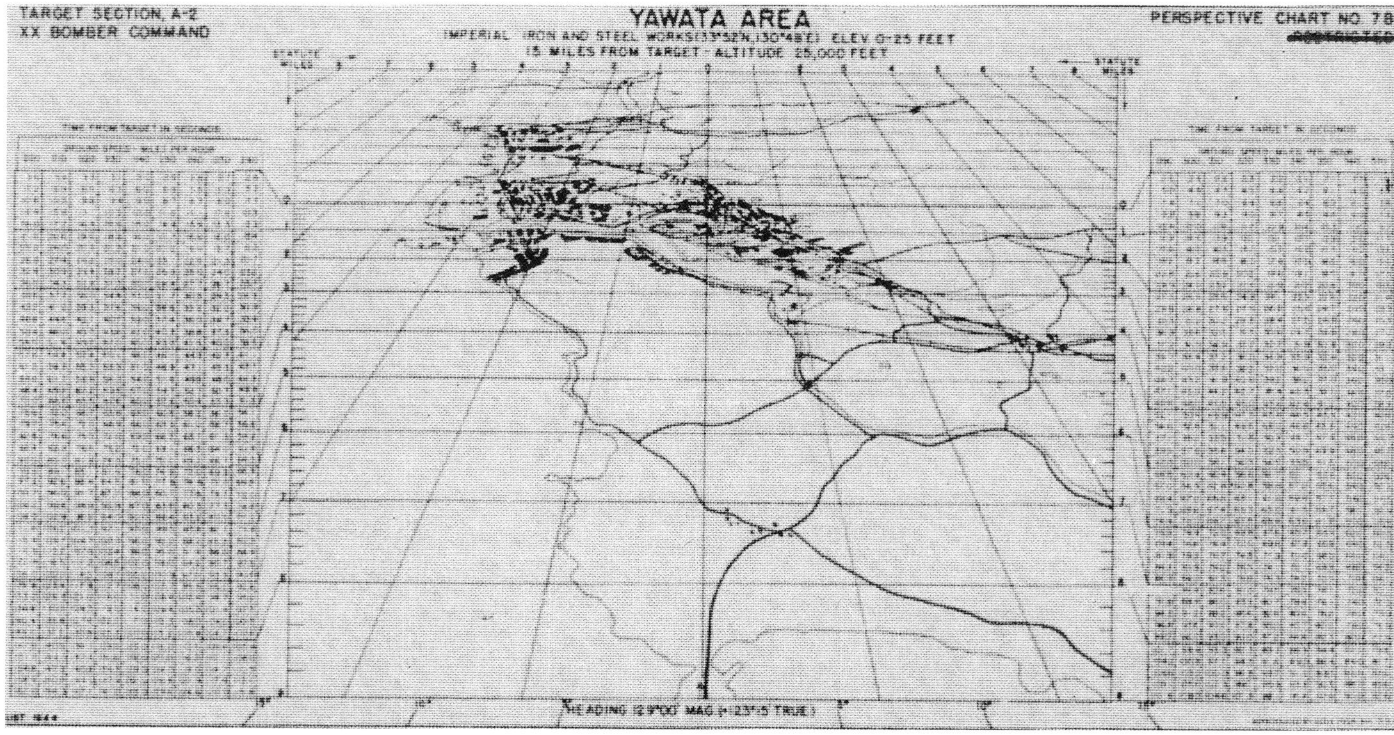

XX BC briefing chart showing pilots and navigators what Yawata, Japan, should look like when approaching from fifteen miles out at 25,000 feet. This particular chart was utilized for Mission #7. (*US Air Force*)

B-29s of the 468th BG preparing to depart to Yawata for Mission #7. (*Schutte via 468th BG*)

The Imperial Iron and Steel Works area—the primary target of Mission #7 to Yawata, Japan. (*US Air Force*)

the crew to abandon the bomber. Seven crew members jumped from the front wheel hatch, five jumped from the rear bomb bay, and the tail gunner leaped from his emergency escape hatch. Chinese peasants gathered the crew and escorted them to a Chinese Catholic priest who assisted them in reaching the group airfield...after being entertained at a party thrown by the local Chinese army commander.[25]

The three bombers that returned to India and one plane that made an emergency landing en route were repaired and arrived in China in time for the operation. Of the 97 bombers listed as ready in China, 75 took off for the daylight segment of the mission (22 from the 40th BG; 18 from the 444th BG; 7 from the 462nd BG; and 28 from the 468th BG). The 462nd BG's #305 crashed at the north end of that group's airfield due to a landing gear failure while attempting to take-off. The pilot throttled back and skidded his bomber to a halt as the gear collapsed. All of the personnel escaped injury, but the wrecked bomber blocked over half of the 462nd BG's planes from launching with the daylight raiders from the other groups. A strong wind prevented the heavily loaded aircraft from taking off in the opposite direction and the 462nd BG needed over six hours to clear the runway. Eight of their remaining thirteen bombers managed to get airborne for a night bombing of Yawata. Five other bombers (three from the 40th BG and two from the 444th BG) that suffered mechanical difficulties earlier in the day joined the 462nd for a night mission of individual aircraft rather than formations over Yawata. One of the 40th BG planes on the night mission returned from the day operation after encountering mechanical problems that were repaired in time for the night raid.[26]

Sixty-one of the seventy-five bombers on the daylight raid visually bombed the primary target with 384 500-pound bombs (ninety-six short tons). The 444th BG's #320 *Flying Stud* developed engine trouble, forcing the twelve crewmen to successfully bail out and return to their base. Four aircraft suffered problems with their bomb release systems and were not able to drop their entire loads on the primary target. One B-29 (#278 *Assid Test* of the 462nd BG) bombed the secondary target due to failure of a fuel transfer pump. The results were unobserved because of undercast conditions. One bomber dropped its ordnance on the target of last resort after developing an oil leak in engine #2. The pilot originally directed a strike on the secondary target, but the radar scope failed approximately eighteen miles from the target and did not begin operating again until the crew was twenty-two miles past the target. The pilot then opted to bomb the target of last resort rather than double back for another run where alerted Japanese defenses could be waiting. The crew bombed via radar and were not able to observe any results. Two aircraft attacked targets of opportunity: the first B-29 (#267 *Winnie* of the 444th BG) lost an engine and diverted from the approach to the primary target. As the crew prepared to jettison the bomb load they spotted a Japanese naval convoy. The bombardier selected a destroyer as his aiming point and offloaded the general purpose bombs as the Japanese vessels initiated light anti-aircraft fire; observed results indicated misses. The second plane (the 468th BG's #284 *The Challenger*) dropped three bombs on an unspecified target of opportunity on Ikishima Island due to an undocumented "personnel error." The bombardier later jettisoned the remaining three bombs in the sea.[27]

The formations experienced intense and fairly accurate anti-aircraft fire in the skies above Yawata; Japanese defenders may have fired at least one ground-to-air rocket at the bombers. One crew reported seeing a "yellow trail of light" as something climbed to over 16,000 feet, although they did not observe any bursts due to cloud cover. Several Japanese aircraft flew parallel to the formations near Yawata and were probably reporting altitudes to anti-aircraft gunners. Strike photos analyzed after the mission verified an increase in anti-aircraft batteries around Yawata since the June 1944 raid by B-29s; post-mission intelligence estimates placed the total at up to 166 guns. Formations also received meager and generally inaccurate anti-aircraft fire from several points along the route. Eight bombers returned with flak damage and #408 *Ready Teddy* of the 468th BG, piloted by Ernest Pickett, fell victim to anti-aircraft fire and crashed in Japan. Crew members in other B-29s witnessed a flak burst that seemed to strike *Ready Teddy*'s flight deck area. One crew member flying in the same formation reported seeing the pilot and co-pilot slumped forward over their controls as the aircraft turned toward the left and almost collided with B-29 #353 *Big Poison*.[28] Maj. John Misterly of the 444th BG flew in the formation behind #408 *Ready Teddy*. He remembered, "The 468th was ahead of us and lower. As we watched we saw one of their planes take a direct flak burst. It was a devastating sight."[29]

#408 *Ready Teddy* fell out of formation and crashed. The 40th BG lost #308 *Feather Merchant* to Japanese anti-aircraft guns and fighters. Flak off the China coast damaged the bomber, wounding Staff Sgt. John Hause, the CFC.

Mission #7 to Yawata viewed from a B-29 bombardier's station. The bomber is twenty-five miles from the target. (*US Air Force*)

The pilot, Capt. Boyd Grubaugh, maintained his course to the target and completed the bomb run. As the pilot turned away from the target area flak struck the bomber again, damaging engine #1 as well as all fuel and oil quantity gauges, cowl flaps, and oil cooler position indicators. A second burst blew pieces of the horizontal tail from the bomber. Grubaugh noted the controls seemed operable and engine #1 continued to function despite the damage. Several Japanese fighters singled out the bomber for attention and attacked. Mechanical problems encountered earlier in the mission left the bottom gun turrets inoperable and the lower portion of the aircraft vulnerable as Japanese pilots placed rounds into the mid-section of the B-29, crippling the fuel transfer and radar systems. Machine gun bullets shattered the rear pressure door into the bomb bay area, forcing the crew to begin utilizing oxygen masks. The B-29 limped back into Chinese air space and then encountered a severe thunderstorm that proved to be too much for the crippled bomber. All but two crew members bailed out. Hause died of his wounds before this point and the tail gunner, Tech Sgt. Roy Hontz, never exited the plane. The Chinese found and assisted the surviving crew members reach a 14th Air Force airfield.[30]

B-29 #332 *Belle of Baltimore* of the 462nd BG crash-landed approximately ten miles from its airfield in China due to a fuel shortage. The crew bombed a target of opportunity and were on the return journey when the fuel tanks emptied; the group later identified flak damage as the primary cause of the fuel shortage and crash. The pilot, Capt. William Sanford, ordered his crew to bail out, but the radio operator reported his parachute had accidently

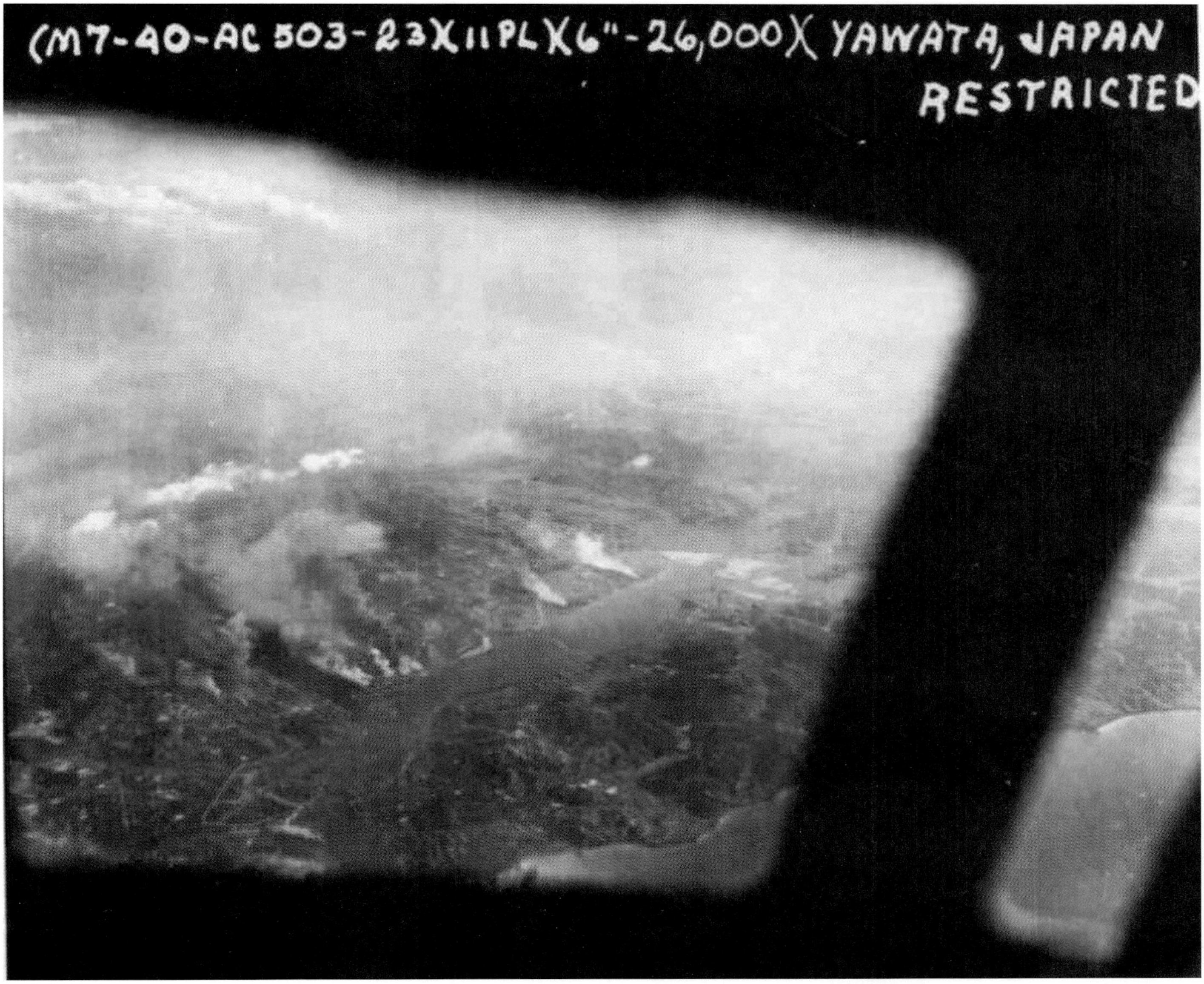

Mission #7 to Yawata as seen from the nose of a B-29. Note the smoke screens ignited over Yawata to obscure the target. (*US Air Force*)

The 40th BG's #342 *Sister Sue* returned early from Mission #7 to Yawata, Japan, due to mechanical issues. (*Brown via 40th BG*)

The 40th BG's #348 *Bengal Lancer* lost engine #4 during Mission #7 to Yawata, Japan. (*40th BG*)

The 468th BG's #272 *Old Campaigner* over Yawata during Mission #7. Note the smoke screens employed by the Japanese to mask the area. (*Schutte via 468th BG*)

opened and spilled inside the aircraft. Sanford gave his parachute to the radio operator, who then jumped from the B-29 with eight other crew members. The co-pilot and flight engineer opted to assist Sanford and ride the plane into a crash landing due to the loss of altitude and increased chance of a mishap if parachuting. Sanford crash-landed his bomber and all crewmen survived the incident.[31] Sanford received the Distinguished Service Cross for his actions.

The crash landing of the 468th BG's #253 *Windy City* can be also attributed to anti-aircraft fire. The bomber returned from the mission with flak damage to the nose wheel door, forcing the plane to make a belly landing, although at least one report attributes the cause to poor weather. The crew members in the aft compartment bailed out prior to the crash landing; those in the forward compartment rode the aircraft through the crash landing due to the inability to lower the nose wheel and parachute though its opening.[32]

Many of the B-29s took evasive action resulting in changes of altitude between 1,000 and 3,000 feet to avoid Japanese flak while on the bomb run and this response contributed to the issues the crews faced accurately placing their general purpose ordnance on the target. Reconnaissance photographs made during the raid captured Japanese barrage balloons on film. (Barrage balloons floated at the end of extremely long cables anchored to the ground that were strong enough to foul propellers and cut wings of passing aircraft at or below the balloons.)

Crews reported they were attacked by approximately fifty Japanese fighters during the mission, yet post-war research indicates the Japanese placed double that number of aircraft into the sky to challenge the XX BC that day. The fighter pilots proved aggressive and their tactics included ramming attacks—the first faced by the XX BC. Sgt. Shigeo Nobe, flying a Nick with his gunner, Sgt. Denzo Takagi, selected a 468th BG formation for a ramming attack as the bombers were directly over the target. Nobe reportedly radioed his flight commander, Lt. Isamu Kashiide, that he intended to ram a bomber. Kashiide called back to halt the sergeant but it was too late; Nobe turned his Nick and aligned the right wing so that it stood

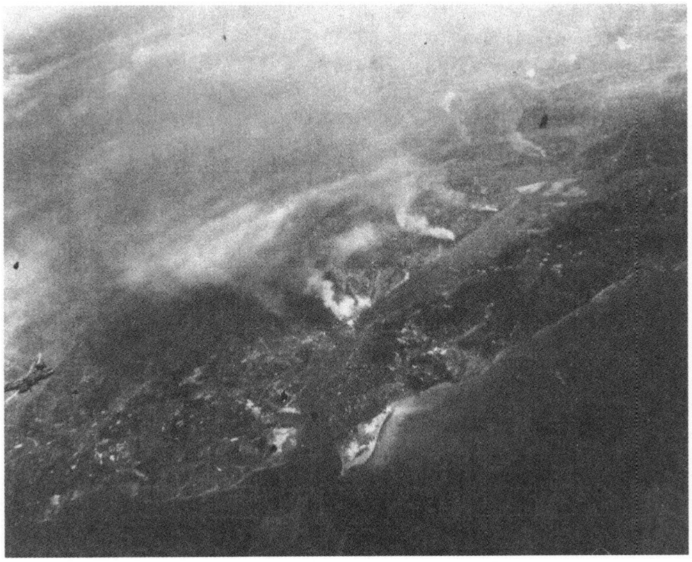

Another view of Yawata during Mission #7. The smoke screens can be seen on the ground and a B-29 is visible in the bottom left corner. (*Schutte via 468th BG*)

Photo taken by a XX BC B-29 during Mission #7 to Yawata. Note the effective utilization of smoke generators by the Japanese to help obscure the area from B-29 bombardiers. (*US Air Force*)

vertical compared to B-29 #334 *Gertrude C*, flown by Col. Robert Clinkscales. The right wing cut through the bomber's left wing, exploding a fuel tank. The Nick cartwheeled over the stricken bomber and #279 *Postville Express*, which was behind *Gertrude C*. Maj. Donald Humphrey, flying *Postville Express*, barely escaped being hit by the flaming debris whirling past him. Capt. Ornell Stauffer, piloting #368 *Calamity Sue*, could not avoid the wreckage; Nobe's out-of-control Nick removed its horizontal stabilizer and the B-29 fell out of formation. One American crewman, Sgt. Austin C. Shott, parachuted from *Calamity Sue* and survived the attack. The Japanese captured Shott, who remained in a prison camp until the end of the war.[33] Wreckage from *Gertrude C* dented the wing and cracked the nose glass of B-29 #217 *Pepper*, which returned safely after the mission. Misterly, flying with the 444th BG, also witnessed the ramming:

> The enemy's propeller cut deep into the wing [Gertrude C], fuel gushed out, and both planes burst into flames. Debris from the crash as the planes disintegrated fell into the path of the slot plane [Calamity Sue] flying in the number four position. The pilot swung up in an attempt to avoid the wreckage, but his vertical stabilizer was sheared off and the B-29 went down in a tail spin... It was difficult to erase the ghastly sight we had just witnessed.[34]

Co-pilot 1st Lt. James DeCoster aboard #281 *20th Century Unlimited* of the 40th BG. (*Schutte via 40th BG*)

#368 *Calamity Sue* of the 468th BG. A Japanese Nick fighter rammed B-29 #334 *Gertrude C* on Mission #7. Capt. Ornell Stauffer, piloting #368 *Calamity Sue*, could not avoid the wreckage and fell out of formation with only one survivor. (*468th BG*)

B-29 #217 *Pepper* of the 468th BG. During Mission #7 to Yawata, a Japanese fighter cart-wheeled and struck #386 *Gertrude C*. Wreckage from *Gertrude C* dented the wing and cracked the nose glass of B-29 #217 *Pepper*, which returned safely after the mission. (*Schutte via 468th BG*)

The 462nd BG's #374, flown by Group Commander Col. Richard Carmichael, crashed due to a combination of mechanical trouble and Japanese fighters. The bomber developed engine trouble and Japanese fighters concentrated on the crippled bomber, hitting the center wing section. The B-29 burst into flames and crashed on Iki Island. Later the downing would be attributed to the dropping of an air-to-air bomb by the Japanese aircraft and presented a rare case where the tactic worked. All of the crew members exited the stricken bomber except radio operator Sgt. Remick Wallace, who may have remained too long at his post trying to make contact with a submarine. Group Gunnery Officer Capt. Chester Tims did not survive the jump and other crew members reported after the war that his parachute did not open. Tims exited the crippled aircraft wounded and his condition, rather than a malfunction, may explain why his chute never opened during the rapid descent. Japanese fighters strafed and killed co-pilot Lt. Carl Skedsvold as he floated to earth. The Japanese captured Carmichael and the other survivors, who were then placed under horrible conditions in a prison camp. The men remained up to six months in solitary confinement cages that were so small they could neither sit up nor lay completely flat in them. They also endured brutal beatings during their captivity.[35]

Three Japanese fighters made a coordinated pass from twelve o'clock toward the B-29 in which Misterly served as navigator. "...Rich opened fire with the six fifties [.50 caliber machine guns] of the two forward turrets. The intense fire forced the enemy fighters to break down and away. Rich had hit at least one as they came through the formation."[36]

Fighters damaged four additional bombers: B-29 #332 of the 40th BG returned with both fighter and anti-aircraft damage. A Japanese fighter placed three holes into the aft turret, six into the tail skid, one in the fuselage, and one into the right wing tip. Anti-aircraft guns deposited several pieces of flak into a wing and one into the vertical fin.

The air-to-air engagements over Japan that day present another opportunity to analyze the conflicting and highly inaccurate victory claims made by both sides due to the confusion of battle. American crewmen claimed seventeen Japanese aircraft destroyed, thirteen probables, and twelve damaged. The Japanese pilots claimed a bomber tally of eleven confirmed destroyed, eleven unconfirmed destroyed, and twenty damaged B-29s. In reality, three B-29s went down over Japan and four returned with fighter damage, while the Japanese losses included two planes destroyed and four with serious damage. Japanese planes with minor damage, if any, were not listed.[37]

The XX BC lost its second crew to Soviet internment when Maj. Richard McGlinn and his personnel bailed out of the 40th BG's #829 *Cait Paomat* after receiving flak damage at Yawata. With diminishing fuel, McGlinn opted to head for the Soviet Union rather than go down in Japanese occupied China. The aircraft crashed and was gathered for parts by the Soviets.[38]

Maj. Richard McGlinn and his crew (40th BG) during a pre-flight check. The XX BC lost its second crew to Soviet internment when Maj. McGlinn and his personnel bailed out of the 40th BG's #829 *Cait Paomat* after receiving flak damage during Mission #7 to Yawata, Japan. (*Caudle via 40th BG*)

The 40th BG lost B-29 #301 on the return flight from Yawata. With the poor visibility during the flight, it is believed a radar error placed the bomber, piloted by Capt. James Slattery, off course and it crashed into the mountains near Kunlien, China. All eleven crew members perished and were buried by the Chinese. Maj. Hamilton Dyer and his 444th BG crew died when their bomber, #286 *Praying Mantis*, crashed onto a remote mountain location approximately sixty-two miles (100 km) from Chengtu. Chinese citizens located the wreck over fifty years later and organized an expedition to retrieve pieces of the aircraft later confirmed to be #286 *Praying Mantis*.[39] Maj. Charles Hansen, pilot of the 444th BG's #330 (now named *Fickle Finger*), also crashed into a mountain during the return flight from Yawata. Hansen aborted two landing attempts and crashed while turning for his third. The pilot and his crew were the first B-29 personnel attacked by Japanese aircraft during World War II and their story is documented in Chapter 1. All perished in the crash except radar operator Virgil Belford. The 462nd BG lost two B-29s on the return flight to India after the Yawata Mission: B-29 #305 *Starduster*, piloted by Miles Thomas, crashed on take-off attempting to return from China and #223 *Lady Bommerang* went down during the flight to its home base in India.[40]

The 444th BG's #330 *Fickle Finger* receiving an engine change. Maj. Charles Hansen, pilot of #330 *Fickle Finger*, crashed into a mountain during the return flight from Mission #7 to Yawata. The pilot and his crew were the first B-29 personnel attacked by Japanese aircraft during World War II. (*Corey via 444th BG*)

Daylight bombing results proved to be better than the previous two missions to Yawata, although the plant remained in operation. Results of the follow-on night raid could not be determined. Reconnaissance from daylight raiders indicated:

> A direct hit on one of the coke installations (which includes 2 batteries of ovens) in the southeast part of the target set it afire. Pinpoints of flame (seen in the strike photos to be astride the ovens at the base of a large plume of dense black smoke ascending therefrom) indicated that coal, or partially coked coal, inside the ovens is burning vigorously. A large building immediately adjacent, probably related to by-products operations, is thought also to be burning...Smoke from the fires mentioned completely obscures the remaining batteries to the south.[41]

The 40th BG's #407 *Shoot You're Faded* after its return from Mission #7 to Yawata. (*Changnon via 40th BG*).

40th BG mechanics stand in front of #254 *Hump Happy Pappy*. Air crews offered frequent praise for their maintenance teams. (*40th BG*)

Chakulia airfield in India, home of the 40th BG. (*US Air Force*)

British anti-aircraft guns defended the B-29s in India. Note the sandbagged gun position in the foreground with the B-29s in the background. There was at least one attempt by Japanese aircraft to raid the B-29 bases in India. (*40th BG*)

Chapter 5

SEPTEMBER 1944: THE MANCHURIAN MONTH

Jap Zeros bombed and strafed our downed plane early the next morning. Then they circled around looking for us as we hid in fox holes.

—JIM ICENHOWER (462nd BG)

American marines landed on the island of Peleliu in the Palau island group on September 15, 1944, commencing a bloody "slug fest" that would span two months. The battle to secure this island inflicted the highest percentage of casualties on American military forces than any other engagement in the Pacific Theater. On September 23, American forces seized Ulithi Atoll in the Caroline Islands for use as a forward naval anchorage for vessels supporting the upcoming invasion of Okinawa. Allied soldiers in Burma continued their slow push toward Rangoon.

The B-29s flying with the XX Bomber Command removed the cannons as tail armament during September; rather than carrying both 20 mm cannons and .50 caliber machine guns, the bombers would carry only the latter in future operations. While a hit from a 20 mm cannon could be devastating to a fighter, a tail gunner was more likely to strike an attacking plane with the machine guns, which could fire more rounds per minute than the cannon. Up to this point, damage to only two Japanese fighters had been credited to B-29 20 mm tail cannons. In addition, the cannon and its ammunition system added considerable weight to a bomber that needed to balance heavy bomb and fuel loads to complete long distance missions.[1]

Gen. Curtis LeMay, who arrived to assume command of XX BC at the end of August, petitioned and received permission to fly on a combat mission to acquire first hand knowledge of the skills of his personnel and the challenges they faced. One week after arriving in the theater, LeMay accompanied his crews on Mission #8 to Anshan, Manchuria. LeMay wrote, "Gen. Arnold had expressly forbidden me to fly any more combat missions. I presented all my arguments and finally got permission to fly one mission."[2]

Mission #8: Anshan, September 8, 1944

Gen. Hap Arnold and the 20th Air Force, desiring to maintain pressure on the Japanese steel industry, ordered another maximum daylight effort against Anshan, Manchuria. The plan identified the harbor area of Dairen, Manchuria, as the secondary target and the railroad yard at Sinsiang, China, as the target of last resort. The Anshan coke plant produced 2,575,000 metric tons of coke annually. Previous bomber raids destroyed one battery out of a total sixteen batteries with 740 coke ovens at Anshan. Further damage would reduce Anshan's coke producing totals even further and hamper this important component of the Japanese steel industry. Dairen harbor handled the export of raw materials to Japan, while the railroad yard at Sinsiang provided key logistical support for Japanese forces operating in China.

Preparing and moving the bombers forward to China proved to be costly in men and equipment; the XX BC lost planes along the Hump or in accidents caused by mechanical issues before many operational missions. Prior to Mission #8 to Anshan, the 444th BG lost #277 *Shanghai Lil* on September 6; pilot Capt. Williams faced a runaway propeller due to an electrical failure while taking off from India. The alarm bell in the aft compartment of the aircraft sounded

Crew shower facilities in China. Note how the buckets of hot water are hoisted with an attached shower head. (*Crocoll via 40th BG*)

The 444th BG's #277 *Dragon Lady*. (*Vaughn via 444th BG*)

Prior to Mission #8 to Anshan, the 444th BG lost #277 *Shanghai Lil* on September 6, 1944. Pilot Capt. Williams faced a runaway propeller due to an electrical failure after taking off from India. A ground maintenance team member on board died in the bail out. (*Steve Kelleher via 444th BG*)

and everyone in that part of the plane bailed out while Williams turned his B-29 for an emergency landing. The plane's right landing gear would not fully extend due to the same electrical problem and the huge bomber swerved off the runway, breaking up as it slid. The damage proved so extensive the plane could not be repaired and bailing out prior to the crash landing may have saved the lives of some or all of the crew members in the rear of the plane. However, a ground maintenance team member, Cpl. Claude Huffine, died in the bail out, possibly due to inexperience utilizing a parachute during an emergency evacuation of an airborne aircraft.[3]

One hundred eight of the 116 B-29s forward deployed into China took off for the September 8 raid on Anshan (29 from the 40th BG; 29 from the 444th BG; 27 from the 462nd BG; and 27 from the 468th BG). Ninety-five bombers carrying 500-pound general purpose bombs reached Anshan and ninety dropped their ordnance on the primary target. Three planes (#279 *Postville Express*, #390 *Gallopin Goose*, and #411 of the 468th BG) off loaded their bombs on an unidentified industrial area near Anshan before reaching the primary target and two were not able to release their bombs: one of the latter (#285 *Ours* of the 462nd BG) dropped its ordnance on a target of opportunity (an airfield near Kaifeng) and the other jettisoned its load. Three planes that bombed Anshan were able to release only a partial weapons load due to mechanical problems. Five B-29s (the 40th BG's #313 *Ding How* and #466 *Able Fox*; the 444th BG's #518; and the 462nd BG's #827 *Cocksure* and #386 *Globe Girdle Myrtle*) bombed the target of last resort: three due to mechanical problems and a formation of the two 462nd BG planes not able to join a larger formation flying to Anshan. The field order called for all formations to consist of at least three B-29s to provide mutual protection against Japanese fighters. Individual bombers or formations of two aircraft were under orders to bomb the target of last resort and return if they could not rendezvous with other aircraft, reducing their vulnerability to fighter attacks in the vicinity of the primary target. Three of these five crews visually observed good to excellent results of their attacks, with bombs falling among warehouses, other buildings, and into the marshaling yards at the target of last resort. Two other B-29s bombed targets of opportunity after encountering mechanical difficulties: a 462nd BG B-29 (#346 *Man O' War*) bombed the Tehsien railroad yard as a target of opportunity and a 468th BG Superfortress (#397 *Million Dollar Baby*) reported excellent results after dropping its load on an airfield west of Anyang.

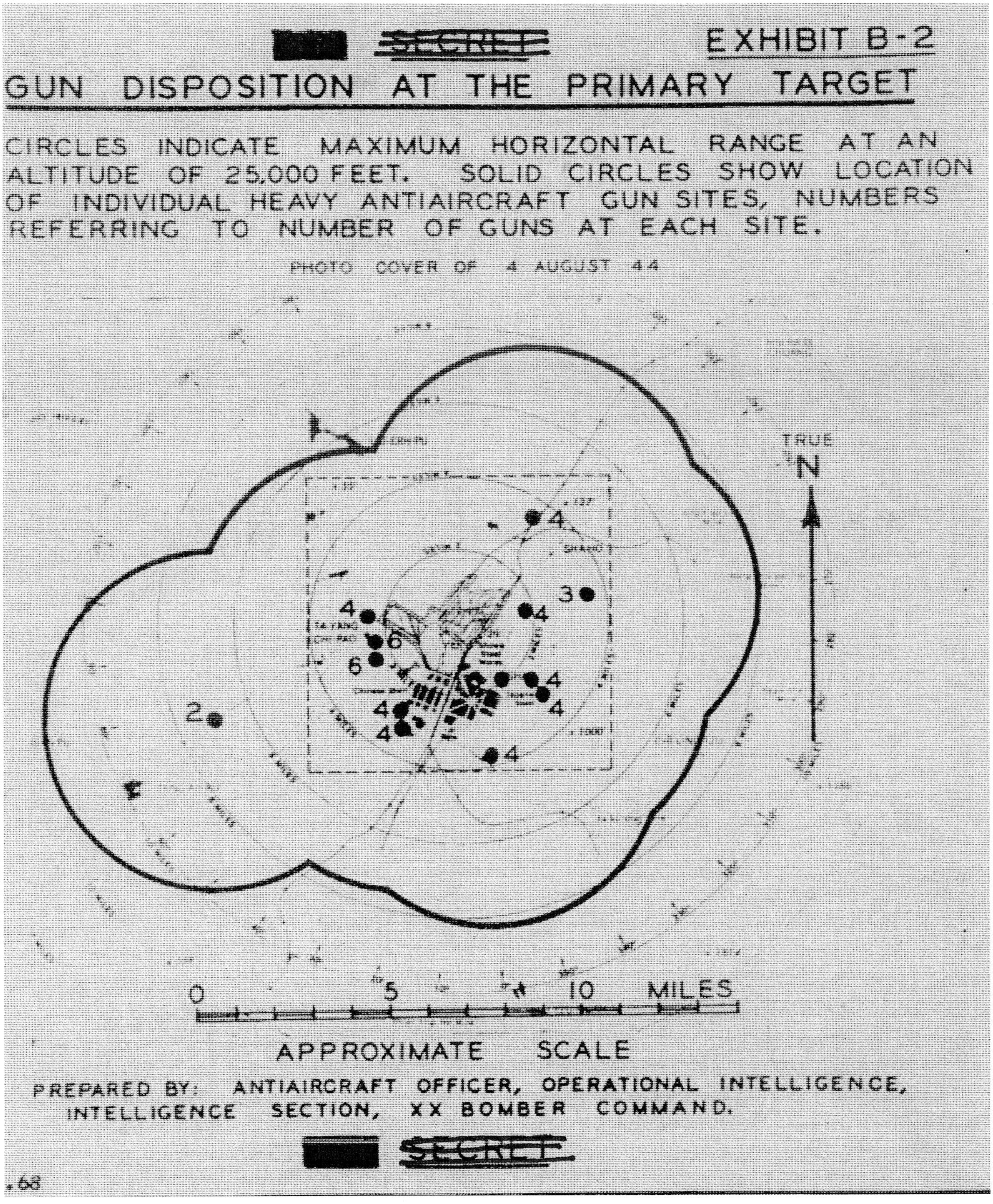

Japanese anti-aircraft gun positions established around the Anshan coke plant, the target of Mission #8. The XX BC utilized this chart to brief crews and help plot the specific direction of the bomb run to minimize exposure of the B-29s to anti-aircraft fire. (*US Air Force*)

Approaching the Showa Steel Works in Anshan, Manchuria, during Mission #8 from the bombardier's position. (*US Air Force*)

Crews reported meager to heavy but generally inaccurate anti-aircraft fire along the route and at the target area. Many indicated the flak was lighter than the previous mission to Anshan. Post-mission analysis attributed the latter comments to better intelligence, permitting planners to route the bombers between anti-aircraft battery coverage areas and over areas of fewer guns. Flak damaged five bombers: #306 *Pampered Lady* (#2 engine) and #503 *Nippon Nipper II* (fuselage) of the 40th BG; #830 *Torrid Toby* (right wing) of the 462nd BG; and #494 *Mary Ann* (right wing) and #504 *Gunga Din* (minor holes in its fuselage) of the 468th BG. B-29 #306 *Pampered Lady* made an emergency landing in Hanchang, China, during the return flight. Gen. LeMay flew on *Nippon Nipper II*, as remembered by the pilot, James Cornett:

> While over the target we were hit with flak. The left waist gunner called and said the CFC [Central Fire Control] gunner had been hit with flak and injured. Further interphone conversation revealed it was not too serious. Then Starkey called and said the RO [Radio Operator] was also hit. I turned to advise Gen. LeMay of this but I couldn't see him. I hollered at Arrington, the FE [Flight Engineer], and asked, "Where the hell is the Gen.?" Answer: "Grabbed a first-aid kit and took off"...Starkey, the Navigator, replied that LeMay had checked the RO. The flak vest was dented in places, but he wasn't cut.[4]

The 40th BG's #322 *Bonny Lee* in flight during Mission #8. (*US Air Force*)

The Japanese employed smoke screens over and around the target area once they identified it as the objective of the B-29s. Approximately one-third of the crews reported seeing smoke billowing from the ground from locations not showing damage from previous bombs.

Japanese fighters made 118 attacks on the bomber force over Anshan with Kawasaki Ki-45 Nicks, Nakajima Ki-44 Tojos, Nakajima Ki-43 Oscars, Kawasaki Ki-100 Tonys, Mitsubishi A6M Zekes, and numerous unidentified aircraft. Post-mission analysis offered a solid assessment of the B-29s' encounters with fighters:

Japanese fighter pilots over Anshan were judged by crew members to be less experienced than those over the Japanese mainland. They were, however, aggressive in some encounters and pressed their attacks with determination. Sixty per cent of the passes and attacks were reported as having been pressed to within 500 yards and 32 per cent to within 200 yards of our planes. Seven enemy aircraft passed down through our formations. Some well executed attacks indicated that about half of the enemy pilots were aggressive and that some were both experienced and aggressive. The pilots of Nicks were thought to be better than those of other enemy aircraft encountered.[5]

The 40th BG's #313 *Ding How* in India during December 1944. During Mission #8 to Anshan, the crew of *Ding How* bombed the target of last resort (the railroad yard in Sinsiang, China) due to mechanical problems. (*40th BG*)

Japanese flak struck the 468th BG's #504 *Gunga Din*, placing minor holes in the fuselage during Mission #8 to Anshan. Note the armory crew assembling fins to bombs and placing them on board *Gunga Din*. A Chinese guard stands at the front of the B-29. (*Schutte via 468th BG*)

The 40th BG's #306 *Pampered Lady* camouflaged in Hangchang, China, after making an emergency landing during the return from Mission #8. Japanese flak struck the B-29, damaging engine #2. (*US Air Force*)

Japanese fighters intercepted the bombers during their flight to Manchuria. A total of fourteen B-29s experienced fighter attacks along the inbound route that resulted in the loss of #360, piloted by Capt. Arthur Hyde of the 462nd BG, and damage to the 468th BG's #272 *Miss Shorty*. In #360's case, the Japanese pilot proved to be aggressive and accurate in his one-pass assault, damaging two engines. Crew member Mel Rosenfeld wrote in his diary, "Intercepted by Jap fighters about 4 hours out. Shot out # 3 and # 4 engines. Salvoed bombs, gas tank, and everything that was loose in the plane."[6]

A Japanese Kawasaki Ki-61 Tony fighter. Maj. John Misterly, a 444th BG navigator, remembered his tail gunner scoring a confirmed kill on a Japanese Tony fighter over Anshan, Manchuria, during Mission #8. (*Lukas*)

The 40th BG's #348 *Bengal Lancer*, not to be confused with #264 *Bengal Lancer* of the 444th BG. There are several examples of aircraft with the same name flying in different groups. (*40th BG*)

Japanese pilots damaged #315 *Deacon's Disciples* of the 444th BG over the target area during Mission #8. (*Gracie via 444th BG*)

The B-29 altered course to limp back to base on the two remaining engines, but the distance proved too great and the pilot made a belly landing at Laohokow. Rosenfeld remembered:

> We went in on our belly in an emergency fighter landing field (just a grass pasture—we called it a cow pasture). After our radio operator located this spot on his books and contacted our weather reporting radio station there we took a vote in the rear compartment on whether to jump or trust out pilot to get us down safely. We reasoned that rather than jump and be scattered or stay with the crew and take our chances. It was stay together or chute down in unknown territory alone.[7]

The landing damaged the underside of the fuselage, the propellers, and the flaps, but all of the crew members survived unharmed. The Japanese located the downed B-29 and bombed the field to destroy the aircraft. One of the crew members, Jim Icenhower, wrote in his diary, "Jap zeros bombed and strafed our downed plane early the next morning. Then they circled around looking for us as we hid in fox holes."[8]

The crew waited at the field—an emergency landing strip with a small American weather detachment—for a few days. While there, they enjoyed the hospitality of local Chinese officials and a Norwegian missionary. They salvaged what they could from their heavily damaged B-29 and destroyed what remained of the plane. The crew departed the air strip in two Douglas C-47 Skytrain cargo planes escorted by 14th Air Force Curtiss P-40 Warhawks.

Damage from a Japanese fighter forced the second B-29 (#272 *Miss Shorty*) to abort the mission and return to its forward base. Enemy aircraft intercepted the bomber at 15,000 feet near Kaifeng. One of the Japanese fighters (an Oscar) attacked from 11 o'clock high out of the sun, inflicting considerable damage as he passed along the top of the bomber and out over the tail. The bomber sustained major damage to the fuselage, electrical system, hydraulic system, and tires. The crew jettisoned their bomb load and successfully retraced their course, landing back at the forward base three hours later.[9]

Major John Misterly, a 444th BG navigator, remembered his tail gunner scoring a confirmed kill on a Japanese Tony fighter over Anshan. "As we bore into the target, the [fighter] attacks were coming from all directions.

B-29s from the 468th BG crossing China in Gen. Curtis LeMay's newly introduced twelve-plane formation. (*Schutte via 468th BG*)

The 40th BG's #222 *Deuces Wild* crash-landed in Chakulia, India, due to fuel starvation on September 11, 1944. (*US Air Force*)

Right at 'bombs away' our tail gunner hit a Tony that burst into flames and disintegrated some 100 yards behind. Our gunners damaged two other fighters."[10]

Two individuals in the 468th BG officially received credit for "probables" in an engagement that illustrated defensive cooperation between bombers flying in a three-ship formation. Bombardier 1st Lt. Archie Damron in #264 *Bengal Lancer* assumed control of the forward guns as a Japanese Tony approached their formation from 11 o'clock low. Damron commenced firing at 400 yards without visible results. As the fighter passed toward the rear of the B-29 the other gunners witnessed black smoke trailing from the fighter after a couple hundred yards. Meanwhile, a second Japanese fighter approached the same formation from 11 o'clock. This time the tail gunner in #370 *Lethal Lady*, flying ahead of #264 *Bengal Lancer*, opened up on the fighter as it reached a point 700 yards behind the bomber. Gunners on all three B-29s witnessed the results. "Left wing burst into flames and was trailing black smoke—some pieces were seen to fly off left wing. The Tony was seen to peel off to left (judged out of control) and dive at an angle of 65 degrees for over 15,000 feet while in sight."[11]

Japanese pilots damaged #315 *Deacon's Disciples* of the 444th BG over the target area. A Japanese Tojo surprised the B-29 crew at Anshan and peppered the bomber with 7.7 mm armor piercing ammunition, damaging engine #3. The crew reported finding bullets in their plane and that flak vests were not a defense against this type of

Another view of #222 *Deuces Wild* of the 40th BG after the crash-landing in Chakulia, India, due to fuel starvation. (*US Air Force*)

ammunition. The senior gunner, Staff Sgt. Saul Miller, died in the attack, which also wounded the radar operator Sgt. Crandall. The bomber, piloted by Maj. Wood, began to fall behind, signaling to other Japanese pilots that easy prey lay in reach. The 444th BG credits Maj. Curtis for saving Maj. Wood and his crew. Curtis dropped back from the formation and provided additional protection for the wounded B-29. The pair provided mutual defensive fire for each other along the entire route home.[12]

Another 444th BG B-29 (#234 *My Assam Dragon*) fell victim to the fighters around Anshan; Japanese fighters pounced on the bomber, knocking out an engine. The pilot, Capt. Overton, managed to reach the coast of Liaotung Bay before beginning to lose altitude. Other crews reported seeing Overton's ship diving at a high rate of speed with fighters on its tail. The last sighting placed #234 at a very low altitude and heading for the Chinese coast. It was learned later that Overton crash-landed at the coast, where seven crew members survived and were aided by the Chinese. Overton and the other six survivors "walked out" of the area with the help of the Chinese and arrived at the 444th BG's forward base on January 23, 1945. The 678th Bomb Squadron reported to the 444th BG, "Upon arrival here they were dressed in the oddest assortment of Chinese clothing imaginable."[13]

Ten Japanese fighters intercepted eight B-29s during the return flight from Anshan. In one case, a Zeke dove from 1 o'clock and closed to within fifty yards while spraying bullets into the vertical stabilizer. A Tojo also approached from 1 o'clock and placed bullets into the right wing of a second B-29. The Tojo closed to an astounding twenty yards as it passed. The B-29's gunners returned fire and reported they hit the fighter as it hurtled past them. The fighter was last seen departing the area and heavily smoking.

The Japanese utilized aerial bombs in their attacks but did not damage any of the B-29s:

> Aerial bombing attacks were experienced by 3 of our aircraft. One of the bombs was released by a single radial-engine fighter making a high frontal approach. The aircraft was first sighted at about 500 yards; it is not known when the bomb was released. It exploded 200 yards off the right wing and inflicted no damage. A second attack was made by a Zeke approaching the rear quarter high and closing to 800 yards. The bomb exploded about 50 feet above and between number 1 and 2 planes of the formation. The third attack was made by an unidentified single-engine fighter coming in from 8 o'clock about 1,000 feet above the formation. The enemy aircraft released a bomb described as "18 inches in diameter and 5 or 6 feet in length." It burst a few seconds after leaving the enemy aircraft and released approximately 12 small bombs. No hits were made.[14]

The four groups expended 25,640 rounds of 50-caliber machine gun and 945 rounds of 20 mm cannon ammunition defending themselves from Japanese fighters. These figures are not as large as they may seem. The groups also expended 19,070 rounds of 50-caliber and 880 rounds of 20 mm ammunition simply test firing their weapons en route to the target.

One of the returning 40th BG planes experienced an emergency—the pilot passed out in the cockpit. The incident was witnessed by James Cornett and Gen. LeMay. Cornett wrote:

I thought the return would be uneventful, as things were chugging along pretty well. Not so. The left waist gunner advised of impending disaster. Sure enough, my left wing man, E.O. Berry's plane, was turning into us. I pulled up slightly to avoid collision, then he leveled out and resumed position. We had not crossed the Yellow River so I could not communicate with Berry effectively. Shortly thereafter light signals were sent to us from Berry's B-29, but we were unable to make out the message. His aircraft started to leave the formation. We signaled back to Berry to stay in formation, but there was no further response. They took up a slightly different heading and left the formation. Starkey assured us that we were on course. Of course Gen. LeMay was aware of the situation and told me to get on the radio and get them back in formation. I explained the Tactical Doctrine prevented radio communication until we had crossed the Yellow River; but if I was ordered to do so I would. He did not do so, but fumed over the situation. We later learned Berry had passed out as a result of amoebic dysentery problems and caused a temporary loss of control of the aircraft, and it had turned into us. The co-pilot had taken over, and being concerned with Berry's condition he had elected to cut across the dog-leg route on a direct heading to our China base. He believed it would reduce flying time and get medical attention for Berry sooner. Perhaps not a good decision, but at least he evaluated the situation and made one. They really didn't precede us by much, but who's to know.[15]

Another B-29 (#212 of the 444th BG) did not make it back to base; the plane lacked sufficient fuel to reach its forward base and the pilot made a belly landing in a river bed. All of the crew members survived.[16]

The B-29s destroyed two coke batteries during the raid. Taking into account the results of the previous attack on Anshan, three of the sixteen coke batteries were deemed out of commission for at least one year. Another three coke batteries sustained sufficient damage to consider them useless for six months to a year. Aerial photographs indicated an additional two batteries may have been damaged by the ground shaking caused by near misses. Initial intelligence estimates—based only on reconnaissance photographs after Mission #8—placed the coke production rate at 65% of output prior to the first bombing attack on the plant.

Re-Organization Under Gen. Curtis LeMay

Flying with Gen. Le May during the Anshan raid presented James Cornett an opportunity to evaluate the new boss who would transform B-29 operations in the China-Burma-India Theater, as well as across the entire Pacific Theater:

> I never learned all that went on between Gen. LeMay and my crew during the mission. I do know that after it, they, to a man, believed he could do no wrong and they had only the highest admiration for him. As for me, I'd already had a high regard for his ability as a Commander, Leader, Tactician, and Specialist in several related fields, but now I had to include a pretty fine human being as well. At no time had he interfered with the operation of the aircraft or mission per se. And to this day I have not changed these personal opinions.[17]

Gen. LeMay ordered an operational "stand down" for training as the logistical network restocked fuel supplies at Chengtu. LeMay brought many battle-tested ideas from his combat commands with the Eighth Air Force in Europe and sought to implement them within the XX BC to improve operations. Hearing about the logistical problems faced by the XX BC may not have fully prepared him for what he discovered upon arriving in India and he certainly realized Wolfe had been handed an "impossible task."[18]

After flying as an observer on Mission #8 LeMay ordered changes in many areas, including formation flying, bombing, intelligence, navigation, and maintenance. The new commander scrapped the old four-plane diamond formations and replaced them with the twelve-plane formations he perfected in the skies above Europe. The larger formations provided greater mutually supporting defensive fire and massed more bombs at one location in the target area to improve accuracy.

LeMay established a "lead crew" system in which each group identified its most experienced six crews for eleven days of specialized training to lead formations. The navigator in the lead crew served the entire formation, while the lead bombardier (or radar operator in poor weather) made the decision when to release the bomb load. The other bombardiers in the formation dropped their ordnance when the lead bombardier (or radar operator) directed. If a lead crew dropped from the formation due to mechanical problems or battle damage another lead-trained crew assumed leadership of the bombers. Operating under a twelve-plane formation with a lead crew required

A twelve-plane B-29 formation introduced to the XX BC by Gen. Curtis LeMay. Operating under a twelve-plane formation with a lead crew required training, including practice in combat, where the fog of war prevailed. (*Bailey via 40th BG*)

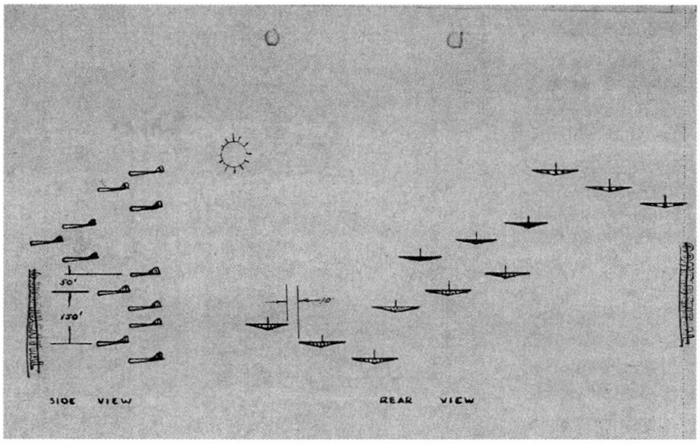

XX BC diagram illustrating the new twelve-plane B-29 formation from the side and behind. The XX BC utilized this type of chart to assist training pilots. (*US Air Force*)

training, including practice in combat, where the fog of war prevailed; the XX BC crews did not have these opportunities to hone their skills. The next mission commenced in two weeks and they had been fortunate to fly more than two missions a month since June.

When LeMay's system worked, it provided superior results compared to the four-plane diamond formations or bombing individually, but when the system collapsed over a target due to lack of training and experience, entire formations could miss the target by miles. The January 6, 1945, mission to Omura is an example of when the system worked exceedingly well. Although one formation missed the target by six miles due to poor weather, another lead crew brought its formation directly onto the target. The bombing results were inconclusive due to weather conditions, but XX BC intelligence analysts believed this second formation placed their ordnance squarely onto the aiming point since they followed the lead bombardier. On January 14, 1945, a lead crew directed a thirteen-plane formation onto Taichu airdrome with excellent bombing results. Examples of formations missing the target include the November 21 raid to Omura: a lead crew escorted its formation to Omuta (beyond Omura) and all of the aircraft bombed the wrong target area. During the same mission, another group scored poor results when their formation collapsed as they attempted to change lead crews during the final bomb run. On December 7, ten B-29s bombed a rail yard nine miles from the primary target in Mukden by following the lead bombardier, who dropped his munitions too early. On December 21, two formations toggled their bombs early due to frosted windshields preventing them from clearly seeing the lead bomber.

LeMay believed daylight raids were required for precision strikes against the industrial targets assigned to XX BC. During night raids, the B-29 crews experienced challenges locating and hitting targets. Bombardiers and radar operators would now work closely together after the bomber formation reached the Initial Point (IP) and commenced the bomb run to the target. If cloud cover obscured the target at any point along the run, the radar operator of a lead or any crew could immediately assume responsibility for releasing the bombs. While the lead crews would direct the formations, it was understood there would be mechanical and other problems on every mission requiring single bombers or small groups to hit the secondary, target of last resort, or even a target of opportunity, during which the crews would be on their own for the bomb run. Bombers also would not deviate their flight paths between the IP and target to avoid anti-aircraft fire. Maintaining a straight course without changing altitude or direction proved important in the European Theater, ensuring the bombs were dropped over the aiming point. As noted on an earlier raid, flight alterations on the bombing run played havoc with the radar operator's

Japanese bombers damaged #254 *Hump Happy Pappy* during a night intruder attack on the 40th BG's forward base in China on September 9, 1944. (*Brusco via 40th BG*)

equipment. If called upon to make the call when over the target, the radar operator might find his equipment still attempting to realign itself after a flight deviation.

During previous missions, the crews learned of their targets and navigation instructions at the forward Chengtu bases prior to launching the mission. During this mandatory training period Gen. LeMay directed the lead crews to study charts of geographical areas and then potential target charts with intelligence staff members. LeMay later wrote that he told the crews, "Take this area, I would say, and study the maps and pictures and everything you can get hold of. I want you to be able to draw your area freehand in your sleep."[19]

The 40th BG's #268 *Good Humpin'* crashed on September 16, 1944, as its crew attempted to land with a fire in engine #2. (*40th BG*)

Many maintenance practices in Europe found their way to the XX BC via LeMay. The Army Air Force functioned with a decentralized maintenance system and LeMay tackled that way of thinking:

> I combined all the supply sections so that supplies were in one place, not stashed in some squadron supply area...I set up a production-line maintenance program for the whole base. We could take the people who knew what they were doing and let them supervise the less skilled personnel so we could get a lot more done. Everyone worked on the airplane that needed to be worked on. In the old system, when one squadron got shot up and had a lot of holes to patch, the sheet metal guys in that squadron would be burning the midnight oil while the next-door squadron would be down at the pub having a beer. The maintenance system I set up in India in 1944 got everyone working.[20]

The 444th BG historical summary for September 1944 provided an interesting examination of Gen. LeMay and the impact of his changes on the group: "Life with the 444th has taken a faster pace since the arrival of Maj. Gen. LeMay, and the first result is the lack of griping which characterized the outfit in the days of more leisure."[21]

The group converted #250 *Bombin' Buggy* to a tanker before sending her back to the United States as "war weary" in November 1944. (*Barnes via 40th BG*)

B-29 engine maintenance. Note the mechanic sitting inside the engine nacelle. (*Hodgdon via 40th BG*)

Col. William Blanchard, commander of the 40th BG, presenting a briefing to his crews before Mission #9 to Anshan, Manchuria. (*40th BG*)

Mission #9: Anshan, September 26, 1944

The damage sustained by the coke plant at Anshan during two previous missions prompted the XX BC to return to Anshan prior to the end of September for a knock-out blow. Damage from the previous attacks had reduced Showa from first to second place in Japanese coke production. Despite the reduction of coke—much of which was exported to the Japanese home islands—Showa's rolled steel production remained at pre-attack levels. The harbor area of Darien, Manchuria, and the railroad yard at Sinsiang, China, remained the secondary and target of last resort. The military value of Darien and Singsiang remained the same as outlined in Mission #8.

One hundred five B-29s launched from the forward bases in China, followed by four other bombers that got off the ground after maintenance repairs. Eighty-eight planes reached the primary target. The XX BC called for each B-29 to carry a load of high explosive bombs and fly in Gen. LeMay's new twelve-plane formations; Mission #9 to Anshan would provide the first B-29 combat test of this formation. The B-29s actually bombed Anshan with nine formations ranging from three to sixteen planes. A single bomber also crossed the plant and dropped its bomb load contradictory to directives, which called for lone bombers to strike the secondary or target of last resort rather than continue to Anshan. Poor visibility prevented immediate crew observations of the bombing results. Reconnaissance photographs, rated from fair to good quality, did not indicate any new damage to the facility.

Two planes dropped their ordnance on the secondary target. One of these bombers experienced mechanical problems and headed to the secondary target while the other crew failed to join a formation. Under mission directives, the crew diverted to the secondary rather than risk flying over Anshan. Four bombers, all with mechanical difficulties, bombed the target of last resort. Nine aircraft off loaded their weapons on targets of opportunity: the 40th BG's #303 *Typhoon McGoon III* (railroad tracks at Changli) and #322 *Bonny Lee* (a dock area); the 444th BG's #510 (a railroad round house and yard near Tsinan); the 462nd BG's #475 *Hoodlum House II* (a road) and #531 (same

An enlargement of the chalk board utilized by Col. Blanchard during his briefing prior to Mission #9. The board illustrates the 40th BG is sending twenty-six B-29s on the XX BC raid: twelve planes are in the group's lead formation and the remaining fourteen are in the second formation. (*40th BG*)

road bombed by #531); and the 468th BG's #284 *The Challenger* (Kaifeng airfield), #362 (Kaifeng airfield), #370 *Lethal Lady* (Loyang military cantonment), and #454 *Totin' To Tokyo* (warehouses near Kaifeng airfield).

A post-mission report reviewed the attempt to utilize Gen. LeMay's twelve-plane formation; the crews met many challenges in assembling and maintaining these formations. The first formation consisted of sixteen aircraft from three different groups. The post-mission report attributed much of the problem to weather conditions. "Because of poor visibility due to cloud coverage and frosting of windows, considerable difficulty was encountered in forming the formations over the rendezvous point. Also, once formed the formations were very loose because of the danger of collision. The wide variance in altitudes and axes of attack reported by aircraft within the same formation is an indication of this."[22]

Japanese anti-aircraft fire over the primary target ranged widely from meager to moderate and inaccurate to accurate. Intelligence estimates placed seventy anti-aircraft guns in the target area. Much of the flak proved to be fairly accurate, despite poor visibility and thick cloud cover, indicating the Japanese probably utilized radar-directed guns to engage the B-29s. The bombers over the secondary target reported meager and inaccurate flak and those over the target of last resort noted a lack of anti-aircraft fire. The bomber formations also flew through anti-aircraft

The crew of #306 *Pampered Lady* released their bombs before reaching the target during Mission #9 to Anshan, Manchuria, due to a miscalculation by the lead bombardier aboard #269. (*Decker via 40th BG*)

The crew of #331 *Gone With The Wind* flew in the fifth formation with five 468th BG B-29s during Mission #9 to Anshan, Manchuria. (*40th BG*)

#303 *Typhoon McGoon III* encountered mechanical difficulties and bombed the railroad tracks at Changli as a target of opportunity during Mission #9. (*Mackey via 40th BG*)

flak at several other locations along the route to and from the primary target. Some crews spotted barrage balloons and there may have been a smoke screen over the Showa plant at Anshan. Thick cloud cover prevented most of the crews from ever seeing the target, but one crew at the end of the bomber stream believed the Japanese had a smoke screen at the plant. Anti-aircraft guns did not bring down any of the bombers, but eight planes did receive damage from exploding flak: the 40th BG's #522 *B-Sweet II* (horizontal stabilizer); the 444th BG's #580 *Flyin' Jackass* (hydraulic system); the 462nd BG's #484 *Our Gal* (nacelle #4, right blister and tunnel), #285 *Ours* (vertical stabilizer), #287 (fuselage, nacelle #1, and left wing), and #463 *Humpin' Honey* (rudder); and the 468th BG's #469 *Blind Date* (fuselage).

Japanese fighters intercepted 84 of the 109 bombers launched for Mission #9. Fighters damaged nine of the B-29s but did not shoot down any Superfortresses. B-29 gunners claimed eleven fighters destroyed, nine probables, and thirty-one damaged. The intensity of the aerial combat can be compared to previous missions with the number of rounds fired by the gunners: 37,125 machine gun (50-caliber) and 281 tail cannon (20 mm) rounds. During the previous mission to Anshan gunners fired 25,640 machine gun rounds in combat. It is interesting to note the tail gunners fired 945 rounds from their cannons on Mission #8—nearly three times as many 20 mm cannon rounds than Mission #9. This may reflect the program to remove 20 mm guns throughout the month.

Crews reported Japanese pilots still seemed to prefer attacking by approaching the front of the bombers. Approximately 10% of the attacks were coordinated, with multiple Japanese fighters in the fray. In one example, "Two Tojos attacked in trail from 2 o'clock low. The enemy opened fire at 800 yards, and pressed the attack to 50 yards, breaking away in power dives. The B-29 returned fire, but it is not believed that any hits were scored. Our aircraft sustained hits in the fuselage behind the radio operator's compartment."[23]

Three Japanese aircraft cooperated to attack another bomber: "Two Nicks and 1 Tony were sitting in the target area waiting for 1 B-29 as it came in towards the aiming point. The 3 fighters attacked in trail from 11 o'clock level, opened fire at 1,000 yards, and closed to 200 yards. The B-29 sustained no damage as a result of the attack, and 1 Nick is claimed as damaged."[24]

Japanese pilots employed aerial bombs during the engagements, including at least one cluster bomb that burst to form approximately six separate, smaller explosions. The Japanese did score a rare aerial bomb hit on a B-29 (#287 of the 462nd BG):

Japanese fighters scored hits on #324 *Three Feathers* during Mission #9 to Anshan. (Archer via 444th BG)

Navigator 1st Lt. Harold Oblender aboard #281 *20th Century Unlimited* of the 40th BG. (*Schutte via 40th BG*)

> Only one B-29 was damaged as a result of these [aerial bombs] attacks, and this instance occurred when a bomb [non-phosphorus] hit the fuselage of aircraft #287 just forward of the Top Gunner's blister and penetrated through to the aft bomb bay where it exploded. The bomb bay doors were sprung and several holes were put in the fuselage, but no further damage was sustained, and there were no injuries to personnel.[25]

Despite the intensity of the aerial combat, Japanese pilots were not able to shoot down any of the B-29s on Mission #9, although they hit nine of the bombers, including #287. The other eight B-29s with fighter damage were the 40th BG's #522 *B-Sweet II* (shell holes in the horizontal stabilizer); the 444th BG's #292 *Black Jack* (holes in the fuselage, stabilizer, elevator, fin, rudder, and tail bulkhead door), #580 *Flyin' Jackass* (damage from a 20 mm explosive shell behind the engineer's panel that wounded radio operator Sgt. Ellis), and #321 *This Is It* (holes in unspecified locations); the 462nd BG's #484 *Our Gal* (left upper aft gun destroyed and holes in the right blister that wounded the right gunner); and the 468th BG's #397 *Million Dollar Baby* (50 holes across the plane that also damaged the upper aft gun turret), #546 (15 holes in the fuselage), and #429 *Blind Date* (unspecified damage).[26] On November 29, Gen. Curtis LeMay personally presented the Purple Heart to Staff Sgt. Arthur Veik, the wounded gunner aboard #484 *Our Gal*. A bullet from the Japanese fighter pierced the blister and destroyed Veik's gun sight. Fragments of the sight struck Veik, causing his injuries.

Defense of XX BC Forward Airfields

The 14th Air Force assumed fighter protection against any Japanese attempt to bomb XX BC's forward airfields in China. In September 1943, Gen. Claire Chennault of the 14th Air Force requested at least one fighter group to accomplish the task handed to him. In response, the chiefs of staff offered to move two P-40 fighter groups (the 33rd and 81st) from Italy and re-equip them with Republic P-47 Thunderbolts. Chennault established the 312th Fighter Wing (FW) to oversee their operations and continued to ask for P-51s, which were more economical on fuel. The XX BC B-29s began arriving before the 312th FW could be fully manned and equipped. While the bomber bases in India lay just beyond the range of Japanese bombers, those in China could be targeted. One of the transferred squadrons from the 33rd Fighter Group flew to China to defend the bomber bases while the other five awaited the arrival of P-47s.

The 444th BG's #292 *Black Jack* returned from Mission #9 to Anshan with holes in the fuselage, stabilizer, elevator, fin, rudder, and tail bulkhead door from Japanese fighters. This was taken in India, as evidenced by the laborers walking in the foreground. (*US Air Force*)

40th BG personnel outside the airfield control tower watch and await the return of B-29s to A-1 in China. (*Changnon via 40th BG*)

Radar at a XX BC airfield near Chengtu, China, provided the XX BC with early warning of Japanese raids. (*40th BG*)

Barrage balloons added a defensive measure against low flying enemy aircraft strafing the airfields. While utilized for defensive purposes, the barrage balloons also posed a challenge to any unsuspecting friendly aircraft. William Holderby, a 468th BG navigator, lamented the balloons were "a menace to local flying."[27]

The 14th Air Force fighters could not be at all places at all times in a country as large as China and the Japanese resorted to night attacks to help destroy American morale. Lt. Robert Schumacher, a flight engineer with the 444th BG, remembered the concern of being caught on the ground by Japanese fighters. "Our stays in China were very limited as the Japanese usually returned the favor after each bombing mission. Early on there were no night fighters available for protection so we refueled and took off for India ASAP."[28]

While the Japanese might not catch any B-29s on the ground, their night bombing could damage runways and buildings, as well as destroy critical stockpiled fuel and supplies. Cpl. B. Vic Dison Jr., a 40th BG tail gunner, hastened with others to the outdoor fox holes the first time he experienced a night raid:

> It seemed that every night we heard the air raid warning sirens. This was the signal to leave our quarters and head for the fox-holes. We complied on the first night when the sirens went off and headed for the open fields and into the fox-holes. After the "all clear" signal we returned to our quarters. Since it was bitterly cold at night we got the charcoal burners out and prepared a fire to warm up. As we warmed up we also caught wind of a terrible odor. We soon discovered that the odor came from our shoes. The Chinese used the fox-holes for outhouses. The second night I stayed in my cot when the alert was sounded. Within a couple of nights everyone stayed in their cots. Although there seemed to be an air-raid alert every night we did not get bombed while we were in China.[29]

At other times the Japanese bombers arrived to find one or more B-29s sitting on a Chinese airfield after delivering supplies or awaiting repairs after a raid. In early 1945, a member of the Air Transport Command (ATC) risked his life assisting two XX BC personnel extinguish a B-29 fire during a Japanese attack. Sgt. Ellwood Smith looked out of his slit trench and saw a B-29 beginning to burn during the raid. Smith and the two XX BC personnel crawled out of their slit trench and rushed to the bomber, grabbed fire extinguishers, and tackled the fire in engine #1. "Leaking gasoline from the left engine could have exploded at any second, but the boys doggedly persisted in their finally successful attempt to kill the flames. As they hit the slit trench the drone of approaching planes signaled the beginning of additional bombing runs..."[30]

468th BG navigator Willard Holderby experienced a Japanese night attack while overnighting in China following the September raid on Anshan, Manchuria, "Tonight we were awakened at about 12:00 PM with a 'two ball' alert which quickly changed to 'three balls' as enemy bombers came overhead. We hit the trenches. A few bombs were dropped, mostly hitting harmlessly in nearby rice paddies."[31]

The number of Japanese raiders in a single night tended to be small to slip through an area undetected. Gen. LeMay noted in his memoirs of the B-29 program, "The bombing the Japanese did against the bomber bases [at Chengtu] was never very good. The raids were light and annoying rather than seriously damaging. We never did lose a B-29, but we lost a C-54 cargo plane once, and we would occasionally lose some gasoline."[32]

Despite the temptation of striking B-29s on the ground in China after missions, the Japanese launched only ten air attacks on forward fields before the bombers departed the country to fly almost exclusively from India in December 1944. The efficiency of Japanese intelligence irritated LeMay more than the night bombing attacks. Japanese intelligence often proved to be accurate and their sources were rarely discovered, but they were naturally assumed to be individuals living in the local area and probably working on or near XX BC airfields. The same individuals hired local Chinese to help direct Japanese bombers to the correct locations for their night attacks. Gen. LeMay wrote these individuals ignited a string of small fires that guided the Japanese bombers to their targets. He also lamented that at least one Japanese agent operated a radio homing beacon from within one of the villages adjacent to a B-29 base.[33]

Japanese bombers struck the Chengtu airfields during the nights of September 8 and 26 after the raids on Anshan, Manchuria, prompting LeMay to request night fighters to protect his bases in China. 40th BG records include a summary of the Japanese attack after the first September bombing mission:

> …a small force of enemy aircraft raided A-1 dropping clusters of fragmentation bombs and several bombs of a 500# G.P. [500-pound general purpose] type. Only minor damage was inflicted on parked aircraft and several personnel sustained minor injuries. The complete absence of ground and air defenses permitted the enemy to drop his bombs from a very low altitude and it is fortunate that more serious damage was not inflicted.[34]

There were anti-aircraft guns at the forward bases, despite the 40th BG headquarters' assertion of their lack. The 40th BG forward detachment prepared the following after the raid:

> Everyone was retired when about 0300 [3 a.m.] in the morning of 9 September, a two ball alert [all personnel should begin moving to sheltered areas due to approaching aircraft] was sounded. Gun crews according to the Base Defense Plan took their stations at their guns around the field. Shortly thereafter, a three ball notice [all personnel should take immediate cover; enemy aircraft are overhead] was given from fighter control. Gas masks and helmets were broken out and nearby slit trenches were occupied when a plane that sounded for all the world like a washing machine began circling overhead. Minutes later a stick of bombs fell across the field. On another run dozens of frag [fragmentation] bombs were dropped on the field. Run number three like the first consisted of 100 or 200 pound demolition bombs that passed in train off the west end of the field in the direction of the combat crew hostel. The last of these landed in a rice paddy approximately 75 yards from the hostel. The three runs resulted in damage to the 45th's [Squadron] tanker #254 and injuries to Staff Sgt. Edward M. Cyrus and Private First Class Venner McNeil. Serious facial injuries were sustained by McNeil and Cyrus was struck in the arm and eye by shrapnel from a bomb that hit the gun pit in which they were stationed. After first aid treatment was administered at the Base Dispensary, the men were evacuated to Chengtu Hospital and thence to India for surgery and treatment.[35]

The 426th Night Fighter Squadron (NFS) arrived in India on August 4, followed by the 427th NFS at the end of September. The 426th NFS personnel waited until September 9 for the first of their night fighters to arrive—the day after the first September Japanese attack on Chengtu. Service personnel assembled the Northrop P-61 Black Widows and installed a radio and radio compass in each. The planes stood ready when LeMay called for night fighter protection of his Chinese airfields. Several P-61s arrived at Chengtu by October 6.

Northrop P-61 Black Widow night fighters being offloaded from a vessel in Calcutta, India, prior to deployment to China. The 426th Night Fighter Squadron (NFS) arrived in India on August 4, 1944, followed by the 427th NFS at the end of September 1944. (*Lukas*)

The Northrop P-61 Black Widow was the first American aircraft designed specifically as a night fighter. Two Pratt & Whitney R-2800-65 Double Wasp 18-cylinder radial engines powered the 49-foot-long Black Widow. It could fly over 1,350 miles at over 220 mph. (*Lukas*)

The Northrop P-61 Black Widow was the first aircraft designed specifically as a night fighter. Two Pratt & Whitney R-2800-65 Double Wasp 18-cylinder radial engines powered the 49-foot long Black Widow. It could fly over 1,350 miles at over 220 mph. The pilot's cockpit was behind the nose, which carried the radar receiving antenna. The gunner sat above and behind the pilot. A turret housing four .50-caliber machine guns was mounted just behind the gunner's cockpit in the early P-61A and late P-61B models. The positioning of the guns permitted them to fire without their flash blinding the gunner at night. The 426th NFS flew late P-61A models in defense of the XX BC's forward airfields in China. These planes did not carry machine gun positions due to troubles with their operation while in flight and a shortage of gun turrets. The P-61 utilized the same gun turret mechanism as the B-29 bombers, which had a higher priority for receiving them. P-61s without machine gun turrets, including those of the 426th NFS, did not fly with gunners and the pilot operated the plane's only armament: four 20 mm cannons in a tub on the belly of the aircraft. The plane could carry 200 rounds of 20 mm ammunition for each gun. The R/O worked from a unique compartment at the rear of the P-61. During flight the radar observer (R/O) faced forward, but could turn in his seat to peer out the Plexiglas behind him. The R/O operated the new SCR-720 radar system with an effective range of around five miles to locate aircraft, but this distance could increase or decrease depending on various conditions.[36]

An important key to successful night fighting involved the coordination of the P-61 pilot, his R/O, and the Ground Controlled Interception (GCI) operator or "controller" at or near the airfield. When an unidentified aircraft approached the area without the proper Identification Friend or Foe (IFF) signal, the GCI would alert the patrolling night fighter or scramble a P-61 sitting on alert status. The GCI operator then assumed control of the P-61 and provided the pilot with a vector to the incoming target. The object was to direct the P-61 to a location where the Black Widow's R/O could acquire a fix on the bogey using the onboard SCR 720 radar system, then the R/O would direct his pilot to a location where the crew could make visual contact with the unidentified aircraft. This was important, because the bogey could be a friendly aircraft with communications and/or IFF problems. After visually identifying the unknown aircraft as hostile, the P-61 crew could then request permission to bring it down. The 426th NFS utilized the same P-61/GCI coordination system to locate and escort lost and/or damaged B-29s to airfields. On more than one occasion P-61s followed GCI vectors until their R/Os picked up the bombers on their SCR-720 radar sets. The Black Widows then made visual contact with the bombers and led them to the safety of their airfields.

Capt. Robert Scott with his R/O, flight officer Charles Phillips, bagged the first kill of a Japanese bomber attacking a XX BC airfield on October 29. The GCI controller identified a bogey approaching Chengtu at forty miles. He directed Scott to a point within three miles of the bogey when Phillips picked up the unidentified aircraft on his SCR-70 radar set. At this point the R/O assumed radar lead and maneuvered his pilot to a position within 1,000 feet of the bogey. Scott identified the aircraft as a Japanese Kawasaki Ki-48 Lily bomber flying at approximately 120 mph. The Black Widow pilot crept to 500 feet from the Lily and opened fire with the 20 mm cannon. The Japanese pilot immediately commenced evasive action and dove to port. Scott pursued the Japanese bomber five minutes before delivering a burst of the 20 mm cannon that resulted in visible hits along the starboard wing and engine as the two planes dived to below 4,000 feet. Scott pulled up his P-61 as the Lily bomber hit the ground, exploding on impact. Upon return to the airfield, the ground crew noticed the P-61 had a nick in a propeller from debris coming off the crippled bomber.[37]

The SCR-720 radar dish housed in the nose of the Northrop P-61 Black Widow. The dish emitted radar signals that were picked up by antenna on the side of the P-61 when they bounced back from an object in the night sky. (*Lukas*)

Members of the 426th NFS in Chengtu, China. The 426th NFS bagged the first kill of a Japanese bomber attacking a XX BC airfield on October 29, 1944. (*Lukas*)

A Japanese Kawasaki Ki-48 Lily bomber. The Japanese dispatched Lily bombers to strike the XX BC forward bases in China during the night of October 29, 1944. A Northop P-61 Black Widow night fighter providing protection for the base intercepted and downed the Japanese raider. (*Lukas*)

While the P-61/GCI coordination and identification system proved reliable most of the time, nothing is perfect. A detachment of the 427th NFS operating in Suichwan, China (not in direct support of the XX BC), dispatched a P-61 to investigate an unidentified bogey in January 1945. The Japanese employed a captured American Consolidated B-24 Liberator in some of their night attacks in the area. Communications could not be established with the bogey, which was not emitting a friendly IFF signal. The Black Widow approached under GCI guidance until the R/O received a signal on his SCR-720 set. The pilot radioed GCI that he could see a large aircraft with four engines and a twin tail in the light of the quarter moon and positively identified it as a B-24; at this point, the bogey turned sharply away from the P-61. The Black

Jing Bow Joyride, a Northrop P-61 Black Widow of the 426th NFS in China. The introduction of American night fighters to Chengtu and the need to support offensive operations in eastern and southern China prompted Japan to divert its night air activities from the B-29 bases by the end of 1944. (*Lukas*)

Widow pilot, R/O, and GCI controller identified this maneuver as an evasive action to avoid the night fighter, so the GCI controller cleared the P-61 pilot to engage the bogey. The Black Widow pilot opened fire with his belly 20 mm cannon and the bogey began burning as two crewmen bailed out of the stricken aircraft before it exploded. However, the event proved to be a tragic mistake, as the P-61 crew learned from the survivors they downed a Consolidated C-87 Liberator Express, the cargo version of the B-24.[38]

The 426th NFS scored its second kill in defense of the XX BC during the night of November 21. Capt. John J. Wilfong and his R/O, Lt. Glenn E. Ashley, launched from Chengtu on a routine patrol that night. The GCI controller radioed Wilfong and vectored him toward an incoming bogey flying at 6,000 feet. Due to the excessive combined speed of the two aircraft as they approached each other the P-61 overshot and missed the bogey without seeing it. GCI called a new heading for a second bogey approaching behind the first and at the same altitude. Ashley picked up the bogey on his SCR-70 radar set as the Black Widow reached a point within four miles of the unidentified aircraft. As Wilfong drew closer the bogey initiated evasive maneuvers and climbed to 14,000 feet. The P-61 crew continued pursuit and moved within 600 feet of the bogey before identifying it as a Japanese Mitsubishi Ki-46 Dinah. (The Japanese employed the two-engine Dinah in night fighter, bomber, and reconnaissance roles in multiple areas during the war.) Wilfong fired approximately forty rounds from his 20 mm cannon and watched as the Dinah exploded in front of him. He noted in his after mission report, "It was a textbook intercept."[39]

The introduction of American night fighters to Chengtu and the need to support offensive operations in eastern and southern China prompted Japan to divert its night air activities from B-29 bases by the end of 1944. As the Japanese shifted their night operations, the 426th and 427th NFS moved their bases eastward to secure better night hunting.

Chapter 6

October 1944: The Formosan Month

I fired at him with both upper turrets and his plane just seemed to stop, and after a second his nose dropped and he went down.

— John Jensen, CFC Gunner (40th BG)

American military forces under Gen. Douglas MacArthur landed on Leyte, in the Philippine Islands, on October 20, 1944, fulfilling the general's promise to return after departing in 1942 prior to their conquest by the Japanese. The United States defeated Japan at the Battle of Leyte Gulf three days later in the largest naval engagement of World War II. In October, President Franklin D. Roosevelt recalled Gen. Joseph Stilwell from China at the insistence of Chiang Kai-shek, who blamed him for the reversals during the Japanese *Ichi-Go* offensive. At the same time, the Allies split the China-Burma-India Theater into two separate theaters: China with American forces under Gen. Albert Wedemeyer and India-Burma with American forces under Gen. Daniel Sultan.

The first B-29s arrived on Saipan in October 1944 under the new XXI Bomber Command (BC) and initiated operations; the Japanese submarine base in the Truk Islands was the first three targets. Plans to establish very heavy bomber bases in the Marianas Islands dated to August 1943, but the idea had been discussed even earlier; the Combined Chiefs of Staff, President Franklin D. Roosevelt, and Prime Minister Winston Churchill approved the plan at the Cairo Conference in December 1943. Initially, they believed capturing the Marianas Islands would be complete by November 1944. At the same meeting, Roosevelt promised Chiang Kai-shek that B-29s would be combat operational in India and China in March 1944. Thus, planning as of December 1943 foresaw B-29 combat operations in the China-Burma-India Theater commencing in March 1944 and from the Marianas by sometime after November 1944, based on the time lag between the actual fall of Saipan in July and the first B-29 combat mission from that island in October. However, delays moving the B-29s to India and beginning combat operations, as well as the acceleration of the American drive in the central Pacific were not foreseen in December 1943. The various acquisition, mechanical, and training issues resulted in a shift to June for the first combat B-29 missions from India and China, while Saipan—the first central Pacific B-29 base—fell to American forces in July. Instead of spreading the start dates for B-29 combat operations between March 1944 from India and China and sometime at the end of 1944 from Saipan (at least nine months), there were only four months between the first combat missions flown from each area.

As early as September, Gen. Hap Arnold began considering moving all B-29 combat operations to the Marianas Islands due to the logistical problems in China. In September, Arnold asked LeMay if he would like to receive additional B-29 reinforcements for XX BC and LeMay declined, noting the logistical system he inherited could barely support the number of B-29s he currently oversaw in the theater.

On October 11, XX BC received official orders to shift combat operations from strategic missions against the Japanese steel and petroleum industries to greater tactical support for the theater commanders, particularly the aircraft industry. The original strategic bombing priorities set the steel industry as the most important target, but

B-29 engine maintenance. (*Bailey via 40th BG*)

B-29 maintenance in Hsinching, China, in the fall of 1944. (Hodgdon via 40th BG)

this shifted as planners elevated strikes against shipping and harbor facilities and the aircraft industry. Some argued successful Allied efforts to sink Japanese merchant vessels and economically choking the home islands made strategic bombing attacks on the steel industry unnecessary. As of October 1944, XX BC flew missions that were more tactically oriented but centered on shipping and the aircraft industry. As a result, XX BC missions primarily turned toward attacking aircraft manufacturing and repair centers, mining harbors and rivers, and bombing naval dry docks. "Training" missions targeted military cantonments and the railroad network. A final decision on the fate of XX BC would arrive early in 1945.

The XX BC flew four combat missions in October, all in support of the American invasion of the Philippines. The primary targets were aircraft assembly and repair facilities on Formosa, off the Chinese coast, and Kyushu in the Japanese home islands.

Mission #10: Formosa, October 14, 1944

Mission #10 directed all four groups to participate in a raid on Formosa with the Okayama Aircraft Repair and Assembly facility as the primary target. Alternate visual targets included the Heito airfield and arsenal as the secondary; shipping targets of opportunity along the coasts of China and Formosa as the tertiary; and Hengyang airfield in China as the target of last resort. The main wharf area of Takao, Formosa, was the alternate radar target in the event of poor visibility over the primary. Okayama was a primary assembly location for Nakajima aircraft trainers, as well as a major repair and modification center for combat aircraft. In addition, aircraft transiting between Japan and the Philippines as well as the Netherlands East Indies stopped there for rest and refueling. A successful raid could impair the manufacturing and repair facilities and destroy or damage aircraft on the ground. Heito served as a major airbase and another staging field for aircraft transiting to the Philippines. The Japanese captured Hengyang airfield—a former American B-25 base—in September 1944. Possession of the field presented Japan a well developed airfield capable of handling bombers in support of their campaigns in China. Takao harbor handled most of the commercial naval traffic for Formosa and provided an assembly point for many of the convoys steaming to Southeast Asia. Reconnaissance photos identified an average of thirty-three vessels in the harbor at any single time during previous weeks. Plans called for the B-29s to carry a mixture of incendiary and general purpose bombs and fly in Gen. LeMay's new twelve-plane formations. Mission #10 and follow-up Missions #11 and #12 supported American operations in preparation for the return to the Philippines and B-29 attacks were carried out in cooperation with strikes by carrier-borne aircraft of the US Navy.[1]

One hundred twenty-three B-29s transited from India to the forward bases in China for Mission #10. Counting aircraft already in China, the strike force consisted of a possible and formidable 132 aircraft (excluding planes designated for photo reconnaissance).

#355 *Bella Bortion* bombed Taichu Airfield while flying Mission #10 to Formosa. The crew are inspecting their survival gear. Note the single 20 mm cannon between the twin 50-caliber machine guns in the tail of the bomber. (*Schutte via 468th BG*)

One hundred thirty of these planes took off for the mission (34 from the 40th BG; 33 from the 444th BG; 29 from the 462nd BG; and 34 from the 468th BG). Photo reconnaissance aircraft (#288 of the 40th BG and #446 of the 468th BG) are included in this total and 104 reached the primary target. One bomber prematurely dropped its load due to a short in the bomb bay doors and the other 103 offloaded 1,035 incendiaries and 1,519 general purpose munitions. The bombers crossed the target in fourteen separate formations ranging from three to seventeen aircraft, causing considerable damage to the target. None of the aircraft bombed the secondary target and five planes hit tertiary targets: the 40th BG's #276 *Black Magic* and #457 *Battlin' Beauty*; #524 Super Mouse of the 444th BG; and the 468th BG's #407 *Lucky Seven* and #365 *General H.H. Arnold Special*. The two 40th BG B-29s

The 444th BG's #524 *Super Mouse* and four other B-29s bombed tertiary targets during Mission #10 to Formosa. The XX BC identified shipping targets of opportunity along the coasts of China and Formosa as tertiary targets for this mission. (*Kelleher via 444th BG*)

During Mission #10 to Formosa, #454 *Totin' To Tokyo* bombed Taichu Airfield with excellent results. Bombs were seen striking hangars and buildings and starting large fires. (*Schutte via 468th BG*)

that struck tertiary targets made late take offs and were not able to join formations. Two planes (#522 *B-Sweet II* of the 40th BG and #386 *Globe Girdle Myrtle* of the 462nd BG) attacked the target of last resort due to mechanical difficulties; results were unobserved due to 10/10 cloud cover forcing them to bomb by radar. Five bombers hit targets of opportunity: the 444th BG's #510 dropped its ordnance on a small city on Nakushu Island with unobserved results, while #355 *Bella Bortion*, #356 *Lassie*, #454 *Totin' To Tokyo*, and #487 *Bengal Lancer* of the 468th BG bombed Taichu Airfield with excellent results. Bombs were seen striking hangars and buildings and starting large fires at Taichu. The remaining aircraft that did not bomb the primary target encountered mechanical issues and returned to forward bases without dropping their bomb loads. The impact of Gen. LeMay's new training and operational procedures can be seen in the post-mission report, with the inclusion of considerably more technical data related to releasing of bombs as well as formation assembly and in-flight conduct.[2]

Two aircraft did not return from the mission due to mechanical problems: the 444th BG lost #280 *Defiant L-assie* early in the mission. Other crews reported seeing #280 *Defiant L-assie* joining a 444th BG formation; the formation flew into an area of overcast and #280 *Defiant L-assie* never emerged. The 40th BG's #513 *Sweater Out* bombed a target of opportunity with one engine inoperable and then disappeared. Later, the pilot, Capt. Charlie Meyer, sent a message through the Chinese military that his crew was safe and "walking out."[3]

The Japanese countered the bombers over the primary target with generally weak and inaccurate anti-aircraft fire, hitting only three of the 104 B-29s. The planes hit by flak were #508 *Ouija Bird* of the 40th BG (propeller #2) and the 444th BG's #399 *The Agitator* (elevator trim tab) and #353 *Big Poison* (left wing and flap). Crews over other targets reported meager and inaccurate anti-aircraft fire. One crew noted the possible utilization of a ground-to-air rocket at Okayama. Barrage balloons were spotted at altitudes as low as 5,000 feet and as high as 24,000 feet. Approximately thirteen Japanese aircraft flew in the

Capt. Charlie Meyer (third from left) and three crew members after returning to A-1 following their bailout over China during Mission #10. The 40th BG's #513 *Sweater Out* bombed a target of opportunity with one engine inoperable before going down. (*Burke via 40th BG*)

The crew of #507 *Bachelor Quarters* jettisoned their bomb load and returned early from Mission #10 due to a loss of manifold pressure in engine #2. (*Harper via 444th BG*)

Japanese flak damaged propeller #2 of #508 *Ouija Bird* during Mission #10 to Formosa. (*40th BG*)

vicinity of the B-29 formations but none attacked, possibly due to the sighting of twelve-plane formations when the Japanese were accustomed to four-plane formations.

Mission #10 destroyed forty-three of the eighty buildings of the Okayama facility, resulting in a very successful raid. The B-29s, along with US Navy carrier aircraft, would return to Okayama two days later and essentially flatten what remained of the plant.[4]

Mission #11: Formosa, October 16, 1944

XX BC continued pressure on Formosa with Mission #11 on October 16, 1944, and Mission #12 the following day. Missions #11 and #12 directed the B-29s to continue pounding Japanese air and naval facilities on Formosa in support of American preparations for a return to the Philippines. The first operation—flown by the 444th BG, 462nd BG, and 468th BG—pitted the bombers against the same targets identified for Mission #10: Okayama was the primary target of the 444th BG and 462nd BG, while the 468th BG received Heito Airfield as its primary. Heito also served as the secondary target for the 444th BG and 462nd BG. The 468th BG marked the Takao port facilities as its secondary target. Hengyang remained the target of last resort for all three groups and planners established Takao as the radar target for all three groups. Rather than attack Hengyang airfield again, crews were ordered to bomb the rail yards in the town itself if forced to hit the target of last resort. As with Mission #10, the B-29s carried a mixture of incendiaries and general purpose munitions.[5]

During Mission #10 #342 *Sister Sue* flew in the eleventh formation to cross the target. (*40th BG*)

Photographic B-29 #288 of the 40th BG followed the main aircraft stream to photograph bombing results during Mission #10 to Formosa. (*Balkinaa via 40th BG*)

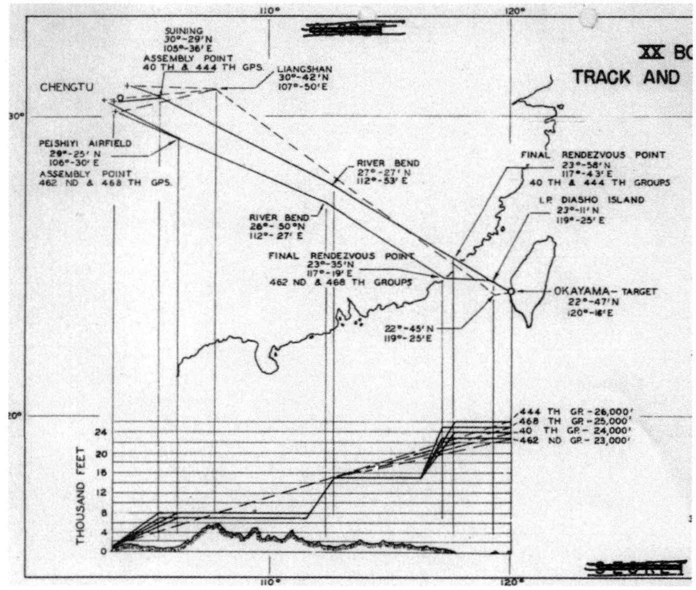

The XX BC utilized this chart to brief pilots and navigators for Mission #11 to Formosa. The chart shows the routes to and from the target as well as prominent navigation locations, assembly points, and rendezvous points. (*US Air Force*)

Col. William Blanchard, commander of the 40th BG, briefing his crews prior to Mission #11. The chart in the background illustrates the expected topographical conditions along the route, including the shape and height of land masses such as islands. (*Schutte via 40th BG*)

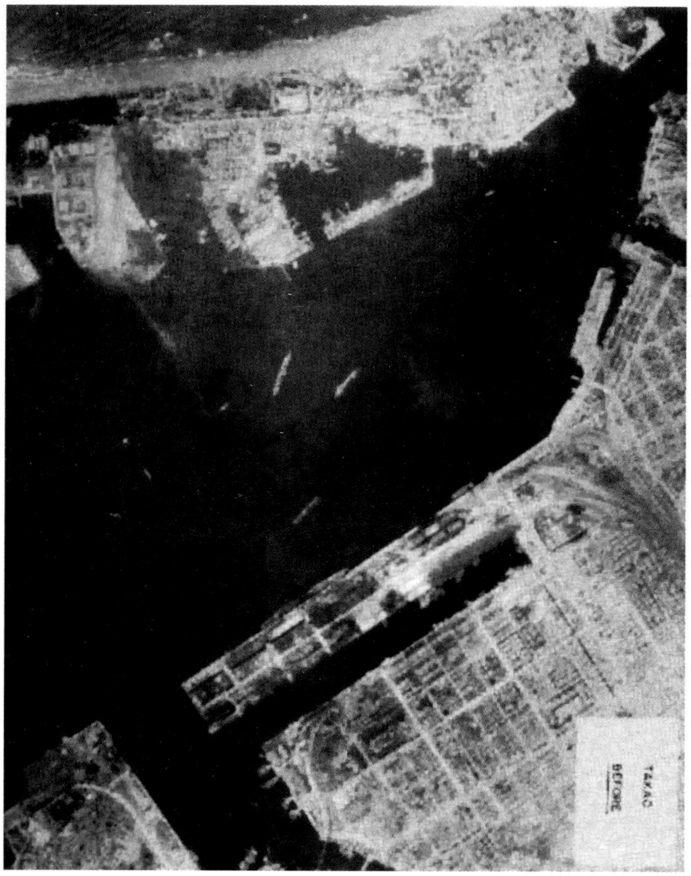

Takao Harbor—the alternate radar target for Mission #11 to Formosa. (*US Air Force*)

The 444th BG's #352 *Fu-Kemal* dropped part of its bomb load on Toshien Harbor with the crew claiming excellent results on Mission #11 to Formosa. (*Miller via 444th BG*)

Crew members with the 468th BG's #390 *Gallopin Goose*, which bombed Amoy Harbor (the secondary target) during Mission #11 to Formosa. (*Schutte via 468th BG*)

Seventy-five bombers launched for Mission #11: 26 flew with the 444th BG, 23 with the 462nd BG, and 23 with the 468th BG. Three additional planes took off late and flew to the target of last resort. Twenty-eight of the forty-nine bombers identified for the primary target bombed Okayama. An additional five B-29s from the 468th BG also bombed Okayama after joining a 462nd BG formation after failing to locate their own planes targeting Heito. Fifteen of the twenty-three 468th BG aircraft bombed that group's primary target, Heito. Ten 444th BG B-29s bombed Heito Airfield after mistaking it for Okayama, for a total of twenty-five aircraft striking Heito; eleven B-29s hit secondary targets. In addition to the ten 444th BG planes bombing Heito, #469 *Blind Date* of the 468th BG dropped ten bombs on Heito and five on the group's secondary target, Takao. Five bombers attacked tertiary targets: the 444th BG's #352 *Fu-Kemal* dropped part of its load on Toshien Harbor and #472 *Sky Chief* bombed Swatow Harbor, claiming excellent results.[6]

B-29 #461 *Haulinas* of the 462nd BG dropped a partial bomb load on Okayama and the remainder of its ordnance on Swatow Harbor. Another 462nd plane (#382 *Big Chief*) dropped its munitions on Sintien harbor and airfield, while #390 *Gallopin Goose* of the 468th BG hit Amoy harbor. Three crews tackled the target of last resort: the 462nd BG B-29s #386 *Globe Girdle Myrtle*, #581, and #362 *Hull's Angels* bombed Hengyang with unobserved results. Four planes, including #382 *Big Chief* over Sintien Airfield, bombed targets of opportunity. The other three were the 444th BG's #307 *Blue Bonnet Belle* (Toshien Airfield) and #204 (an unnamed airfield) and the 462nd BG's #285 *Ours* (Namao Airfield). All three crews reported hitting runways and/or buildings at the airfields.[7]

Crews noted Japanese anti-aircraft fire over Okayama and Heito was meager and inaccurate, with none striking any of the B-29s. The flak over Takao ranged from meager to moderate and from inaccurate to accurate. All of the bombers returned from Takao without anti-aircraft damage. Japanese flak did hit one B-29 over Toshien. Official post-mission records note two bombers returned from Mission #11 with flak damage, but state it was not known where and when each sustained the damage. This is especially interesting since the Japanese anti-aircraft gunners at Toshien are credited with hitting only one bomber and its group is not recorded. The two bombers damaged by flak were the 444th BG's #462 *Princess Eileen II* and #360 *Slow Freight*.

There were approximately fifty-one attacks by Japanese fighters against the B-29s on Mission #11. Three bombers received damage from fighters and gunners claimed three Japanese fighters destroyed, three probably destroyed, and nine damaged. The fighter-damaged bombers were all from the 462nd BG: #456 *The Shrike* (small hole in the fuselage), #329 *Ding Hao* (puncture in the right nose wheel tire and a hole in the nose section), and #311 *Night*

Japanese flak damaged #462 *Princess Eileen II* of the 444th BG during Mission #11 to Formosa. (*Archer via 444th BG*)

The 444th BG's #360 *Slow Freight* returned with flak damage from Mission #11. (*Corradina via 444th BG*)

Mare (damage to the fuselage and lower aft turret). A bullet from the fighter attacking #456 *The Shrike*, flown by Maj. C. Kolander, entered the radar compartment, penetrated the armor plate, and passed into the central fire control compartment, striking the left gunner Tech Sgt. Harry Green.[8] Japanese pilots employed aerial bombs and rockets in their attacks. They proved to be aggressive and pushed their attacks to within 250 yards of the bombers in 40% of the cases. The post-mission analysis recorded one coordinated attack:

> 2 Oscars approached simultaneously, one from 11 o'clock high and the other from 12 high. Both opened fire at 1,000 yards, the Oscar from 11 crossing over to 1 o'clock and then pressing the attack to within 200 yards at which point he was hit by the bombardier and went out at 4 o'clock in flames. This plane is claimed as destroyed. The other Oscar pressed his attack to 100 yards and dived, going out low at 6 o'clock.[9]

At least nine Japanese attacks included the utilization of aerial bombs. The post-mission analysis pays careful attention to two unique aerial bomb attacks:

Two observations were unusual in that the bombs appeared to explode immediately after release. A Tony pulled ahead of the formation, turned, and approached from 12 o'clock. When about 1,500 yards from the formation, the fighter broke into an abrupt dive. Immediately afterward, a large patch of white smoke, with streamers, appeared in the sky at the exact spot where the Tony had begun his dive. In the other instance, a ball of white smoke with streamers suddenly appeared immediately astern of a Tony and seemed to have been ejected from the tail of the fuselage. Tony had been pacing the formation out of range on the right beam.[10]

Two bombers came under aerial rocket attack by Japanese fighters:

> An Oscar approached from 5 o'clock low and was first sighted at 1,200 yards. When about 1,000 yards out, the fighter fired a rocket. The tail gunner saw the projectile for a split second, and described it as having a red tail. It exploded with a red and yellow flash mixed with white smoke and then emitted white streamers. The explosion occurred 100 feet behind, 100 feet below, and 200 yards to the right. The tail gunner opened fire at about the time the projectile was released and the Oscar is claimed as destroyed. Another B-29 reported a Tojo which fired 5 rockets, 3 in one burst and 2 in another. The fighter approached from 2 o'clock high and when 1,000 yards out, was about 1,000 feet above the B-29. The fighter drifted back as he closed the attack, and was 400 yards out and 200 feet above when the first rockets were released. 2 projectiles came from under 1 wing and 1 from under the other wing. Seconds later, 2 additional rockets were released. The trajectory was flat; the trail and ensuing bursts were white.[11]

The 40th BG's #275 *Snafuper Bomber* flew in the eleventh formation over the target during Mission #10. (*Claypool via 40th BG*)

The 40th BG's #344 *Princess Patsy* undergoing an engine change. During Mission #11 to Formosa #344 *Princess Patsy* flew in the first formation over the target. (*40th BG*)

During Mission #11 to Formosa, the 444th BG's #464 *Flying Stud II* jettisoned its bomb load and returned early due to problems with a generator. (*Read via 444th BG*)

Missions #10 and #11, combined with the US Navy carrier aircraft strike, destroyed 74 of 80 buildings and 69 aircraft at Okayama Assembly plant and an additional 16 buildings (of 32) and 47 aircraft at Okayama Airfield. The raids proved to be some of the most successful of the B-29 attacks in the China-Burma-India (CBI) Theater. Intelligence estimates noted it could take Japan four to six months to replace the aircraft production and repair capacity lost at Okayama. The bombers also scored significant hits at Heito, Takao, and Toshien.

Mission #12: Formosa, October 17, 1944

XX BC continued its series of raids on Formosa the next day, with the 40th BG targeting the Einansho Aircraft Depot; the Takao Harbor area was the secondary target and the tertiary and targets of last resort were the same as Mission #11. Einansho Aircraft Depot was one of the largest Japanese airfields on Formosa and included extensive billeting and supply storage areas. Recent photo reconnaissance estimates placed an average sixty-one aircraft at the airfield daily. Destroying or damaging this target could have an important impact on Japanese attempts to marshal air power in the defense of the Philippines, as well as repair damage to planes assigned to that sector.

Inside an airfield control tower in China. The individual on the right is sighting a signal light; the box in front of the man on the left (next to the canteen) is a small telephone switchboard. (*468th BG*)

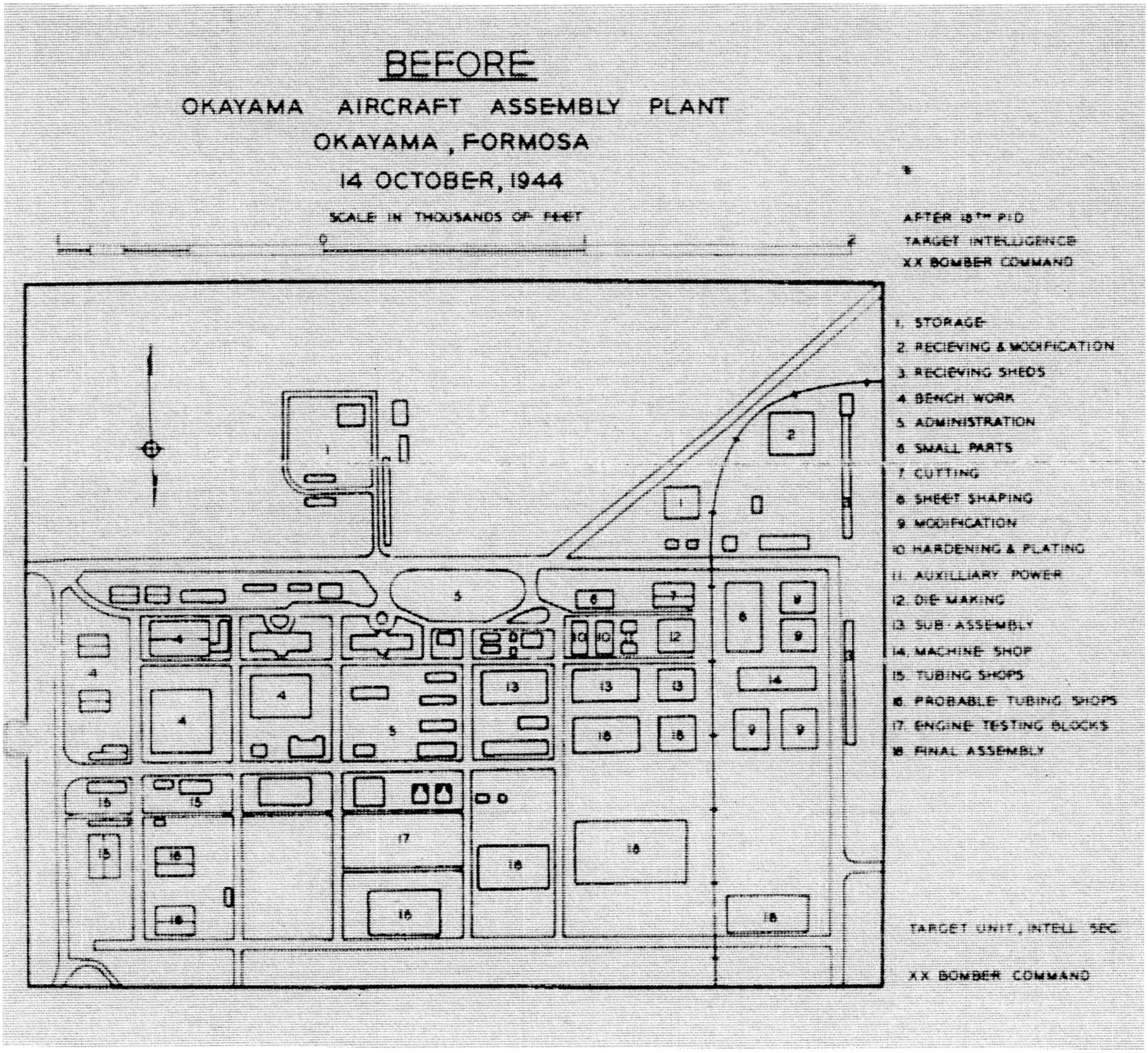

Diagram of the Okayama Aircraft Assembly Plant on Formosa. This plant was the target of Mission #11. (*US Air Force*)

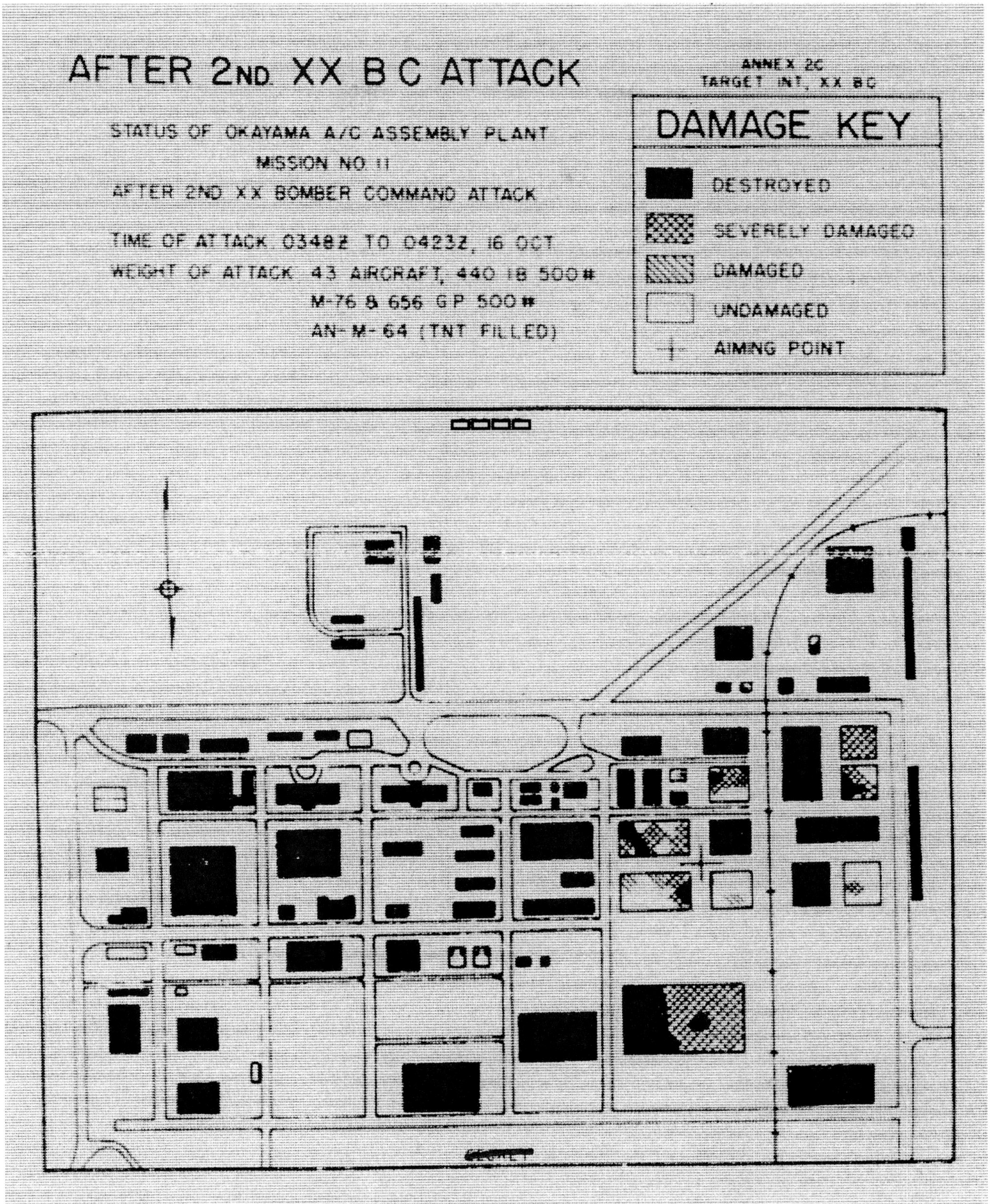

Diagram showing the extent of damage to the buildings of the Okayama Aircraft Assembly Plant on Formosa after Mission #11—the second XX BC attack on the plant. (*US Air Force*)

The 40th BG's #276 *Snafuper Bomber*. The crew in this B-29 flew in the third formation over Takao during Mission #12. (*Changnon via 40th BG*)

The 40th BG's #303 *Typhoon McGoon III* bombed Amoy during Mission #12 to Formosa as a tertiary target due to a fuel transfer problem. (*Bozzuto via 40th BG*)

As on Mission #11, the B-29s carried a mixture of incendiaries and general purpose bombs. Thirty 40th BG B-29s launched from China in support of Mission #12: seven of these planes returned due to mechanical problems. One of these (#303 *Typhoon McGoon III*) bombed Amoy as a tertiary target due to a fuel transfer problem. One aircraft (#342 *Sister Sue*) crashed attempting to safely return. Only ten of the twenty-three B-29s over Einansho actually bombed the primary target due to cloud cover; the other thirteen proceeded to the secondary target and bombed Takao Harbor. Bombing results at Einansho were not included in the post-mission analysis due to lack of visual information caused by cloud cover.[12]

The 40th BG reported meager and inaccurate flak over Einansho and along the flying route and meager and accurate anti-aircraft fire over Takao. Japanese gunners struck four bombers on Mission #12: flak hit #322 *Bonny Lee* near the naval base at Toshien, resulting in a cracked window panel in the nose section and a hole in the horizontal stabilizer. Flak over Takao also found #363 *Marietta Misfit*, placing several holes in the aircraft, including the aft pressurized compartment, left wing, and a wheel nacelle. B-29 #466 *Able Fox* made an emergency landing at an alternate airfield after losing engine #2 to flak and #295 *Monsoon Minnie* returned with unspecified flak damage.[13]

The group encountered enemy fighters at both Einansho and Takao; at each location Japanese pilots attacked the bombers after they dropped their ordnance. Fighters targeted fourteen of the twenty-three B-29s, making twenty-eight attacks on the bombers; 50% of these were directed against the front of the aircraft. B-29 gunners claimed eight fighters destroyed and seven damaged. Crews noted the Japanese pilots seemed more aggressive than on any previous mission, with 75% of the attacks pressed to 250 yards or less. According to the post-mission analysis:

> The enemy made 3 aerial bombing attacks, all employing phosphorus bombs, none of which damaged any of our aircraft. One enemy plane approached from 2 o'clock high and released a bomb when about 1,000 yards above the formation. The bomb exploded 500 feet above and 200 feet to the left. Another fighter approaching from 2 o'clock high released a bomb while in a dive. The bomb exploded wide of its mark, and the Jap continued his dive through the formation, firing with machine guns. The third attack occurred when an Oscar approached high from 7 o'clock. The bomb was released while in a dive 200 yards above the formation, and burst 100 yards to the left and 50 feet above. Again, the enemy plane continued its dive through the formation but in this instance did not open fire with machine guns.[14]

Japanese fighters damaged four B-29s, three of which were also hit by flak: the latter bombers were #295 *Monsoon Minnie*, #466 *Able Fox* (both with unspecified fighter damage), and #363 *Marietta Misfit* (forward bomb bay holed). The fourth plane (#269 *Smokey Stover*) received a bullet puncture in the center pressurized compartment. Edward Hornyai, a replacement gunner, died in the attack on #295 *Monsoon*

The 40th BG's #269 *Smokey Stover* returned from Mission #12 to Formosa with a bullet puncture from a Japanese fighter in the center pressurized compartment.

A Japanese fighter hit the 40th BG's #295 *Monsoon Minnie* with a 20 mm explosive shell during Mission #12 to Formosa. (*Kulicka via 40th BG*)

Minnie piloted by Robert Moss. *Monsoon Minnie* flew in a formation with a lead crew that called for a second run over the target due to misalignment of the first bomb run from the IP. Co-pilot Carter McGregor recalled the flak being "thick and heavy" as the bombardier released the bombs based on the lead plane. McGregor remembered being hit by fighters immediately after "bombs away":

> The best way to spot them [Japanese fighters] at a distance was by their vapor trails, and then when they would get a little closer you could see the leading edges start blinking, and you knew their calling cards were on the way. Suddenly, there was an explosion, and the interior of the plane filled with fog. I didn't know what the noise was, but I knew that we had taken some kind of hit and had depressurized, causing the warm air inside the airplane to vaporize. For a few seconds, the fog was too thick to see anything, but I yelled for everyone to get on a mask at the same time I was grabbing for mine and hooking it to my helmet. We knew from past experience that if the hole in the plane was not too big, we could put something over it—a magazine, a cushion, anything that would cover the space and then the pressure would build back quickly, so I wanted everyone to look for holes. At the same instant, [Ralph] Weinberg [navigator] said, "I'm hit," and Sgt. [Royal] Klaver [radio operator] said, "I'm hit too, but I can't tell how bad." I looked around me to see if we had any holes in the front end, and I just happened to look up, right over my seat, and saw blue sky through a hole about four inches in diameter, just above my head. I turned to see where the shell had hit, and there was a big scar on the armor plate behind my seat, about six inches behind me. Later, we surmised that when the 20 mm shell hit the armor plate, the bullet shattered, and the fragments ricocheted back and hit the navigator and radio operator. I could not believe I was not hit too, but I couldn't feel anything hurting, although there was no way some of that shrapnel could have missed hitting me, somewhere.[15]

Gunner Edward Hornyai died when his blister blew out on the 40th BG's #295 *Monsoon Minnie* during Mission #12. This photo of the XXI BC's #593 *American Maid* shows how this could happen. Sgt. James Krantz dangled for fifteen minutes but survived due to his personally designed safety straps. (*US Air Force*)

One of the lower gun turrets resounded with a steady stream of fire; the command crew called for the gunners to shift to firing bursts rather than burning up ammunition. A reply on the intercom informed Moss and McGregor that the gun could not be halted and explained that Hornyai was gone. Puzzled replies were met with an explanation that the left blister had been blown out in the explosion, sucking Hornyai and his gun sight out of the B-29. The slipstream pinned the gun sight to the aircraft with a depressed trigger. The still-functioning gun sight remained connected to its control cables, which in turn kept firing the guns in the turret. Tail gunner Sgt. Joe Duemig broke into the conversation:

> I saw him go out and watched his chute open, but some of the fighters left us and started making passes at him. I can still see him floating down.[16]

The left gunner assumed control of the gun turret and halted firing. McGregor later reported what happened to Hornyai:

> The gunner did not have his seat belt fastened or he would never have been pulled out of the plane. In his excitement about the fighters, he had unfastened his belt so that he could turn and fire more easily without being hindered...There was never any report on the fate of Sgt. Edward Hornyai; the last any of our crew had seen of him, he was floating down in his chute with the fighters making passes. We did not know whether he opened his chute or whether the force of being sucked out of the plane opened it, but in any event, his chances for survival were nonexistent. We had been about halfway between Formosa and the Chinese mainland over the Yellow Sea when the incident occurred; and although he was wearing a Mae West, to survive the initial attack, the fighter target shooting, and then land in the Yellow Sea would have been a miracle.[17]

Approximately forty minutes after launching, #342 *Sister Sue* approached the airfield with the intention of landing following a loss of engine #4; the crew extinguished the fire but was unable to feather the propeller. The pilot, Ernest Turner, aligned the aircraft to land but aborted the attempt; he then brought the plane around the field for a second landing attempt from a different direction. During this approach the fire ignited again in engine #4. CFC gunner Calvin Brown recorded what happened:

> We were about 20 miles from base when no. 4 started to burn again. The fire suppressant system was used up and we could not put the fire out. Our altitude was about 600 or 700 feet. I never did hear the order to bail out but I got into my chute and everyone in the gunnery compartment was gone. I went to the rear hatch and [Walter] McCarthy [radar operator] sat in the hatch with his chute on. I helped him out with my boot. I sat in the hatch and watched the engine burn. Eventually the wing burned off from the engine and went sailing away. The plane rolled to the right and I jumped. Being at such a low altitude, I pulled the ripcord as soon as I left the hatch. My chute opened in the slipstream and the way the harness was connected to the shroud lines, it hit me in the back of the head and I was out. Just as I hit the ground I came to and went out again...When I came to this time, there were about 8 or 10 Chinamen standing around me, laughing and giggling and pointing at me with no effort to help. After I regained my senses I gathered my chute and started down a trail and ran into Tom Sample [bombardier] and Captain Turner. The plane was down just over the hill from where we were. The ammunition was cooking off from the fire.[18]

Before the crash, Turner ordered the left gunner, Ted Urban, to manually jettison two of the bombs that could not be dropped by the bombardier:

> When Turner decided to abort the mission after the initial #4 engine fire, he was concerned about other B-29's flying behind us as we still were on instruments in overcast. When he turned around and headed back to the airfield and before the fatal fire, he gave the order to salvo the bombs. The bomb bay doors were opened and the bombs were released. Visual verification that the bombs were away showed that two shackles malfunctioned resulting in two 500 lb bombs dangling in the bomb bay each held by only one of two shackle hooks. The fused end of the bombs were facing downward and arming wires were withdrawn allowing the arming process to proceed. Turner ordered me to go into the bomb bay and mechanically release the bombs. He emphasized to take my parachute. I was already in full emergency gear with parachute on and emergency tool kit strapped to my belt. As I approached the entrance to the bomb bay, I saw flames shooting by the right gunner's blister. The right gunner yelled "plane on fire, bail out". I stepped into the bomb bay

> and knowing the doors were open, jumped, counted a quick 10 count and pulled the rip cord. After one or two swings with the open parachute, I landed in a dry field with the only injury being a cut tongue.[19]

Nine men safely bailed out of the aircraft, but two died as the bomber crashed ten miles from the airfield. Brown noted the loss of his fellow crewmen:

> Captain Turner told us that "Popeye" [radio operator Elwyn Gardner] and [Clark] Rauth [flight engineer] went down with the plane. They helped everyone else out and they didn`t have their chutes on. Captain Turner had a broken jaw because his chute just cracked and he hit the ground. "Popeye" had gotten off a mayday message so our base knew we were down.[20]

The 40th BG lost #342 *Sister Sue* shortly after take-off for Mission #12. Nine men managed to safely bail out of the aircraft, but two died as the bomber crashed ten miles from the airfield. (*40th BG*)

Flight engineer Mst. Sgt. Harry Miller aboard #281 *20th Century Unlimited* of the 40th BG. (*Schutte via 40th BG*)

The 468th BG's #494 *Mary Ann* during Mission #12 to Formosa. (*Schutte via 468th BG*)

Crash site of the 40th BG's #288. This photographic B-29 crashed on take-off from China on October 22, 1944. (*US Air Force*)

Another view of the crash site of #288 of the 40th BG. (*US Air Force*)

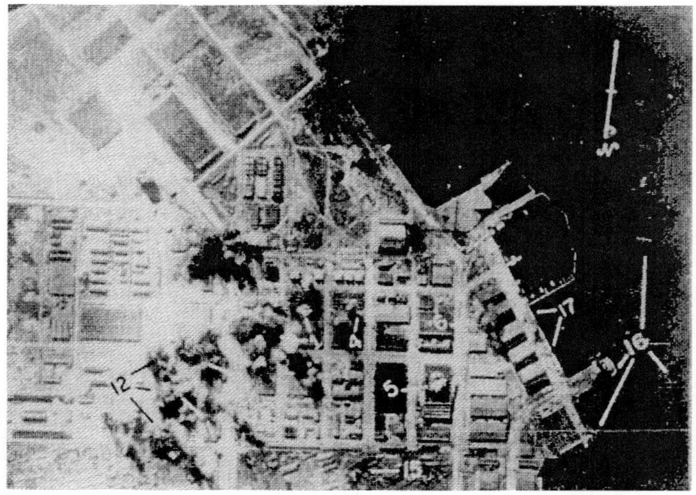

Pre-mission photograph of the Point Island Storage Area in Shanghai, the secondary target of Mission #13. Note the bomb explosions near the number "12." (*US Air Force*)

Mission #13: Omura, October 25, 1944

Two weeks later, after restocking fuel in China, XX BC flew to Omura, Japan, still in support of the American return to the Philippines on October 20. As with the raids against Formosa prior to the landings, XX BC targeted aircraft repair/assembly/transit fields. Any damage or destruction caused by the B-29s at these facilities meant fewer Japanese resources in the Philippines campaign. All four groups identified aircraft for Mission #13, a maximum effort day raid with the Omura Aircraft Assembly Plant as the primary target. The Point Island storage area in Shanghai, China, was the secondary target and the dock area and warehouses of Hankow, China, were the target of last resort. The Omura Plant manufactured Mitsubishi A6M Zeke, Aichi B7A Grace, and Mitsubishi F1M Pete aircraft and repaired Zekes and Aichi E13A Jakes; the plant also made aircraft engines. The secondary target served the Japanese army and navy as a transshipment point away from Chinese populated areas and Allied prisoner of war camps. Vulnerable to incendiaries, destruction or damage could disrupt Japanese operations in China. Destruction of the dock area in Hankow could impede the flow of Japanese military supplies up the Yangtze River in support of Japanese military forces.[21]

Plans called for the 40th BG, 444th BG, and the 462nd BG to carry general purpose and incendiaries and the 468th BG to haul cluster bombs, providing a mixture of ordnance to cause the greatest possible destruction at the Omura Plant. Seventy-nine B-29s launched for Mission #13 (14 with the 40th BG; 26 with the 444th BG; 20 with the 462nd BG; and 18 with the 468th BG). Of the seventy-nine airborne aircraft, fifty-nine reached and bombed Omura. Although smoke obscured most of the strike photos, numerous hits were recorded on buildings in the Omura Plant complex, including two directly on the aiming point building. Two B-29s bombed the secondary target. The 444th BG's #492 *Deacon's Disciples II* developed engine trouble and proceeded to the secondary target, where the crew dropped their munitions by radar through complete cloud cover and without observable results. B-29 #338 *Patches* of the 462nd BG also experienced mechanical difficulties and opted to bomb the secondary through cloud cover. Aircraft #204 of the 444th BG could not locate a formation to join and diverted to the target of last resort. Again, the crew bombed by radar through thick clouds and was not able to observe results.[22]

During Mission #13 to Omura, the 40th BG's #579 *Eddie Allen* found itself alone after the other two bombers in its formation turned around due to mechanical problems, so it diverted to a Japanese airfield on Saishu Island, where the bombardier visually dropped the ordnance. (*Changnon via 40th BG*)

The 444th BG's #422 *Little Mike* bombed three different targets of opportunity in China during Mission #13 to Omura, Japan: two different trains and the Pengpu Marshalling Yards. (*Evans via 444th BG*)

Nine bombers selected targets of opportunity in China. The 40th BG's #579 *Eddie Allen* found itself alone after the other two bombers in its formation turned around due to mechanical problems. Three bombers remained the minimum number for the assembly of a formation; if there were less than three B-29s flying together, orders called for a decision to bomb the nearest target and return to forward bases to reduce vulnerability to Japanese fighters. The pilot of #579 *Eddie Allen* diverted to a Japanese airfield on Saishu Island, where the bombardier visually dropped its ordnance; the crew reported seeing bombs falling among the hangars and other buildings at the airfield. Four 444th BG aircraft bombed targets of opportunity. Aircraft #419 and #507 *Atsall Bro's* bombed a large vessel off the Chinese coast; the vessel commenced evasive maneuvers and avoided being hit by the bombs. Plane #411 *Duchess* dropped its load on a bridge near Pengpu with all of the bombs landing on the end of the structure. B-29 #422 *Little Mike* bombed three different targets of opportunity: the crew dropped five bombs on a long train with good results; three bombs on another train, destroying a coach; and five bombs on the Pengpu Marshalling Yards, with hits on a building and tracks. The crew in #411 *Duchess* witnessed the second bombing by #422 *Little Mike* and reported the coach literally blew apart.

Three 462nd BG B-29s also bombed targets of opportunity: aircraft #456 *The Shrike* offloaded on the Kioshan Railroad Yards with unobserved results; B-29 #461 *Haulinas* bombed petroleum tanks and buildings at Kuchen with poor results (None of the bombs were seen to strike any of the tanks or buildings.); and Plane #213 *Carlalani* bombed the railroad marshalling yards at Laoyao. (Reported results were excellent, with hits in various "choke points" in the yards.) The ninth aircraft—the 468th BG's #272 *Miss Shorty*—bombed the Chinchow bridge with unobserved results. The other aircraft not striking Omura returned due to mechanical problems and did not bomb any targets.[23]

Japanese anti-aircraft fire over Omura was classified as meager to moderate but inaccurate. Crews reported seeing Japanese aircraft, including a biplane, flying parallel with them and probably directing flak. The B-29s also encountered flak near Sasebo and Nagasaki—both previous targets of the bombers—as well as at other areas along the route. Japanese naval vessels in the vicinity of the bomber stream added to the flak. Crews spotted barrage balloons and smoke screens as part of the Japanese defenses.

Japanese fighters attacked forty-three of the B-29s on Mission #13, shooting down one and damaging twelve. B-29 gunners claimed seven fighters destroyed, five probables, and eighteen damaged. The fighter attacks occurred en route to the target, over the target, and on the way back to forward bases, but most of the fighters concentrated on the bombers around Omura and at Saishu Island during the return flight. The first attack came near Nanyang, China, at night. Crews never saw the fighter, but witnessed tracer bullets zipping by them. As in past

During Mission #13 to Omura, Japan, the 468th BG's #272 *Miss Shorty* experienced mechanical problems and bombed the Chinchow Bridge in China as a target of opportunity with unobserved results. (*Schutte via 468th BG*)

engagements, frontal assaults proved the most popular conducted by the aggressive Japanese pilots. There were several coordinated attacks by multiple fighters, including one involving seven Japanese aircraft:

> 7 Tojos entered in trail from 11 and 10 o'clock. The first 4 attacked at 11 o'clock high; the other 3 attempted to follow from the same direction, but drifted back to 10 o'clock. The 4 from 11 opened fire at 750 yards and the 3 from 10 began firing at 1,000 yards; all 7 closed to about 200 yards and broke away in fast vertical dives. Our aircraft opened fire on all planes at 1,000 yards but no damage was done on either side... In a [more] typical 2-plane attack, 2 Tonys entered in trail at 12 o'clock high. The first fighter opened fire at about 800 yards, closed to 400, and broke in a dive. The second Tony fired to 400 yards, pressed the attack to 100, at which point fire from the upper forward turret knocked pieces off the fighter and caused it to burst into flames. The Tony apparently intended to zoom from its dive and go over the B-29, but after being hit, appeared to dive directly at the B-29, missing the wing by only a few feet as it passed underneath. The fighter by this time was in flames from nose to tail, and was completely out of control.[24]

Japanese fighters heavily damaged the 40th BG's #281 *The Heavenly Body*, flown by Capt. Jack Ledford, during Mission #13. Ledford managed to crash-land the B-29 in China. (*40th BG*)

Japanese pilots employed aerial phosphorus bombs in some of the attacks against the B-29s:

> In a typical attack of this kind, a Tony came in from 1 o'clock, dropped 2 small bombs from 150 yards above and 400 yards out, after which he pulled up and to his left. The bombs exploded just off the B-29s wing tips. Almost immediately another Tony followed from 1 o'clock high, firing steadily from 800 to 400 yards. The number 3 engine was hit and the prop had to be feathered. Fighters immediately concentrated on the crippled plane until another B-29 dropped back to lend its assistance.[25]

Bomber crews noted the Japanese pilots attempted a new tactic: they made spirals or corkscrews as they approached the bombers from above. This proved to be useful, because it made tracking by the B-29s' gunners difficult. In turn, one B-29 pilot employed his own new tactic. With fighters continuing to attack from in front and high, the pilot slightly elevated his nose, allowing his bottom turrets to join the defense. This tactic was reportedly successful in deterring some of the Japanese fighters from pressing their attacks too closely. Many of the B-29 gunners complained that rain water and mud had splashed onto their blisters at take-off, obscuring their vision during engagements with fighters.

Japanese fighters shot down #281 *Heavenly Body* of the 40th BG flown by Capt. Jack Ledford, who remembered the incident in which he and the central fire control (CFC) gunner were wounded:

> After bombs away, the formation turned to the right, away from the target. We were under fairly heavy fighter attack at this time since [Thomas] Clark, our CFC gunner was calling out targets and allotting gun control. As we turned right away from our target, our aircraft was hit. As soon as I realized we had been hit, I pulled away from the formation in order to minimize a possible collision. I also yelled at [1st Lieutenant James] DeCoster [co-pilot] to take the controls. The next few minutes were hectic. My legs were paralyzed, and [Master Sgt. Harry] Miller, our flight engineer, was unconscious from a severe head wound. We had cabin explosive decompression, and everyone was busy with oxygen masks and trying to take care of Miller and me. Since we were already out of formation with #3 engine useless, DeCoster and I decided to take our aircraft down and ask other aircraft to drop down with us for cover. A couple did for a short time but they had to climb back up to a higher altitude to save their own fuel. Our #3 engine was windmilling, but we didn't feather it right away so we wouldn't attract any more enemy fighters.[26]

Other crew members added more details to those first critical seconds, including gunner Sgt. Gilbert Rodencal:

> The fact that Ledford had his back pack chute on had helped to prevent more damage. The whole bottom corner of the chute was blown to shreds. Miller was unconscious. [Sgt. D.] McCullough [radio operator] and [1st Lieutenant Howard] Oblender [navigator] had laid him on top of the wheel well hatch. The only visible wounds were three very deep scalp wounds over the right ear where shrapnel had penetrated his skull. He was wearing his flak helmet, and the wounds were away from the explosion. I could not figure how he got hit on his right side.[27]

Navigator 1st Lt. Howard McCullough added:

> Shortly after bombs away, there was a loud "ping" sound, and someone on the intercom said, "We have been hit; put on your oxygen mask." At that moment I looked over at Oblender and noticed that he had pieces of dried prunes all over his face that had come from a box of prunes that was apparently blown away. I asked if he was OK, and he said he was. He pointed to Miller. I leaned over to check on Miller and found him slumped forward with mucus running from his nose. I immediately put a small oxygen tank on and started to get Miller out of his seat and on the floor over the wheel well hatch, but because he was much larger than I, I had some difficulty getting him laid down properly and an oxygen mask put on him. I went back to my position, and Ledford instructed me to contact the lead plane to request two planes be assigned to fly protective formation with us. I'm not sure how long the other planes stayed with us.[28]

Tail gunner Tech Sgt. Jack Halpern:

> I noticed fighters in the area. They were doing "rollover" maneuvers, but they were far out of range of my guns. Soon after bombs away, I saw those same fighters. This time I noticed small flashes of light coming from the underside of their wings. At that moment, the inside cabin pressure of 8,000 feet immediately went to our bombing altitude pressure of 20-22,000 feet. My tail gunner's compartment fogged up. My ears popped like they were going to burst.[29]

The crew members assessed their situation during the short period of time while other B-29s dropped out of formation to help cover them. DeCoster maintained control of the bomber while Rodencal treated Miller and bandaged his wounds; he then turned to assist Ledford. Shrapnel tore a huge hole in the pilot's side and grazed his spinal column, explaining the paralysis in his legs. The damage to the aircraft and the subsequent loss of fuel meant they would not be able to make it back to forward bases in China. The crew considered heading to Russia, but Ledford remarked that would be his last option, due to intelligence briefings on the other crews who had previously diverted to Russia after suffering damage. Ledford refused morphine for his wound and continued to direct emergency planning. Co-pilot DeCoster, still in control of the aircraft, called for Halpern to leave his tail gun position and assist at the flight engineer's panel. Halpern recalled:

> DeCoster called for me to come up and man the flight engineer's position. I could not leave the tail gunner's position right then because a number of enemy fighters were now coming in around the tail. I fired my guns in a scatter fashion to ward off any penetrating attack. I admit firing guns in this matter could be ineffective in downing any enemy aircraft, but it had the effect of dispersing the Jap fighters.[30]

Halpern transferred the remaining fuel from the bomb bay tanks into the wing tanks and called for the bombardier, 2nd Lt. William Gardner, to jettison the former to reduce the weight of the aircraft, but a system failure meant someone would have to hand-release them over the open bomb bay doors. Gardner called out for Halpern:

> After failing to salvo the tanks Gardner told me to go into the bomb bay and salvo them manually. Without my parachute I crawled out into the forward bomb bay. Gardner had already opened the bomb bay doors. The wind turbulence added to the "fright factor" of going out into the bomb bay at 10,000 feet with the doors open. I struggled across the narrow metal structure and pulled the emergency release lever. Down dropped both fuel tanks. The resulting vacuum made me feel like I was being sucked out of the bomb bay. I hung on to a stanchion with all the muscle I could muster. I then crawled back into the cockpit and resumed my seat at the engineer's panel.[31]

As McCullough attempted to make radio contact with an Allied airfield he received several bogus Japanese messages masquerading as friendly posts attempting to persuade the crippled bomber to land. He ignored these, having been warned of such ruses during intelligence briefings. The radio operator finally made contact with a legitimate airfield and transmitted a distress message while the other crew members prepared to bail out. A spare parachute in the aircraft saved Ledford:

> By a stroke of great good fortune, we had a spare chute. Our guys put this chute on me and then used the shroud lines of my damaged chute to make a static line so that we could open Miller's chute after dropping him. By this time DeCoster was down to two engines and nervously encouraging us to get out. The guys dropped Miller and then carried me over to the nose wheel well and dropped me. I was still paralyzed in my legs. As I fell, I delayed opening my chute in order to slow

> down my forward speed and have as gentle an opening shock as possible. I also hoped I could get on the ground before Harry and see where he landed.[32]

Halpern encountered numerous challenges in his bail out:

> I pushed my way through the opened door into the 200 mph slip stream. I held onto my rip cord and, as a result, the wind yanked my right arm, pulling my rip cord and opening my parachute. My right foot caught underneath the rear entrance door jam. I was being bashed against the right side of the fuselage by the wind. My opened chute dragged across the right horizontal stabilizer and elevator. Gardner leaned down and untwisted my right foot, allowing me to fall free of the plane. Luckily, my chute did not become entangled with the stabilizer.[33]

Rodencal experienced his own problems and added to Halpern's story:

> Clark had a little problem with the idea of jumping, but a stiff push helped in a hurry. My first attempt wasn't too good. I stuck my head out, lost my glasses, and got slammed against the door frame. The second time I made it. I could see the plane leaving with puffs of smoke coming from the engines. I am now alone, flat on my back at 10,000 feet, and I open my chute. What a jolt. It was very quiet, just the swish of air from the chute. Sounds from very far away could be heard. I heard Halpern hollering way up the valley that he is in a thermal and going up. First to jump, last to get down.[34]

Capt. Jack Ledford and his crew with Chinese military and civilian personnel after their rescue. Japanese fighters shot down the 40th BG's #281 *The Heavenly Body* during Mission #13 to Omura. (*Gardner via 40th BG*)

Left gunner Staff Sgt. Russell Elwell noted:

> The crew in the back of the plane bailed out a little sooner than the crew in front; thus, when they got on the ground the two segments of the crew were separated by a mountain. I remember Clark stepping into the door opening and having the slip stream pin the door between his body and backpack chute and not allowing him to jump or move back. Since I was behind him, and anxious to jump, I gave him a push and then dove out myself. As I rolled face up and saw the tail assembly pass over, I pulled the rip cord. Still in the slip stream, the chute opened with a hard impact, straps slamming against the back of my head. I believe I was knocked unconscious, because there was a period of time I don't remember. I also had cuts on my neck and head. The next moment I remember floating down not far from Clark and trying to make conversation but not saying much.[35]

Miller died a few minutes after landing; a Norwegian missionary took care of his body and buried him the next day. After numerous adventures the other crew members returned to forward Chinese bases.

The next day, the 40th BG dispatched #582 *Little Clambert*, piloted by Maj. John Eigenmann, for a post-mission photographic reconnaissance of Omura. The photographic mission evolved into a running gun battle with Japanese fighters.

CFC gunner John Jensen prepared a brief summary of the air battle after the war that is a classic review of how the centralized fire control system worked on a B-29. Other bombers, including the Boeing B-17 Flying Fortress and the Consolidated B-24 Liberator, carried machine guns that were either manually operated or electronically fired (for example, the chin guns on the B-17 G) by one person. The B-29's central fire control system permitted different individuals to assume control and fire the weapons; thus, whoever had the best visual angle of a fighter could assume control of a gun turret. The early "A" and late "B" models of P-61 Black Widows carried an upper machine gun turret that operated with the same system utilized on B-29s. Any crew member on those aircraft (pilot, gunner, or radar operator) could assume control of the turret. In fact, the late "A" and early "B" models did not carry a machine gun turret because B-29 production took priority and there were not enough turrets available for installation on both aircraft. Jensen recorded:

> Just as we turned north, Bell reported 9 fighters coming up through the clouds behind us, and while they were climbing up to get in front of us, he reported 7 more coming up. As we approached the new target, the first 9 were in position to attack. [Owen] Donahue [bombardier] and I coordinated the use of the upper forward turret so we could use it to the maximum. The first group came at us singly and in pairs so we each used it at different times. The first pass was a single and he came in at 12 o'clock level. Donahue took both forward turrets, and the fighter made the mistake of climbing so Donahue could get both turrets on him. He was smoking as he passed just over our right wing—so close, in fact, Eigenmann said he could almost read his dog tags. This was very likely the one damaged plane which Donahue got credit for. On the next pass two came in, one high and one low. Donahue took the lower turret and I the upper turret. The one that came in high rolled over and started into us just as I fired both upper turrets. He never made it all the way around before his nose dipped down and he went into a dive, straight down. In the meantime, Donahue had gotten his fighter, as confirmed by [William] Douglas [left gunner]. As this was happening one of the second group attempted a tail attack, and Cliff Bell shot him down. Another one came in on us from 12 o'clock high, and as he rolled over and started his attack, I fired at him with both upper turrets and his plane just seemed to stop, and after a second his nose dropped and he went down...At this time, or just shortly afterward, three came in from one o'clock level, and here is where Eigenmann's ability came to the fore. He either turned right or left, went up or down, and adjusted the speed either faster or slower to either throw off the timing of the attack or to bring into play the upper turrets' fire power. Donahue fired at all three and hit every one hard as we saw smoke streaming from all of them. We are certain that he got all three. However, the powers that be credited him with two shot down and one damaged. Right after this, one came at us from 10 o'clock high, and I shot him down. When he passed over us, he was so close that he hit our radio antenna and snapped it off. If my memory is right, this was all of the first 16 to come up, and the rest were far less aggressive in their attacks than they had been. With some time to think now, I became concerned about our ammo supply, primarily in the upper and lower forward turrets, so we decided that Donahue and I would just fire at the fighters that posed a threat to us. We all felt that if we had more ammo we could have gotten some more of their fighters. Later, when I did check the ammo supply, the upper turrets were almost out, and the lower forward had no more than 100 or 200 rounds left.[36]

The attacks continued later over the South China Sea:

> Up to this time [David] Lagoy [right gunner] and Douglas really had not had many chances to shoot at anything, but the change in tactics now gave them several good chances. Lagoy reported that one was coming up from six o'clock low and he had him in his sights. I remember thinking after a while, "My God, why doesn't he shoot?" However, when he felt he had him in range, he fired at him and down he went smoking badly. Douglas got his about this time, and I remember the fighter just nosed over and went down. Lagoy shot at one of the last ones to come up and hit it really hard as we saw him going down smoking very badly.[37]

The pilot and his crew returned safely, receiving credit for nine fighters destroyed and two damaged. Eigenmann received the Silver Star in December 1944 for his actions during the October mission. The citation records the multiple fighter attacks and states, "Maj. Eigenmann displayed cool courage in piloting his aircraft during these attacks and successfully accomplished his missions without loss of a crew member or damage to the airplane."[38] The other crew members received either the Distinguished Flying Cross or the Air Medal for their achievements during the mission.

The 40th BG's #404 in China. (*40th BG*)

Chapter 7

November 1944: Missions in Support of Tactical Operations in Burma and the Philippines

It seemed that out of nowhere, about 10 or 12 Chinese guerrilla soldiers appeared in the ditch beside us, started shooting back at the Jap patrol with three or four of them making motions for us to run down the ditch with them.

—Staff Sgt. Dwight Collins (40th BG)

The Allied campaigns on the island of Leyte and in Burma continued in November 1944. The United States announced it had finally secured the island of Peleliu on November 27 after a long, bloody engagement. In China, the Japanese *Ichi-Go* offensive threatened the city of Kunming and its largest airfield.

A major milestone in B-29 history occurred in November, when Superfortresses with XXI Bomber Command (BC), based in the Marianas islands, bombed the Japanese capital Tokyo—the first aerial bombing of Tokyo since the Doolittle Raid, with aircraft carrier-launched North American B-25 Mitchell medium bombers in 1942. XXI BC B-29s returned twice to bomb Tokyo and other areas on the island of Honshu before the end of the month. While the XXI BC hit targets on Honshu, the XX BC under Gen. Curtis LeMay conducted five tactical support missions during November: two of these missions provided support for Gen. Douglas MacArthur's campaign in the Philippines; two can be attributed to assistance operations for the Allied operations in Burma; and the fifth can be seen as beneficial to both Allied campaigns. The missions flown to assist MacArthur targeted Japanese aircraft assembly and repair facilities on Formosa; those benefiting Allied forces in Burma hit targets related to the railroad transportation network in Burma and Thailand; and the fifth mission struck the Japanese naval repair docks in Singapore. Although the strikes against the Japanese railroad network in Burma and Thailand assisted Allied efforts in Burma, the XX BC viewed them as training missions, since the crews continued to learn and perfect the new operational techniques introduced by Gen. LeMay in mid-September. The missions flown against the aircraft plants on Formosa and the docks in Singapore supported October 1944's revised strategic bombing priorities emphasizing shipping and the aircraft industry.

XXI BC B-29s were now bombing Tokyo and other targets on the island of Honshu while XX BC bombers were still logistically hard pressed to hit targets on the southwestern edge of Kyushu Island. Gen. LeMay and his XX BC staff could see the handwriting on the wall and initiated the planning process for ceasing operations through China.

Mission #14: Rangoon, November 3, 1944

Gen. Curtis LeMay originally planned a training mission for October 4, 1944; the XX BC would fly a mission from India against a target in Southeast Asia to hone its new formation and lead crew techniques under combat conditions not as intense as a mission to Japan or Manchuria. However, the directive to support Gen. MacArthur's upcoming return to the Philippines by hitting Japanese aircraft assembly and repair facilities on Formosa forced the scrubbing of a local training mission. Throughout October, B-29 crews continued developing their new skills with longer and more intense operations to Formosa and Kyushu in support of the American invasion of the Philippines that same month.

Gen. Curtis LeMay (back to camera) presenting awards to 40th BG personnel in November 1944. (*Taylor via 40th BG*)

A view of #298 *Katie* after she ground looped while attempting to take off from Hsingchin, China, on November 3, 1944. (*US Air Force*)

Tires on #298 *Katie* of the 40th BG blew while attempting to take off from Hsingchin, China, on November 3, 1944. The B-29 was considered "totaled" and did not fly again. (*Franks via 40th BG*)

At the opening of November, LeMay could finally dispatch his bombers on a "training" mission to hone formation flying, radar, and bombing techniques under a less intense combat environment. Planners selected Burma for the training mission to preserve fuel supply stockpiles in China, support tactical military operations in Burma as long demanded by the theater commander, and hit a target where anti-aircraft defenses would be lighter. Mission documents identified the Malagon Railroad Yards in Rangoon as the primary target and the Taungup Military Storage Area as the target of last resort. Malagon served the Japanese as the primary rail yard in Rangoon. Military supplies and troops passed through Rangoon from Thailand and Burmese ports in support of operations in Burma. At any one time, up to 300 rail cars and five locomotives could be in the rail yard. Malagon also performed limited maintenance on locomotives following the Japanese loss of the Insein Repair Shops to Allied air attacks. The Taungup storage facility was one of the largest Japanese military storage areas in western Burma at this time. Destruction of either location could hamper Japanese military operations in Burma.[1]

LeMay's plan called for B-29s to assemble in three-plane elements over their bases and then join to form twelve-plane formations, permitting the bombers to practice assembling and flying as formations to the targets. In other raids utilizing LeMay's twelve-plane formations, the aircraft assembled prior to reaching the target area and did not fly the entire mission together. Plans designated each group provide twelve aircraft for the mission. The

Another view of the 40th BG's #298 *Katie* at Hsingchin, China, on November 3, 1944. (*US Air Force*)

Crew of the 40th BG's #579 *Eddie Allen* pull props prior to Mission #14 to Rangoon. (*Changnon via 40th BG*)

The primary target of Mission #14 to Rangoon, Burma. The Malagon Railroad Yards served the Japanese as the primary rail yard in Rangoon. Military supplies and troops passed through Rangoon from Thailand and Burmese ports in support of operations in Burma. (*US Air Force*)

The 40th BG's #407 *Shoot You're Faded* could not drop nine of its bombs due to a rack failure during Mission #14 to Rangoon. The pilot diverted to the target of last resort (the Taungup Military Storage Area) on the return flight. (*Conley via 40th BG*)

40th BG B-29s dropping their ordnance during a 1944 mission launched from India. (*Changnon via 40th BG*)

Shell casings fired by B-29 gunners fell and struck #574 *293* of the 40th BG during Mission #14 to Rangoon, Burma, scarring the Plexiglass on the nose of the aircraft. (*40th BG*)

B-29s carried general purpose bombs for maximum destruction of tracks, rail cars, and buildings. Each Group placed twelve bombers into the air except the 40th BG, which launched thirteen planes without explanation for the odd plane; it could have been for photographic reconnaissance but was not listed under that mission. Of the forty-nine Superfortresses, forty-four reached and bombed the primary target. Three aircraft experienced rack failures and dropped only partial bomb loads—a problem seen on nearly every mission. The primary target sustained considerable damage; photographs confirmed the destruction of the round house and all but one building around it, the damage or destruction of seventy-four pieces of rolling stock and four locomotives, and the destruction of the main rail line and spur lines in multiple locations. Two of the aircraft bombed the target of last resort: the 40th BG's #407 *Shoot You're Faded* could not drop nine of its bombs due to a rack failure. The pilot diverted to the target of last resort on the return flight and managed to drop them, although he needed two runs to offload the munitions. Results were not observed. Aircraft #202 *Satan's Angel* of the 444th BG bombed the target of last resort after developing mechanical problems en route to the target area. The crew reported seeing hits in an area that contained small sheds.[2]

Japanese flak over Rangoon proved to be surprisingly accurate, with fourteen B-29s returning with damage. Crews spotted aircraft obviously flying as anti-aircraft spotters parallel to their formations. Any combination of chance, gunner skill, accurate spotting, and/or large twelve-plane formations moving as one big target could have accounted for the high percentage of flak hits. Thirteen of the fourteen bombers received minor damage. The one aircraft with significant flak damage (#279 *Postville Express* of the 468th BG) landed with a gash in a propeller and holes in the right wing. The crews over the target of last resort reported meager and inaccurate flak; twelve of the forty-nine bombers on the mission were attacked by Japanese fighters. All of the attacks occurred in the primary target area. B-29 gunners claimed to have damaged two fighters and all of the bombers returned without being hit by fighters.[3]

Three B-29s were damaged by other bombers during Mission #14; shell casings fired by B-29 gunners struck #574 *293* of the 40th BG and scarred the Plexiglass on the nose of the aircraft. Shell casings also fell on another 40th BG aircraft (#394 *Last Resort*), breaking the bombardier's Plexiglass and placing a hole in the leading edge of the left wing. Meanwhile, a gun on #444 *Humpin' Honey* of the 462nd BG shot rounds into its own forward bomb bay door.[4]

The 444th BG lost #518 en route to the target; a search by all available assets commenced after the mission and a B-24 Liberator bomber flown by the 40th BG spotted the ditched B-29. The incident is recorded in the post-mission intelligence analysis:

> The first indication of trouble came when two undecipherable calls from the tail gunner [Sigmund Kohn] were heard on the inter-phone. It was afterward determined that he had evidently screamed, "Fire in the tail gunner's position" but for one of two reasons the message was garbled; since the radar operator had already experienced trouble with the inter-phone that may have caused the distortion of the message or it may have been the result of the shouting of the tail gunner. As soon as the plane was depressurized the radar operator went back to see what the difficulty was. He stated that the gunner's door was open about two inches, flames could be seen and the density of the smoke made it impossible to tell whether or not the tail gunner was still in the compartment. Later observations showed the compartment completely gutted and that the fire had burned through the fuselage. The tail gunner is still unaccounted for. No chutes were reported by other planes of the formation. The plane was at 15,000 feet when the pilot decided to ditch. The fire and smoke prevented some members from taking their conventional ditching position. However, a successful ditching was made...and the only injury was a possible cracked vertebra suffered by the right gunner. Two life rafts were successfully inflated, and additional supplies were dropped to the crew. The survivors were rescued by a 72-foot motor launch of the Royal Indian Navy. The crew spent about 36 hours in the rafts and were in good condition with the exception of the injured right gunner. It is believed that the tail gunner was severely burned and jumped prior to the ditching.[5]

The post-mission analysis noted the training apparently went well; all of the aircraft except one assembled into their assigned twelve-plane formations and bombed the target together. The one exception joined another formation.

The 40th BG's #579 *Eddie Allen* during Mission #14 to Rangoon. (*Changnon via 40th BG*)

Pilot Capt. Jack Ledford (left) chats with bombardier 2nd Lt. William Gardner (with cigar) aboard #281 *20th Century Unlimited* of the 40th BG. (*Schutte via 40th BG*)

Mission #15: Singapore, November 5, 1944

The XX BC flew its first mission to Singapore on November 5, 1944. Over the next few months, the command would return to Singapore many times and pilots considered it a tough and well-defended target. The British surrendered Singapore to the Japanese on February 15, 1942. In the process, the Japanese received British naval facilities, including the King George VI graving dry dock and the Admiralty IX floating dry dock. The former lay as a permanent fixture to the wharf, while the latter actually floated in a manner similar to a pontoon boat. Each could be flooded to allow a vessel to enter for repairs. Upon securing the vessel, the water in both docks would be pumped out, permitting crews to conduct work on the hull in a dry environment. Singapore served as the main Japanese repair facility for large vessels outside the home islands, with the King George VI dry dock at Singapore being one of the world's largest repair facilities and capable of handling multiple ships, including the largest Japanese naval vessels. Destruction of the dry docks at Singapore could seriously hamper Japanese efforts to repair damage to military vessels and delay their return to service against the Americans in the Philippines.[6]

Each B-29 group identified aircraft to participate in the raid targeting the dry dock at the Singapore Naval Base. The Fourth Senoko Oil Depot at the Singapore Naval Base was the primary radar target in the event poor visibility prevented bombardiers from spotting the dry dock. The secondary target was the Pangkalanbrandan Oil Refinery on Sumatra, with a military storage area at Taungup, Burma, as the target of last resort. The Fourth Senoko Oil Depot consisted of thirty-nine oil tanks and two pumping stations. The Pangkalan Brandan Oil Refinery produced 19% of Japan's fuel oil and a successful bombing could seriously impact the Japanese military's access to it. The target of last resort was one of the main Japanese military storage locations in western Burma.[6]

Planners laid out the mission as a daylight raid with 1,000-pound general purpose bombs due to the steel and reinforced concrete construction of the primary target. A later decision called for adding 500-pound general purpose bombs to some of the aircraft loads. With the mission to Singapore following closely on the heels of the Rangoon operations, each group was requested to dispatch a minimum of fifteen aircraft on the raid. The command conducted a change to the new policy on formation flying; plans called for aircraft to establish formations of three planes within one flight circle above the assembly point. At that time, any planes not able to join a formation were ordered to proceed to the primary target and not the target of last resort as on previous missions. The XX BC launched a total of seventy-six B-29s for Mission #15 (17 from the 40th BG; 19 from the 444th BG; 20 from the 462nd BG; and 20 from the 468th BG). Twenty-three of the aircraft did not bomb the primary target: seven bombed the secondary; three bombed the target of last resort; one bombed a target of opportunity; ten returned for various mechanical issues; and two crashed. Seventeen B-29s bombed Singapore individually and the others attacked in formations ranging from two to eight bombers, indicating problems attempting to follow formation assembly plans. Cloud cover proved to be mixed over the target, necessitating only one plane to bomb by radar. Smoke and fire at the target helped to obscure it from later planes crossing the area.

Seven aircraft bombed the secondary target; weather over the Pangkalanbrandan Oil Refinery proved excellent for bombing, with clear skies and unrestricted visibility. Crews declared good results, with bomb hits ranging from the aiming point itself. Aircraft over the secondary target were the 40th BG's #508 *Ouija Bird*; the 444th BG's #524 *Super Mouse*, #580 *Flyin' Jackass* , and #267 *Winnie*; and the 468th BG's #365 *General H.H. Arnold Special*, #429 *Blind Date*, and #284 *The Challenger*. Three bombers (#394 *Last Resort* of the 40th BG, along with the 462nd BG's #830 *Torrid Toby* and #329 *Ding Hao*) diverted to the target of last resort. All bombing results were unobserved. The 40th BG's #582 *Little Clambert* bombed a Japanese air field as a target of opportunity; bombs were seen to strike up to 1,000 feet from the target due to a malfunction of the bomb release system.[8]

Anti-aircraft fire over Singapore ranged from meager to moderate and inaccurate to accurate; at least one Japanese cruiser and one destroyer joined the ground units defending the target. The Nachi class cruiser steamed from the area to avoid being a target as it engaged the bombers and the Takamami class destroyer lay in a nearby dry dock, undergoing repairs at the time of the attack. Post-mission analysis indicated the B-29 crews offered considerable respect to the skill of the naval gunners and noted anti-aircraft accuracy noticeably decreased when the cruiser departed the area. In fact, post-mission statistics presented a quantitative decrease in flak accuracy after the sailing of the cruiser:

> One aircraft reported that "ground fire seemed low whereas naval fire was in heavy concentrations quickly climbing to altitude in cone shaped clusters. Thirty to fifty bursts were seen in the air at one time and the bursts could be heard"...It was also stated that "two crews of damaged aircraft thought the naval vessels to be using barrage type of fire with as many as 150 bursts reported covering an air volume approximately 5,000 feet in diameter."[9]

The small light-colored circles on the tail of the 444th BG's #251 *Old Battler* are patches covering holes made by Japanese flak. (*Kenney via 444th BG*)

Seven B-29s sustained flak damage; none of the B-29s passing the target after the departure of the cruiser were damaged. Flak over the secondary target also ranged from meager to moderate and inaccurate to accurate. One aircraft (#429 *Blind Date* of the 468th BG) received anti-aircraft damage while bombing the oil refinery. B-29 crews bombing the target of last resort in Burma did not encounter any anti-aircraft fire. Two aircraft spotted anti-aircraft balloons over Singapore.

Aircraft #444 *Humpin' Honey* of the 462nd BG crashed approximately thirty minutes after take-off. Ten minutes after lifting from his Indian air base the pilot, Capt. Simpson, lost engine #3 at 2,500 feet and turned the B-29 to return as he began to rapidly lose altitude. The bombardier salvoed the bomb load and the pilot ordered the crew to bail out. The bomber crashed between twenty and twenty-five miles from its base and all of the crew members survived except the radio operator, whose parachute did not open.[10]

B-29 #370 *Lethal Lady*, flown by Lt. Ike Eigler with a crew that included 468th BG commander Col. Ted Faulkner, the group staff navigator, and the group staff bombardier ditched en route to Singapore. The 40th BG's #582 *Little Clambert* reported seeing another B-29 burst into flames; this aircraft is presumed to have been #370 *Lethal Lady*. The pilot of #582 *Little Clambert* diverted toward this location and the crew claimed they spotted a "white light"

Loading bombs bound for a B-29 onto a trailer. (*US Air Force*)

that might have come from a life raft. The radio operator aboard #582 *Little Clambert* signaled a submarine posted in the area for a crew rescue, but neither the plane nor its crew were ever found.

Several aircraft experienced fuel shortages due to the long mission and landed at either China Bay on Ceylon (from where the wing launched Mission #5 to the oil refinery at Palembang) or Cox's Bazar. Each aircraft refueled and returned to its Indian base the same or next day.

Reconnaissance photographs returned by a 468th BG B-29 on November 8 showed a breach in a sliding caisson gate with water in the King George VI dry dock; damage to a 465-foot freighter in the dry dock; and several support buildings destroyed or damaged. Intelligence estimates rated the damage extensive enough to require up to three months for repairs and depriving the Japanese of 50% of their dry dock capabilities south of Japan.[11]

Mission #16: Omura, November 11, 1944

All four groups returned six days later on Mission #16 to Omura, Japan, in continued support of Gen. MacArthur's campaign in the Philippines. The Omura Aircraft Plant was the primary target for the daylight operation, with the Sasebo Aircraft Factory the secondary. The field order identified the Point Island Storage Area in Shanghai, China, as the secondary target for bombers facing mechanical issues and not able to reach Japan. The wharf area of Nanking, China, was the target of last resort. The Omura Aircraft Plant built Mitsubishi F1M Pete observation and Aichi B7A Grace carrier attack aircraft. The Grace served the Japanese Navy as a newly introduced carrier-borne aircraft and destruction of its assembly area could delay its incorporation into Japanese forward defenses. The Omura Plant also repaired Mitsubishi A6M Zeke fighter and Aichi 13A Jake observation aircraft. The Sasebo Aircraft Factory assembled Pete aircraft and produced engine assembly mounts. The Point Island Storage Area in Shanghai was a large storage and trans-shipment facility for the Japanese Army and Navy. It lay over three miles from populated areas, making it an ideal target for incendiary bombing with slight chance for collateral damage to non-combatants. The Japanese utilized Nanking as a major barracks, storage, and trans-shipment location for its forces in China. Destruction of the supplies along the wharf area could hamper Japanese operations against Chinese forces.[12]

This mission to Omura was actually part of a "double strike" plan that began with Mission #13, targeting Omura at the end of October. Originally, the second strike should have occurred two days after the first, but it had to be delayed due to insufficient fuel stocks in China. Hauling the fuel across the Hump remained a slow process and the XX BC dispatched more B-29s on the October Formosa raids than previously planned. More aircraft on the Formosa missions meant greater demand for the fuel supplies stockpiled in China. The B-29s on Mission #16 carried a mix of incendiary and 500-pound general purpose munitions. The Command launched ninety-six aircraft to Omura (25 from the 40th BG; 28 from the 444th BG; 16 from the 462nd BG; and 27 from the 468th BG). Less than one-third (twenty-nine aircraft) bombed the primary target and only one dropped its load visually due to cloud cover. Photographic reconnaissance on November 17 revealed no new damage at the Omura Aircraft Plant since the October raid. Several barracks and other buildings were destroyed or damaged. None of the aircraft bombed the secondary target at Sasebo, but twelve dropped their ordnance on the secondary at Shanghai; results were not reported. Twenty-four B-29s bombed the target of last resort in Nanking. A photographic reconnaissance mission on November 16 indicated a warehouse and a few buildings near a railroad terminal were destroyed or damaged and a small vessel in the river showed apparent damage. Fifteen planes dropped their munitions on targets of opportunity, with three of these B-29s also offloading their bombs on both an assigned and target of opportunity. The most common targets of opportunity were airfields, bridges, and shipping.[13]

The 40th BG's #331 *Gone With The Wind* bombed the target of last resort (the wharf area in Nanking, China) during Mission #16 to Omura, Japan, then landed at Kwanghan due to low fuel on the return leg of the operation. (*Hilyard via 40th BG*)

Deteriorating weather conditions was the factor for so many aircraft not proceeding to Omura. Many pilots made individual command decisions to divert from Omura to another target and many others were contacted and directed to change course. Tom Carroll, the 40th BG weather officer, remembered the mission after the war:

> [Weather] forecasts were based on maps which were 12 to 24 hours old and on which the reports were scanty. From the latest maps available, we determined that the weather would be suitable for this mission to Kyushu. I had just finished briefing the crews when I received a phone call from the weather office saying that some reports had just come in indicating a disturbance northeast of Formosa. I asked if they had notified the Command Weather Officer and was told that he had been notified by telephone, but considered the reports of no significance to the operation. I decided to investigate the weather reports for myself, so I went to the Weather Office where the reports had already been entered on a map. After an analysis of the data, I concluded that a typhoon of moderate intensity was centered northeast of Formosa, that it was moving north-northeast in the direction of Kyushu and would be affecting that area by target time. Kyushu would be covered by several layers of clouds, and visual bombing would be impossible. Meanwhile, there was the fact to consider that the reports upon which this decision was based were so scanty that there was reasonable doubt as to the existence of the typhoon at all and considerable more doubt as to the position, intensity and movement. In view of the scanty data on which the forecast was based, I knew that there was a strong possibility that Kyushu might not be affected by the typhoon, in which case it would remain clear. Worse yet, Nanking would be overcast. If Kyushu were clear and Nanking cloudy, and I gave the commanders a forecast contrariwise, the entire effort of hauling gas, bombs and other supplies over the Hump to China and the risks of the men who were flying the mission would be wasted. Nevertheless, my decision was that Kyushu would be obscured by cloud and that Nanking would be clear. I started for the control tower to tell [Group Commander] Col. Blanchard of this situation. By the time I arrived, the last plane was lining up for takeoff. I explained the meteorological situation to the colonel. He told me to repeat the story to the Gen. LeMay was also in the control tower. LeMay was furious when I gave him the disturbing news about the typhoon. He did not immediately change the plan. He calculated how much time he would have before he had to radio the crews to change targets and asked me to stay close to the situation in the interim and come back in about three or four hours to see if there was any change. I thought this was a shrewd decision. At that time I woke up the Bomber Command weather officer and got him back on the job, too. As can be imagined, he was somewhat displeased, but in the face of the evidence, he had to go along with my forecast.[14]

Gen. LeMay altered the target based on weather conditions; the 40th BG sent messages to its aircraft mandating a change in target from Omura to Nanking. Many reported receiving it, while other pilots diverted on their own command decision. Some command aircraft did not receive any messages and as a result continued to Omura, where one-third of the force dropped its bomb load by radar and, in two cases, dead reckoning of position by the navigators.

Crews noted flak over Omura to be meager, ranging from inaccurate to accurate. Anti-aircraft fire did not damage any of the planes bombing the aircraft plant, although two B-29s were rocked by close blasts. Japanese gunners must have utilized radar directed firing to locate the bombers through the cloud cover. The bombers also encountered flak from sites near Nagasaki. The B-29s

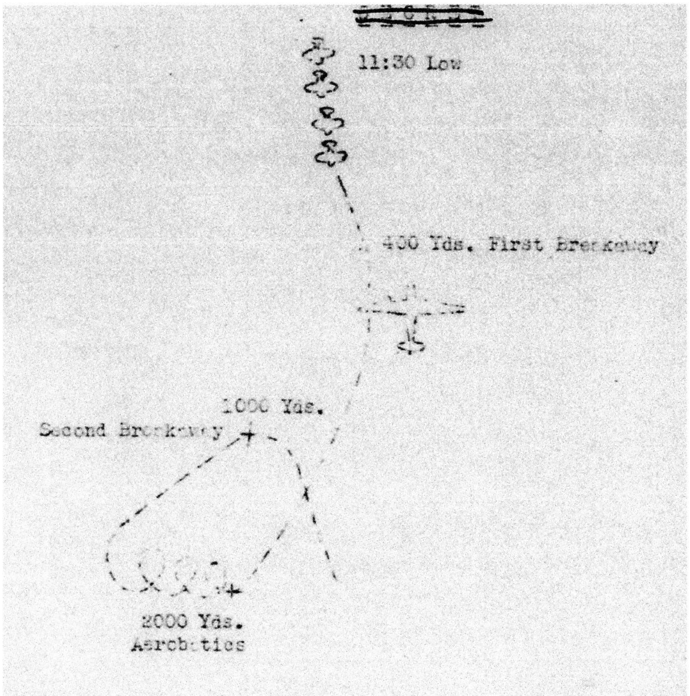

This post-raid XX BC intelligence drawing illustrates a B-29 crew's description of a Japanese fighter attack during Mission #16; four Japanese Nakajima Ki-43 Oscars attacked the B-29. After passing the bomber, the fighters performed a series of acrobatics and then assaulted the B-29 again. (*US Air Force*)

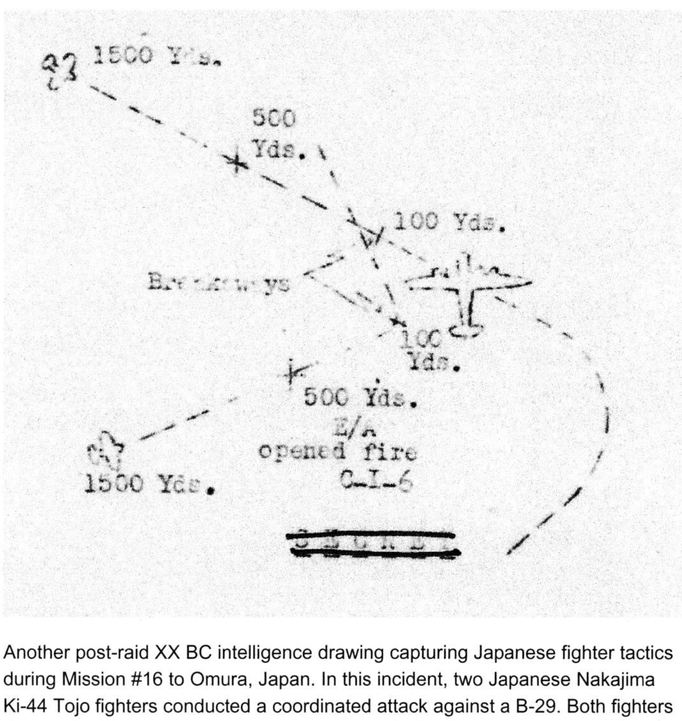

Another post-raid XX BC intelligence drawing capturing Japanese fighter tactics during Mission #16 to Omura, Japan. In this incident, two Japanese Nakajima Ki-44 Tojo fighters conducted a coordinated attack against a B-29. Both fighters departed the area after making a single pass. (*US Air Force*)

over the secondary target at Shanghai reported meager flak from land and naval based weapons. Two or three destroyers escorting a small Japanese convoy engaged up to fourteen bombers between five and ten miles south of Saishu Island. The destroyers struck one B-29 (#424 *Hap's Characters* of the 468th BG) and inflicted minor damage to the horizontal stabilizer. Individual bombers encountered meager and inaccurate flak at other locations along the briefed flying route or near targets of opportunity. One B-29 crew reported possible utilization of phosphorus-based anti-aircraft flak at Nanking:

> The tail gunner of aircraft 251 [Old Battler] of the 444th Group, while over Nanking...observed 3 white bursts, much larger than the ordinary flak burst. Two bursts were first observed at 8 o'clock and approximately 1,500 feet below the aircraft with the third burst appearing very shortly thereafter in approximately the same position. Together the 3 bursts formed a triangular pattern in the sky. Before the bursts occurred, a round glowing ball was seen and a very short time later the burst appeared developing into trails of white (possibly phosphorus) in all directions. The ball first seen was still visible after the burst occurred.[15]

Crews described total Japanese air opposition as "weak," although individual pilots were aggressive, with a total of twenty-nine bombers intercepted by fighters, including the Kawasaki Ki-61 Tony, Nakajima Ki-44 Tojo, Nakajima Ki-43 Oscar, Kawasaki Ki-45 Nick, Zeke, and a single Nakajima J1N1-S Irving. Three B-29s received fighter damage, while gunners among the entire command claimed two fighters destroyed, two probables, and twelve damaged. Nearly all of the attacks (92%) occurred away from the assigned targets.

At least one coordinated aerial attack employed aerial bombs, as noted in the post mission intelligence analysis:

> The use of aerial bombs was observed in only one encounter with enemy aircraft. In this instance, 3 bombs were released in a coordinated attack by 3 Tojos, in what was described as a possible combination bombing and gunnery attack. The B-29, on its way back to the Chengtu area, was flying at 15,000 feet at a point approximately 100 miles north and slightly west of Hankow. Three bombs were observed falling well in front of the airplane, continuing down without exploding. No enemy aircraft were seen at this time. (The bombs were described as shaped like US practice bombs, but

smaller in size, and were judged to weigh about 60 pounds.) A minute or two later, 3 Tojos were sighted, high, 4,000 yards ahead, coming in line abreast from 11:30, 12:30, and 1:30 o'clock. The enemy pilots opened fire at 1,000 yards, and the B-29 returned it at 800 yards. The Tojos closed to 400 yards, then broke away in peel-offs, two to the right and one to the left. No hits were claimed on the Tojos, nor was the B-29 reported damaged.[16]

The XX BC lost five B-29s during the mission. Aircraft #300 *Round Robin Rosie* with the 444th BG dropped from its formation due to an oil leak in engine #3. Another crew heard the crippled B-29 trying to radio a rescue submarine in the area. Later, the crew members of another B-29 sighted a ditched Superfortress and took photographs of the aircraft showing the bomber afloat with a large oil slick surrounding it. Although there were no life rafts visible in the photograph, white specks on the aircraft itself could have been crew members. The same photographs included images of two single-engine Japanese float aircraft in the vicinity of the B-29. Neither the crew members nor their remains were ever recovered, and after the war memorials were established in the American cemetery in the Philippines to honor them.

The 468th BG's #365 *General H. H. Arnold Special* radioed a low fuel status after bombing Omura and then went silent. Group personnel listed the aircraft, piloted by Capt. Weston Price, as "missing in action," but rather than crashing somewhere in China, Price opted to become the third B-29 pilot interned in the Soviet Union. Calculations indicated the bomber had sufficient fuel for a diversion to Vladivostok and Price chose to join the other crews there rather than risk a crash-landing or parachute jump in Japanese occupied China. Price inherited his B-29 from the squadron commander and maintained the plane's name, the *General H. H. Arnold Special*. When Gen. Arnold visited the Boeing B-29 plant at Wichita, Kansas, on January 11, 1944, he pointed to the 175th fuselage in the assembly line and literally signed it, proclaiming he wanted the bomber ready for flight, along with the preceding fuselages, on March 1, 1944. During the disassembly to reverse engineer the B-29 for the production of the Tupolev Tu-4 bomber, Soviet technicians found a plaque near the bombardier's area proclaiming the naming of the aircraft by Boeing personnel in honor of Gen. Arnold. Price and his crew were allowed to "escape" through Iran in 1945 with the personnel of the other interred B-29s.[17]

The 444th BG's #300 *Round Robin Rosie* dropped from its formation due to an oil leak in engine #3 during Mission #16 to Omura, Japan. Neither the crew members nor their remains were ever recovered. (Kelleher via 444th BG)

The 444th BG's #307 *Blue Bonnet Belle*, piloted by Capt. Bill Wyatt, crashed in China following severe ice build-up on the wings during Mission #16. Seven crew members bailed out and four perished in the crash of the B-29. (*58th BW*)

The 444th BG's #307 *Blue Bonnet Belle*, piloted by Capt. Bill Wyatt, crashed in China following severe ice build-up on the wings; seven crew members bailed out and four perished in the crash of the B-29. The Chinese collected the survivors and assisted in their return to Chengtu. Another 444th BG B-29 (#419, piloted by Capt. Milton Levitch) also developed icing problems and crashed in China; most of the crew survived the crash. This aircraft was mentioned in the chapter reviewing the August 11 mission of the XX BC. At some point, a possible post-mission typographical or administrative error changed the date of this crash from November 11 to August 11, 1944. Subsequently, most published sources list the loss as August 11. However, careful examination of records from the XX BC and the 444th BG clearly indicate Capt. Levitch and his crew crashed during Mission #16 on November 11.[18]

The tail section of #237 *Sir Trofrepus* of the 40th BG. #237 *Sir Trofrepus* crashed while on the bombing run during Mission #16. As the bombs dropped at least two collided in mid-air and exploded, sending shrapnel into the B-29. (*Albert via 40th BG*)

The 40th BG lost #237 *Sir Trofrepus*, piloted by 1st Lt. Richard Vickery, due to an unusual accident while on the bombing run at Nanking. As the bombs dropped from the aircraft at least two collided in mid-air and exploded, sending shrapnel into the B-29. Left gunner Sgt. Watson Lankford related the accident after the war:

> We headed for the target which appeared cloud covered so the radar operator was told to prepare for a radar bomb run. About two minutes from the target, the target appeared clear so the bombardier told radar that he would take over. We had been instructed as gunners to watch for the bombs hitting. Immediately after the bombardier said, "Bombs away," he called, "Any of you see where the bombs hit?" Almost immediately thereafter the explosion of the bombs under the plane took place. The right wing tanks ruptured, and the wing caught fire. We got a message on intercom from the co-pilot to stand by. Our radar man decided he was going to get out. He took an ax to cut an opening in the bulkhead which depressurized the plane. Carlton, Rieger and I formed up to go out the rear hatch. We were sort of taking our lead from Carlton since he was the CFC gunner. I was at the hatch when suddenly I was pushed out. Rieger followed and then Carlton. All four engines were still going. We never got a bailout order.[19]

Sgt. Carl Rieger, the right gunner, added to the story:

> After releasing the bombs in salvo, they were about 50 to 75 yards below the plane when they exploded. Shrapnel hit the right wing, setting us on fire. I was the only one in position to check for other damage, and I found fire in the bomb bay. I returned to my position to contact others by intercom. I could get no answer, and there was mass confusion by this time. After six to eight minutes, I went to the rear door and jumped. I was the last to leave the waist section.[20]

Maj. Francis Morgan, assigned to XX BC, flew aboard #237 as an observer and offered details related to the crew members in the nose section of the B-29:

> We wanted to stay with the plane as long as possible to get away from the Japanese around Nanking. Tokyo Rose had warned us several times that any captured B-29 fliers would be executed, and we had heard about men being tortured by the Japanese. [Second Lieutenant William] Warburton [flight engineer] called all crew members to alert them for bailout, and they responded. Vickery turned over the plane to Page to fly. Warburton had problems in lowering the nose wheel which took a few minutes to get down. We were losing altitude but not rapidly and were at probably 19,000 feet when the plane lurched to the right. Warburton called the men in the rear, but only [Sgt. George] Schuchardt, the tail gunner, replied, leading us to assume the gunners and radar operator had already jumped. When the lurch occurred, [1st Lt. Felix] Sinicrope, the navigator, dropped thorough the wheel well followed by Warburton. [2nd Lt.] Cassidy, the bombardier, [co-pilot Second Lieutenant Bernard] Page and Vickery were forward and ready to jump, but another lurch threw us around. Both [radio operator Staff Sgt. Dwight] Collins and I were thrown into the engineer's compartment with Collins on top of me. The plane was now on its side, and I was standing on the flight engineer's window, looking up at the nose wheel. The plane continued to roll over and then over again. Then it exploded.[21]

Crew members landed scattered among the rice paddies and surrounding terrain in the area. Morgan continued:

> My last conscious recollection was that I was attempting to reach the nose wheel which was above my head. Sinicrope later reported that shortly after his chute had opened, he observed the plane pass over him in a gentle turn to the right; then it rolled completely over twice. The flames from #4 engine appeared to sweep through the plane and over to the left wing. Then it exploded. Upon return to consciousness, I found myself about 2,500 feet above ground. When I pulled the ripcord, it took a couple of tugs to open the chute. After clearing blood from my eyes, I observed two sections of the plane on the ground to my left, both blazing. Fragments from inside the plane—pieces of aluminum and odd bits of debris—were falling down beside me. I landed in a rice paddy, which was filled with water, some 65 miles northwest of Nanking. I had seen three other chutes descending so I headed for them. Within 300 yards, I met Collins, Schuchardt and Warburton. Collins was very dazed and suffering from shock, having had as miraculous escape as I. Warburton appeared to be the only one who was not injured. Schuchardt was limping, and I had several facial cuts, broken teeth and a ragged gash on my right wrist.[22]

Radio operator Staff Sgt. Dwight Collins explained why Morgan mentioned he looked "very glazed":

> Needless to say, I was in shock. Lt. Warburton was first to reach me. According to him, I was sitting on the bank of the rice paddy, my elbows on my knees, my chin in my hands and a dazed stare in my eyes. He told me to get up and bury my chute so we would not be strafed by enemy planes. I did not respond, so he pulled me up, slapped me a couple of times, and that brought me around.[23]

Some of the crew members from B-29 #237 *Sir Trofrepus* were halted and handed over to Japanese soldiers by armed Chinese, while others encountered Chinese Communist forces that actively defended them from the Japanese and helped them return to their unit. The United States had cultivated a working relationship known as the "Dixie Mission" with Mao Tse-tung and his Communist guerrillas since the summer of 1944, for the purpose of several military and political goals, including the recovery and safe delivery of downed American air crews in China. Gen. LeMay added a personal touch to the Dixie Mission by sending his own team to meet with Mao and the two men exchanged personal gifts. Many American air crews owe their recovery and protection to Chinese Communist forces under Mao. More details on this working relationship will be covered in chapter 8.

The group that parachuted from *Sir Trofrepus* and were on the ground with Maj. Morgan encountered Communist Chinese troops while under fire from Japanese soldiers. Staff Sgt. Collins remembered his rescue by the Communist soldiers:

> Lt. Warburton was applying a compression bandage in the area of my temple to stop blood flowing from a cut along the hairline above my left eye when we heard shots, and the ground near our feet was scratched up by bullets. We could see a Japanese patrol running down a hill perhaps 500 yards away, shooting at us as they came our way. We jumped into a ditch, not knowing what to do next. It seemed that out of nowhere, about 10 or 12 Chinese guerrilla soldiers appeared in the ditch beside us, started shooting back at the Jap patrol with three or four of them making motions for us to run down the ditch with them. This certainly seemed like the better alternative so we did not hesitate. As I recall, this all took place somewhere around 11:00 a.m. The Chinese guerilla troops ran us as hard as possible the rest of the day. A certain number stayed at the rice paddy where we landed, fighting the Jap patrol until we could gain distance.[24]

Rieger, the right gunner, fell into the hands of an armed Chinese group that handed him to the Japanese; he endured a series of Japanese prisons along with Lankford and Sgt. Frederick Carlton, the central fire control gunner, until the end of the war. Rieger noted a few details of his capture:

> I landed on the bank of a rice paddy badly spraining my left knee and right ankle. The chute dragged me through to the other side of the rice paddy before I could get it collapsed. It was the only paddy to have water in it. Immediately about 12 Chinese soldiers ran up. I thought I was in good hands, but I found out differently. They searched me and marched me to a small compound about two miles away. After two hours a group of Jap soldiers arrived and marched me to a Jap compound six miles away near a railroad. That was hell because of my sprains. With my hands behind my back, they tied me to a post in a small room and

left me there all night. They questioned me early the next morning, and I would give them only my name, rank and serial number, even when they held bayonets four inches from my eyes and threatened to throw powder in my eyes to blind me. I felt certain at least part of the crew eluded capture at that time. Later in the morning they took me outside, and there was Watson Lankford. We were placed on a train and, after approximately an hour and a half, we arrived at Nanking. There we were paraded through the streets still with our hands tied. We walked at first, but when I could no longer walk because of the sprains, they put us in rickshaws. While in the rickshaw, a Chinese boy ran up and hit me a good blow on the head. The Jap in charge beat the hell out of the boy.[25]

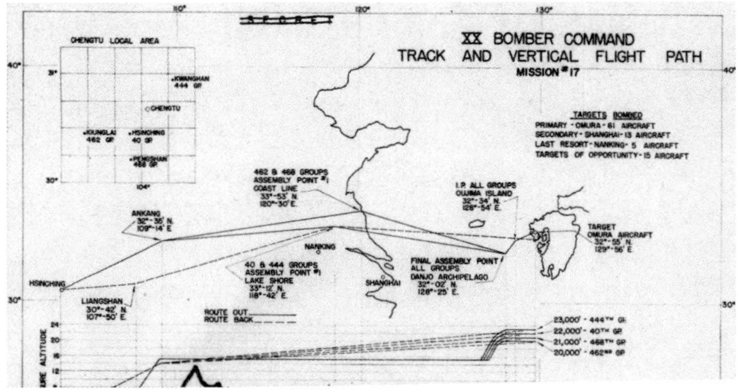

The XX BC utilized this chart to brief pilots and navigators for Mission #17 to Omura, Japan, which shows the routes to and from the target, as well as assembly points and the Initial Point (IP) from which the B-29s would begin their bomb run against the target. (*US Air Force*)

Mission #17: Omura, November 21, 1944

Ten days later, XX BC returned to Japan with the Omura Aircraft Plant as the primary target again. Operational plans for the primary target were nearly identical to those in Mission #16, but in contrast, planners designated Kiangnan Dock and Engineering Works in Shanghai, China, as the secondary target. The wharf area in Nanking, China, remained on the target list as the last resort. The Kiangnan Dock and Engineering Works included a dry dock and served as a major ship building and repair facility for the Japanese. Warships up to the size of a light cruiser could be serviced within the dry dock. Small ore carrying vessels originated in the shipbuilding yard. Destruction of the area could deny the Japanese of not only a ship repair facility, but also limit their ability to replace smaller commercial vessels destroyed by the Allies. The Japanese utilized Nanking as a rail and river transportation hub for its forces operating in China.[26]

The command lost one bomber in the forward movement from India to the staging bases in China: B-29 #531 of the 462nd BG experienced a fire that erupted beneath the radar compartment. All of the crew members except the tail gunner bailed out. One hundred nine bombers launched from China for Mission #17 (28 from the 40th BG; 29 from the 44th BG; 30 from the 462nd BG; and 22 from the 468th BG). B-29 #362 of the 468th BG crashed upon lifting off from the airfield. The plane struck trees near the south end of the runway, crashing on its left wing and bursting into flames. Only the tail gunner survived the crash, although severely injured. Of the remaining 108 aircraft, sixty-one bombed the primary target from between 20,000 to 24,000 feet with a mixture of demolition and incendiary weapons.

The crews encountered thick cloud cover over Omura that forced them to bomb by radar rather than visually. Strike photos showed bomb craters on the airfield, but there were no damaged Japanese aircraft present. The bombs missed the main aircraft plant, falling 1,000 feet from the aiming point. Thirteen B-29s attacked the secondary target at Shanghai due to mechanical problems and/or inability to join a formation. Crews reported clear weather over Shanghai. Photographs recorded numerous hits on buildings and warehouses, but the report does not mention any damage to the dry dock. Five aircraft bombed the target of last resort at Nanking and fifteen dropped their ordnance on targets of opportunity in China and Japan. Photographs from Nanking showed damage to buildings and warehouses. The targets of opportunity included Omuta (not to be confused with Omura) and Nagasaki, Japan, as well as bridges and an airfield in China. A formation bombed Omuta when the lead crew became confused and led them to the wrong target (due to navigation and not confusion with the similar spelling of names in English).

The Omura Aircraft Plant in Omura, Japan, was the primary target for Mission #17. The Omura Aircraft Plant built Mitsubishi F1M Pete observation and Aichi B7A Grace carrier attack aircraft. (*US Air Force*)

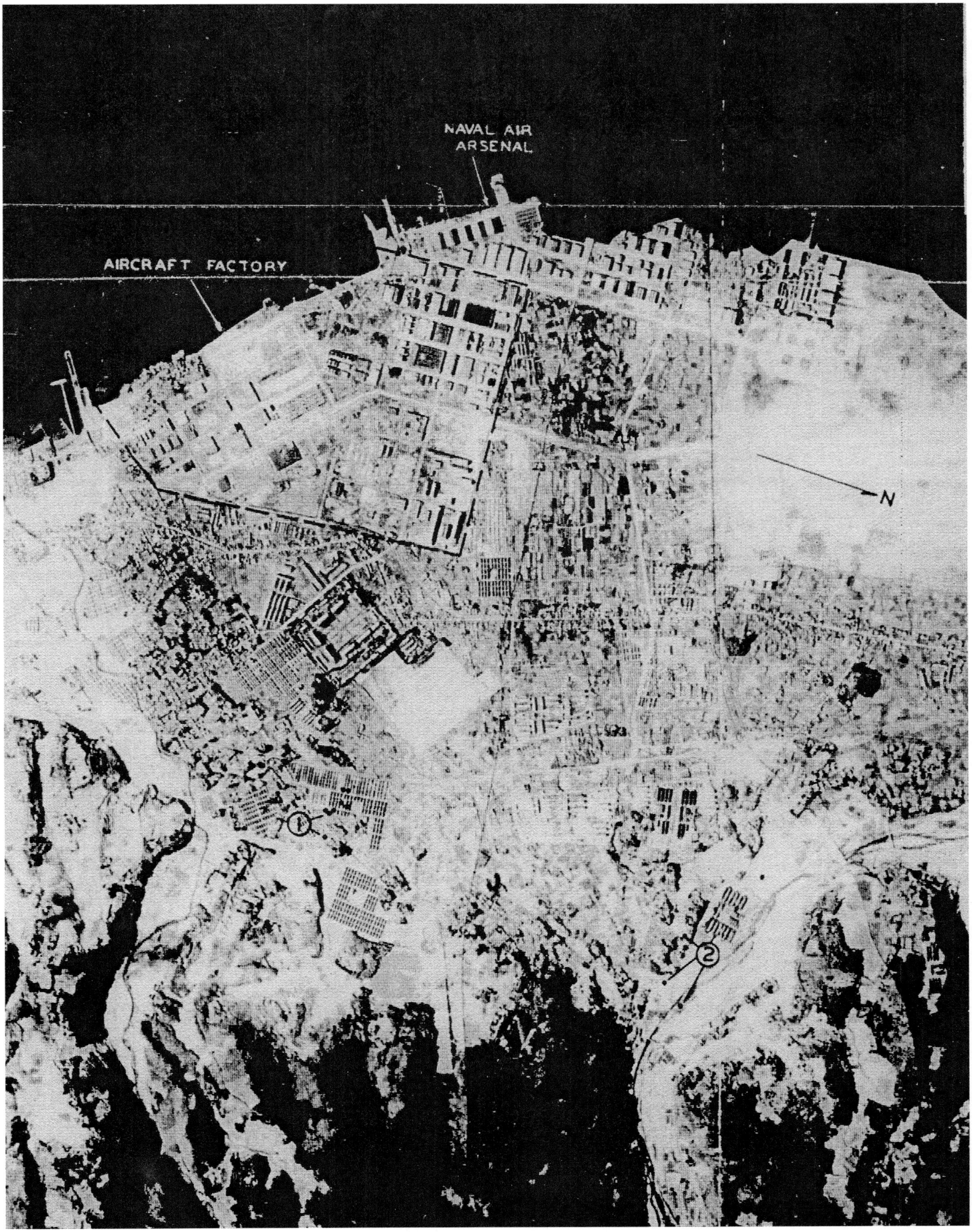
NAVAL AIR
ARSENAL
AIRCRAFT FACTORY
N
1
2

A crew member of the 468th BG's #409 *The Uninvited* stands with two Chinese soldiers. *The Uninvited* returned with Japanese flak and fighter damage after Mission #17 to Omura, Japan. (*Harper via 468th BG*)

The 40th BG's #579 *Eddie Allen* in November 1944. *Eddie Allen* landed with flak damage to the cowl flap, exhaust collector ring, and right horizontal stabilizer after Mission #17. (*Mahli via 40th BG*)

Japanese anti-aircraft artillery at Omura proved to be meager and generally inaccurate during Mission #17; crews also reported meager to moderate but inaccurate flak over Omuta, Nagasaki, and Shanghai. Only two bombers sustained flak damage during the operation: the 468th BG's #409 *The Uninvited* reported flak as well as fighter damage, but post-mission studies did not distinguish the source of the damage on various aircraft components and just attributed each to enemy action. The plane returned with holes in the fuselage, horizontal stabilizer, and bomb bay doors, as well as a severed elevator trim tab cable. The 40th BG's #579 *Eddie Allen* landed with flak damage to the cowl flap, exhaust collector ring, and right horizontal stabilizer.[27]

While Japanese flak can be considered meager, their fighter opposition should be viewed as strong and aggressive during this operation and led to some of the most intense air-to-air combat involving the XX BC flying from China and India. Japanese fighters intercepted two-thirds of the total bomber force at some point along its flight path. Enemy fighter action resulted in the downing of two B-29s in the target area, with four crash-landing due to battle damage, one plane diverting and landing in the Soviet Union, and other bombers returning with various categories of damage. B-29 gunners claimed the destruction of twenty-seven fighters as well as nineteen probables and twenty-four damaged. Crews estimated the Japanese engaged them with approximately 100 different fighters of various types across China and Japan, although 85% of the encounters occurred in the target area.

Japanese tactics included phosphorus aerial bombs in forty-six attacks. The fighter pilots continued to "flip" the aerial bombs from the bellies of their aircraft rather than drop them conventionally. Some of the aerial bomb bursts were described as much larger than usual, with centers varying from white to dark grey and black. White phosphorus streams stretched from 150 to 500 feet from the center of the explosions. One B-29 crew reported flying through a phosphorus streamer. The explosion occurred approximately 100 feet to the left of the bomber and spewed phosphorus streamers in a circular pattern. The left wing of the bomber knifed directly through one of the streamers without sustaining any damage.

One B-29 avoided the phosphorus streamers of an aerial bomb by flying up and over the bursting explosion. In a coordinated aerial bombing attack on a single B-29, two Oscars approached in trail from three o'clock high and closed to within 200 yards, where they conducted tight turns and "flipped" their bombs from the underside of the aircraft. The B-29 gunners opened fire at 300 yards and claimed a "probably destroyed" on the second Oscar. The aerial bombs did not damage the bomber.

The Japanese possibly launched at least two air-to-air rockets at the bombers. In one attack, a rocket from an unobserved aircraft trailing a thin stream of white smoke passed close to a B-29 without exploding. A Japanese twin-engine fighter approximately 2,000 yards in front of a bomber launched the second rocket attack. A small explosion and smoke emerged from under the left wing of the fighter, quickly followed by a loud explosion over the tail of the bomber. The crew never saw the rocket itself and the bomber did not sustain any damage.

Japanese pilots conducted thirty-three coordinated attacks against the B-29s. In one case, three Oscars approached a B-29 at 1,700 yards from 11 o'clock high. The fighters, flying in trail out of the sun, opened fire at 300 yards and closed to within fifty feet of the bomber. They broke the attack at this distance by diving to the 5:30 position, leaving a hole in the radar compartment of the B-29. In another coordinated attack, three Japanese Tojos conducted a "belly button" assault on a single B-29. The Japanese fighters approached the bomber abreast from 6 o'clock level. At 2,000 yards, the fighters broke into a dive and then went for the tail of the bomber, opening fire at 1,000 yards. They closed to 800 yards and then dispersed, with one fighter passing beneath the B-29, one to the right, and one to the left. The attack did not result in damage to either side.

Seven Japanese fighters launched a coordinated attack known as a "chow line" by the bomber crews. The fighters—possibly Oscars—flew in line and to the right and rear of a ten-ship B-29 formation. The Japanese pilots reduced their visibility by maintaining positions within the sun. The fighters, flying in trail behind each other, moved toward the front of the bomber formation, banked sharply, and turned to attack the B-29s from positions ranging between 1 and 3 o'clock high. Several of the fighters flew through the bomber formation in their breakaway moves. Both sides exchanged gunfire, but there were no reports of hits.

The Japanese also employed the "chow line" tactic to deliver aerial bombs. This assault consisted of three fighters: one acting as a decoy and two flying in a "chow line" formation to the right and rear of a bomber formation. The decoy approached from 12:30 high to attract the attention of the bombers. As the decoy attacked the formation, the other fighters pulled forward and banked into the formation. The two fighters flew over the B-29s and flipped their aerial bombs before breaking away by diving into the 8 o'clock. Again, no damage was reported to either side.[28]

Two 462nd BG B-29s crashed in the target area following attacks by Japanese fighters: Capt. Joseph Killebrew piloted #278 *Assid Test* of the 462nd BG when two Japanese Mitsubishi J2M Jack fighters jumped the bomber at Omuta, near Omura. Six other crews observed the B-29 spinning out of control and crashing into Omuta Bay. The precise details of this engagement are not known due to the loss of all eleven crew members in the crash. The 462nd BG also lost #848, piloted by Capt. Richard McMillan, and his crew on their first combat mission. Three crew members died in the engagement and the other eight men bailed out of the doomed bomber. Half of these crew members successfully evaded capture and the other four fell into Japanese hands, becoming prisoners of war. The Japanese executed three of the prisoners and released the last man at the end of the war.[29]

Japanese fighters critically damaged the 40th BG's #275 *Snafuper Bomber*, piloted by Capt. James Cowden, in the target area. Projectiles entering the B-29 killed the bombardier and wounded the co-pilot, 1st Lt. Leland Jones, who vividly remembered the action:

> Shortly after bombs away, the flak stopped, and almost instantly the fighter planes came swarming in...we made a breakaway formation turn, and, while turning, we also started descending at the rate of about 1200 feet per minute, and of course we were gaining speed. Ballistically speaking, this maneuver makes it very difficult for a fighter pilot to aim properly to hit a target that was changing so many ballistic factors, such as speed changing, turning, and altitude changes, and so on. In spite of these difficulties a fighter shot us up pretty badly. Our bombardier, [First Lieutenant] Ira Redmon, got credit for shooting down two Zeroes, including the one that shot us up. Observers in the formation stated in the debriefing that the Jap fighter plane blew up at the same time that we were hit. One of the shells blew our nose out, and Redmon was instantly killed. [First Lieutenant] Dick Steiner, the navigator, and I were wounded. The next thing I

Japanese fighters critically damaged 40th BG's #275 *Snafuper Bomber*, piloted by Capt. James Cowden, near Omura, Japan, during Mission #17. The pilot ordered the crew to abandon the bomber and the ten survivors parachuted safely and returned to base. (*Bozzuto via 40th BG*)

> remember, I was still in my seat with our first-aid man, the radio operator [Staff Sgt. Bill Salmon], and someone else, treating my wounds. I had my hand holding my head at the left temple, and when I tried to move the arm and hand, they wouldn't move. One of my wounds was at the temple, and I apparently had grabbed my head, and my blood froze my hand to my head. Dick Steiner told me later that the temperature inside the nose section dropped immediately to the outside temperature, which he said was -55 centigrade. And, of course, it didn't take much time for the blood and the hand to freeze. Bill Salmon used his knife and pried my hand away from my head.[30]

Navigator Dick Steiner added his perspective:

> I recall a perfect picture of the target on my radar scope. The run looked good to me. Redmon opened the bomb-bay doors, and I felt the usual lurch as the bombs were released. Many fighters were being called in by the gunners, and the bombardier immediately after the release. As the bomb bay doors closed, the forward turrets began firing almost without interruption. I heard Red ask for control of the upper and lower forward guns and could see him hunched over the gun sight. There was a sharp explosion in the front cockpit, and the air inside turned foggy as we lost pressure. Shell fragments were flying around the cockpit. One hit my flak vest just under my left rib cage and lodged in my vest. It felt as if someone had slapped me. One fragment hit my wooden sextant box on the desk in front of me and shattered a lens in the sextant. Looking forward I could see Red's gun sight swinging free and Red, with flak helmet fallen down over his face, slumped in his seat. [Co-pilot] Leland Jones, who had been flying the plane while in formation, was slumped in his seat with blood pumping from the side of his head onto the aisle stand.[31]

Cowden dropped from formation but maintained control of the wounded bomber as other aircraft maneuvered to provide cover. Cowden summarized the situation to this point:

> Now that we were in the clouds, we could assess our damage beyond the cockpit. The left wheel well and tires were blown apart and were dragging in the wind. The radio compartment was blown apart with heavy shrapnel, and the intercom system was out completely. At this point the radio man and the radar operator pieced together a radio with which we could reach the other planes in the formation. When the squadron found us, they circled once to let us join the formation for added security on the way home.[32]

Harry Changnon flew as a co-pilot on another 40th BG B-29 that offered to fly "shotgun" over Cowden and help his crew return safely. Changnon recorded:

> Cowden peeled out of the formation right in front of us when he was hit, but there was no smoke or flames. The Japs were tossing phosphorous bombs at us, but they weren't making contact. Now and then we could feel and hear a few pieces of flak rattling against the planes. We had several waves of fighters attack our formation and later were told 85 Nips were in on the defense of the area. During those hectic few minutes, Cowden was able to regain control of his plane. Woolsey and Lanzoni dropped down to help him drive off fighters who might have taken a cripple, and then the three of them pulled back into formation as Doyle slowed down for them. I could see Cowden's nose and fuselage shot up, and he was leaking oil out of his #2 nacelle which also had holes in it.[33]

The pilot nursed his crippled bomber on three engines back across China while remaining in formation with the assisting B-29s and the protection they provided. As the bombers neared their base in China, Cowden struggled to remain in formation and disappeared in a cloud bank. Losing altitude and flying alone, the crew reached a point within thirty miles of their base where the loss of fuel related to damage necessitated a bail out. Cowden ordered the crew to abandon the bomber and the ten survivors successfully parachuted and returned to their base. Cowden continued his narrative:

> I had spotted a nice long valley. I gave the signal for the crew to drop the co-pilot. Then the alarm was given for the crew to jump. I jumped last. As soon as my chute opened, I started counting the line of white chutes against the rice field. The farmers in the fields were very excited and came right over to where I had landed. They picked up my chute and gear and pointed to the hill where the plane had crashed. I went with them to make sure that no one had frozen in the jump. All was O.K. I had hit the ground at 4:30 pm. The Chinese farmers escorted me to a little village where I caught up with the crew. This was about 9:30 that night. By the time I got there, the crew had arranged to have Leland attended to by the Chinese doctor.[34]

Flight Engineer 1st Lt. Leonard Koenig recalled the bailout:

> Leland was the first to jump, and he is correct when he says he fell a long way. Steiner, Salmon and I were sweating him out all the way, and there was one big sigh of relief when that white blossom appeared. Steiner and Salmon followed; then it was my turn. I didn't like the idea of trying to jump from those close quarters, so I climbed down the ladder, hung on with one hand and swung out, dangled there until I had a good hold on the ripcord handle and let go. The descent was uneventful, but I wound up hanging upside down from a low tree. I was still trying to get out of my harness when some Chinese arrived and extricated me.[35]

Cowden offered a conclusion to the operation:

> The next morning we caught up with a small army of Chinese who helped the crew get the body of Ira Redmon out of the wreckage and to wrap him in his chute to be carried back for burial. There was also the matter of destroying the bomb sight which was attended to. Then we got to the only telephone in the area and gave our base the message that we needed to be picked up and that we needed an ambulance. After the call, we kept walking toward our expected pick-up point. When we met up with our rescuers, we put Leland in the ambulance to be taken to the university hospital in Chengtu. The rest of us piled in a troop carrier of some sort. We were starved and were looking forward to a big turkey dinner because it was Thanksgiving Day this date in 1944. When we got to the mess hall, we were disappointed to discover that we were too late and all the turkey was gone. It turned out it was the day after Thanksgiving when we got back. We had forgotten about the extra day's travel. But Big Joe, the Chinese cook, said he would fix us all the eggs and toast we wished. We settled for that. It had been a long mission.[36]

The 40th BG lost another B-29 (#290 *Wempy's Blitzburger*) in a collision with a 444th BG aircraft at an emergency airfield near Ankang. B-29 #290 *Wempy's Blitzburger*, piloted by Maj. Joseph White, landed at the grass airfield near Ankang due to a fuel shortage. Before the bomber could be refueled (often accomplished by Chinese labor utilizing cans), the 444th BG's #321 *This Is It* approached the airfield; a Japanese fighter had targeted the 444th bomber, piloted by Capt. Dunn, over Omura and damaged the bomber's aileron controls. At the same time, a falling shell casing from the air battle around the bomber defied astronomical chances and struck one of the nacelles, damaging the engine. Dunn was unable to feather the propeller on the engine. The formation leader directed him to ditch the aircraft, but Dunn opted to maintain control of his crippled bomber and attempt to reach friendly Chinese territory, where the crew would have a better chance for survival and recovery. Although American submarines were alerted of the mission before it was flown, B-29 crew members surviving a ditching at sea in the waters off northeast China faced near certain capture by the Japanese if they were found alive. The pilot diverted his B-29 to the emergency grass airfield near Ankang, where Maj. White of the 40th BG had already landed. Dunn's bomber touched down on the wet grass and the plane raced toward the end of the strip. The wet grass and windmilling damaged propeller negated the ability of the pilot and the brakes to halt the skidding B-29, which struck Maj. White's bomber. The impact crushed the forward compartment of Dunn's aircraft, killing the pilot and the other three men within. The other crew members of #321 *This Is It* survived the ordeal. Dunn received a posthumous Distinguished Service Cross for his efforts that resulted in the survival of most of the crew. Fortunately, none of White's crew members were aboard their bomber, which was also destroyed in the mishap. The XX BC officially listed the loss of #290 *Wempy's Blitzburger* as an "accident" and the loss of #321 *This Is It* due to "enemy action."[37]

The 40th BG lost #290 *Wempy's Blitzburger* in a collision with the 444th BG's #321 *This Is It* at an emergency airfield near Ankang, China, after Mission #17 to Omura, Japan. (*40th BG*)

The 444th BG's #321 *This Is It* slid into #290 *Wempy's Blitzbuger* of the 40th BG during an emergency landing at Ankang, China, following Mission #17. (*Archer via 40th BG*)

The 444th BG lost two other B-29s on this mission to Omura, including #510, which made a crash landing in China. Japanese fighters attacked #510 during the bomb run, destroying flight instruments, pilot controls, the fuel transfer system, radio, radar, the gun operating system, and engine #4. The pilot flew the doomed bomber to China and crash-landed on the beach at Changtsun. All of the crew survived and were transported by the Chinese to Chungking. Many published sources do not include this aircraft as a Mission #17 casualty. At least one claims it crashed on November 23, while others simply do not account for the bomber. However, XX BC in its December 1, 1944, post-mission report and the 444th BG in its historical report dated December 13, 1944, list #510 as a combat casualty on the November 21 raid on Omura.[38]

The 444th BG also lost #204, piloted by Capt. Hutchinson, on this mission. A Japanese fighter struck the bomber in the central fire control compartment, killing one gunner, blowing another out of an observation blister, and wounding the tail gunner. The attack crippled the central gun system and damaged the rudder. To maintain straight and level flight the "controls had to be roped down." Further damage included engine #1 with a propeller that could not be feathered. Despite the damage, Hutchinson flew the B-29 to the emergency landing field at Ankang. As the pilot set the plane down in an attempt to land, he spotted the other bombers that had already crash-landed at the field. After the tragic accident involving #290 *Wempy's Blitzburger* and #321 *This Is It*, the remains of the aircraft blocked part of the grass field. Thinking quickly, Hutchinson retracted his landing gear, barely cleared the wreckage, and then crash-landed on the grass field without injury to his crew.[39] He received a Distinguished Flying Cross for his quick reaction that certainly saved the lives of his crew members.

A 468th BG B-29 originally listed as missing in action flew to the Soviet Union, rather than risk going down in Japanese controlled territory after a duel with fighters over Omura. Japanese fighters knocked out an engine on #358 *Ding How* piloted by 1st Lt. William Mickish. (There were at least three B-29s named "Ding How" or "Ding Hao" in three different XX BC groups.) Strong headwinds from the west reduced any chances for the crew to reach friendly territory before needing to land or bail out. Mickish opted to head to Vladivostok rather than risk losing his crew in Japanese controlled territory. This bomber became the third and last intact B-29 held by the

Soviet Union. Mickish and his crew were permitted to "escape" with the other three XX BC crews (two who crash-landed and one who parachuted into Soviet territory) to Iran in January 1945.[40]

Published sources vary when listing the number of aircraft lost on Mission #17, with one publication stating the XX BC lost only two B-29s. The latter is an accurate figure, if only the two B-29s downed by the Japanese over the target area are counted, but does not present a clear picture of the losses connected to this operation. The XX BC lost ten aircraft related to Mission #17, including #531 of the 462nd BG, which went down en route to China; #362 of the 468th BG, which crashed on take-off from Chengtu; and #204 of the 444th BG, which crash-landed at an emergency field. The other seven planes are the 40th BG's #275 *Snafupuper Bomber* and #290 *Wempy's Blitzburger*; the 444th BG's #321 *This Is It* and #510; the 462nd BG's #278 *Assid Test* and #848; and the 468th BG's #358 *Ding How*.

Twelve other aircraft returned safely after sustaining battle damage. Japanese fighters accounted for ten of these bombers. Two 40th BG B-29s received fighter damage on the mission: #276 *Black Magic* (bullet holes in the fuselage, elevator, and lower rear gun turret) and #394 *Last Resort*. The latter aircraft, piloted by Maj. Donald Roberts, landed at an emergency field on two engines after a Japanese fighter placed a bullet hole in engine #4's propeller dome. Radio operator Howard Anderson remembered the attack:

> When we departed the I.P. (initial point), I climbed up in the tunnel and looked through the astro-dome to watch for enemy fighters, and I noticed several making passes at other planes in the formation. I did not see any anti-aircraft bursts. By now, the bomb bay doors were open. The gunners were very busy, with their turrets swinging around, and the intercom chatter was beginning to build up. As I recall, it was the radio operator's duty to observe (through the window of the bomb bay hatch) the release of the bombs, which I knew would be momentarily. So I slipped down to my radio position, and then "all Hell broke loose." It seemed that the entire Japanese air force had hit our B-29, and the aircraft just seemed to shudder and shake. I heard Elmo Gray [flight engineer] tell the Major that he had lost #4 engine and to feather it.[41]

As Gray attempted to feather the propeller, another Japanese fighter hit engines #1 and #2 during a pass. The crew feathered the propeller on engine #1 but had to leave the other propeller windmilling. The B-29 rapidly dropped from formation after releasing its bomb load. Roberts returned power to engine #1 and managed to start it. Anderson continued his narration from the point of the second attack:

> Then another wave of fighters pounded us and I knew that we had lost cabin pressure by the number of holes which I saw. I also became aware that we were fast losing altitude when I heard that #2 engine was being feathered, and then the bombs went out of the bomb bay. However, I did not know that #1 engine also had failed for a short period before Elmo got it back to producing power again. We were still under attack as there was a lot the turrets and lots of chatter on the intercom. So I climbed back up into the tunnel and almost passed out as I saw two clean bullet holes down through the exact position where I had been only minutes before. Looking through the astro-dome I could see that the Japs were intent on finishing us.[42]

With two engines turning, the B-29 pilot leveled the bomber after dropping 6,000 feet from his formation. Japanese fighters continued to assault the wounded bomber, which was now flying at a much slower speed and without the mutual support of a formation and its massed guns. During the next fifteen minutes, the bomber and fighters dueled in a vicious air battle that left the B-29 gunners claiming two enemy planes destroyed, one probably destroyed, and one damaged. The Japanese fighters abandoned the fight and the B-29 crew limped home. After seven hours of keeping his B-29 aloft despite the plane's damage, Roberts made a safe landing on two engines at an emergency airfield; he received the Silver Star in February 1945. Under normal circumstances the crew would have been stuck at this location until the 40th BG could dispatch maintenance personnel and spare parts to repair the B-29, but another XX BC B-29 had crashed nearby and the Roberts crew was able to salvage the parts they needed, including a propeller, to return to their forward base in China. Fourteenth Air Force fighters maintained protective cover over the airfield as Roberts and his crew repaired their bomber utilizing any field technique that seemed appropriate. The crew placed the new propeller on their aircraft with a sledge hammer and returned safely to their Chinese airfield.

Japanese fighters damaged three 444th BG planes: #353 *Big Poison* (nacelle #4); #462 *Princess Eileen II* (an intercooler); and #267 *Winnie* (holes in the fuselage and damage to wiring). Two B-29s from the 462nd BG landed with fighter damage: #463 *Humpin' Honey* (fuselage, horizontal stabilizer, and a control cable) and #338 *Globe Girdle Myrtle* (bullet holes in nacelle #2 and the fuselage and a blown observation blister). Three planes flying with the 468th BG received fighter damage: #407 *Lucky Seven* (20 mm shell in engine #1 and damage to the lower rear turret); #279 *Postville Express* (blown observation blister and holes in the right wing, tail, nacelle #2, and a fuel tank); and #409 *The Uninvited*. The latter plane also returned with flak damage and post-mission reports did not distinguish the source of the specific damaged areas across the bomber.[43]

Japanese fighters damaged the #4 nacelle of the 444th BG's #353 *Big Poison* on Mission #17 to Omura, Japan. (*Bessler via 444th BG*)

The Japanese launched a night intruder raid against the B-29 bases November 21 in retaliation for the raid on Omura. The night intruders dropped incendiary clusters that damaged three B-29s and a Consolidated C-109 (a fuel tanker version of the B-24 Liberator). The incendiaries also ignited drums of gasoline that burned brightly, with flames leaping up to 100 feet. Lt. Col. John Seeley, the 40th BG forward commanding officer, was injured in an accident when his jeep wrecked into a deep ditch as he raced to the scene of the fires. The 426th Night Fighter Squadron scored its second Northrop P-61 Black Widow kill in defense of the XX BC forward bases in China during this night (see chapter 5).

The 468th BG's #232 *Kickapoo II* arrived in India on April 21, 1944, and returned home as "war weary" on November 25, 1944, after flying only two combat missions, but she made thirty-seven trips across the Hump. (*Schutte via 468th BG*)

Mission #18: Bangkok, November 27, 1944

The XX BC flew its next mission from India as aircraft restocked aviation fuel in China following the two missions to Omura, Japan. The command considered this operation another training mission that also benefited Allied soldiers battling the Japanese in Burma. All four groups participated in the raid, with the Bansue Marshaling Yard in Bangkok, Thailand, as the primary target, Mergui Harbor in Burma as the secondary, and a military storage area at Taungup, Burma, as the target of last resort. Bansue was the primary railroad switching yard for trains moving south and west of Bangkok. The facility also housed a locomotive repair shop and maintained the highest count of rail cars in the Bangkok area. Mergui was the most northern harbor utilized by the Japanese for the landing of military supplies in Burma. Many small vessels lay in the harbor area on a daily basis and the area hosted warehouses for the storage of offloaded military supplies. Taungup served as a principal military storage base for Japanese forces operating in western Burma.[44]

During Mission #18 to Bangkok, Thailand, the 40th BG's #319 *Himalaya Hussy* bombed an industrial site in Bangkok as a target of opportunity when a technical issue prevented dropping its ordnance on the Bansue Marshaling Yard. The crew recorded poor results from the bombing. (*40th BG*)

The 444th BG's #464 *Flying Stud II* sustained flak damage during Mission #18 to Bangkok, Thailand. (*Vaughn via 444th BG*)

The 444th BG's #524 *Super Mouse* returned from Mission #18 with flak damage to the bomb bay doors, engine #2, the radar compartment, wing tip, and the leading edge of a wing. (*Rich via 444th BG*)

Each group launched fifteen B-29s (sixty bombers airborne) bound for Bangkok; fifty-five of them reached and bombed the primary target with general purpose ordnance in clear weather conditions with good results. Both aiming points and several other buildings in the complex were destroyed. The bombing also destroyed four locomotives and damaged five. Ninety pieces of rolling stock were either destroyed or damaged. One B-29 (#217 *Pepper* of the 468th BG) bombed the secondary target. The crew reported half of the twenty-four bombs hit the water and the other half struck the wharf area. B-29 #457 *Battlin' Beauty* of the 40th BG hit the target of last resort visually, reporting good results. Another 40th BG plane (#319 *Himalaya Hussy*) bombed an industrial site in Bangkok as a target of opportunity when a technical issue prevented the dropping of its ordnance on the Bansue Marshaling Yard. The crew recorded poor results from the bombing.

Although Japanese anti-aircraft fire was categorized as weak and inaccurate, flak struck four bombers in the target area. Two of these B-29s flew with the 40th BG: #276 *Black Magic* (holes in the cowl flap and nacelle of engine #1, the left horizontal stabilizer, rudder, and radar compartment) and #522 *B-Sweet II* (damage to the right horizontal stabilizer, leading edge of a wing, engine #3 nacelle, and cracked glass near the bombardier's station). Both of these aircraft also reported receiving hits from a fighter and post-mission analysis did not specifically attribute damaged areas to either flak or fighters. Two 444th BG bombers also landed with flak damage: #375 *Her Majesty* (engine #4 nacelle) and #524 *Super Mouse* (bomb bay doors, engine #2, the radar compartment, wing tip, and the leading edge of a wing). Two other 444th BG bombers (#464 *Flying Stud II* and #462 *Princess Eileen II*) may have sustained flak damage, but mechanics and crew members could not be certain if the damage originated from flak or bomb explosions underneath the aircraft.[45]

Following Mission #18 targeting Bangkok, the 40th BG's #276 *Black Magic* returned with fighter damage, including holes in the cowl flap and nacelle of engine #1 and the left horizontal stabilizer, rudder, and radar compartment. (*40th BG*)

Large fuel drum storage in China. Note the B-29 on the runway in the distance. (*US Air Force*)

The command lost one B-29 on this mission to Bangkok: the 40th BG's #452 *Devil May Care* piloted by 1st Lt. Carl Blackwell. Fighter opposition flown by both Japanese and Thai pilots proved to be weak, although the only loss of a B-29 during the mission was attributed to fighter damage from a Thai pilot. Information is sketchy, but the Royal Thai Air Force Museum and other sources credit Thai pilot Flight Lt. Therdsak Worrasap, flying a Japanese manufactured Nakajima Ki-43 Oscar, with damaging a B-29 during the November 27 air raid. Worrasap flew with six other Thai pilots in cooperation with fourteen Ki-43s of the Imperial Japanese Army Air Force to counter the B-29s over Bangkok that day. While Thailand credits Therdsak with the destruction of a B-29 (presumably #452), this cannot be proven due to the disappearance of the bomber and the "fog of war" when attempting a post-mission analysis. B-29 gunners damaged Therdsak's fighter, forcing him to bail out. He landed with severe burns from the engagement. Lt. Blackwell piloted his stricken B-29 with wounded crew members toward India and radioed for permission to land at the closer airfield of Chittagong, rather than proceed farther to his 40th BG base. After receiving permission no one heard from the bomber again, and it presumably crashed into the sea. An extensive search did not discover the wreck or any debris. The 20th Air Force attributed damaged fighters to #276 *Black Magic* and #522 *B-Sweet II* as well as #452 of the 40th BG. Another B-29 (#484 *Our Gal* of the 462nd BG) returned with damage to its horizontal stabilizer from a falling shell casing. Shell casings falling from aircraft in these air battles proved to be metallic rain, as they dropped among all of the participants. While a shell casing striking a plane in flight was rare, the incidents over Bangkok and Omura during the previous raid demonstrated it was certainly not impossible. B-29 gunners claimed the destruction of seven fighters as well as three probables and six damaged.[46]

Chapter 8

December 1944: Tragic Losses Over Rangoon and Mukden

My God! The sky's turning red!

—Tail Gunner (40th BG) over Rangoon

December 1944 witnessed continued Allied offensives against the Japanese. American and Filipino troops landed on Mindoro, in the Philippines, in support of the campaign to liberate the islands. The slow advances in Burma progressed as the British 36th Division made contact with the Indian 19th Division near the town of Indaw, in the northern area of the country, as two Chinese divisions pushed south from Myitkyina and Commonwealth forces drove eastward from the Indian border. Allied aircraft, including B-29s of the XXI Bomber Command (BC) in the Marianas Islands, initiated the bombardment of Iwo Jima in preparation for a landing by the United States Marines in February 1945.

On 4 December, Gen. Albert Wedemeyer, commander of American forces in the China Theater, requested Gen. George C. Marshall, Army Chief of Staff, to remove the XX BC B-29s from China as early as possible after January 15, 1945. Wedemeyer saw few benefits of the B-29s in his theater, with the XX BC striking targets outside China and in turn siphoning fuel allocations carried by aircraft of the Air Transport Command (ATC) across the Himalaya Mountains from India. A departure of the XX BC from their forward bases in China would increase ATC's tonnage of fuel and supplies destined for the 14th Air Force and Chinese forces. It would also free the 312th Fighter Wing from defense of Chengtu airfields and at least temporarily allow Gen. Chennault to utilize them as 14th Air Force assets to stem the Japanese *Ichi-Go* offensive. In anticipation of the inevitable, XX BC staff completed their field order overseeing the cessation of operations staged through China on December 15, 1944.[1]

Mission #19: Mukden, December 7, 1944

The field order for Mission #19 identified the Manchuria Airplane Manufacturing Company in Mukden, Manchuria, as the primary target, with the Manchuria Dockyard Company, Drydocks, and Shipping in Darien, Manchuria, the secondary. The railroad yards in Chenghsien, China, were the target of last resort. With this raid, the XX BC shifted from strategic attacks against Japanese heavy industry in Manchuria and conducted a raid against aircraft production facilities in the country. The primary target served the Japanese in the assembly of aircraft trainers and possibly produced engines. Destruction of the facility could halt the production of aircraft trainers there by up to six months and hamper the ability of the Japanese to train new pilots. The secondary target included three dry docks and several shipbuilding slips. The company also constructed engines for commercial vessels. The target of last resort provided a critical alternative transportation link for Japanese military forces in China; its disruption could slow the movement of Japanese troops and military supplies in the country. The XX BC originally planned a third raid to Omura after the two raids on that city in November in support of American efforts to liberate the Philippines, but predictions for poor weather resulted in a change to Mukden as an alternative target. The final decision to make the change occurred only hours before commencement of the operation.[2]

One hundred twenty-one bombers arrived in China from India, including a 40th BG plane that ground looped on landing. Counting aircraft already at the forward bases,

Gen. Albert Wedemeyer with a Chinese man. On December 4, 1944, Gen. Wedemeyer, commander of American forces in the China Theater, requested Gen. George C. Marshall, the army chief of staff, to remove XX BC B-29s from China as early as possible after January 15, 1945. (*US Army*)

108 B-29s launched for the mission to Mukden: the 40th BG (30 planes), 444th BG (31 planes), 462nd BG (28 planes), and the 468th BG (34 planes). Eighty-nine B-29s bombed the primary target with a mixture of incendiary and high explosive ordnance. The weather was clear, but smoke screens and icing on aircraft windshields hindered visual sighting of the target area. Ice completely covered the Plexiglass of many aircraft, forcing 1st Lt. Tom Young in the 468th BG's #536 *Mammy Yokum* to depressurize his bomber and open a side window, allowing the wind to clear his windshield.[3] Photographs of the primary target indicated bombs were scattered around the complex, with the greatest damage at an adjacent arsenal, including warehouse buildings, machine shops, and a storage area. Only one formation scored hits on the aircraft manufacturing facility. Strike photos indicated hits or near misses on an aircraft assembly hangar, two propeller mounting hangars, and a large final assembly building. Three formations scored hits on the arsenal, while the bombs of another formation struck a barracks and administrative area. Three formations missed the primary target area.

Ten 40th BG bombers dropped their loads early on the Suhuton Railway Yards, nine miles short of the primary target; the lead bomber accidentally released early, causing the other nine planes to drop their munitions. One B-29 crew in the eleven-plane formation did not release early and continued to the primary target. Most of the bombs landed on open ground, but several hits destroyed or damaged rail lines and rolling stock. Three B-29s bombed the secondary target: the 40th BG's #331 *Gone With The Wind* and the 468th BG's #409 *The Uninvited* and #284 *The Challenger*. Three aircraft hit the target of last resort: #420 *Rankless Wreck* of the 40th BG, #352 *Fu-Kemal* of the 444th BG, and #272 *Miss Shorty* flying with the 468th BG. Two B-29s bombed targets of opportunity: the 40th BG's #294 *Monsoon* bombed an airfield one mile from Hsuchang with unobserved results, and B-29 #324 *Three Feathers* of the 444th BG dropped its load on the dock installations at Tsingtao. The crew observed direct hits on buildings along the dock.[4]

The Manchuria Dockyard Company, drydocks, and shipping in Darien, Manchuria—the secondary target for Mission #19. (*US Air Force*)

During Mission #19 to Mukden the 40th BG's #331 *Gone With The Wind* bombed the secondary target—the Manchuria Dockyard Company, drydocks, and shipping in Darien, Manchuria. (*40th BG*)

The 40th BG's #294 *Monsoon* bombed an airfield one mile from Hsuchang, China, as a target of opportunity with unobserved results during Mission #19 to Mukden, Manchuria. (*Seith via 40th BG*)

Crews recorded the anti-aircraft fire over the primary target area as meager to moderate and generally inaccurate, with four B-29s receiving flak damage. Two 444th BG aircraft were hit by flak: #423 *Urgin' Virgin* (horizontal stabilizer) and #226 (horizontal stabilizer and leading edge of a wing). The other two planes flew with the 468th BG: #411 (engine #4 nacelle) and #208 *Andy's Dandy* (right flap and fuselage). Meager to moderate flak over Darien resulted in damage to the 468th BG's #409 *The Uninvited* (wing). Bombers also encountered anti-aircraft fire at numerous other locations during the mission but crossed these areas without damage. The Japanese employed an effective smoke screen over the primary target area, obscuring it from B-29 bombardiers. The post-mission analysis reviewed the smoke screen:

> For the first time an effective smoke screen was used by the enemy. Several ineffective attempts at screening had been noted before, notably at Yawata, Anshan, and Nanking using in nearly every case white smoke. At Mukden black smoke was used emanating from a number of double slit trenches roughly circling the arsenal and aircraft factory. Apparently the generator is housed in one of the slit trenches while the other is used by personnel. The screen was put into operation very quickly and intelligently taking maximum advantage of the prevailing wind.[5]

The 444th BG's #423 *Urgin' Virgin* returned from Mission #19 to Mukden, Manchuria, with flak damage to a horizontal stabilizer. (*Howe family via 444th BG*)

Engine maintenance on the 468th BG's #208 *Andy's Dandy*. This B-29 returned with damage to the right flap and fuselage inflicted by Japanese flak over Mukden during Mission #19. (*Schutte via 468th BG*)

The term "Japanese" in this air engagement actually refers to both Japanese and Manchurian Air Force (officially known as the Manchukuo Imperial Air Force) opposition to the XX BC. While Manchurian Air Force fighters probably engaged B-29s in earlier missions, they were confirmed to have fought during this mission. Manchuria (Manchukuo) was an area of northeast China seized by Japan in 1931, which then established a "puppet" state under the nominal leadership of Puyi, the last Chinese emperor. Despite the claim of an independent state, Puyi actually ruled as a figurehead for the Japanese military establishment. The Japanese formed a small "independent" air force in the state and armed it with obsolete aircraft, including the Nakajima Ki-27 Nate fighter. The Manchurian Air Force fell under the command structure of the Japanese Second Air Army and flew in the defense of Manchurian territory in which lay Mukden.[6]

Japanese fighter defenses proved to be fairly effective against the B-29s, with four falling in the target area and another eleven returning with fighter damage. Fighters attacked seventy-seven of the bombers, with B-29 gunners claiming twenty aircraft destroyed, ten probably destroyed, and thirty damaged. Post-mission analysis indicates 20% of the fighter attacks were coordinated and conducted by two or more Japanese pilots.

A variety of Japanese fighter aircraft, including Manchurian-flown Nates, engaged the bombers over Mukden. The majority of fighter attacks originated from above and in front of the bombers in a pattern repeated during the previous ten missions. Analysts believed Japanese tactics from high frontal positions included an attempt to injure the cockpit crew and thus disable the bomber by removing the pilot and co-pilot. During the Mukden mission, high frontal attacks resulted in an unforeseen benefit for the Japanese pilots: the frosting of windshields inhibited many bombardiers from assuming control of the forward gun turrets to counter Japanese fighters. The same weather conditions aided the B-29 crews when it came to spotting the Japanese: the fighters produced bold vapor trails in the cold sky, permitting B-29 gunners to spot and track them. Records indicated the gunners could even locate Japanese pilots attempting to utilize the sun to mask their movements.

A Japanese Kawasaki Ki-45 Nick fighter. Pilot Sgt. Shinobu Ikeda rammed #390 *Gallopin Goose* of the 468th BG with a Nick fighter during Mission #19 to Mukden and both planes crashed; Ikeda did not survive the encounter. (*Lukas*)

The fighter pilots were very aggressive and even employed ramming tactics against the B-29s targeting Mukden. Five of the Japanese attacks included aerial bombs, with phosphorous striking the wing of a bomber:

> All 5 of the aerial bombing approaches were made from the front, 1 at 10 o'clock, 1 at 11 o'clock, 2 at 1 o'clock, and 1 at 2 o'clock. "Flipping" as well as "dropping" tactics were used, and both explosive and phosphorous types were reported. A Kawasaki Ki-45 Nick dropped a cylindrical object about 18 inches long with strips of tinsel or shackles dangling from the bomb; it was dropped about 250 yards above the formation, and was not seen to explode. 4 bombs about the size of hand grenades were dropped by another plane and were reported as exploding with red bursts. 1 B-29 was hit in the right flap and wing root with phosphorous particles, but major damage was not done despite the fact that the phosphorous was still burning and the holes being enlarged when the B-29 landed at base.[7]

Ground crew members pose with #390 *Gallopin Goose* of the 468th BG. A Japanese Kawasaki Ki-45 Nick fighter rammed its tail during Mission #19 to Mukden, Manchuria. Staff Sgt. Arnold Pope was the only crewman who managed to parachute from the stricken bomber. (*Schutte via 468th BG*)

Japanese pilots also utilized several "chow line" attacks against the bomber formations. One assault involved fourteen fighters coordinating their runs against a twelve-bomber formation:

> A "chow line" attack was executed by 7 Nicks and 7 Nakajima Ki-43 Oscars flying in a line astern to the right of a formation of 12 B-29s. The enemy fighters were positioned high and in the sun; they accelerated, moved ahead of the formation, banked to the left and in rapid succession dove on the B-29s from 1 and 2 o'clock. Attacks were aimed particularly at the lead element and the lead plane of the C element. The Jap pilots opened fire at about 1,200 yards and pressed their diving attacks as close as 25 yards. Most of the fighters leveled off and went out over the formation, others dived below it, and 3 flew directly through the formation. 1 B-29 sustained minor damage while 1 Nick is claimed as destroyed and 2 Nicks as damaged.[8]

Japanese fighter pilots downed two B-29s utilizing ramming tactics over Mukden. The first bomber to fall (#390 *Gallopin Goose* of the 468th BG) encountered a Japanese fighter approximately fifteen minutes prior to the target. Japanese pilot Sgt. Shinobu Ikeda first initiated an attack against the tail section of #486 *Windy City*:

> The fighter then approached the formation from the rear at about 7 o'clock on #486. The tail and left gunners of #486 fired when the Nick was about 200 yards out. His right engine began to smoke and part of the canopy was seen to fly off. 3 other B-29s in the formation observed that #390's tail gunner was also firing on the Nick at this time. It was observed that the Nick's nose appeared to be bashed in. The enemy plane dropped down apparently out of control, then seemed to recover itself and pulled up towards the tail of #390 with left wing high. The Nick crashed into the tail of the B-29 shearing off the vertical fin and left stabilizer. The Nick broke up in mid-air. #390 maintained fair control for 2,000 feet, then spun over on its back and dropped straight to the ground.[9]

Only one crewman (Staff Sgt. Arnold Pope) parachuted from the stricken bomber. Sgt. Ikeda died in the crash of his crippled Nick.

A Nakajima Ki-44 Tojo targeted another B-29 (#299 *Humpin Honey* of the 462nd BG). Although described by some postwar sources as a ramming attack, the B-29 crews who observed the action questioned this analysis at the time of the mission:

> The Tojo approached the formation at 11 o'clock on aircraft #395, passed under #395, approached aircraft #424 also at 11 o'clock direction. The Tojo then banked to his own right and passed under #424, approaching #299 level at 1 o'clock to 11 o'clock direction, and collided with the left wing of the B-29. The bombardier of #395 fired on the Tojo and saw the enemy plane break into flames; the bombardier of #424 fired also but claims no hits, as was the case with aircraft #439. The top gunner of aircraft #411 fired and observed pieces flying off the Tojo. It is probable that #299 fired at the enemy plane also, although no fire from the destroyed B-29 was observed. Aircraft #417, #469, and #353 witnessed the collision but did not observe enough of the action to supply evidence as to whether or not the Jap pilot rammed intentionally. Aircraft #265, however, reported that the Tojo appeared to "blow up" just prior to the collision. The crew of aircraft #424 believes that it was not intentionally ramming as the Tojo apparently attempted to lift his wing to avoid #299 and get out of the formation. It appeared to observers on #429 that the Tojo didn't attempt to ram, but that there wasn't enough space to maneuver out of the formation. Analysis of all of the factors indicates that the Tojo was hit prior to the collision, probably was out of control, and possibly even disintegrated immediately prior to the collision. There is even evidence that he attempted to avoid the collision.[10]

The B-29 either exploded or broke apart at its mid-section, hurling two survivors—Staff Sgt. Walter Huss and Tech Sgt. Ken Beckwith—into the sky, where they employed their parachutes. The Japanese captured both men and charged them with "crimes" related to bombing civilian targets. Both men endured solitary confinement in prison until liberated by Soviet forces at the end of the war.

The death of the Tojo pilot eliminated any post-mission analysis of the attack by the Japanese and prevents developing a definitive answer as to whether he intended to ram #299 or his aggressiveness and/or battle damage resulted in an unintentional collision. One piece of evidence that could favor an intentional ramming is confirmation by at least one B-29 crew member that the Japanese pilot attempted to lift his wing. Ramming attacks against the bombers over Mukden were not intended to be automatic suicide runs like the "kamikaze" dives against American ships off Okinawa the following year; the tactic for ramming involved slicing the bomber and surviving the attack by bailing out, if possible, and fighting another day.

Second Lt. Fumiro Sou targeted the 468th BG's #356 *Lassie* flown by Maj. Douglas Hatfield; the Japanese fighter flew directly at the front of the bomber in an apparent ramming attack. Gunners aboard the B-29 hit the Oscar's engine, setting it on fire. Second Lt. Sou banked his aircraft and struck the propeller on engine #1; the fighter began cartwheeling and hurled the Japanese pilot from his cockpit. Sou parachuted to safety and claimed he downed #356 *Lassie*. Meanwhile, Hatfield and crew returned to northwest China despite the propeller damage.[11]

The 444th BG lost B-29 #262 *Round Trip Ticket*, piloted by Maj. Carl Barnes, possibly to a Japanese Nick fighter. Other crew members remembered seeing the aircraft

A Japanese pilot targeted #356 *Lassie* of the 468th BG during Mission #19. The fighter pilot banked his aircraft and struck the propeller on engine #1. Hatfield and crew returned to northwest China despite the propeller damage. (*US Air Force*)

The 444th BG possibly lost #262 *Round Trip Ticket* to a Japanese fighter. Other crew members on Mission #19 to Mukden, Manchuria, remembered seeing a fighter diving at the same location as the missing bomber. (*444th BG*)

immediately after the bomb run, and then it disappeared. One reported observing a Nick diving at the same location as the missing bomber. The 40th BG's #322 *Bonny Lee*, piloted by Capt. Robert Tisserat, made a two-engine emergency landing at Ankang due to combat damage.[12]

Capt. Robert Tisserat, pilot of the 40th BG's #322 *Bonny Lee*, made a two-engine emergency landing at Ankang due to combat damage on Mission #19 to Mukden, Manchuria. (*Barnes via 40th BG*)

Three B-29s crashed as non-combat losses on the return flight from Mukden. The 468th BG's #395, piloted by Capt. Martin, overshot the runway when landing after the mission and was written off as a total loss. The nose section was completely iced, adding weight and reducing cockpit visibility. The plane actually fell the last forty feet with the right wing sagging. The bomber struck the ground, causing it to swerve to the right. All of the crew members survived. B-29 #359 *Missouri Queen* of the 462nd BG crashed due to fuel exhaustion on the flight back from Mukden. The crew radioed the plane was low on fuel and the pilot planned to land at an emergency field; nothing was seen nor heard from the B-29 again. The 468th BG's #389 *Party Girl*, flown by 1st Lt. Calvin Lyons, flew with a formation on the return leg from Mukden. Approximately one hour and fifteen minutes from their base, the formation leader directed the other pilots to disperse and begin their descents to the airfield. When the formation leader dropped his altitude he encountered heavy icing and opted to order all planes to regain altitude and make quick and steep landing approaches, avoiding prolonged exposure to ice. Meanwhile, the formation lost all contact with Lyons, whose plane

The 468th BG's #395, piloted by Capt. Martin, overshot the runway when landing after Mission #19. The nose section was completely iced and the plane actually fell the last forty feet, striking the ground and causing it to swerve. All of the crew members survived. (*US Air Force*)

The 468th BG's #395 photographed during its crash landing after Mission #19 to Mukden. (*US Air Force*)

apparently crashed due to the weight and loss of stability caused by heavy ice deposits on the surface of the bomber.[13]

The 40th BG lost #363 *Marietta Misfit*, piloted by Capt. George Varoff, after the bomber sustained fighter damage near Mukden. Varoff joined the military following a career as a pole vaulter. He set a world pole vaulting record in 1936, but did not qualify for the 1936 Olympics in Germany. The cancellation of the 1940 and 1944 Olympic games due to World War II ended his Olympic hopes and resulted in a stint in the Army Air Force as a pilot. A Japanese fighter jumped Varoff's B-29, damaging an engine during the Mukden mission. The 40th BG record relates the tale:

> The Formation Commander immediately assigned two other planes to escort the cripple [Varoff's B-29]. Everything seemed to be all right until position 36 30'N – 113 00'E was reached at 0553Z. At this time #363 was seen to lower its landing gear and open the bomb bay doors. The altitude of the plane was 14,000 feet and the terrain below was rugged and mountainous with steep river gorges and sheer cliffs. Then Captain Varoff called Major Wemple in #729 [*Nippon Nipper III*], one of the escorting planes, and in an unruffled matter-of-fact voice stated that #1 propeller was getting ready to fly off and that they were abandoning the plane. The crews of the escorting planes watched what they described as a "heart-breaking scene" as they saw the #1 prop fly off and saw the crew bailing out. Eleven chutes were seen to open but the observers reported that one chute was seen to collapse when the strong wind blew it against a sheer cliff. Number 363 was seen to crash into a mountain and explode.[14]

All eleven crew members survived the bail out and were rescued by Chinese Communist forces, who escorted them to where they could be picked up by an aircraft. The XX BC maintained a liaison presence with the Chinese Communists and their leader Mao Tse-tung (briefly mentioned in chapter 7). An American intelligence officer from the XX BC named Louis Jones worked with the Chinese Communists as a liaison officer in December 1944, when Varoff and his crew parachuted from their

The tail section of #395 of the 468th BG after the crash landing following Mission #19. Note the tail guns have already been salvaged from the wreck. (*Schutte via 468th BG*)

B-29. Jones wrote about the frustrations behind transporting the Varoff crew back to American control:

> When the first rescue attempt was made, Varoff's crew was not there. They had gone to a neighboring village to be wined and dined as guests of the communists. Once it was determined the crew was not at the strip, the rescue plane took off immediately. They could not afford to stay on the ground any length of time because the Japanese fighter bases were too close. There were nothing but pleas over the communist [communications] network to come again. The second attempt went smoothly. The entire crew of 11 got out safely.[15]

40th BG records included a lamentation of concern for the condition of the Varoff crew after their bail out, but also an interesting comment that the generosity and banquets of the Chinese Communists resulted in weight gain for most of the personnel:

> Capt. George Varoff and his entire crew (44th Squadron) returned to Chakulia from China on 9 February. This crew had to bail out behind the Jap lines in North China when returning from Mukden, Manchuria, while on the 7 December mission, and had been walking out with the help of Chinese Communists in bitterly cold weather and more than once in danger of being captured by the Japanese during this elapsed time. Despite the strenuous journey they all returned to their outfit in excellent condition, most of them having put on weight since the time of their bailout. Once again the 40th Group was indebted to the Chinese Communist Forces who in all likelihood had suffered casualties in their successful efforts to return this crew.[16]

American military aid supported Gen. Chiang Kai-Shek and his nationalist forces, but not Mao and the Chinese Communists in their mutual fight against the Japanese; both Chinese parties looked toward fully renewing their conflict as soon as the Allies defeated Japan. Gen. Curtis LeMay wholeheartedly supported and nurtured the relationship established between XX BC and the Chinese Communists. Crews parachuting into communist-held territory needed the assurance of Chinese protection and support to return to Allied control, which could only be accomplished through direct communication with Mao and the Chinese Communists. Mao and LeMay exchanged messages and gifts, with the former receiving a pair of binoculars and providing the latter with a Japanese sword. LeMay assigned his personal North American B-25 Mitchell bomber outfitted as a transport to ferry gifts of medical supplies to the communists and fly downed crewmen back to American bases. LeMay wanted sufficient medical supplies on hand to ensure his crewmen would receive adequate attention if injured.

Gen. Curtis LeMay receives a Japanese sword sent to him by Mao Tse-tung. LeMay supported and nurtured the relationship established between XX BC and the Chinese Communists. B-29 crews parachuting into Communist-held territory needed assurance of Chinese protection and support to return to Allied control. (*40th BG*)

Duty as a XX BC liaison officer with the Chinese Communists had its rewards and interesting memories. After World War II, Louis Jones remembered a meal during which he sat next to Mao:

> Once a week Chairman Mao would invite the American Mission Commander to have dinner with him and other political and military leaders. During one of these meals I was sitting next to Chairman Mao. I reached over toward the center of the table with my chop sticks to try a succulent-looking meat dish. Mao put his chop sticks on top of mine and spoke to me in Chinese. Since I did not understand him I turned to my interpreter who told me that Mao realized that in my country the dog was a pet, but that in China the dog was a meat animal and that I did not have to eat it if I did not want to. I started to pull back, but when I looked up I saw that everyone had stopped eating to see what my reaction would be; therefore, I went ahead and ate the dog meat and everyone went back to eating and appeared satisfied with my reaction. Nevertheless, for the rest of the meal I dodged this local delicacy.[17]

Second Lt. Sou's claim of downing #356 *Lassie* in a ramming attack permits a brief review of the claims for destruction of enemy aircraft by both sides during Mission #19. While inflated claims could be morale boosts for crews and civilians at home, they could also exaggerate the success of specific tactics or even the attrition of opposing forces. Sorting these claims at the end of the war proved to be challenging, since it required the accurate and official records of both sides in the same air battle. Researchers Koji Takaki and Henry Sakaida—the former Japanese and the latter American—managed to compare the Japanese records to those of the United States for this air battle over Mukden. Although the XX BC lost four B-29s to Japanese fighters, Japanese pilots claimed to have downed fifteen bombers. On the other side, American gunners claimed the destruction of twenty fighters and the probable destruction of ten more; Japanese records indicate an actual loss of only six fighters, including one Manchurian Nate, in the engagement over Mukden.[18]

Mission #20: Bangkok (Rangoon), December 14, 1944

One of the XX BC's most tragic operational accidents occurred over Rangoon during Mission #20. The mission was intended as a training exercise in support of Allied tactical operations in Burma and called for all four groups to return to Bangkok, Thailand, with the Rama VI Bridge as the primary target; the Central Railroad Station in Rangoon, Burma, as the secondary; and the railroad yards in Bassein, Burma, as the target of last resort. With Bangkok serving as the principal supply route from Malaya and Indo-China to Japanese troops in Burma, Allied planners wanted to drop the Rama VI Bridge into the river. The Rama VI Bridge was a five-span, steel girder, lattice-style bridge 1,456 feet long and forty-five feet wide. The bridge utilized shore abutments and four masonry piers to support the structure. Each masonry pier was formed by two round columns approximately twelve feet in diameter sixteen feet apart. Rail traffic from Thailand bound to Rangoon and the Japanese front in Burma moved through the Central Railroad Station in Rangoon. Destruction of this facility could disrupt Japanese supplies destined for front-line troops in Burma. Bassein was not an active military supply point in December 1944, but planners thought bombing the railroad yards at Bassein could discourage the Japanese military from shifting traffic to the yards. With the Rama VI Bridge laying as a small target, plans called for the pilots to proceed to the secondary target if cloud cover prohibited visual bombing at Bangkok, since the size of the bridge would not permit effective radar bombing through cloud cover.[19]

Each group launched twelve aircraft for a total of forty-eight airborne B-29s. The field order called for each aircraft to carry high explosive bombs. Some bombs packed the new Composition B—a mixture of TNT and RDX (Research Department Explosive) much more powerful than TNT alone. (At the same time, Composition B is more volatile than TNT.) The B-29 crews raised concerns when they realized the 500-pound Composition B bombs hung underneath the 1,000-pound TNT weapons and argued the bombs could collide and explode when released due to their instantaneous fuses, rather than dropping at a constant speed. 40th BG Commander Col. William Blanchard ordered the mission flown with the mixed load, although XX BC granted him permission to change it. The decision cost the group four downed aircraft, four crews either killed in action or captured, and one dead crewman on a damaged bomber that struggled back to India.[20]

Thirty-three B-29s bombed the primary target in Bangkok. The bridge remained intact, although the bombs destroyed many small buildings in the area and caused slight damage to both approaches to the bridge. As the cloud cover increased, the 40th BG aircraft diverted to the secondary target at Rangoon. Eleven aircraft bombed the secondary target with considerable accuracy. The destruction included the main station building, passenger loading platforms, receiving sheds, miscellaneous shops, and thirty-five pieces of rolling stock. Two bombers (#859 *Shag'n Home* of the 40th BG and #415 *Jolly Roger* of the 468th BG) hit the target of last resort due to mechanical issues and the results were not observed. One 468th BG plane bombed a target of opportunity in Bangkok by mistake; due to improper target identification, the crew bombed the Phra Buddha Yodfa Bridge, with hits observed on two spans.

The tragic accident occurred in the skies over Rangoon. As the 40th BG B-29s passed over the target and dropped their ordnance an explosion rocked all of the bombers: four planes crashed in or around Rangoon, six made emergency landings at Allied fields, and only one bomber returned to the 40th BG's home field. The latter bomber brought home one crew member fatally wounded in the accident. Post-mission analysis and interviews determined that one or more of the bombs dropped by the low formation exploded, probably from contact with another bomb, leading to a terrible tragedy affecting every plane in the formation. Ignoring the pre-mission warnings about mixing the bomb loads resulted in the deaths of seventeen crew members and another twenty-seven men held prisoner of war until May 1945.[21]

The 468th BG's #415 *Jolly Roger* bombed the target of last resort on Mission #20 to Rangoon due to mechanical issues; results were not observed. (*Schutte via 468th BG*)

Four 40th BG B-29s crashed immediately or within minutes after the accident. Capt. Howard Gerber, pilot of #726, died along with his entire crew over Rangoon. Capt. Bob Shanks, pilot of #574 *293*, and his crew bailed out and were captured by the Japanese. Sgt. G. M. Etherington, the flight engineer on #574 *293*, remembered the incident:

> Seconds after bombs away there was a tremendous explosion. I guess all four engines had been hit. Two engines were on fire—#3 and one other. My first concern was to get these fires out, which fortunately I was able to do. One of the other two was running so rough that we decided to feather it. The gunners reported there was a big hole in the right wing and the control surfaces were badly damaged. Bob and [Co-pilot Harold] Fletch had a lot of trouble flying the plane but managed to control it. There were several holes in the plane, but miraculously nobody was seriously hurt. I had a scratch on my left arm and [Navigator] Julian Cochran had a small piece of metal in the sole of his shoe and a small wound on his leg. His parachute had been shredded, and he went through the tunnel to get a spare chute which just happened to be in the back.[22]

The ordnance mishap during Mission #20 to Rangoon brought down the 40th BG's #573 *293*. Shanks and his crew bailed out and were captured by the Japanese. (*Slonina via 40th BG*)

Navigator Julian Cochran added his perspective:

> The explosion beneath us was of gigantic proportions. I immediately felt something hit my right ankle on the inside about one inch above the top of my GI shoes. My left shoe had a hunk of the sole knocked out just in front of the arch. A small piece of metal, probably skin of the plane, was just under my skin. It bled little and did not hurt. I picked up my chest chute from the floor and found it blossomed out in white. The whole bottom was shredded. I announced on the intercom that my chute was ruined, and [Central Fire Control Gunner] Nick [Oglesby] came on to say there was an extra chute in the radar room. I immediately flew through the tunnel to get it, and when I got back up front, I was out of air and quickly hooked on the oxygen at the front of the tunnel.[23]

Shanks fought to maintain control of the crippled bomber and fly to the Bay of Bengal, where the crew would have a good chance of rescue. The crew re-started one of the feathered engines, giving the B-29 two power plants to reach the Bay of Bengal. This engine soon began running rough and had to be feathered, leaving the crippled ship flying on only one engine. As the plane crossed the Irrawaddy River Delta, the final engine died. Etherington continued:

> I switched on the autopilot to give the pilots a better chance to get out and told Bob and Fletch to come right behind me. Then I jumped and pulled the rip-cord. There was quite a jolt as the chute opened—but it sure looked good to me. Several chutes were open in the direction we had come from. After what seemed like too long a time, two more chutes opened. Soon the plane turned to the left and started toward me, with #2 engine now burning fiercely. It turned again to the left, losing altitude, and as it was flying away from me, crashed and burned.[24]

Cochran jumped after Etherington:

> I don't remember the order to bail out nor any discussion as to who would go first. I know the nose wheel was lowered, and I immediately climbed down straddling the hole and standing on the handholds, pulled my legs together and dropped out. I thought I was first out, but two chutes were already open. Two of the guys in the back moved even faster than I did. I remember looking up toward the plane and pulling the cord as soon as I was clear. I never remember seeing the rip cord handle in my hand; I apparently simply pulled it and dropped it. I landed in an irrigation ditch, in waist-deep water and up to my knees in mud. Mine was probably the softest landing of anyone.[25]

Three crew members landed near a Burmese village, where the inhabitants emerged and escorted them to shelter. Someone apparently informed the local Burmese authorities of their presence, as a group of pro-Japanese Burmese soldiers apprehended the Americans and handed them to the Japanese. By the fourth day, the entire crew found themselves in the hands of the Japanese and remained prisoners of war (POWs) until the end of hostilities in Burma. They endured terrible conditions, as related by Cochran:

> Many had beri-beri; everyone had malaria; everyone had lice to a degree. By wearing only a loin cloth, I gave the lice no place to hide. We all lost weight. Those weighing 180 pounds lost as much as 60; I lost only about 10, for I weighed only 128 when I went down. You were required to bow to the guards, and if caught not bowing, you were forced to stand at attention in the sun for hours.[26]

Norman Larson flew as the navigator on B-29 #831 *Queenie*, piloted by 1st Lt. Wayne Triemer. Six crew members got out of the plane and became prisoners of war; the other five men died in the accident. Larson recalled his initial day as a prisoner of war in Rangoon's New Laws County Jail:

> I was alone, scared, and down in the dumps. I didn't know who on the crew had made it and who had not. I saw no one except the odd guard going by. The cuts under my chin and on my wrist were minor, but my ribs ached. That evening I had my first taste of POW cuisine. A tin dish was shoved into my cell. It held a small portion of rice liberally mixed with small pebbles and dead bugs and covered with a thin watery liquid which I subsequently found out was called "soup." I wasn't given a spoon or a fork so I drank the liquid and shoved some of the rice in my mouth. The rest of it went into the binjo [slang for a box or hole for relieving oneself]. It actually takes a day or so before you get hungry enough to eat swill like this.[27]

The Japanese later transferred Larson to the main prisoner facility in Rangoon, where he joined his other surviving crew members:

> At the POW camp, after some nonsense about "voluntarily" signing a statement giving our parole not to escape, we were brought to the cell block and placed in cells on the second floor. In my cell were Bert Parmalee, Karnig Thomasian and Richard Brooks. There was nothing in the cell, which was about 9½ feet square, except the inevitable binjo box. We were issued two burlap rice sacks which had been opened and which were full of holes, two tin dishes for our food (one of mine was a rusty old sardine can) and a prison-made spoon. We were also issued a small piece of cloth and a pin. On the cloth was written our POW number. It had to be worn at all times.[28]

A tragic accident occurred in the skies over Rangoon during Mission #20, when bombs collided and exploded, sending four B-29s into crashes. Six crew members got out of the 40th BG's #831 *Queenie* and became prisoners of war. The other five men died in the accident. (*40th BG*)

Capt. Cornelius Meyer and the other ten crew members of B-29 #457 *Battlin' Beauty* parachuted from their doomed bomber and fell into the hands of the Japanese military. Lt. Marion Burke, navigator aboard #457 *Battlin' Beauty*, peered at the meager anti-aircraft fire over Rangoon as his bombardier dropped their bomb load. Suddenly, the bomber shook and he heard the tail gunner scream into the intercom, "My God! The sky's turning red!" Burke immediately turned around to face his navigation table, only to find it did not exist; something had passed through the bomber and smashed the table. A warning indicated the bomb bay was burning and the flight engineer called out to the pilot that engine #3 had been ripped from the wing. Meyer ordered his crew to abandon the bomber. Burke glanced at radio operator Sgt. Richard Montgomery and realized his hand had been severed and was hanging by a single tendon; Burke pushed Montgomery out the nose wheel well. The radio operator actually tried to climb back into the B-29, forcing Burke to shove Montgomery again and follow him as the plane began a fatal spin.

Burke and Montgomery landed near a Japanese camp at a Burmese village. Burke bandaged Montgomery's arm, realizing he could not save the hand but needed to cover the wound. Japanese soldiers quickly captured the two men and two other crew members and forced them, including Montgomery, to stand all night with their hands bound. They kicked any prisoner who began to collapse. The crew endured forty-eight hours of interrogation and torture, including beatings by the non-sharpened back edge of a samurai sword. Two days later the Japanese hauled them to an old British prison, where they were reunited with their other crew members.

Co-pilot Lionel Coffin on #457 *Battlin' Beauty* resisted the Japanese interrogators. His refusal to answer any questions beyond the standard name, rank, and serial number earned three days in a cage so small he could not even sit up. The Japanese finally gave up and transferred him to a cell. Others were placed into small cells without food or water for days. One group of five American prisoners remained without food until Christmas, when they were tossed some raw meat. Interrogations and beatings continued for all of the prisoners. After three weeks, the B-29 crew members joined the general prisoner population in larger open-bay cells but remained separated from non-flying prisoners. The guards administered especially harsh punishments to the bomber crews. One guard forced Burke to stand on top of a seven-foot high metal fence. After falling from the fence due to pure exhaustion, the guard ordered him to stand up at attention, despite being barely conscious. A British soldier saved Burke's life at this point. When the guard looked away, the British soldier took Burke's hat and put it on his own head and assumed his position. The Japanese guard did not recognize the switch and tormented the British soldier, thinking it was Burke, who managed to move away unnoticed.

Inadequate food proved to be a way of life in the camp. When rations were not cut the prisoners received a cup of rice in the morning, a cup of rice with a few vegetables at lunch, and a cup of rice at dinner. Occasionally a fish head or perhaps even a piece of meat might be thrown into the bowl. By one account, the camp commandant's cat opted to stroll across the prison yard one day and the prisoners enjoyed a little meat at dinner.[29]

Mission #21: Hankow, December 18, 1944

Four days after the Bangkok/Rangoon mission, the XX BC initiated a series of three strikes that would cover targets in China, Japan, and Manchuria over a four-day window. Chiang Kai-Shek continued to call for B-29 strikes directly supporting his forces fighting the Japanese in China. Hitting secondary targets, targets of last resort, and targets of opportunity in China with bombers not able to reach primary targets in Japan, Manchuria, or Formosa did not satisfy Chiang nor American Maj. Gen. Claire

The 468th's briefing prior to Mission #21 to Hankow. Note the ninety-second take-off intervals for individual aircraft written on the chalk board. (*Schutte via 468th BG*)

Chennault, commander of the 14th Air Force. Chennault had demanded a large American incendiary strike against Hankow as far back as June 1944. As discussed earlier, the Army Air Force intended to employ the B-29s as a strategic resource against Japanese industry, not as a tactical asset in support of a ground campaign. The establishment of the 20th Air Force under command of Gen. Hap Arnold with the XX BC in India was a means to keep the B-29s separate from the demands of local commanders. Wedemeyer echoed the demands for B-29 strikes in support of the campaign in China as soon as he arrived in Chungking on October 31, 1944. Gen. Curtis LeMay continued the policy of citing previous directives for the B-29s to operate as a strategic air asset. LeMay wrote after the war, "[Wedemeyer] was also badgering me in China to help the theater of operations. Their intelligence said there was a Japanese build-up being made for a drive on western China aimed at capturing Chungking, and he wanted me to stop this with the B-29s. I, of course, refused because it wasn't in line with my orders."[30]

Everything changed when the Joint Chiefs of Staff ordered XX BC to cooperate with Wedemeyer in a massive raid on Hankow. LeMay met Gen. Chennault in China to plan the combined XX BC and 14th Air Force mission. After considerable debate, LeMay agreed to an incendiary raid. Scheduling Mission #21 served as an appeasement to Chiang, Chennault, and Wedemeyer, as well as a test for a new type of bombing strategy—incendiary munitions against highly flammable Asian cities. Gen. LeMay would later utilize this tactic to destroy Japanese cities as he directed the B-29 campaign from Saipan and the Tinian Islands.

The docks and adjacent storage areas of Hankow, China, were the primary target of the mission, with the railyard and storage area of Yochow, China, and the airfield storage area of Tangyang, China, as the target of last resort. Hankow served as a major military base and storage area for the Japanese. Supplies were offloaded at Hankow and transshipped into the interior of China by small vessels or rail. Up to 20,000 tons of military supplies were temporarily stored in Hankow on any particular day. The Japanese utilized Yochow as a supply base along the Wuchang-Hengyang railway. The storage area at Tangyang supported Japanese aircraft operating along the Yangtze River area. Successful strikes on any of these targets, but especially the primary target Hankow, could serve to disrupt supplies flowing to the Japanese military operating in China.[31]

Successfully hitting Hankow was considered so important that the mission was coordinated with an attack by 14th Air Force Consolidated B-24 Liberators, Martin B-26 Marauder medium bombers, and North American P-51 Mustangs. Plans called for the B-29s to hit the dock area with incendiary bombs. As the B-29s turned for home, 14th Air Force aircraft would attack Hankow and Japanese airfields in the area, catching fighters on the ground refueling and preparing to launch and intercept the Superfortresses departing the area. Originally scheduled for December 15, the mission date changed twice before settling on December 18. XX BC staff divided the Hankow docks into four distinct areas targeted by different Bomber Groups carrying different ordnance: planes in Component A carried M-76 500-pound incendiary bombs; Component B loaded M-76 500-pound incendiaries and M-47 100-pound incendiaries; Component C had M-47 100-pound incendiaries; and Component D hauled M-17 500-pound cluster bombs. The latter opened in the air and scattered smaller "cluster" munitions across a wide area. All aircraft in each component carried the same munitions load.[32]

Ninety-four B-29s launched from Chinese bases for Mission #21 (16 from the 40th BG, 25 from the 444th BG, 23 from the 462nd BG, and 30 with the 468th BG). The smaller number of 40th BG aircraft reflects the operational limitations placed on the group by downed

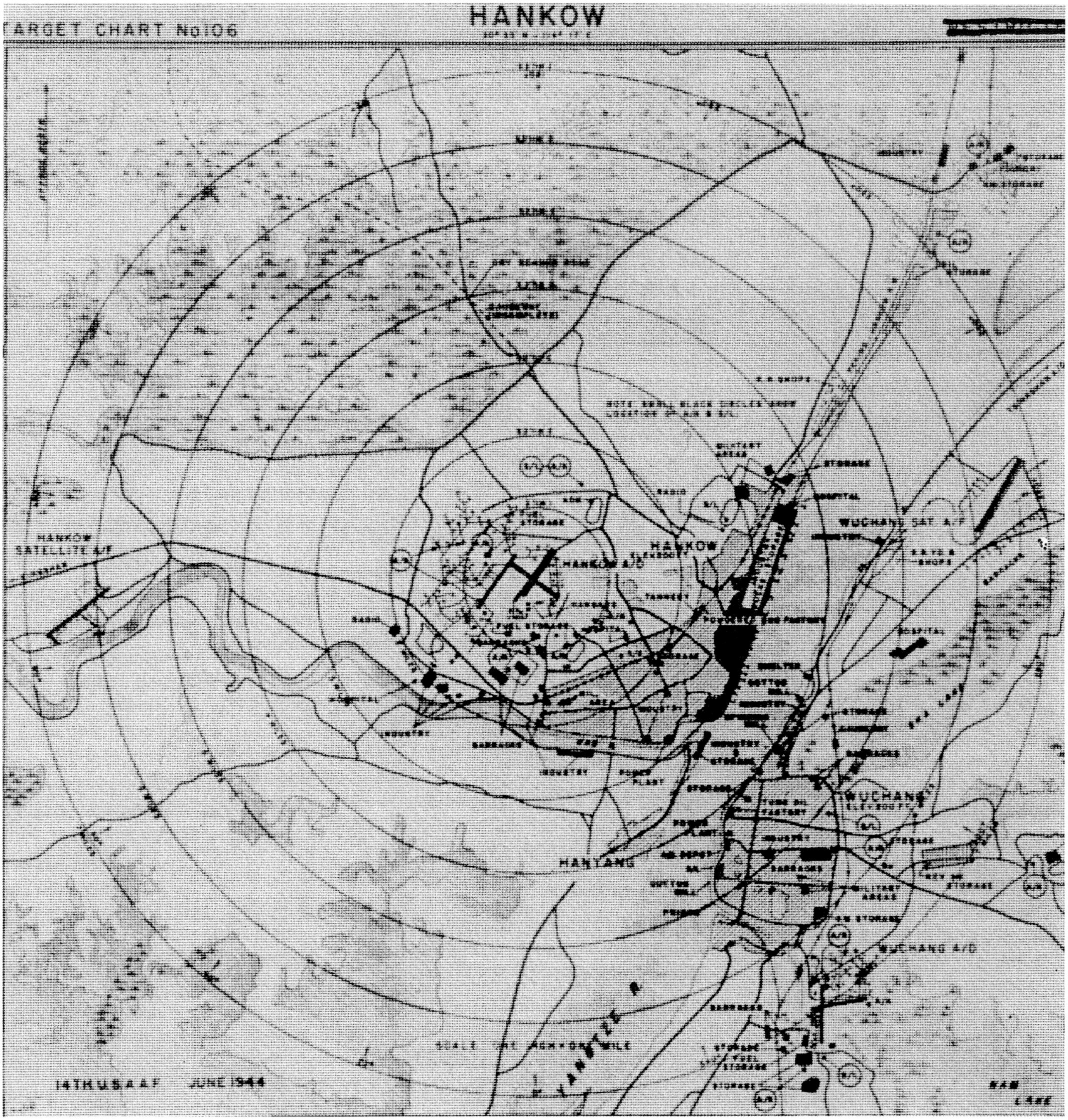

Military bombardment target chart for Hankow, China, the primary target of Mission #21. (*US Air Force*)

Japanese flak scored major damage on the 444th BG's #399 *The Agitator* during Mission #21 to Hankow. Flak struck this bomber along the fuselage just behind the cockpit area, but the B-29 returned home. (*Wilkins family via 444th BG*)

and damaged aircraft that flew the Rangoon mission four days earlier. Eighty-four bombers hit the primary target. Three 468th BG bombers (#546, #494, and #424 *Hap's Characters*) released incendiaries on the secondary target with poor to fair results. Three planes dropped incendiary ordnance on the target of last resort: #461 *Haulinas* and #362 *Hull's Angels* of the 462nd BG and #411 of the 468th BG. Two crews reported not seeing results and one noted excellent hits on the target. The 468th BG's #354 dropped part of its load on Hankow and part on a target of opportunity at Lehang with unobserved results.[33]

The bombers encountered meager to moderate anti-aircraft fire over Hankow. Two B-29 crews reported seeing phosphorous anti-aircraft shells mixed with the usual exploding high explosive shells that struck nine planes. Only one of these bombers (#399 *The Agitator* of the 444th BG) received significant damage. Flak struck this bomber along the fuselage just behind the cockpit area. Japanese gunners also engaged but did not hit bombers at Yochow and three other locations.[34]

Crews reported Japanese fighter opposition as weak. The Japanese made only six coordinated attacks and one included an aerial bomb. Four bombers sustained minor damage from fighters and gunners claimed to have destroyed one fighter, as well as the probable destruction of three more and damage to an additional ten fighters. Japanese fighters damaged #451 *Black Jack Too* of the 444th BG (holes in the radio compartment and emergency hydraulic system), the 462nd BG's #362 *Hull's Angels* (a wheel well, cooling duct, and wing panel) and #505 *Wild Hair* (hole in the bomb bay), and the 468th BG's #397 *Million Dollar Baby* (throttle control cable and fuselage). B-29 #691 *Fast Company* of the 468th BG returned with friendly fire holes in its bomb bay. All aircraft returned safely after the mission.[35]

Bombing results in Hankow were classified as excellent, despite the estimation that only thirty-three B-29s placed bombs into the designated strike area. Gen. Chennault requested a last minute change in the departure time for the B-29s and one group did not receive the message, throwing the formation arrival times out of sequence. Heavy smoke rising from the fires ignited by the first formations greatly obscured the area for the later bomber formations. The incendiary bombs destroyed between 40–50% of the entire strike area, which burned for three days, as winds helped spread the flames outside the target area. LeMay credited the results of the Hankow raid with confirming incendiary bombing as an effective strategy against Japanese cities. He noted, "...its success gave us a great deal of useful information about the effects of incendiaries on the highly flammable wood and paper construction common to the housing stock of the Far East."[36]

Mission #22: Omura, December 19, 1944

The XX BC maintained its aircraft in China after Mission #21 and launched them against Omura, Japan, the next day, with the Omura Aircraft Plant as the primary target. Mission plans listed the Kiangnan Dock and Engineering Works in Shanghai, China, as the secondary target and the Nanking Wharf in China as the target of last resort. The Omura Aircraft Plant continued to produce Japanese Mitsubishi F1M Pete reconnaissance and Aichi B7A Grace attack aircraft while repairing Mitsubishi A6M Zeke fighters and Aichi E13A Jake reconnaissance aircraft. The Kiangnan Dock and Engineering Works included the city's largest dry dock and served as the most important shipbuilding (merchant vessels) and repair facility outside Japan. The target of last resort provided the Japanese with a location for transloading military supplies from large vessels to smaller ones, as well as rail lines in support of their forces operating in the interior of China.[37]

The command originally planned this mission for October and then November as a double-strike operation, with

The Japanese Omura Aircraft Plant on Formosa repaired the Aichi E13A Jake observation aircraft. The XX BC targeted this plant during Mission #22. (*Lukas*)

A mess hall in China. (*40th BG*)

one group of B-29s hitting Omura and another group bombing a different target. Due to the constant stream of engine troubles on the B-29, XX BC decided to utilize only bombers with recently modified engines for the long distance mission to Japan. Mission #22 also incorporated changes from the other operations flown against Omura, including altering routes, moving the formation assembly points to provide more flight time at night during the outbound journey and to save fuel, the dissolving of formations on the return leg to provide pilots practice instrument flying when approaching to land, and the setting of specific times over the target to better coordinate the bombing runs of each formation.[38]

Thirty-six B-29s departed from China carrying a mixture of high explosive and incendiary bombs. All four groups launched B-29s for the operation (12 from the 40th BG, 10 with the 444th BG, 9 from the 462nd BG, and 5 with the 468th BG). Less than half of these planes (17) bombed the primary target by radar. Thirteen B-29s visually bombed the secondary target and two planes (the 444th BG's #202 *Satan's Angel* and the 40th BG's #582 *Little Clambert* flown by Capt. Graham Bleiler) visually dropped their ordnance on the target of last resort. Damage to the primary target could not be assessed at the time of the mission due to the thick cloud cover. A reconnaissance mission returned with photographs that did not show any new damage since the last raid on the plant. Strike photos at the secondary target showed a river steamer blazing after a bomb hit and flooding within the dry dock. Near misses were scored against another steamer, a destroyer escort, and a mine layer vessel. Several buildings and shops were hit as well. Results at the target of last resort were not observed.

Crews experienced meager and generally inaccurate anti-aircraft flak over Omura and Shanghai. All aircraft returned without flak damage. Crews reported Japanese fighter defenses ranging from weak to moderate. Fighters attacked twenty-one of the thirty-six airborne bombers without inflicting any damage, while B-29 gunners claimed five destroyed, four probably destroyed, and twelve damaged. Japanese fighters did not engage any bombers over Omura, but were present in the clear skies over Shanghai and along the route back to western China. The B-29 crews noted the Japanese fighter pilots seemed to be less aggressive than in engagements during earlier missions. Ten of the Japanese attacks included aerial bombs, according to post-mission analysis:

> An interesting coordinated attack in which aerial bombs were used was reported by a 3 plane formation of B-29s flying over Shanghai at 20,000 feet, with the sun at 6 o'clock. Three Oscars were sighted at 2,000 yards approaching in line astern from 12 o'clock high. The lead B-29 opened fire at 1,200 yards. The Oscars returned the fire at 1,000 yards and kept coming in. Each Oscar, as he cleared the top of the formation by about 100 feet, dropped a phosphorous bomb, then staying on course, headed directly into the sun. No B-29s were reported damaged nor were any claims made against the Oscars.[39]

The 40th BG lost #466 *Able Fox* of the 40th BG, piloted by Capt. Chester Woolsey, due to engine problems. The propeller could not be feathered, and the crew abandoned the aircraft near Ankang due to excessive vibrations. All of the crew members returned safely. (*Clendenen via 40th BG*)

A streamer from a phosphorous bomb did strike one bomber. "One B-29 reported an attack with phosphorous type bombs in which 2 bombs exploded about 400 feet above a formation, with streamers spreading out to cover the B-29s. The crew of the airplane reporting the attack stated that its left wing was hit by the streamers but the embers slid off inflicting no damage."[40]

Two Japanese Kawasaki Ki-61 Tony pilots coordinated an attack on a B-29 that placed each of the fighters on opposite sides of the B-29 from the perspective of the cockpit crew:

> Two Tonys were sighted at 2,000 yards, low; one coming in from 11 o'clock and the other from 1 o'clock. It appeared like a well timed attack with the Tony at 11 o'clock just a few seconds ahead of the other. Each Tony in his pursuit curve opened fire at 1,000 yards, closed to 500 yards, then broke away under the formation. The B-29 opened fire at 800 yards and claimed damage on the 11 o'clock Tony. The other was not hit. No damage was reported to the B-29.[41]

Four Japanese Nakajima Ki-44 Tojos conducted a succession of coordinated attacks:

> Four Tojos executed approximately 15 attacks in a chow line maneuver, but with a slight variation – a low approach instead of the usual high. The attacks were directed principally against a B-29 flying in No. 3 position of a 3 plane formation. Each Tojo made 3 to 4 individual passes in such rapid succession that it was impossible to keep an accurate count, and the total of 15 attacks was an estimate. All approaches were from 3 o'clock low, and the first enemy aircraft was sighted at 1,200 yards. After each Tojo banked in to attack, the enemy pilot opened fire at 900 yards, continued on to 400 yards, then broke away to 5:30 o'clock. The B-29 fired at 600 yards, and claimed 1 destroyed and 1 probably destroyed. No damage was reported to the B-29.[42]

B-29 #678 *Kickapoo Lou* of the 468th BG returned with a self-inflicted wound in the bomb bay by one of its own lower gun turrets. Two planes were operational losses during the mission: the 40th BG lost #466 *Able Fox*, piloted by Capt. Chester Woolsey, due to engine problems. Approximately two hours after take-off engine #1 suffered a leak and lost all of its oil. The propeller could not be feathered, and the crew eventually had to abandon the aircraft near Ankang due to excessive vibrations. All of the crew members returned safely.[43] The 462nd BG's #452, piloted by 1st Lt. Walter Romaniw, lost engine #2 between the second assembly point and the initial point near the target; the crew jettisoned the bombs and turned back. However, the lack of fuel forced the crew to bail out and all returned safely.[44]

The 40th BG lost another B-29 the next night while Maj. Robert Moss and his crew flew #331 *Gone With The Wind* from China to India. As the B-29 passed through the night skies over Burma, a British Bristol Beaufighter night fighter pilot intercepted the bomber. Moss and his crew asserted the plane carried an operable Identification, Friend or Foe (IFF) box that emitted a signal indicating it was an Allied aircraft, but the XX BC, as a separate strategic Air Force, did not always coordinate the movement of B-29s across the Hump with other Allied air units. It should be added that Allied air units did not fully coordinate their flights with the XX BC as well. The descent of the bomber alarmed American ground units, which fired anti-aircraft guns as a possible air raid warning and in turn caused greater confusion for the Beaufighter pilot, who claimed he did not receive an IFF signal from the B-29. The British pilot fired his cannon and crippled the bomber. As a wing burst into flames, the fighter pilot could see the American insignia on the bomber. All eleven crew members jumped from the bomber, but the parachute carried by navigator 1st Lt. David Lustig did not open; ten men survived the friendly fire incident. Co-pilot 1st Lt. John Elliott recalled the tragic incident:

The 40th BG lost #331 *Gone With The Wind* the night after Mission #22 to Omura, as Maj. Robert Moss and his crew flew from China to India. A British Bristol Beaufighter night fighter pilot intercepted and shot down the bomber over Burma. (*US Air Force*)

We were not carrying any bombs nor were our guns loaded since we did not believe we were in any danger. Some crew members, not essential to the operation of the plane, were relaxing. We were equipped with IFF. It was operating properly and was set on the designated code channel for that day. At the time we were flying at approximately 10,000 ft. The full moon was about halfway down in the west. The first indication that anything was amiss was the rat-tat-tat of bullets hitting the plane. I looked out the right side of cockpit and saw our #3 engine on fire. I told Bob, and he told me to feather the engine. After feathering and activating the fire extinguishers, heavy flames continued to trail from the engine. With the danger of the plane exploding, Bob gave the order over the intercom to bail out and, at the same time, rang the alarm bell. I lowered the landing gear so that the crew in the forward compartment could go out through the nose wheel well. I'm not certain, but I believe Chuck Biehle [bombardier] was the first one out. I followed him, and when I hit the airstream feet first, I began to tumble head over heels. I pulled the ripcord, and my chute opened, stopping my tumbling. I looked down and saw that I was over the large estuary of the Ganges River, about a half mile in width. It was quite difficult to judge distance in the light of the moon, which was about 30 degrees above the western horizon. Coming down from 10,000 ft., I drifted over Sandwip Island. In landing, I sort of slid down the side of a springy tree which slowed my speed, and I landed with little jarring.[45]

Elliott learned that friendly fire incidents were more common than one might imagine:

> A few days after the episode, Charles Biehle, Robert Helfrich [radar operator], and I, the only ones not injured, were called upon to accompany some of our ranking staff officers on a trip to Chittagong to meet with some British military officials regarding the shoot down. While at Chittagong, we met with some members of a USAF P-38 outfit who were assigned there to fly cover for Allied shipping convoys plying the Burma coast. All of these pilots were interested in our escape from the burning plane. To commiserate with us, they told us, "Don't worry, boys, we shot down two Beaufighters in the past month." They had a strict "no fly" zone over the convoys with orders to shoot down anyone who flew into this zone.[46]

The downing of #331 *Gone With The Wind* was not the only "friendly fire" incident involving a XX BC B-29. In September 1944, a 444th BG B-29 (#262 *Round Trip Ticket*) flown by Maj. Jack Blackwell encountered six unidentified fighters while flying across the Hump to China. The apparent leader of the fighters approached the bomber. A gunner aboard the B-29 opened fire, damaging the wing and retracted landing gear of the fighter, which then departed the area with the five other aircraft. Several days later, the group learned the fighters were British Supermarine Spitfires and the pilot of the damaged plane was a squadron commander. In a "matter of fact" style, the 444th BG historical report for the month notes, "The Maj. [Blackwell] was absolved from all blame naturally."[47] The 444th BG lost B-29 #262 *Round Trip Ticket* on December 7, 1944, during the mission to Mukden. Maj. Carl Barnes and his crew were flying the aircraft on that mission, having "borrowed" it from Maj. Blackwell.

Mission #23: Mukden, December 21, 1944

The Command returned to Manchuria two days after Mission #22 to Omura. Again, planners selected the Manchurian Aircraft Manufacturing Company in Mukden as the primary target. The secondary target included two options: shipping in the port of Darien or the South Manchurian Railway and piers and facilities in Darien. The railroad yards at Chenghsien were selected as the target of last resort. The primary target produced training aircraft for the Japanese and its destruction could hinder pilot training programs. The best port facilities north of Shanghai could be found in Darien, the secondary target. Destruction in the port could hinder the movement of supplies to Japanese forces in the area, as well as manufactured goods and raw materials bound for Japan. The tertiary target served the Japanese as an important alternate supply line for troops in China. Disruption of the rail yards could result in bottlenecks along other rail lines utilized for the transport of supplies and troops.[48]

The XX BC launched forty-nine B-29s carrying a mixture of high explosive and incendiary bombs from its forward bases in China: twelve planes each from the 40th BG, 444th BG, and 462nd BG and thirteen planes from the 468th BG. Forty of the B-29s arrived at the primary target, but only nineteen bombed the plant. Heavy frosting of cockpit windows prevented bomber crews from clearly seeing other bombers, especially the lead planes. The planes in two formations dropped their ordnance up to nine miles from the target, leaving only the lead bombers to drop munitions on the aircraft plant. In these cases, one bombardier would believe he saw the lead plane drop its load and then release his ordnance and the surrounding planes would dump their loads upon seeing the errant bomber release its munitions. A post strike analysis indicated the primary target did not sustain any new damage since the last bombing mission to Mukden, but errant incendiary bombs hit the arsenal located 2,000 feet from the aircraft plant, gutting workshops. Other errant bombs cratered the nearby runway and struck the Mukden Railroad Yards.

B-29 #228 *Earthquake McGoon* of the 444th BG bombed the secondary target due to a blown gunner's blister and two planes (#487 *Bengal Lancer* and #704 *The Gear Box* of the 468th BG) hit the target of last resort. Five B-29s dropped ordnance on targets of opportunity: the 40th BG's #718 *Black Magic II* bombed Tiahlu with poor results and #538 *Beter 'N' Nutin* of the 444th BG hit an industrial facility in Luchou with excellent results. The tail gunner on this aircraft lost his parachute at take-off and the pilot opted to strike a target of opportunity rather than risk falling to anti-aircraft flak or fighters and needing his crew to bail out. Crew members reported seeing bombs striking the main concentration of buildings at the Luchou plant. Three planes (#461 *Haulinas* and #463 *Humpin' Honey* of the 462nd BG and the 468th BG's #208 *Pioneer*) bombed the rail yards at Tsanghien. B-29 #461 *Haulinas* experienced a mechanical problem and the formation leader directed #463 *Humpin' Honey* to escort the former back to their forward base. The 462nd crew on #461 *Haulinas* noted good bombing results, but the crew on

The Manchurian Aircraft Manufacturing Company in Mukden, Manchuria—the primary target for Mission #23. Note the intelligence annotations on the photograph, including dots showing bomb craters, the location of smoke generators, and the precise location of the plant adjacent to the airfield. (*US Air Force*)

#463 *Humpin' Honey* declared poor results due to a momentary problem that caused a delay in the bomb release. Strikes from #208 *Pioneer*, which bombed the target of opportunity after not being able to locate the target of last resort, were not observed.[49]

Anti-aircraft fire over Mukden ranged from meager to moderate and inaccurate to accurate. Some B-29 crews noted many of the flak bursts appeared to be phosphorous. Japanese anti-aircraft gun crews also engaged the bombers over Darien and other points along the flight path of the bombers. Flak damaged seven bombers on Mission #21: the 462nd BG's #232 returned with minor flak damage to its left horizontal stabilizer. Six 468th BG planes sustained anti-aircraft damage. Five received minor damage: #417 *Rushin' Rotation* (right outboard wing and horizontal stabilizer), #464 *Belle Ringer* (propeller #3, the underside of the left wing, a bomb bay door, and the leading edge of both wings), #691 *Fast Company* (#2 oil cooler flap and engines #3 and #4), #546 (two propellers and holes throughout the aircraft), and #487 *Bengal Lancer* (nose glass). The sixth 468th BG plane (#737 *Pioneer II*) limped home with major damage after an anti-aircraft shell pierced a center wing section. Each of these 468th BG B-29s (except #487 *Bengal Lancer*) also landed with fighter damage. The Japanese set a successful smoke screen that covered two miles, obscured the target from view, and contributed to the failure to hit the primary target; many of the errant bombs hit other legitimate, if unintentional, military targets. Post-mission analysis noted:

> The smoke screen employed by the Jap was even more effective than that of the first attack due to an earlier warning and the construction of a number of new generating sites...the entire arsenal and aircraft factory as well as the airfield were effectively screened by the time the second wave of aircraft appeared...This smoke screen hampered bombardiers necessitating off-set bombing methods and prevented visual observation of bomb strikes.[50]

Japanese fighter coverage, including Manchurian aircraft, was rated as moderate to strong over Mukden and "nil to weak" in other areas. Two B-29s crashed due to fighters during the operation and fifteen others landed with fighter damage. B-29 gunners claimed the destruction of twenty-two fighters, as well as six probably destroyed and nineteen damaged. One Japanese fighter succumbed to a unique quirk of war: two single-engine fighters attacked a B-29 at the moment the bombardier released the plane's bomb load. The radio operator, watching the progress of the falling bombs through the open bomb bay doors, saw one of the bombs strike a fighter. He noted the impact caused a "big explosion and the immediate disintegration" of the fighter. The official post-mission analysis listed the confirmed destruction of the fighter as "bombed." A Japanese fighter attacked B-29 #404 of the 40th BG during the bomb run; a 20 mm shell pierced the bomber, blowing out the left gunner's blister. The 40th BG headquarters praised crews of the 444th BG for remaining with the damaged B-29 and ensuring the crew returned to the forward base.[51]

Japanese pilots employed phosphorous aerial bombs in seven fighter attacks: four phosphorous bombs missed the bombers; two hit B-29s but did not cause any damage; and one can be attributed to the destruction of #505 *Wild Hair*, piloted by Capt. John Campbell, of the 462nd BG. Two phosphorous bombs were employed in the loss of #505 *Wild Hair*: one bomb struck the right wing of the bomber but bounced off the plane; the second hit the nose section. The crew on an adjacent B-29 witnessed the loss of #505 *Wild Hair*:

> Aircraft No. 4505 was flying in #2 position in the lead element, en route from the initial point, at 0150Z, about 8 minutes before bombs away. Two Tojos, in a coordinated attack, came in from 11 o'clock, high, in line astern – each dropping a phosphorous bomb on the B-29. One bomb hit the right wing and bounced off, but the other was thought to have hit the nose section, and inflicted damage. The B-29 slid out of the formation and went into a slight dive, trailing smoke from #3 and #4 engines. It leveled off about 1,500 feet below the formation and 5 chutes appeared. A few moments later the nose wheel came down and 5 more chutes appeared. The aircraft then went into a slow spiral, losing altitude, and apparently under control. All 4 propellers were turning but smoke and fire were observed coming from the right wing section. Just as the B-29 leveled off again to lower its landing gear, 3 enemy aircraft were seen to make several head-on attacks. Aircraft #4505 was finally seen to hit the ground and explode at 0156Z.[52]

The second B-29 lost to fighters fell to a ramming attack by a Manchurian pilot flying an obsolete Nakajima Ki-27 Nate. Second Lt. Tahei Matsumoto died when he rammed the 468th BG's #715 *Old Campaigner* flown by Capt. Charles Benedict. Only the radio operator, Staff Sgt. Elbert Edwards, survived the crash:

The crew of the 40th BG's #276 *Black Magic* bailed out over the Hump in late December 1944 due to a fuel problem. All eleven were rescued. (*Lundquist via 40th BG*)

> All reports agree that the enemy aircraft struck A/C 715 from between number 1 and 2 engines. One wing and the right horizontal stabilizer were seen to have been sheared off. A/C 715 was seen to circle under the formation and go into a spin. One crew member [on another B-29] reported that the aircraft exploded before it struck the ground. Crews of 4 aircraft reported that one parachute was seen to open, while one crew reports observing 2 parachutes. Three planes in the formation were all firing at the enemy aircraft as it came into the formation, but without apparent effect. The enemy aircraft disintegrated as it struck the B-29. Two crews reported that the enemy aircraft was the third of 5 enemy planes which flew through the formation. One crew reported that each of the 5 Japanese aircraft executed a slow roll as it went through.[53]

Staff Sgt. Edwards became a Japanese prisoner until the end of the war. In October 1945, he provided an official statement for inclusion in the missing air crew report on #715. According to Edwards, the B-29 immediately depressurized upon being rammed by the Nate, adding to the confusion of the incident. He managed to drop through the bomb bay and lost consciousness after opening his parachute. Edwards did not see any of the other crew members and learned they were dead when a Japanese interrogator asked him why he was the only person to bail out of the aircraft.[54] 1st Lt. Warren Dailey and 1st Lt. Tom Evans—the bombardier and navigator on #715, respectively—were brothers-in-law, having married twin sisters. Both men died in the attack with the eight remaining crew members. A second Manchurian pilot (2nd Lt. Naruo Nishihara) attempted to ram another B-29 but fell to its gunners.[55]

Following Christmas 1944, the XX BC launched its next mission the second day of 1945—another training operation to drop the Rama VI Bridge in Bangkok while restocking the fuel supply in Chengtu.

Chapter 9

January 1945: The Last Missions Launched from Chengtu

Shrapnel had cut the rudder cables and damaged the tail. I righted the plane with the ailerons and pushed the nose down to prevent a stall.

—Maj. McPherson (468th BG)

In January 1945, American forces landed on Luzon Island in the Philippines as Gen. Douglas MacArthur continued his offensive to liberate the area from the Japanese. Operating from the Marianas Islands, XXI Bomber Command (BC) B-29s flew against sixteen targets in the Japanese home islands, Iwo Jima, and smaller islands in the Marianas and near Truk.

During the first week of January, Gen. Curtis LeMay, commander of XX BC, flew to Saipan to meet with Gen. Haywood Hansell, commander of XXI BC, for early preparations of the former to assume command of the XXI BC. LeMay returned to India with XXI BC Chief of Staff Gen. Roger Ramey, who would assume command of the XX BC upon the departure of the former. On January 12, Gen. Albert Wedemeyer, commander of American forces in the China Theater, again requested the removal of XX BC B-29s from China no later than February 1. Gen. "Hap" Arnold—the commander of the Army Air Forces as well as the 20th Air Force, under which the XX and XXI BCs operated—concurred, and three days later the Joint Chiefs of Staff agreed to the request. Gen. LeMay departed for the Marianas Islands on January 18 and Ramey assumed command of XX BC. Nine days later, the XX BC evacuated its forward airfields in Chengtu, China.[1]

During January, the XX BC flew one "training" mission against the railroad network (Rama VI Bridge) in Thailand and eight missions targeting the Japanese aircraft industry and naval facilities in accordance with strategic bombing priorities.

Mission #24: Bangkok, January 2, 1945

The XX BC targeted Bangkok, Thailand, for the first B-29 bombing mission of 1945. All four groups dispatched bombers on this training mission, which doubled as an attempt to drop the Rama VI Bridge, the primary target for Mission #24. Field orders identified the Central Station and Yards in Rangoon, Burma, as the secondary target and the railroad yards and warehouses in Bassein, Burma, as the target of last resort. At this time, Bangkok was the central point for the movement of supplies and troops to Burma. Mining the Manam River reduced water-borne traffic and increased the utilization of land routes across Thailand to Burma. The Japanese moved much of the traffic to the Thai rail network. One rail line ran from French Indo-China to Bangkok, where it split into three separate lines, with one leading to Burma, one to the north, and one to the south into Malaya, and eventually Singapore. Cutting the Rama VI Bridge would halt rail traffic from French Indo-China and disrupt the movement of military supplies to Burma. The secondary target supported all of the rail traffic between Thailand and Rangoon. Damage to the target would hinder the movement of Japanese supplies bound for Burma and destroy rail cars and equipment currently at the station. The target of last resort did not serve as a major Japanese transit point for Rangoon, but its destruction could prevent utilization by the Japanese military in the future as the campaign shifted.[2]

The 40th BG's #752 *Wichita Witch* targeted the primary target (the Rama VI Bridge) during Mission #24 to Bangkok. (*40th BG*)

The 468th BG's #494 *Mary Ann* with her ground crew. A gunner aboard #494 *Mary Ann* shot his own bomb bay during a battle with Japanese fighters on Mission #24. Alignment of the lower guns to not fire into the bomb bay doors proved to be an ongoing problem. (*US Air Force*)

Forty-nine B-29s departed India for Bangkok (13 from the 40th BG and 12 from each of the other groups) and forty-four visually bombed the primary target. The 40th BG's #582 *Little Clambert* blew a cylinder; #738 *Honeywell Honey* suffered a malfunction of an engine prop governor, and an engine on #579 *Eddie Allen* swallowed a valve, forcing the pilot to feather the propeller. The latter B-29 bombed a target of opportunity at Pagoda Airfield and the other two bombers jettisoned their ordnance and returned to the group airfield in India. Two 462nd BG B-29s did not make it to the primary target due to mechanical difficulties. The group's #472 returned with engine trouble after jettisoning its bomb load and #590 *Celestial Princess* experienced a malfunctioning engine but bombed the target of last resort before flying back to India. The B-29s flew in group twelve-plane formations, with two groups short of that number and in smaller formations due to aborts. The target assessment indicated at least one bomb hit the bridge and others were near misses, rendering the structure temporarily unserviceable but not destroyed. The bombing destroyed or damaged numerous buildings near the bridge.[3]

Post-mission reports noted Japanese flak at the primary target to be meager and inaccurate. Two bombers spotted what they described as phosphorus flak bursts; each displayed the characteristics of phosphorus, including "tentacles" that extended above white spherical explosions. None of the bombers reported damage from phosphorous flak. Crews spoke of one "sausage shaped" barrage balloon at 5,000 feet and anti-aircraft fire from Don Muang Airfield as inaccurate, with the exception of one burst series that damaged a B-29, while the other shells exploded within 150 feet of other aircraft. Twelve bombers recorded being attacked by Japanese fighters in thirteen separate and unaggressive engagements, including eleven by Nakajima Ki-43 Oscars, one by a Kawasaki Ki-61 Tony, and one by an unidentified single-engine aircraft. The first B-29 formation bombed without fighter opposition, which commenced with the second formation. All fighter attacks except one originated above and half from the left of the bomber formations. Three bi-wing Japanese fighters attacked one group from behind but could not catch the faster bombers. Japanese pilots directed most of their attacks against the 468th BG, which expended 6,120 machine gun rounds defending its bombers. In contrast, the 444th BG fired 662 rounds and gunners of the other groups did not engage any Japanese fighters. A Japanese pilot placed bullets into the left wing of the 468th BG's #487 *Bengal Lancer*, which returned safely to India. Both #494 *Mary Ann* and #429 *Blind Date* from the 468th BG shot holes into their bomb bays with their own guns while fighting Japanese fighters. Alignment of the lower guns to not fire into the bomb bay doors proved to be an ongoing problem, as seen in several previous missions. The B-29 gunners claimed the probable destruction of one fighter and damage to two other aircraft.[4]

Bombs bursting from 444th BG B-29s at one end of the Rama VI Bridge during Mission #24. (*US Air Force*)

Post-mission intelligence photograph of the Rama VI Bridge after Mission #24. The black and white dots indicate craters or locations in the river where bombs fell. The bridge remained intact after the operation. (*US Air Force*)

Mission #25: Omura, January 6, 1945

All four groups of the XX BC returned to Japan for Mission #24 on January 6, 1945. The command targeted the Tachiarai Machine Works as the primary visual and the Omura Aircraft Plant as the primary radar objective on the Japanese island of Kyushu. The Nanking wharf area was the secondary target, with the airdrome storage area in Tangyang, China, as the target of last resort. The Japanese were known to assemble and repair aircraft components at the Tachiarai Machine Works, but intelligence believed it also assembled Mitsubishi Ki-15 Babs, a single-engine light bomber and reconnaissance aircraft. Although this facility did not assemble or repair large numbers of aircraft compared to the Japanese total, it lay within B-29 range from China while larger facilities did not. Despite its comparatively small capacity, bombing the plant could result in the destruction of numerous Japanese aircraft and reduce its ability to support assembly and repair. The Omura Aircraft Plant constructed Mitsubishi F1M Pete reconnaissance and Aichi B7A Grace attack aircraft while repairing Aichi E13A Jake reconnaissance and Mitsubishi A6M Zeke fighter aircraft. The secondary target, Nanking, held many barracks and storage buildings as a center for the Japanese military in China. Supplies transported by river vessels were transloaded to railroad cars in Nanking for movement to the front line troops. Bombing the wharfs could destroy military supplies awaiting rail movement. The target of last resort served the Japanese as a forward airfield in the Yangtze River region.[5]

Plans called for sixty aircraft (15 from each group) to bomb the target, but only forty-nine B-29s took off from the forward bases in China for the operation and twenty-eight bombed the primary radar target due to 9/10 cloud cover. Thick clouds obscured mission photographs taken for a post-strike assessment. Calculations indicated the 40th BG's ordnance hit approximately five miles from the target; 462nd BG bombs probably fell within the target vicinity; and the results of the 444th BG and 468th BG could not be estimated from their photos.

Eleven aircraft bombed Nanking due to various mechanical issues; three returned to the forward bases after jettisoning their loads; and one returned with its ordnance. B-29 #208 *Pioneer* of the 468th BG experienced a fire en route to Omura and the pilot, Capt. Fouts, turned to bring his bomber back to the airfield in China. As Fouts approached the field, he ordered nine members of the crew to bail out while he and the navigator made an emergency night landing after jettisoning bombs.[6]

Crews reported meager and generally inaccurate anti-aircraft fire in the various target areas, as well as along the flying routes. Japanese guns fired at least two phosphorous anti-aircraft rounds in the primary target area. Two 462nd BG crews spotted a dozen barrage balloons when bombing Laoyao as a target of opportunity. Two B-29s sustained minor damage from flak. The 40th BG's #522 *B-Sweet II* returned with a hole in its right wing tip from flak near Nanking and the Japanese gunners at Nagasaki placed a hole in the left wing of #457 *Battlin' Beauty* of the 462nd BG. Bomber crews described Japanese fighter opposition as meager but improved over previous encounters in the area. The majority (68%) of the fighter attacks occurred within a thirty-five-minute widow over the primary target area; the remaining assaults were flown by fighters at the secondary target and along the flying routes. Most of the Japanese fighters continued the pattern of attacking the B-29s from a high, frontal position. B-29 gunners claimed they shot down four fighters, along with six probably destroyed and ten damaged. Japanese pilots downed one B-29 (#254 of the 462nd BG piloted by Maj. Slack) and damaged five others. Three 40th BG bombers returned with fighter damage: B-29 #505 *Draggin' Lady* arrived with two machine gun rounds in the upper forward turret; #738 *Honeywell Honey* accumulated numerous bullet holes; and #589 *Calamity Jane* landed with a rip in its right elevator. The 462nd BG's #728 sported bullet holes across its left wing and #703 *American Beauty* of the 468th BG returned with bullet damage to a propeller.[7] The post-mission intelligence assessment noted the following reference to the loss of #254:

> A/C 254 (462nd) was attacked by a fighter just after bombs away. Number 3 and 4 engines were shot out, but the only injury sustained by personnel was a slight nick in the bombardier's arm. The aircraft lost too much speed and altitude to be escorted, but radio contact was maintained by aircraft 457 [*Battlin' Beauty*] and 448. Aircraft 254 was on fire and the crew thought it would be necessary to bail, but later indicated maybe they could ditch. Aircraft 448 gave the position of 254 to a submarine and received acknowledgement. Sometime later, at 0400Z, aircraft 457 received a message purportedly from the submarine stating it had found the wreck of 254, and still later a garbled message was received by aircraft 457 asking if there were 12 chutes aboard. The observations made by 3 different crew,

The 40th BG's #522 *B-Sweet II* returned from Mission #25 to Omura, Japan, with a hole in a wing tip from Japanese flak near Nanking, China. (*Schaal via 40th BG*)

although apparently in conflict as to time and location, bear out the fate of aircraft 254. Aircraft 457 reported the aircraft to have been shot down at...0140Z. An aircraft of the 468th Group saw a B-29 that was smoking drop out of a 6-aircraft formation about 30 miles NW of Sasebo. About 10 minutes later the B-29 was surrounded by 5 to 6 fighters and disappeared into the overcast at 13,000 feet. The third observation by aircraft 724 was of a B-29 from the 462nd Group going down in flames...at approximately 0215Z.[8]

The 40th BG's#738 *Honeywell Honey* returned from Mission #25 targeting Omura with numerous bullet holes from Japanese fighters. (*Buzza via 40th BG*)

Mission #26: Formosa, January 9, 1945

The XX BC set the Heito Airfield and arsenal as the primary visual and the wharves at Keelung Harbor as the primary radar target for Mission #26, bound for the island of Formosa. Shinchiku Airdrome was the secondary target, with port facilities along the Chinese coast as targets of last resort. The airfield at Heito served as one of the primary staging fields for Japanese aircraft flying to the Philippines and Netherlands East Indies; it also hosted an arsenal and facilities for the assembly and repair of military aircraft. The primary radar target provided berthing for the transshipment of military supplies to Japanese forces in Southeast Asia. An attack on this facility could destroy or damage any ships at the berths, as well as warehouses holding military supplies. The secondary target mirrored the services provided by Heito Airfield and attacks on any targets of last resort could destroy, damage, or interrupt the movement of military supplies flowing inland to Japanese forces in the interior of China. Attacks on the bases on Formosa supported American efforts to liberate the Philippines, and the raid of January 9, 1945, operated in coordination with American carrier-based aircraft also scheduled to strike air and naval targets on the island.[9]

The XX BC launched forty-six out of a planned forty-eight aircraft for Mission #26 (12 planes each from the 40th BG, 444th BG, and 468th BG and 10 from the 462nd BG). Two of the originally planned aircraft failed to take-off due to engine problems. Thirty-nine B-29s bombed

The 468th BG's #703 *American Beauty* returned from Mission #25 with bullet damage to a propeller. (*Schutte via 468th BG*)

Keeping warm on the flight line with a Chinese guard. (*US Air Force*)

the primary radar target at Keelung Harbor with a mix of incendiary and general purpose munitions due to cloud cover, including a seven-plane formation of the 40th BG that dropped its ordnance eight to ten miles short of the airfield due to a malfunction of the bomb release mechanism in the lead aircraft. Six B-29s bombed targets of last resort along the Chinese coast because of engine problems; most of the mechanical issues related to loss of oil pressure or oil leaks. Aircraft #740 *Harry Miller* of the 40th BG struck the port of Foochow, while the other five and one from the 462nd BG bombed Amoy. The latter planes included the 444th BG's #376 *Miss N.C.* and #507 *Atsall Bro's*; the 468th BG's #525 *Mary K* and #719 *The Uninvited II*; and the 462nd BG's #456 *The Shrike*. One B-29 (#691 *Fast Company* of the 468th BG) returned early without reaching a target due a loss of oil pressure in an engine.[10]

The B-29s did not encounter any anti-aircraft fire over any of the targets due to heavy cloud cover, and the crews did not see any Japanese aircraft. Bombing results were not clear due to undercast that obscured the target from strike photos, and the XX BC did not fly any immediate post-strike reconnaissance missions to Formosa.[11]

Mission #27: Singapore, January 11, 1945

Two days later, B-29s from all four groups flew to Singapore for Mission #27, with the Admiralty Floating Drydock and King George VI Drydock facilities as the primary targets. The Swettenhum and Victoria Piers at Penang Harbor in Malaya were the secondary target, with Mergui Harbor in Burma as the target of last resort. Although the XX BC raid on November 5, 1944, damaged the Admiralty Floating Drydock, repair facilities at the location still served major Japanese naval vessels. Poor weather conditions over Singapore delayed a return mission to the drydock throughout November and December 1944.

Emptying fuel drums into more permanent storage in China. (*US Air Force*)

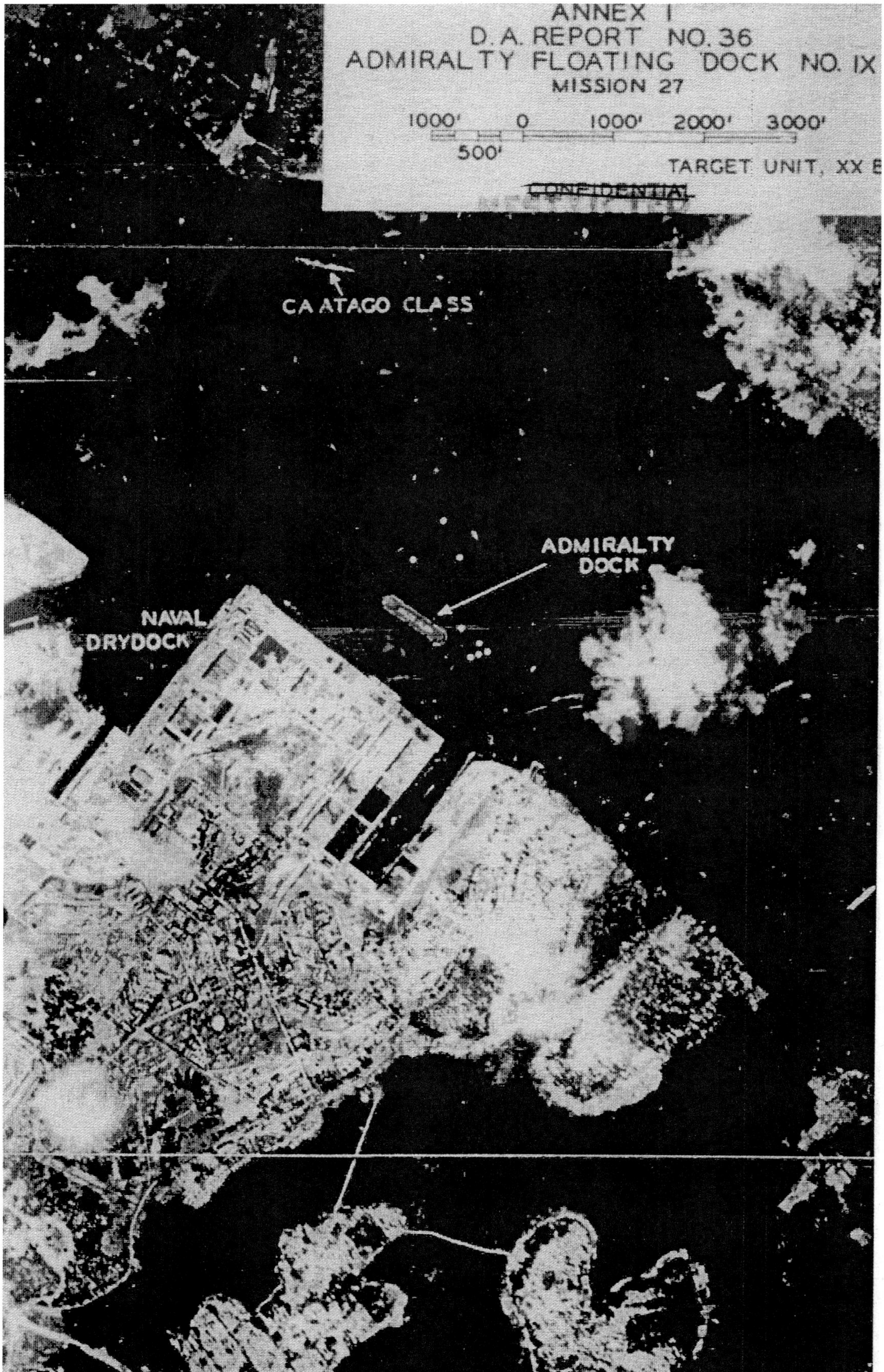

Aerial intelligence photograph of the Admiralty Floating Dock in Singapore—the primary target of Mission #27. Note the presence of a Japanese Atago Class cruiser ("CA" means cruiser) above and to the left of the floating dock. (*US Air Force*)

Crews were designated to bomb the Admiralty Floating Drydock and switch to the King George VI Drydock if the former lay under cloud cover or submerged due to earlier damage. Penang served as the major base for Japanese, German, and Italian submarines operating in the Indian Ocean. The base also supported the transshipping of supplies bound for Japanese forces operating in Burma. The Japanese utilized the target of last resort as a major location for offloading military supplies from vessels for movement by rail through Thailand.[12]

Forty-seven B-29s launched, with 10 from the 40th BG, 12 from the 444th BG, 12 from the 462nd BG, and 13 representing the 468th BG. Sixteen bombers dropped their general purpose ordnance on the floating drydock, nine bombed the King George VI Drydock, nine B-29s bombed the secondary target, four attacked the target of last resort, and three planes deposited their munitions on targets of opportunity. Plans called for the B-29s to fly in three-plane formations, but the crews over the drydocks bombed as individual aircraft with the exception of a single two-plane formation. The bombers experienced extremely poor visibility as they approached their initial assembly points to establish formations after take-off. Forced to fly by instruments rather than visually, the crews set courses for Singapore as individual aircraft rather than the planned formations. A few of the B-29 crews experienced heavy turbulence. Capt. Bores, pilot of the 468th BG's #487 *Bengal Lancer*, reported severe turbulence in his debriefing:

> At 0152Z, we hit a storm, and we were caught in a downdraft which sent us from twenty-four thousand feet to twelve thousand feet at the rate of six thousand feet a minute or better. We were in a spiral to the left. An up-draft hit us and we ascended from eighteen thousand feet (where we had finally managed to climb under some control) to twenty-five thousand feet at the rate of six thousand feet a minute or better. Our air speed went from three hundred and ten miles per hour to one hundred and eighty on the down-draft. Both pilot's and co-pilot's gyro horizons and pilot's gyro-compass went out. Both the pilot and co-pilot fought the controls to keep the plane out of a spin, and the pilot attempted to de-pressurize at twenty-five thousand feet...The radar operator's seat was torn from floor before the operator had a chance to put on his [oxygen] mask. He held onto the table, but the table also jarred loose. He unbuckled his safety belt and crawled back to right gunner who attempted to give him oxygen and finally succeeded. The top-turret gunner suffered shock from severe jolting and crawled down later with an upset stomach. Bombs were sheared from their shackles and driven through the bomb bay doors at approximately 0200Z. The pilot and co-pilot finally affected a recovery at approximately 0210Z, and at 0241Z the navigator took a bearing from the southwest tip of an island which could be seen through a hole in the clouds. The plane then turned west southwest and headed for base.[13]

Many planes received meager and inaccurate anti-aircraft fire from batteries along the route to and from Singapore. All of the B-29s experienced meager and inaccurate to accurate flak over Singapore. The Japanese maintained "barrage"-style flak over the Admiralty Floating Drydock. Bomber crews reported a circular series of fifteen to twenty flak bursts every half second around the drydock, indicating a precisely choreographed anti-aircraft defense. Other Japanese batteries employed a "continuously pointed" style of flak, in which gunners trailed a specific bomber while attempting to adjust fire and move the bursts onto the moving aircraft. The Japanese followed the 444th BG's #375 *Her Majesty* with this type of anti-aircraft fire; its crew reported after the mission they received "AA [anti-aircraft] fire in two parallel rows about 30 feet apart," with bursts that followed them. One aircraft (B-29 #475 *Hoodlum House II* of the 462nd BG) suffered a hole in the wing and a cracked tail gunner's window. In addition to black flak bursts spewing pieces of exploding metal across the sky, crews noted the Japanese also employed phosphorous anti-aircraft fire, which could burn holes through the outer layers of a plane. The pilot and co-pilot of #472 of the 462nd Group reported several unusual white phosphorous flak bursts, as well as another odd device associated with the round.[14] Post-mission intelligence analysts noted the following:

> The [phosphorous] bursts would explode in a normal manner with white streamers arching up and down. Both [pilot and co-pilot] state that they saw a black object immediately after the flak explosion. It appeared to be about 12-18 inches long and about as large around as a man's wrist. It would disappear one to three seconds after the bursts with no apparent explosion. Both the pilot and co-pilot seemed to think that the object appeared to unfold or unravel. Approximately ten of these were observed in the primary target area.[15]

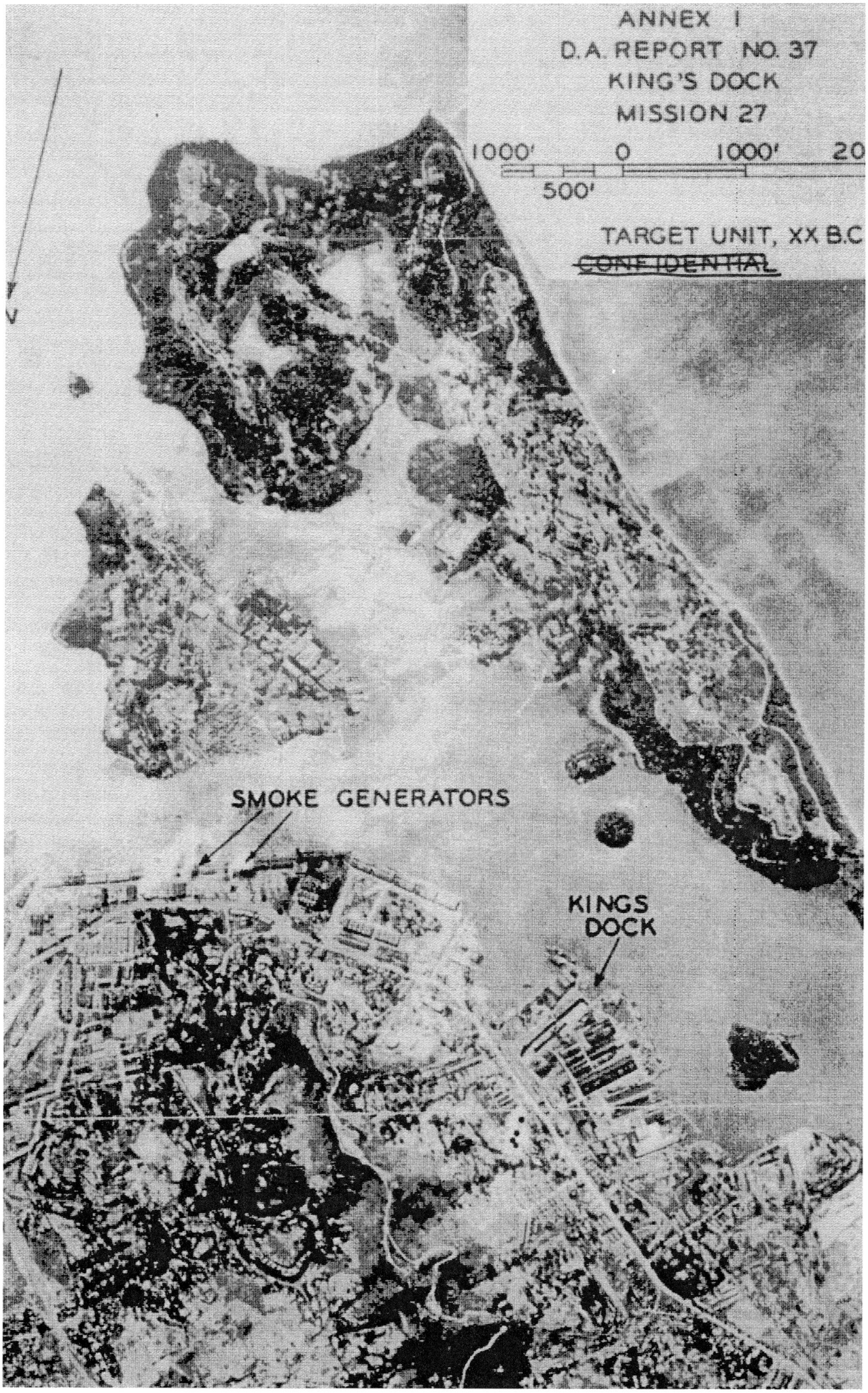

Mission #27 to Singapore. Japanese smoke generators are in operation and specifically marked to the left of the King's Dock. (*US Air Force*)

Although described as "weak," the Japanese fighter opposition manifested as ninety-nine recorded individual and coordinated attacks by many types of fighters against the B-29s over Singapore and two fighter attacks against the planes bombing Penang. B-29 gunners expended 19,590 rounds of ammunition. One Japanese pilot may have attempted to ram a B-29 as recorded by post-mission analysts: "The fighter approached from 12 o'clock level and the B-29 dropped sharply in evasive action; the fighter passed over the B-29 in level flight at a distance of about 20 yards. The B-29 crew believed that the enemy pilot intended to ram, but this view is open to question in that the fighter preceded on course in level flight."[16]

The 462nd BG's #475 *Hoodlum House II* suffered a hole in the wing and a cracked tail gunner's window from Japanese flak during Mission #27 to Singapore. (*462nd BG*)

Many of the Japanese fighter pilots coordinated their attacks against the bombers as described in a post-mission summary:

> In a typical 4 plane attack, 2 Oscars came in at 10 o'clock level and pressed their attacks to 200 yards; at the same time 2 Oscars approached at 2 o'clock level, broke off at 800 yards, went into a shallow sliding dive to their left, then pulled up in a steep climb to attack again from 3 o'clock to 5 o'clock level. All 4 flights broke away in split S's. The B-29 opened fire on both strings at about 1,000 yards, but no damage was done on either side.[17]

In other coordinated attacks by fighters:

> 4 Oscars executed a typical "sidewheeler" attack, 2 coming in at 3 o'clock low and 2 at 9 o'clock low. Again, the attacks from the left were closely pressed while the 2 planes from the right beam broke off at 700-800 yards. Fire on both sides were ineffective... One coordinated tail attack was reported in which a [Nakajima Ki-44] Tojo approached at 6 o'clock low, followed immediately by an Oscar at 7 o'clock high out of the sun. Both fighters pressed the attack to about 100 yards and went out in sharp dives toward 11 o'clock.[18]

Japanese pilots employed aerial phosphorous bombs as well as their guns. They seemed to pay special attention to a lone B-29, as multiple fighters (one estimate places the total at twenty-two separate aircraft) worked together in an unsuccessful attempt to bring her down with phosphorus bombs during a seventeen-minute running battle. Six B-29s returned with battle damage from Japanese fighters, although none were hit by phosphorous bombs, including the 40th BG's #582 *Little Clambert* (hole in the top elevator) and #394 *Last Resort* (holes in tank #4 and the right flap, with the aileron trim tab cable severed); #720 *Fu-Kemal-Tu* of the 444th BG (bullet hole in the leading edge of the horizontal stabilizer with damage to the ribs, spars, and the right elevator); #472 of the 462nd BG (holes in the gas tank and top of the wing); and the 468th BG's #678 *Kickapoo Lou* (engine #1 and nacelle damaged, a throttle shot out, and damage to the nose wheels and doors) and #546 (damage to the upper blister and a hole through the radar compartment). Gunners claimed to have destroyed six fighters, with one probably destroyed and seventeen damaged.[19]

Two B-29s did not return to India: the first was #226 of the 444th BG piloted by Maj. J. H. Wilson:

> This aircraft was last heard from on voice at 0145Z near the initial point. Nothing definite has been established regarding the fate of this aircraft. However, one B-29 on course just off the coast of India was seen jettisoning its equipment. This ties in with a British report that an aircraft near the coast dropped out of radar scope that was tracking it. It is thought that this may have been A/C 226, but a search has revealed no signs of the missing aircraft.[20]

And then B-29 #704 *The Gear Box* (468th BG):

> This aircraft was last heard from at 0230Z when it gave a "bombs away" message over the PT [Primary Target]. No definite facts regarding its fate are available. It is possible that this aircraft may have been lost over the target (an aircraft of the 444th Group reported from 20 miles from the PT seeing an unidentified aircraft explode over the target at 0211Z) but it is more probable that A/C 704 is the plane that was last seen just off the coast of the Malay Peninsula with 2 engines probably feathered. It was last seen at 15,000 feet and losing 500 feet a minute. Two aircraft of the 444th Group headed for China Bay tried to contact the plane on the 468th Group frequency with no success.[21]

Maj. Donald Humphrey piloted the 468th BG's #704 *The Gear Box* on the Singapore mission. He leveled the bomber over Malaya and prepared his crew to bail out upon spotting cultivated terrain where they would have the best chance for safe parachute landings. As Humphrey prepared to bail out the plane plunged sharply downward at approximately 15,000 feet and threw him against the controls. The pilot jumped from the crippled bomber but never remembered how he exited the aircraft. As he drifted to earth, Humphrey watched as the damaged left wing broke off his bomber, followed by the other wing and tail. Finally, the fuselage broke into two pieces before striking the ground. Four crew members died; the Japanese captured four men; and four evaded capture with the assistance of Malayan Communist guerillas. The Japanese held the captured crew members in the Saigon Prisoner of War (POW) camp until the end of the war.[22]

Many published sources confuse B-29 #704 *The Gear Box* (crashed on Mission #27 to Singapore) with B-29 #279 *Postville Express*, the first B-29 to bomb Japan during Mission #2 to Yawata. Maj. Humphrey flew both aircraft and named his first B-29 (#279) *Postville Express*, which was "retired" as a war weary bomber in November 1944. The plane Humphrey flew in January 1945 was not the aircraft in which he bombed Yawata in June 1944. At least once in postwar years, Humphrey referred to #704 as *Postville Express* and this may have been a slip or an indication he intended to give #704 the same name as #279. XX BC and 468th BG records indicate #704 carried the name *The Gear Box*.[23]

Post-mission reconnaissance photographs indicated the Admiralty Floating Drydock and King George VI Drydock both lay undamaged by bombs. Some bombs fell as close as 250 yards from the former and over five miles from the latter. The bombing at Penang damaged buildings and warehouses. Intelligence analysts noted the poor bombing results could be attributed to icing and enemy fighters. The B-29s experienced severe icing, and some bombardiers reported lack of visibility through the nose glass. Second, flying their bomb runs individually rather than in small formations made the B-29s more vulnerable to Japanese fighters. The fighters tended to attack toward the front of the B-29 and the bombardier sits in the most forward section of the nose, surrounded by Plexiglass.[24]

Mission #28: Formosa, January 14, 1945

The 40th BG suffered one of its greatest tragedies on January 14, as maintenance and armament crews feverishly worked to keep up with the increased mission schedule in January and an accident occurred in India while offloading fragmentation cluster bombs from B-29 #582 *Little Clambert*. Either the top or third cluster on a rear rack broke and one or more cluster bombs fell on a cement doughnut placed beneath the bomb bay. The bomb (or bombs) exploded on contact with the doughnut, igniting a fire in the bomb bay where the other cluster bombs remained. A crash crew quickly arrived and moved to extinguish the fire, despite knowing bombs remained in the bomb bay. Other maintenance and armament crew members sprang forward to assist the crash personnel. Nine men died in the accident and another twenty-one were injured when the bombs inside the plane exploded. Many men were later decorated for risking, and in some cases losing, their lives to save others. The 40th BG records pick up the story at this point:

> Before the fire could be extinguished, it ignited some of the fragmentation clusters and a series of explosions occurred which completely demolished aircraft #42-24582 [*Little Clambert*], so damaged aircraft #42-63394 [*Last Resort*] that it had to be salvaged and inflicted varying degrees of damage on four other B-29 aircraft and one B-24 aircraft which were parked in the vicinity… The exploding fragmentation clusters wrecked terrible havoc among these [maintenance and armament] personnel…[25]

The XX BC returned to Formosa three days after the Singapore mission in continuation of the raids to support the American forces fighting in the Philippines. Planners reversed the target order from Mission #26 and identified

The 40th BG suffered a tragedy on January 14, 1945, when a bomb rack broke and one or more cluster bombs fell from #582 *Little Clambert*, striking a cement doughnut. The bomb (or bombs) exploded, igniting a fire in the bomb bay among the remaining cluster bombs. (*US Air Force*)

Shinchiku Airfield as the primary target. The alternate primary visual targets were the Heito Air Arsenal (the primary on Mission #26) and Kagi Airfield, while the shipping facilities and harbor of Takao were the alternate primary radar target area. Chinese ports remained the secondary targets and Hengyang, China, was annotated as the target of last resort. The air bases and air arsenal supported aircraft flying to and from the Philippines and Netherlands East Indies. Hengyang lay on the Hankow – Canton rail line and served the Japanese as a major transportation and communications hub in Southern China.[26]

Eighty-two B-29s launched from forward staging bases in China, carrying a mix of incendiary, general purpose, and fragmentation bombs on January 14, including 20 from the 40th BG, 26 representing the 444th BG, 19 flying with the 462nd BG, and 17 with the 468th BG. In a last minute change, the XX BC commander selected Kagi Air Base—an alternate visual target—as the primary destination of the bomber force headed across China to Formosa. Of the eighty-two airborne B-29s, fifty-four bombed Kagi Air Base, one (#739 of the 40th BG) dropped its ordnance on Heito Air Arsenal, four targeted Chinese ports (#738 *Honeywell Honey* of the 40th BG and the 468th BG's

A crash crew quickly arrived and moved to extinguish the fire in the 40th BG's #582 *Little Clambert*. Nine men died in the accident and another twenty-one were injured when the bombs inside the plane exploded. (*US Air Force*)

#275 *Lassie Too* and #534 *Pioneer III* hit Amoy and B-29 #463 *Humpin' Honey* of the 462nd BG at an unidentified port), five struck the target of last resort, and thirteen went after targets of opportunity (with twelve bombing Taichu Airfield and one bombing an unknown air field). Nine 40th BG B-29s bombed Taichu Airfield after becoming disoriented following a navigational error. Three planes from the 462nd BG mistook Taichu for the primary target at Kagi and bombed the former airfield.[27]

The Japanese fired meager and inaccurate to accurate anti-aircraft fire over Formosa. B-29 crews spotted at least twenty-seven different Japanese aircraft, but none attacked the bombers, including three fighters over the Chinese port of Amoy. One fighter over Formosa did approach to within 1,200 yards but turned away. All of the bombers returned without battle damage. Good quality photographs helped make the damage assessment from the raid:

> A heavy concentration of bombs fell over the target [Kagi airfield] area and resulted in visible damage to 46 per cent of the 844,300 feet of area covered by buildings. Previous attacks had caused 9.7 per cent damage. This attack caused 42 per cent damage, the total of 46 per cent including damage reported by this attack on previous damage. To date 20 per cent has been destroyed, 25 per cent severely damaged, and 3 per cent slightly damaged...Each of the 9 hangars shows severe damage but no collapse. Eleven barracks

Records of the 40th BG include a description of what happened during the January 14, 1945, accident: "The fire ignited some of the fragmentation clusters and a series of explosions occurred which completely demolished aircraft #42-24582 [*Little Clambert*] and critically damaged aircraft #42-63394 [*Last Resort*]." (*US Air Force*)

The 40th BG's #394 *Last Resort* displaying the damage she received during the explosion of #394 *Little Clambert*. (*US Air Force*)

> buildings were completely gutted by fire and a varying degree of damage was sustained by the remaining warehouses, sheds, and administration buildings. Approximately 16 aircraft were destroyed or damaged.[28]

Mission #29: Formosa, January 17, 1945

Three days later, the XX BC repeated the raid to Formosa. B-29s from all four groups targeted Shinchiku air base on Formosa from the advance bases in China during Mission #29. The alternate primary targets were the Heito Airdrome and air arsenal, Einasho airport, and the Takao main wharf area (the alternate radar target). Dock areas in Chinese coastal ports were secondary targets, with the city of Hengyang, China, as a target of last resort. Shinchiku served as a major transit base for aircraft passing to the south and contained important aircraft repair facilities. Intelligence estimates noted many Japanese aircraft should be at the field during the attack due to planes flying between Japan and the battle areas of the Philippines to the south. Japanese shipping and supplies could be found in the secondary targets and they utilized Hengyang as a major communications and transportation center for offensive operations in China. The Japanese captured the town four months earlier, in September 1944. Early plans called for the bombers to return to bases in Kunming, in southwest China, after the raid, but low fuel stocks in the country prevented this scenario and shifted the location to the bases at Chengtu. The theater directed a maximum effort for all agencies to haul additional fuel across the Hump to support this mission. The operation called for two separate wing formations, with four twelve-plane formations within each. The scheduled group participants were the 40th BG (23 aircraft), 444th BG (22 aircraft), 462nd BG (29 aircraft), and the 468th (21 aircraft) for a total of ninety-five B-29s.[29]

Ninety-two bombers carrying general purpose, fragmentation, and incendiary bombs took off for the mission and seventy-eight reached the primary target. The 468th BG's #719 *The Uninvited II* experienced a bomb arming in the rear bomb bay and dropped its load 10,000 feet short of the target. The 462nd BG's #475 *Hoodlum House II* hit a secondary target facility in Amoy, China. Five aircraft hit the target of last resort due to various oil leaks and mechanical problems: the 40th BG's #757; the 462nd BG's #502 *Long John Silver*, #873, and #461 *Haulinas*; and the 468th BG's #276 *Raiden Maiden II*. Two struck targets of opportunity: #277 *Shanghai Lil* of the 444th BG (a bridge at Foochow, China) and #230 of the 462nd BG (a warehouse in Leiyang, China).[30]

Crews faced meager and inaccurate black and white flak bursts with no reported damage over the primary target. Two of the five B-29s striking the target of last resort also experienced meager and inaccurate anti-aircraft fire. The

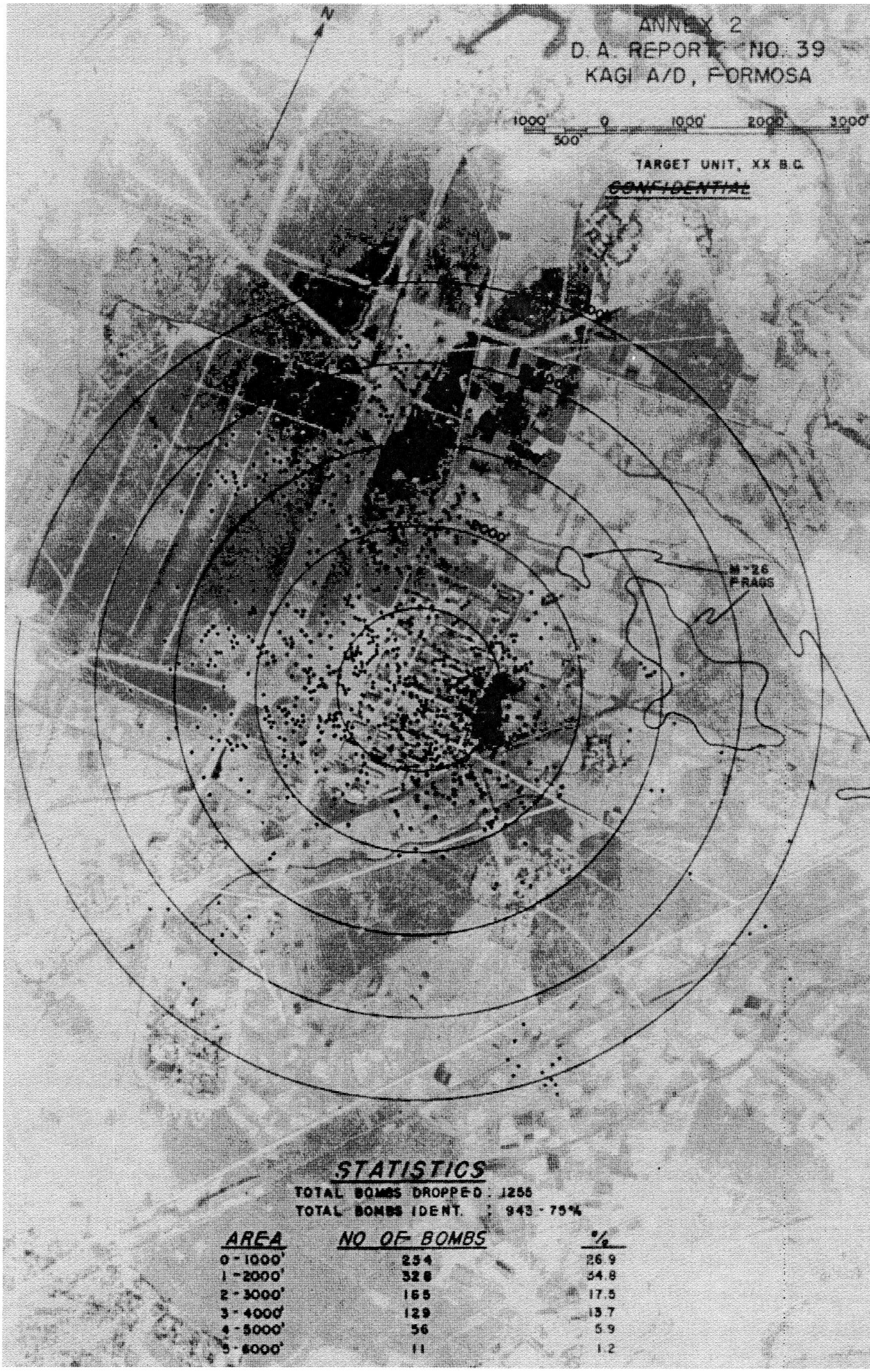

Post-mission intelligence photograph marking the locations of bomb craters at Kagi Airfield, an alternate visual target for Mission #28 to Formosa. (*US Air Force*)

raiders spotted eleven enemy aircraft: three over the primary target, one at the last resort target, and seven along the Chinese coast; the latter included a Mitsubishi G4M Betty bomber. None of the aircraft engaged the B-29s and remained well out of gun range.

The 40th BG's #729 *Nippon Nipper III* flew in the fourth bombing formation during Mission #29. (*Wemple via 40th BG*)

The XX BC lost one aircraft. The 468th BG's #494 *Mary Ann*, piloted by Maj. McPherson, crashed six miles east of Hsinching one hour after takeoff. Shortly after launching the pilot lost an engine and opted to return to the airfield. A second engine suffered a runaway propeller as the plane approached the base. The bombardier dropped the bomb load six miles from the base and in an unusual accident, the resulting explosions damaged the control surfaces of the low-flying B-29. McPherson later reported they replaced the bomb pins before dropping so the ordnance would not explode, but as he noted:

> When the bombs struck the ground part of them exploded and the blast was terrific. The front bomb bay bulk head door was blown in, shrapnel shattered against the plane and fire flashed ahead and around us. I felt the blast through my open window, the plane lurched violently to the right and lifted and the right rudder pedal went loose under my foot and the left rudder appeared to be locked. Thought the plane was going in immediately and ordered co-pilot to bail out then I flipped the emergency bell on and the co-pilot dropped the landing tear. Shrapnel had cut the rudder cables and damaged the tail. I righted the plane with the ailerons and pushed the nose down to prevent an immediate stall. Force of blast raised us from two hundred fifty feet above the terrain to one thousand feet.[31]

The 468th BG's #494 *Mary Ann* crashed six miles east of Hsingching, China, during Mission #29 to Formosa. The bombardier dropped the bomb load and in an unusual accident, the resulting explosions critically damaged the low-flying B-29. (*Schutte via 468th BG*)

The crew bailed out but four men died on impact with the ground due to the low altitude at which they jumped. McPherson was the last to depart the crippled B-29:

> I grabbed the control column and leveled the plane momentarily, threw off my head set, jerked the cord free of my parachute harness and left the seat just as I thought I saw a hill loom in front of the plane. Pulled my rip cord ring free of the container on my way back to the wheel well, dropped down to the bottom rung and fell free of the plane facing the rear. As soon as I felt the slip stream I jerked my rip cord and saw the chute stream out behind me but not open. Kicked my feet twice and heard the chute open with a sharp crack and felt my body jerk and do a flip...I saw the plane go into the ground in a diving turn, right wing low, and explode. The sound of rending metal, oxygen bottles, and ammunition exploding, and a sheet of flame filled the air.[32]

The crew of the 40th BG's #407 *Shoot You're Faded* jettisoned their bomb load early and safely returned due to mechanical issues encountered on Mission #29. (*Mahli via 40th BG*)

Three B-29 crews (the 40th BG's #407 *Shoot You're Faded* and #505 *Draggin' Lady* and #227 *Lady Be Good* of the 468th BG) jettisoned their loads early due to mechanical issues and safely returned. The mission resulted in 99,000 square feet of damage to buildings and the cratering of runways, which was added to the existing 331,700 square feet of damage from earlier raids. Damaged or destroyed structures included hangars, warehouses, and other support buildings.[33]

Mission #30: Saigon, January 25–26, 1945

The XX BC flew its first mission to Saigon, in French Indo-China (Vietnam in this case), during the night of January 25–26, 1945. It should be noted that French Indo-China secured independence a decade after WWII ended as four separate states: Vietnam (which originated as North and South Vietnam pending a failed referendum and then merger in 1975 after many long years of war), Laos, and Cambodia. The mine laying operation (Mission #30) targeted waters around Saigon (Ho Chi Minh City today) and Cam Ranh Bay by B-29s from the 462nd BG. During the same night, 444th and 468th BGs laid mines around Singapore on Mission #31. The primary targets in Saigon were Cape St. Jacques, Canhrai Bay, and Song Soirap, with secondary targets along the Mekong River. The Japanese plotted convoys through Saigon traveling to and from Singapore. Saigon also served as a major port for the movement of supplies and troops to Burma and the export of raw materials to Japan. Six months earlier, the Japanese reduced the utilization of Saigon as a convoy assembly point due to bombing by the 14th Air Force and shifted to the Philippines. However, with the American invasion of the Philippines in October 1944, the Japanese again increased vessel traffic in Saigon and Cam Ranh Bay. Mining the water around Saigon and Cam Ranh Bay north of the city could further impede Japanese convoy traffic between Japan and Singapore, as well as disrupt port operations in support of the fighting in Burma and the Philippines. Placing mines at the secondary targets would produce mine fields in the Mekong River, which the Japanese utilized as a significant means of transportation between Saigon and Phnom Penh, where supplies were transloaded for movement by rail through Thailand to Burma.[34]

Twenty-six B-29s from the 462nd BG departed India for French Indo-China. Crews recorded anti-aircraft fire around Saigon as meager and inaccurate, while those over Cam Ranh Bay did not encounter any anti-aircraft opposition from the ground. Crews spotted eleven enemy aircraft but none engaged the bombers. One bomber crew reported seeing a Japanese fighter mounting a searchlight fifty miles north of Saigon. The fighter did not approach closer than one mile, but the crew informed post-mission intelligence collectors it was evident the plane utilized the searchlight in a vain attempt to locate them or another B-29. Another crew witnessed eight fighters taking off from an airfield near Saigon, but the fighters did not locate nor engage any bombers.[35]

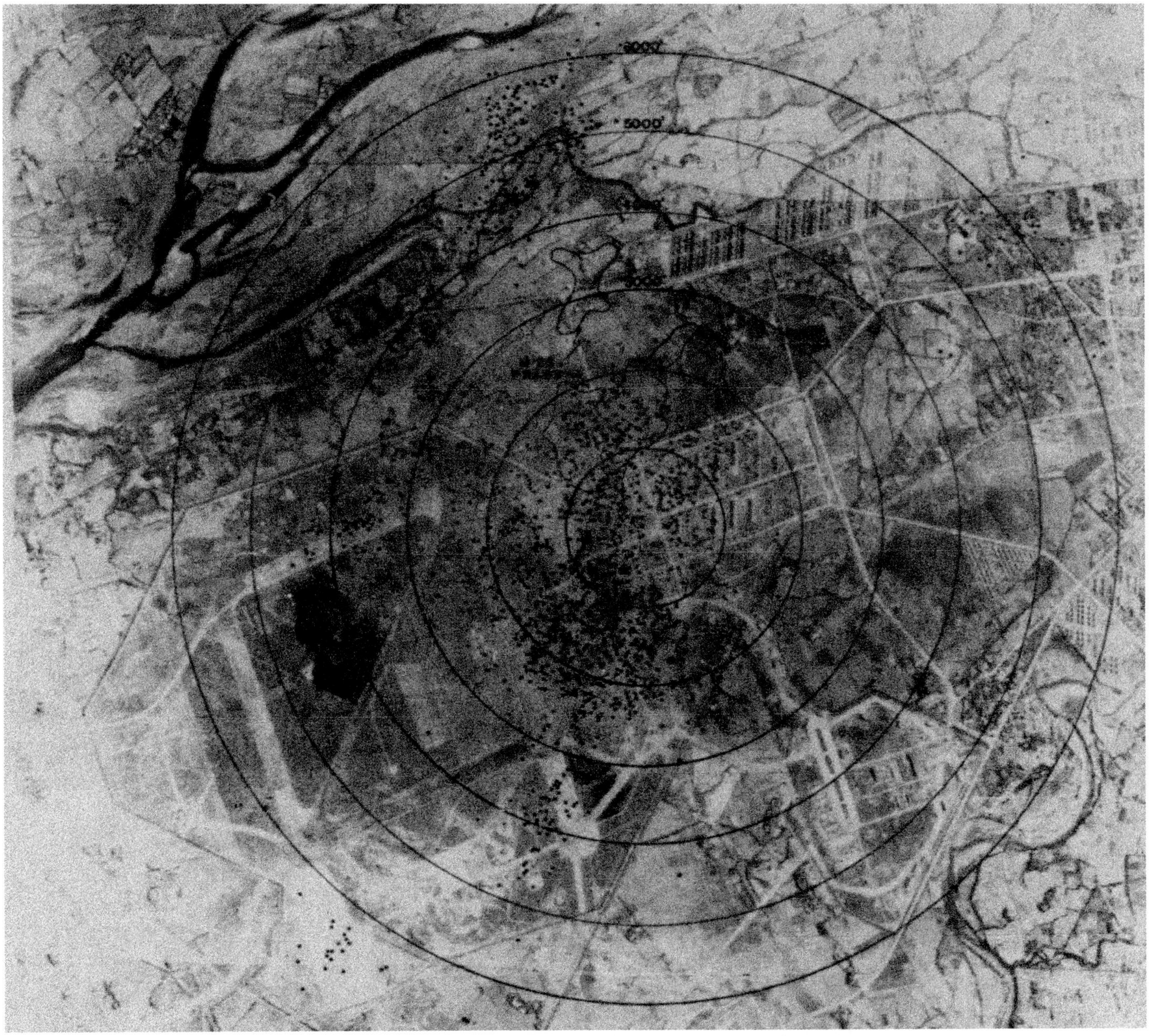

This photograph assesses the bombing conducted against Shinchiku air base on Formosa during Mission #29. Each black dot indicates a bomb crater and a review of where each dot is located within the concentric circles, permitting XX BC to determine bomb patterns and estimate the effectiveness of the raid. (*US Air Force*)

Note the missing propeller and multiple gashes on the side of this B-29; this is what could happen when a crew was unable to feather a propeller on a damaged engine. The propeller could rip off the engine and fly into the bomber itself. (*Schumacher*)

The 462nd BG laid sixty-four mines in fields around Saigon and thirty-four mines at Cam Ranh Bay. B-29 #801 *Phony Express* could not locate the target area due to undercast conditions, forcing the crew to mine a target of opportunity at Navan Bay. B-29 #463 *Humpin' Honey* laid four mines at Cam Ranh Bay—its primary target—and two mines along the Mekong River at the Goh Si Chang Channel (a secondary target).[36]

Mission #31: Singapore, January 25–26, 1945

While the 462nd BG laid mines along the coast of French Indo-China, B-29s from the 444th and 468th BG sowed mine fields near Singapore, with the primary targets at the Johore Strait, Inner Middle Channel, Outer Middle Channel, Rhio Strait, Inner Main Strait, and the Outer Main Strait. The secondary targets were Penang Harbor, the Pakchan River, and Mergui Harbor. In January 1945, Singapore remained one of the most important shipping centers in the Southwest Pacific. The Japanese army and navy retained their southern headquarters in the city. Many military supplies destined for fighting in Burma arrived in Singapore, where they were transloaded to rail for travel along the Malay Peninsula or to smaller vessels destined for ports closer to Rangoon. Singapore provided one of the only areas beyond Japan for the docking and major repair of ships. Japanese naval vessels that fled the American invasion of the Philippines sought anchorage around the city. The harbor and local straits hosted oil tankers bound for Japan and vessels carrying other raw materials for the war effort. Mining the area could impede the passage of Japanese shipping and damage or sink warships and cargo vessels.[37]

The selection of Penang Harbor, on the Malay Peninsula, as a secondary target is interesting. Penang served as the Indian Ocean port under Tokyo's control for Japanese, German, and Italian submarines attempting to run the gauntlet of Allied air and sea power as they traveled between Asia and Europe carrying personnel, strategic raw materials, and technology between the two Axis states. The Germans based submarines of its *Monsun Gruppe* (Monsoon Group) in Penang beginning in 1943, with satellite facilities at other locations in the area. Many of the submarines assigned to this group sank due to Allied attacks en route or after arriving in Asia, but a few did make Indian Ocean patrols. Japan assumed control of six boats when Germany surrendered in May 1945 (four U-Boats and two former Italian cargo submarines that were seized by Germany when Italy surrendered to the Allied powers earlier). XX BC plans for Mission #31 specifically mentioned the secondary target of Penang as a base for German and Japanese Indian Ocean naval forces.[38]

The 444th BG launched twenty-four B-29s and the 468th BG placed an additional twenty-six bombers in the air. Aircraft flew individually rather than in formation, as well as the one bound for Saigon and Cam Ranh Bay. The 444th BG laid 36 mines in the Johore Strait, 12 in the Middle Channel, and 53 in the Outer Middle Channel. The 468th BG deposited 24 mines in the Rhio Strait, 12 in the Inner Middle Channel, 33 in the Inner Main Strait, and 21 in the Outer Main Strait. Two 444th BG B-29s and one 468th BG bomber laid a total of fifteen mines in the Pakchan River (secondary area), while another 468th BG B-29 left six mines in Penang Harbor. 444th BG aircraft #277 *Shanghai Lil*, #507 *Atsall Bro's*, #375 *Her Majesty*, and #268 *Airborn* returned with mines due to mechanical difficulties, while #584 *Lucky Lady* jettisoned its payload before landing.[39]

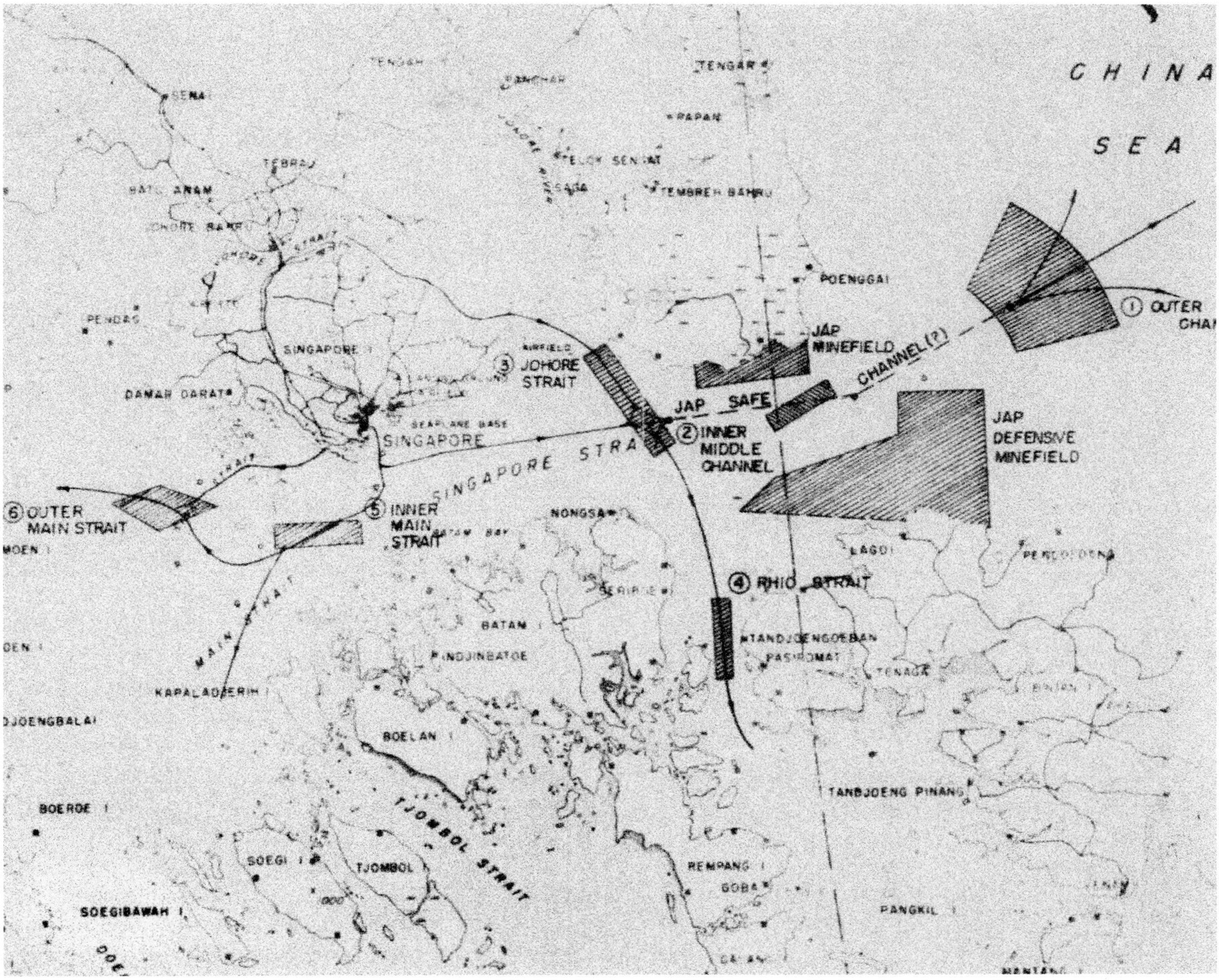

This map shows the Japanese defensive mine fields near Singapore, as well as the six areas marked for American mines dropped by XX BC B-29s during Mission #31. Each of the areas selected for mining by the B-29s is located adjacent to a number within a circle for easier identification.
(*US Air Force*)

Imperial Japanese Navy Submarine I-10 at Penang in 1942. Penang served as the main Japanese submarine base on the eastern Indian Ocean and also supported German and Italian submarines either transiting or patrolling the Indian Ocean. XX BC designated Penang as the secondary target for Mission #31 to Singapore. (*Lukas*)

The 40th BG's #859 *Shag'n Home* experienced an oil leak and needed to jettison its bombs prior to reaching the target during Mission #32 to Saigon. (*40th BG*)

The 40th BG's #274 *Bad Penny* flew in the second formation during Mission #32 to Saigon. (*40th BG*)

Five bomber crews reported meager and inaccurate heavy anti-aircraft and smaller caliber automatic weapons fire near Singapore. Automatic weapons fire also greeted two B-29s over Penang Harbor. Japanese anti-aircraft fire did not damage any of the bombers. The Japanese tethered a single 2,000-foot barrage balloon to an aircraft carrier in Singapore that was spotted by at least one B-29 crew. The balloon did not serve as an obstacle for the bombers, since they were mining nearby waters and were flying higher (between 3,000 and 6,000 feet) than the barrage balloon. A Japanese fighter did approach a B-29 from the tail position over Singapore. XX BC records indicate the fighter flew within 100 feet of the bomber without either aircraft opening fire.[40]

Mission #32: Saigon, January 27, 1945

With three of the XX BC's groups recovering from night mining missions the previous day, the 40th BG flew Mission #32 on January 27, 1945, to bomb shipping in the waters off Cape St. Jacques, near Saigon, where convoys formed or refitted for journeys to and from Japan and Singapore. Planners identified the Saigon Navy Yard and arsenal as the alternate target, the Rama VI Bridge in Bangkok as the secondary target, and the rail yards and jetties in Martaban, Burma, as the last resort target. Japanese military and merchant vessels frequented the waters near Saigon as they formed and concluded convoys. Bombing this area provided an opportunity to hit and destroy vessels as they lay at anchor off Cape St. Jacques. The Saigon Navy Yard serviced and repaired medium size vessels and included storage for naval supplies and munitions. The Rama VI Bridge still remained intact after attempts to destroy it during earlier missions, including Mission #24 on January 2. Martaban—the target of last resort—included jetties for small vessels to offload supplies that would depart the area via rail.[41]

Twenty-five B-29s launched with general purpose bombs and twenty-two dropped them at the primary target area for a combined total of 75.36 tons of high explosives. One bomber (#685) targeted the alternate following a failure of the fuel transfer system and two planes (#396 *Marietta Belle* and #859 *Shag 'n' Home*) jettisoned their loads due to mechanical problems. The 40th BG flew across the primary target area in two formations: one of nine planes and one of thirteen. Crews classified the undercast cloud cover at 10/10, meaning zero visibility

The 40th BG's #328 *Eight Ball Charlie* was flying with the XXI BC at this time. In January 1945, while with the XX BC, #328 *Eight Ball Charlie* encountered a problem with its bomb bay doors during Mission #32. (*Coppola via 40th BG*)

B-29 #505 *Draggin' Lady* developed a problem during Mission #32 to Saigon, forcing the plane to burn excessive fuel. #233 *Superstitious Aloysious* (seen here) slowed and remained with #505 *Draggin' Lady*, providing escort and helping protect the plane and crew. (*Watkins via the 40th BG*)

of the ground. Bombardiers dropped their ordnance by radar without viewing the results. B-29 #505 *Draggin' Lady* developed a problem while dropping its bombs; three remained in the bomb bay and had to be jettisoned later. The bomb bay doors would not fully close, forcing the plane to burn more fuel. B-29 #233 *Superstitious Aloysious* slowed and remained with #505 *Draggin' Lady* to escort and help protect the plane and crew. Both bombers initially landed at Cox's Bazar due to fuel shortage before returning to their base in India.[42]

The bomber force did not encounter any anti-aircraft fire. Crews spotted three Japanese fighters taking off from the Saigon area but none of these aircraft approached or engaged the bombers. Post-strike reconnaissance photographs also did not indicate any damage to vessels in the area. Hitting a vessel from a level bomber at high altitude was very challenging and was even more difficult by radar through cloud cover.[43]

The 40th BG's #798 *Ole Gas Eater* undergoing an engine change at Cox's Bazar following an emergency landing returning from Mission #32 to Saigon. (*Poplaski via 40th BG*)

Chapter 10

February 1945: Missions in Support of Southeast Asia Command

I know that you can never give up or you're lost, but I was ready to give up when this giant submarine surfaced directly in front of me.

—John Topoloski (40th BG) after spending thirty-six hours in a Mae West alone in the ocean

February 1945 opened with an unopposed American landing southwest of Manila, in the Philippines, and an insertion of Australian troops onto New Britain, east of New Guinea. American forces recaptured the Bataan Peninsula in the Philippines on February 17 and American Marines landed on Iwo Jima, northwest of the Marianas Islands, two days later. XXI Bomber Command (BC), now under the leadership of Gen. Curtis LeMay, continued its aerial offensive against the Japanese aircraft industry and other targets in the Japanese home islands, Iwo Jima, and "training" missions to locations near Truk for newly arrived crews.

February 1945 was the first month XX BC did not stage through airfields in Chengtu, China. The command flew seven missions against shipping/naval facilities, military supply dumps, and the railroad network in support of the Allied South East Asia Command (SEAC), which oversaw operations in Southeast Asia, which the United States had designated its China-Burma-India and later India-Burma Theaters for command and planning purposes. The Allies established SEAC in 1943, to provide strategic oversight of military air, land, and sea operations in Southeast Asia, including India, Burma, Ceylon, Malaya, Sumatra, Thailand, and French Indo-China, with the rest of the Netherlands East Indies added just prior to the end of the war in 1945. British Admiral Lord Mountbatten commanded SEAC from its inception until 1946, with American Gen. Joseph Stilwell as his first deputy supreme allied commander.

Mission #33: Singapore, February 1, 1945

Mission #33 was not only the first, but also the costliest operation in terms of B-29s lost and damaged during February 1945. XX BC targeted the Admiralty floating drydock in Singapore and alerted all four groups for this important mission. The King George VI drydock at the same naval base served as the alternate target, with the piers at Penang as the secondary target and the rail yard and jetties of Martaban, Burma, as the target of last resort. The B-29s targeted the drydocks in Singapore on January 11, but did not score any visible hits in post-mission reconnaissance photographs.

One hundred twelve planes (twenty-eight from each group) launched in a maximum effort to hit the drydock and ensure its unavailability to repair Japanese vessels. Approximately half of this force (sixty-seven B-29s) attacked the Admiralty floating drydock with 143.66 tons of general purpose bombs and twenty-one dropped 47.89 tons of ordnance on the alternate target, the King George VI drydock. Fifteen bombers targeted the secondary area with 32.10 tons, while five aircraft dropped 10.69 tons of bombs on the target of last resort. One B-29 (#456 of the 468th BG) bombed a warehouse in Bassien, Burma, as a target of opportunity.[1]

The bombers received moderate anti-aircraft fire ranging from inaccurate to accurate targeting. The crews of the

462nd BG's #454 *Thunderbird* and #711 encountered the possible utilization of concussion munitions by the Japanese. Both planes flew in the tenth formation to pass over the target, with #454 slotted as the lead bomber. The ordnance, possibly fired from the Japanese naval base, appeared to emit a strong concussion following a blinding flash with a red center, yet without the metal fragments and smoke common with most flak. Post-mission intelligence noted the following after debriefing other crews who witnessed what happened with #454:

> As the formation passed over the target and during fighter and ground AA attack, an unusual explosion was observed on the top of the left horizontal stabilizer of A/C 454. The explosion consisted of a blinding flash with a red center, not unlike a gigantic fire cracker, which lasted a fraction of a second and left no smoke. No damage could be observed immediately after the explosion.[2]

The crew of the 462nd BG's #711 reported being rocked by a similar type of concussive explosion while flying in the same formation. The intelligence summary noted:

> The gunner's blister of this aircraft [#711] was blown inward [underline emphasis in the original], hitting the gunner, and then forced out by suction which also propelled the gunner against his gun sight. No observations relating to the characteristics of any burst prior to the loss of the blister are available. It was reported, however, and the only appropriate explanation is that the primary cause was the result of an exterior concussion. Subsequent examination on the ground again revealed no fragment damage to the aircraft nor was the gunner injured except from the sudden contact with the blister and gun sight.[3]

(The 7th Air Force tactical reconnaissance aircraft experienced a similar phenomenon in August 1944, while photographing Japanese assets on Pagan Island, in the Marianas Islands.) Two other B-29s in formation with #454 and #711 received damage from conventional flak at the same location. Flak is attributed to downing (via crash landing) the 444th BG's #736, piloted by Capt. Knott, as well as damaging eight other B-29s. Aircraft #736 caught a flak explosion that knocked out engine #1 and damaged the prop governor on engine #2; the latter propeller continued to turn at 2,000 revolutions per minute. The pilot returned to India, where he crash-landed the bomber at his home base.[4] As Knott initiated a final approach for an emergency landing a dust storm obscured the end of the runway:

Japanese flak hit a main spar and fuel cell on the 444th BG's #464 *Flying Stud II* during Mission #33 to Singapore. (*Schutte via 468th BG*)

> A 28 mile per hour cross wind shifted the aircraft approximately 50 feet to the side of the runway. With insufficient power to go around, Captain Knott had no alternative but to raise the landing gear and crash land alongside the runway. He narrowly missed an anti-aircraft position and trees and finally stopped on clear ground with no injury to personnel and very little structural damage to the aircraft.[5]

The B-29s damaged by flak included the 444th BG's #720 *Fu-Kemal-Tu* (engine #1 controls and the outboard wing), #464 *Flying Stud II* (a main spar and fuel cell), and #451 *Black Jack Too* (engine #4 nacelle and the left wing). Those returning with flak damage from the 462nd BG were #711 and #590 *Celestial Princess* (holes in the left outboard wing and a ring cowl). The 468th BG planes flying home with damage included #275 *Hi Stepper* (radar compartment and vertical fin), #536 *Mammy Yokum* (left flap), and #719 *The Uninvited II* (vertical stabilizer and flap). Lt. Edward Wilfinger—radar operator on #275 *Hi Stepper*—died from wounds he received when flak hit his B-29.[6]

Japanese fighters intercepted half of the bomber force. Attacks were generally described as weak, but individual fighter pilots displayed skill and coordination, resulting in the downing of one B-29 (#589 *Calamity Jane* of the 40th BG) and damage to seven other bombers. B-29 gunners claimed the destruction of three Japanese fighters (two Nakajima Ki-44 Tojos and one Mitsubishi A6M Zeke), as well as four "probables" and fourteen damaged.

A Japanese Tojo fighter jumped Capt. Aubrey Richard and crew in the 40th BG's #589 *Calamity Jane* shortly after bombs away on Mission #33. The plane and crew disappeared attempting to return to India. (*Changnon via 40th BG*)

A Japanese Tojo fighter jumped the 40th BG's #589 *Calamity Jane*, piloted by Capt. Aubrey Richard, shortly after bombs away. The fighter damaged the B-29, forcing Capt. Richard to assume the lead position in a four-bomber formation for protection. Richard requested crews in the other planes to provide their observations of the fire and smoke emanating from the right wing section. Aircraft #498 *B Sweet III* confirmed seeing smoke and gasoline pouring from the wing between engines #3 and #4. Soon after this conversation, #589 *Calamity Jane* turned from the formation and took a heading between 25 and 30 degrees. The crew of B-29 #498 *B Sweet III* later reported they could still see smoke but no flames and radioed #589 *Calamity Jane* to determine its intention. The crew on #589 *Calamity Jane* responded they were headed to pre-arranged coordinates where a submarine was patrolling on air-sea rescue duty. #589 *Calamity Jane* appeared to not be in distress and maintained altitude as it increased its distance from the formation. The air-rescue submarine never found the bomber. The military later noted a piece of the B-29 may have been displayed in Singapore, but the wreck and remains of the crew were never found.[7]

Japanese fighters displayed keen coordination in numerous attacks on the bomber force; post-mission records specifically annotate the following coordination between two fighters:

> Two single engine fighters (Oscars or Zekes) attacked in line astern from 1 o'clock high. It looked like a typical frontal attack until one of the fighters broke off, still some distance out, and slipped and skidded in a possible attempt to draw fire from the center of the formation. One crew reported that two 20 mm wing guns were firing as it skipped off to the side. The other fighter kept coming in, and before breaking off at about 250 yards dropped an aerial bomb near the formation. No claims were made against the enemy aircraft nor was damage from the attack reported by the B-29.[8]

At one point during the passage over Singapore, B-29 crews witnessed five Japanese fighters working together:

> [A] coordinated attack was made by five Oscars, and described as a "strafing" attack. The enemy fighters circled high above the formation and when reaching a position between 10:30 and 11:00 o'clock nosed down toward the formation and sprayed it with gunfire. Each Oscar attacked once (one dropping aerial bombs in addition to shooting), opened fire at 1,500 yards and closed to about 400 yards before peeling off to a breakaway. One B-29 reported damage to a prop governor from enemy gunfire. There were no claims against the Oscars.[9]

Cpl. Robert Asbury, tail gunner on #714, received a slight wound when a bullet from a Japanese fighter hit his gun sight. Post-mission analysis recorded the following results:

> Immediately prior to the attack, the Admiralty floating drydock was partially submerged and a 460-foot engine-aft cargo vessel therein had steam up and was slightly askew, apparently getting ready to depart. In the course of the attack, the dock received 5 hits between the bulkheads, probably seriously damaging the bottom of the deck and setting the cargo vessel afire. In addition, 1 hit was scored on the top of the port bulkhead admidships, resulting in a 15 by 30 foot hole. Five near misses were close enough to have caused underwater damage to the plates. Reconnaissance several hours after the attack showed the dock to be under water for approximately three-quarters of its length and the vessel aboard burning furiously in two places.[10]

Reconnaissance photos taken four days later indicated the dock lay partially submerged and the cargo vessel had sunk.

Mission #34: Saigon, February 7, 1945

On February 7, XX BC simultaneously struck two targets: Saigon and Bangkok. The 444th and 462nd BG flew Mission #34 with a mixture of general purpose and incendiary bombs to Saigon, with the Navy Yard and harbor as the primary target. Planners selected the Royal Ordnance factory in Bangkok as the secondary target and the Martaban railroad marshalling yards in Burma as the target of last resort. The Navy Yard in Saigon handled medium-sized vessels and contained various repair facilities. Disruption of the naval installation at Saigon and damage to any vessels berthed there would support Allied operations in Burma and the Philippines.[11]

The 462nd BG's #393 *Rush Order* returned to base early with its bomb load due to a blown exhaust stack on one of its engines during Mission #34 to Saigon. (*US Air Force*)

Sixty-seven B-29s (32 from the 444th BG and 35 from the 462nd BG) launched. Forty-two bombers attempted to attack the primary target, while twenty flew to Phnom Penh as a target of opportunity and two dropped their loads at Martaban due to mechanical problems. Eleven B-29s of the 444th BG released their bombs too early on the approach to the primary target in Saigon. One of the bombers flying over Phnom Penh could not bomb due to faulty bomb bay doors and later jettisoned the load before returning to India. B-29 #393 *Rush Order* of the 462nd BG returned to base early with its bomb load due to a blown exhaust stack on one of its engines.[12]

This photo of #757 of the 40th BG was probably taken when the 40th BG flew with the XXI BC from the Pacific after March 1945. During the XX BC Mission #34, #757 flew in the seventh bombing formation to cross the target. (*Changnon via 40th BG*)

Weather conditions over Saigon were extremely unfavorable; the area experienced 9/10 to 10/10 (complete) undercast, preventing bombardiers from seeing the target and forcing them to rely on radar sets for bombing. Poor radar pictures of the area below complicated the process. Two formations from the 462nd BG made two dry runs over the target area to accurately locate the navy yard. After the second attempt the crews opted to fly to Phnom Penh as a target of opportunity. A 444th BG formation made one dry run and then changed the lead aircraft. This formation discharged its load during the second run. Another 444th BG formation changed lead aircraft between the initial point and the target. As the original lead bomber relinquished its position the bombardier accidentally released three bombs. Eleven other bombers did not receive the order to change the lead aircraft and dropped their loads upon seeing the accidental discharge, again demonstrating inexperience in large formation tactics.[13]

Only four of the B-29s encountered anti-aircraft fire over Saigon and the crews noted it as meager and inaccurate. The aircraft over Phnom Penh did not receive any anti-

The 462nd BG lost the only bomber to not return from Mission #34 to Saigon. B-29 #461 *Haulinas*, piloted by Harold Kinreed, made a crash landing at Dum Dum airfield in India at the end of the mission due to low fuel. Three crew members died and three were injured. (*462nd BG*)

aircraft fire, while the bombers at Martaban reported meager fire ranging from inaccurate to accurate. Three B-29s flying off their briefed course toward Saigon spotted anti-aircraft flak near Rangoon. Other bombers reported briefly coming under fire at other locations along the flight route and five received minor damage.

Approximately five Japanese fighters made nine approaches toward the B-29s; all of the attacks occurred at Phnom Penh and Saigon. Crews reported the attacks as timid and only two fighters (both Tojos) pressed within 1,000 yards, opening fire on the bombers. The crew of the 462nd BG's #484 *Our Gal* watched as a Zeke flew within 300 yards of their bomber from 11 o'clock. At this distance the B-29 gunners commenced firing and the Zeke broke away in a sharp dive without ever firing on the bomber. A gunner on #801 *Phony Express* of the 462nd BG claimed credit for damaging a Tojo attacking from 9 o'clock. The gunner fired on the fighter at approximately 1,200 yards. Rounds appeared to strike the Tojo, which broke contact at 1,000 yards without returning fire. The 462nd BG received the brunt of fighter attacks and expended 2,025 rounds, compared to sixty rounds fired by the 444th BG. The 462nd's total is actually small based on the number of bombers firing on fighters and confirms gunners were mainly placing warning shots at fighters outside optimum engagement distances and Japanese fighters were not pressing attacks against the bombers.[14]

The 462nd BG lost the only bomber on Mission #34. B-29 #461 *Haulinas*, piloted by Harold Kinreed, made a crash landing at Dum Dum airfield in India at the end of the mission due to low fuel. As the B-29 approached the airfield all four engines ceased functioning, forcing the pilot to crash-land the plane. The bomber did not touch down until reaching the last third of the runway and slid off the end, demolishing the plane. Three crew members died and three were injured.[15]

Post-mission reconnaissance confirmed poor bombing results in Saigon. Dropping loads by radar through a complete undercast proved challenging for the crews and resulted in missing the Saigon target by over 3,000 feet. In densely packed Saigon, missing the navy yard and arsenal by this distance resulted in heavy damage within a residential and business district of the city. The first formation over Phnom Penh scored better results due to dropping visually. The B-29s destroyed jetties along the river front, but also damaged or destroyed residential and business structures within the city. Bombing results of the second formation could not be determined.[16]

Mission #35: Bangkok, February 7, 1945

The 40th and 468th BG bombed the second target scheduled for February 7. Planners again selected the Rama VI Bridge in Bangkok as the primary target, with the Martaban jetties and marshalling yard as the secondary. By February 1945, Bangkok had emerged as the central point for collecting and forwarding supplies destined for Japanese forces in Burma. Material traveled by rail from Phnom Penh and the coast to Bangkok for further rail movement westward to Burma. All rail traffic from French Indo-China had to cross the Rama VI Bridge and destruction or damage to the bridge could disrupt Japanese supplies flowing by rail from the east.[17]

Original plans called for a 112-plane strike against the Rama VI Bridge, but XX BC believed the mission could be accomplished with fewer aircraft and altered this plan to split the groups between the previously discussed mission to Saigon (Mission #34) and the Bangkok strike (Mission #35). Fifty-eight of sixty-four airborne bombers hit the primary target and one 468th BG B-29 (#895 *City of Pittsburgh*) struck the secondary due to engine trouble. The 40th BG approached the primary target at approximately 20,000 feet and the 468th BG at approximately 18,000 feet in eighteen formations (two to five planes per formation). Each B-29 carried twelve 1,000-pound general

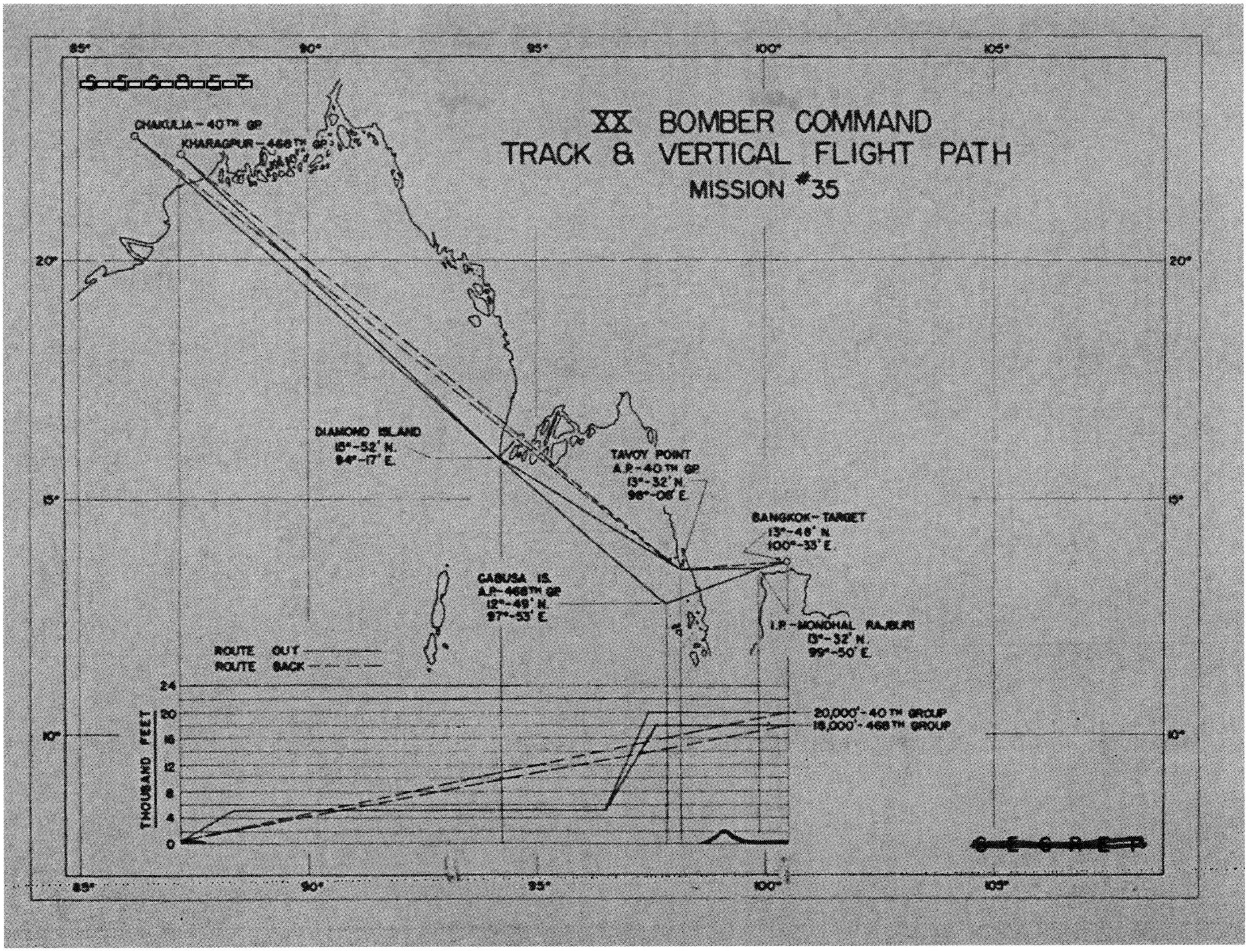

XX BC utilized this chart to brief pilots and navigators on the route to and from Bangkok for Mission #35. (*US Air Force*)

purpose high explosive bombs with the center of the Rama VI Bridge serving as the visual aiming point and the center of Bangkok as the radar aiming point in the event of poor weather. Two spans of the bridge could be brought down if the central piers collapsed as a result of high explosive shock waves from the onslaught of the bombing raid. With clear weather over the target the bombardiers in the formations utilized visual bombing techniques.[18]

Seventeen of the B-29 formations encountered meager flak ranging from inaccurate to accurate bursts. One of the 40th BG B-29s (#527 *Devilish Snooks*) sustained major damage to an engine and the rear bomb bay. Four bombers from the 40th BG (#894, #374 *Tabomma II*, #587 *San Antonio Rose*, and #462 *The Lemon*) and two from the 468th BG (#542 *Lady Hamilton II* and #714 *Robert J. Wilson*) returned with minor flak damage. Flak blew out the right gunner's blister of the 468th BG's #542 *Lady Hamilton II*, wounding the gunner, Cpl. Jack Shanker. Fellow crew members treated the wounded gunner and radioed the 468th BG in India for medical advice.[19] The following exchange of radio transmissions illustrates the attempt to treat the gunner while applying medical advice from the Group in India (the following repeats the transmissions word for word without punctuation):

The 468th BG's #471 *Chattanooga Choo Choo* from the cockpit of another B-29. *Chattanooga Choo Choo* experienced engine problems and returned early to India, rather than continue with Mission #35 to Bangkok. (*Schutte via 468th BG*)

The 40th BG's #620 *Sleepy Time Gal* flew as the lead bomber in the fifth formation over the target during Mission #35. (*40th BG*)

#542: Wounded man on board shot in neck can't move right arm think collar bone broken advise if possible ETA 1010Z.

468th BG: Keep man quiet give one tube only of morphine and plasma as necessary.

#542: Having trouble giving plasma it won't flow into vein and makes swelling just above needle advise.

468th BG: Put in other arm in vein reason for swelling first time was that needle not in vein pinch back the rubber tubing above the needle to determine if blood is drawn into the glass tube this proves the needle to be in vein if bleeding put on pressure bandage.

#542: Have done so.

468th BG: Is he in shock what is pulse?

#542: Unable to give plasma pulse is normal man is resting.

468th BG: How much blood has he lost moderate or severe mix all plasma in plane right away.

#542: Bleeding is moderate pulse is 89.

468th BG: Keep patient warm also on oxygen report pulse rate every ten minutes.[20]

The 40th BG's #908, taken on Tinian Island sometime after March 1945, when the 40th BG operated under the XXI BC. In February 1945, #908 flew in the fifth bombing formation during the XX BC's Mission #35 to Bangkok. (*Fearsad via 40th BG*)

Personnel of the 25th Squadron pose with #374 *Tabooma II* of the 40th BG. During Mission #35 to Bangkok, the bombardier encountered problems with the bomb bay, forcing him to individually salvo when the bomber passed the target. (*40th BG*)

During Mission #35 to Bangkok, #527 *Devilish Snooks* of the 40th BG sustained major flak damage to an engine and the rear bomb bay. (*40th BG*)

Japanese flak damaged the 40th BG's #587 *San Antonio Rose* during Mission #35 to Bangkok. (*40th BG*)

Capt. Ira Matthews, pilot of the 40th BG's #579 *Eddie Allen*. Matthews' B-29 flew as the lead bomber and his bombardier, 1st Lt. Marshall "Shorty" Norton, served as the formation's lead bombardier in the operation to drop the Rama VI Bridge during Mission #35. (*US Air Force*)

Bomber crews spotted numerous Japanese fighters, but none attacked the formations. Crews also reported six cigar-shaped barrage balloons anchored to vessels in the Tavoy River that rose to 2,000 feet and one formation noticed four possible barrage balloons tethered over central Bangkok. Four B-29s returned early to India due to engine problems (#445 *The Craig Comet*, #471 *Chattanooga Choo Choo*, and #532 *Million Dollar Baby II* of the 468th BG and #455 *Genie* of the 40th BG). One 468th BG bomber (#663 *Hero Haters*) attempted to bomb the primary and secondary targets, but failed each time due to bomb release failures.[21]

Post-strike reconnaissance photographs indicated at least four bombs made direct hits on the Rama VI Bridge, resulting in an approximately 65% loss of the center span, and near misses damaged the extreme end of the northwest span. Bombs also cut the rail lines, siding tracks, and small support buildings. Pilot Ira Matthews of the 40th BG reported the B-29s of his formation dropped the center span of the Rama VI Bridge thanks to the skill of his bombardier, 1st Lt. Marshall "Shorty" Norton. Matthews's B-29 flew as the lead bomber in the formation and Norton served as the formation's lead bombardier. Other bombardiers released their ordnance upon seeing the bombs dropped by Norton in a textbook example of defensive formation tactics. According to Matthews:

> The ten B-29s were in a tight formation when Shorty Norton took control at the Initial Point, and he made such smooth course corrections on the bomb run that we never seemed to change heading. As always, Shorty ignored the flak and fighter opposition we met on the way to the bomb release point. The other Bombardiers released their bombs when they saw Shorty's bombs leave our bomb bays. By the time the last bomb had exploded, the center span of the Rama VI Bridge was on the bottom of the river. Strike photos showed a perfect bomb pattern that was every Bombardier's dream.[22]

Norton retained a copy of the post-strike reconnaissance photograph of the Rama VI Bridge with the gap in its center span as a souvenir. Upon rotating back to the United States a few weeks later, a customs and security search discovered the classified photo and it was confiscated.

Medical personnel remove Cpl. Jack Shanker from the 468th BG's #542 *Lady Hamilton II* after Mission #35. Flak blew out a gunner's blister, wounding Shanker. (*Schutte via 468th BG*)

Mission #36: Rangoon, February 11, 1945

The XX BC tapped all four Bomb Groups for Mission #36, to bomb the Japanese supply dumps north of Rangoon, Burma, on February 11, 1945, in support of Allied operations. The dumps lay north of Rangoon near Lake Victoria and provided critical military supplies and equipment for the Japanese forces fighting in Burma. The raid occurred in cooperation with Consolidated B-24 Liberators of the 14th Air Force that attacked the supply dump one hour prior to the arrival of the B-29s. Planners identified Area "F" at the supply dump as the primary target and did not establish secondary or last resort targets. Plans called for the crews to return with their bomb loads if unable to hit the supply dump.[23] According to XX BC, "This decision was made in view of the fact that there were no suitable secondary or last resort targets for the bomb load carried, and because the primary target does not offer a sufficient radar return to insure any degree of success of radar bombing."[24]

The XX BC tested another change during Mission #36: during the previous thirty-five operational missions, B-29 pilots assembled into group formations in the vicinity of specific ground locations. According to mission reports, "Another change from previous missions was that each

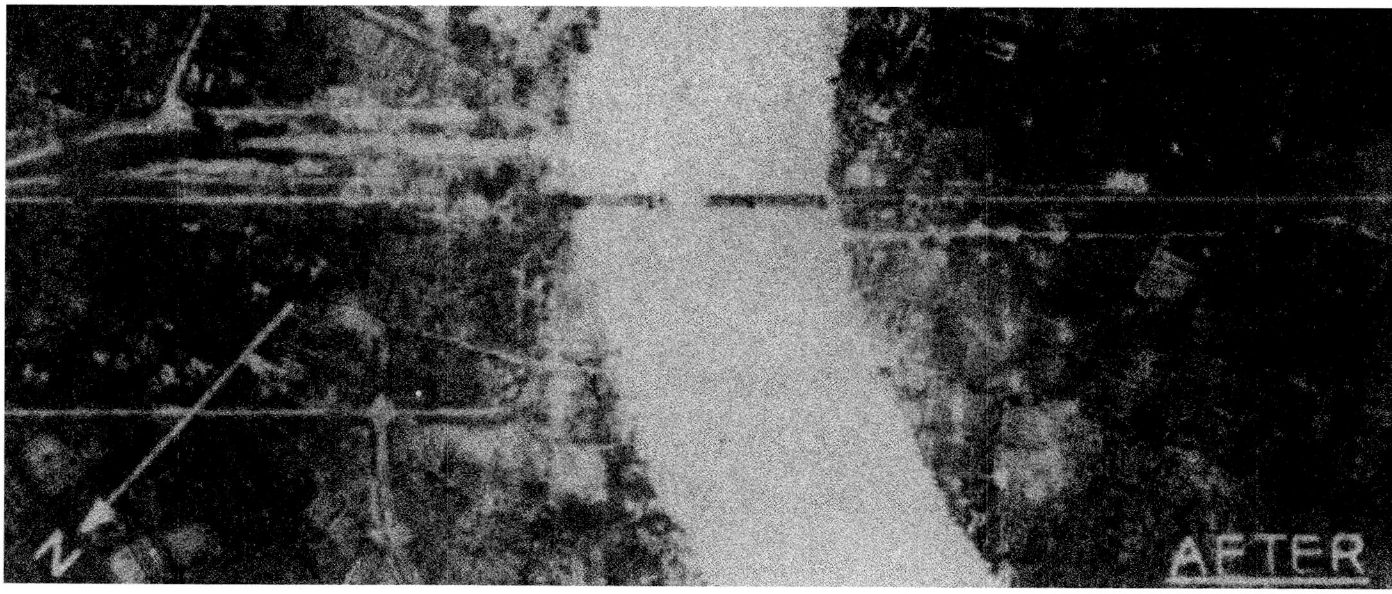

The destruction of the Rama VI Bridge after Mission #35 to Bangkok, Thailand. Lead Bombardier 1st Lt. Marshall "Shorty" Norton retained a copy of this photograph as a souvenir until it was confiscated weeks later during a customs and security search upon returning to the United States. (*US Air Force*)

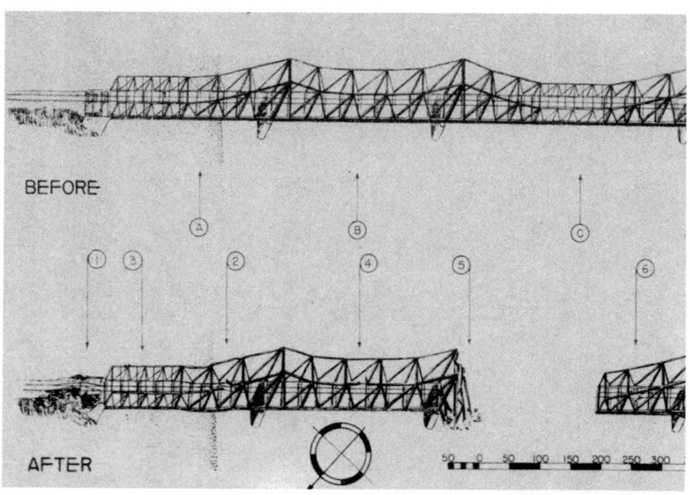

A post-raid diagram showing the specific destruction caused to the Rama VI Bridge during Mission #35. (*US Air Force*)

Group had an individual over-water assembly point. This innovation was an experiment to determine the feasibility of assembly over water."[25]

The 40th and 468th BG carried incendiary bombs while the 444th and 462nd BG hauled fragmentation bombs. Supply dump "F" included ammunition hidden beneath a covering of palm trees and brush, as well as within small revetments. The varied ordnance allowed the bombers to place a mix of fragmentation and incendiary bombs on the area for maximum effectiveness against the target. The 40th BG, 444th BG, and 462nd BG placed fifteen aircraft each in the air, while the 468th BG launched fourteen B-29s. The 468th BG's #530 *Totin-To-Tokyo II* lost an engine prior to takeoff and aborted the mission. Fifty-five of the fifty-nine B-29s bombed the supply dump from altitudes ranging from 17,400 feet to 21,280 feet. Each group struck the target as a separate formation. Planners wanted the fragmentation bombs dropped first, but this directive was omitted from the mission order, resulting in the groups carrying the incendiary ordnance hitting the supply dump first. Twelve of the bombers reported some type of malfunction with bombing systems upon their return: one B-29 (#463 *Humpin' Honey* of the 462nd BG) experienced a total failure of the bombs to drop but managed to clear and deposit them on Hmawbi Airfield. The crew opted to hit the airfield despite the original directive to return unused ordnance to India due to the bombs having been already armed for the run over

Two crew members of the 468th BG's #530 *Totin-To-Tokyo II* review a chart in China sometime in the summer or fall of 1944. #530 *Totin-To-Tokyo II* lost an engine prior to take off and aborted Mission #36 to Rangoon, Burma. (*Schutte via 468th BG*)

the supply dump. Three bombers aborted after takeoff: the 40th BG's #757 experienced a frozen propeller governor; the 462nd BG's #560 lost an engine due to a rocker arm failure and jettisoned its bombs; and #417 *Rushin' Rotation* of the 468th BG jettisoned its load and returned after losing oil pressure in an engine.[26]

All of the B-29s encountered moderate and accurate heavy anti-aircraft fire over the Rangoon area. After the mission, crews noted that the flak over Rangoon was actually more accurate and intense than over Anshan, in Manchuria. The 468th BG formation led the command across the target. Flak initially tended to be to the right and behind the formation, but began to move toward the formation itself, as the gunners adjusted their weapons and were better prepared when the 40th BG flew into the target area:

> All anti-aircraft bursts observed were reported to be black. Fire throughout the whole encounter was Continuous Directed with tracking being easily recognized by the "trail" pattern of bursts. Initial bursts were encountered about 1 1/2 minutes before bomb release time and continued without let up until 0540Z, time that the last aircraft in formation broke off to the left after the strike photo run. The greatest intensity of bursts encountered came about one-half minute before to one-half minute after 'bombs away"...The first guns to engage our formation were off in altitude by about 2,000 feet, but quickly corrected until bursts were for most part level. Formation #3 [462nd BG] observed fire directed against #2 [40th BG] and reported that "bursts were all through the formation with more outside its limits. Just after [formation] #2 dropped it bombs, there was one very large white burst in the center of the formation. The burst was 5-10 times as large as the ordinary black AA [anti-aircraft] and had many long streamers." This was probably phosphorous AA as no air-to-air bombing attacks were reported.[27]

Twenty-nine B-29s (51% of the attacking force) sustained minor flak damage over Rangoon, although none of the bombers returned with what would be classified as major damage. Lt. Francis McCann, bombardier on #460 *Lassie Too* of the 468th BG, sustained a superficial arm wound from a flak burst that struck his bomber. The Japanese gunners proved to be better prepared and quicker to adjust fire as each successive bomber formation flew across the target: the first B-29 formation returned with one aircraft damaged, but there were seven damaged in the second formation, nine in the third, and thirteen in the fourth, so thirteen of the fifteen bombers in the 444th BG formation—the last group over the target—sustained flak damage.[28]

Japanese fighters attacked two of the four formations with eight Kawasaki Ki-61 Tony and one Nakajima Ki-43 Oscar. Fighters made nine single and three coordinated attacks and the pilots proved to be more aggressive than many encountered in other missions outside Japan and China. Ten of the attacks occurred with pilots closing to within 300 yards and four of those were within 100 yards of the bombers. During the air engagements, bullets fired from the upper turret of #463 *Humpin' Honey* of the 462nd BG struck #590 *Celestial Princess* of the same group, which was flying to the left and in front of the former B-29. A post-mission review blamed the incident on the failure of a limit switch, rather than personal error on the bombardier who controlled the upper turret while it was firing. B-29 gunners claimed to have damaged two Tonys (claims by #897 *Jokers Wild* of the 444th BG and #590 *Celestial Princess* of the 462nd BG) and the Oscar (claimed by #711 of the 462nd BG), while one B-29 sustained major damage from a fighter attack. The 462nd BG's #590 *Celestial Princess*, piloted by Maj. Bagby, battled a Japanese Tony that attacked from a position forward of the bomber and placed machine gun bullets into the left wing of the B-29. The bomber returned to India under escort by #463 *Humpin' Honey*, piloted by Capt. Waller, and #503 *Sky Scraper*, flown by Capt. Sullivan, with damage to its engine #1 and propeller, as well as the pilot's window, the upper forward turret, and the fuselage. All personnel returned safely.[29]

A post-strike target damage assessment could not be made independently of the 14th Air Force B-24s that bombed one hour prior to the B-29s. Dump "F" included seventy-five hutments and thirty-five miscellaneous buildings destroyed and at least ten others damaged. Bombs falling outside the "Dump F" area destroyed ten to fifteen buildings and revetments in "Dump A" and seventeen small buildings in "Dump K," as well as several buildings at the Insein Railroad Workshops and at a mental hospital converted for supply storage, according to intelligence sources.[30]

Mission #37: Kuala Lumpur, February 19, 1945

XX BC tapped the 444th and 468th BG for Mission #37 to the Central Railroad Repair Shops in Kuala Lumpur, Malaya. The mission, set for February 19, 1945, established Alor Star Airfield in Malaya as the secondary target and the Martaban Railroad Marshalling Yard as the target of last resort. The Central Repair Shops in Kuala Lumpur comprised a large and well equipped facility for the maintenance of the entire Malayan rail system and performed the only major maintenance on rail cars and engines. The shops could assemble locomotives from imported components and was the only installation of its kind in Malaya. Destruction of the facility would decrease the efficiency of the railroad system in Malaya and its ability to transport raw materials to Singapore for ships bound for Japan. A successful raid would also support Allied military efforts in Burma by hampering the movement of Japanese military supplies from Singapore to Thailand for transshipment to Burma. Each group earmarked thirty B-29s for the mission.[31]

The 468th BG's #272 *Miss Shorty* bombed the secondary target (Alor Star Airfield in Malaya) because of mechanical issues while flying Mission #37 to Kuala Lumpur. (*Schutte via 468th BG*)

During Mission #37, four 444th BG B-29s, including #730 *High and Mighty*, bombed the Malayan Collieries at Batu Arang as a result of human error; the lead crew in this formation thought they were bombing the primary target. (*Kelleher via 444th BG*)

Forty-nine B-29s visually dropped 346 general purpose 1,000-pound bombs on the primary target in formations ranging from two to five planes, with one aircraft flying by itself. Three B-29s (#417 *Rushin' Rotation*, #272 *Miss Shorty*, and #532 *Million Dollar Baby II* of the 468th BG) bombed the secondary target because of mechanical issues and one 444th BG plane (#580 *Flyin' Jackass*) attacked the target of last resort due to a faulty fuel transfer unit. Four other 444th BG B-29s (#730 *High and Mighty*, #422 *Little Mike*, #237, and #524 *Super Mouse*) bombed a target of opportunity identified as the Malayan Collieries in Batu Arang as a result of human error. The lead crew in this formation thought they were bombing the primary target and the other crews dropped ordnance on their lead bombardier's signal. One bomber (#891 *Monsoon Goon II* of the 444th BG) experienced mechanical problems and returned to India after jettisoning its bomb load while another 444th BG B-29 (#897 *Jokers Wild*) returned with its bombs.[32]

The 444th BG's #422 *Little Mike* mistakenly bombed the Malayan Collieries at Batu Arang, which was later categorized as a target of opportunity during Mission #37 to Kuala Lumpur. She was one of four 444th BG bombers, including #730 *High and Mighty*, that made this error. (*Evans via 444th BG*)

Although the bombers did not encounter anti-aircraft fire at any of the targets, the Japanese did engage them with heavy flak from batteries near Penang. Approximately fifteen Japanese aircraft, including obsolete planes such as the Aichi D3A Val attack, Mitsubishi A5M Claude fighter, and Nakajima Ki-27 Nate fighter aircraft, along with more up to date Oscars, made twenty-seven attacks against the bombers in the primary target area Kuala Lumpur. Crews rated the fighter opposition as weak, with nearly all of the attacks coming from the front of the

Although the name is written as *Monsoon Goon*, this B-29 is #891 *Monsoon Goon II* of the 444th BG, which returned early during Mission #37 due to mechanical issues. (*Kelleher via 444th BG*)

Japanese Aichi D3A Val dive bombers. The Japanese employed the obsolete Val dive bomber to attack B-29s over Kuala Lumpur during Mission #37. B-29 gunners claimed they damaged four of the Vals during the engagements. (*Lukas*)

bomber formations. This attack position seemed logical to everyone, since the more obsolete Japanese fighters would not be able to catch the faster B-29s from behind. Most fighters made a single pass at a bomber and then broke away to attack a plane in the formation behind it. B-29 gunners engaged the fighters in twenty-five of the twenty-seven attacks and noted a lack of aggressive tactics among the Japanese pilots, who tended to break contact over 500 yards from the bombers. The fighters employed at least five aerial bombs against the bombers as reported by crews:

> Two unusual types of bombs were used in several attacks. The first was described as a cluster of three bombs shaped like flat boards which were wired together. It was dropped from about 1,000 feet above in a head-on attack, and tumbled down without exploding. The second resembled a piece of stove pipe, from eight to ten inches in diameter and four feet long, with a cable, about 12 feet long, dangling from the end. Two of these bombs were dropped but neither exploded.[33]

Gunners made initial claims for the destruction of a Claude and damage to another Claude, two Oscars, and four Vals. All of the B-29s returned without battle damage. Approximately 57% of the buildings at the Central Rail Shops were structurally damaged and 9% received superficial damage. Post-strike photographs also indicated the B-29s damaged or destroyed 105 pieces of rolling stock and six locomotives.[34]

Mission #38: Singapore, February 24, 1945

Mission #38 targeted the Empire Dock area in Singapore with a daylight raid by all four groups on February 24, 1945. The Malayan Collieries lay between Singapore and India as a secondary target, while the field order identified a supply hut area in Khao Huagang, Thailand, as the target of last resort. (XX BC and group documents spelled this area as "Khoa," but this book utilizes the more common transliteration "Khao.") The Empire dock comprised the greatest single berthing space (one-third of the total) for ships and warehouses in Singapore Harbor. Large vessels moored at the berth while workers transferred military supplies to warehouses or moved raw materials or other commercial stores onto the ships. Destroyed military supplies would be difficult to replace, with American forces in the Philippines intercepting Japanese vessels sailing between the home islands and Southeast Asia. Khao Huagang, the target of last resort, lay at the western terminus of the Kra Isthmus Railroad, which connects the Bangkok-Singapore Railroad with the Bay of Bengal via the Pakcham River.[35]

The B-29s carried incendiary cluster bombs to ignite fires in the Empire Dock area, as well as a few delay fused general purpose bombs; the latter were set to detonate one-half hour after dropping to maim and hamper fire fighting crews. One hundred fourteen bombers initially took off on this mission (30 from the 40th BG; 29 from the 444th BG; 27 from the 462nd BG; and 28 from the

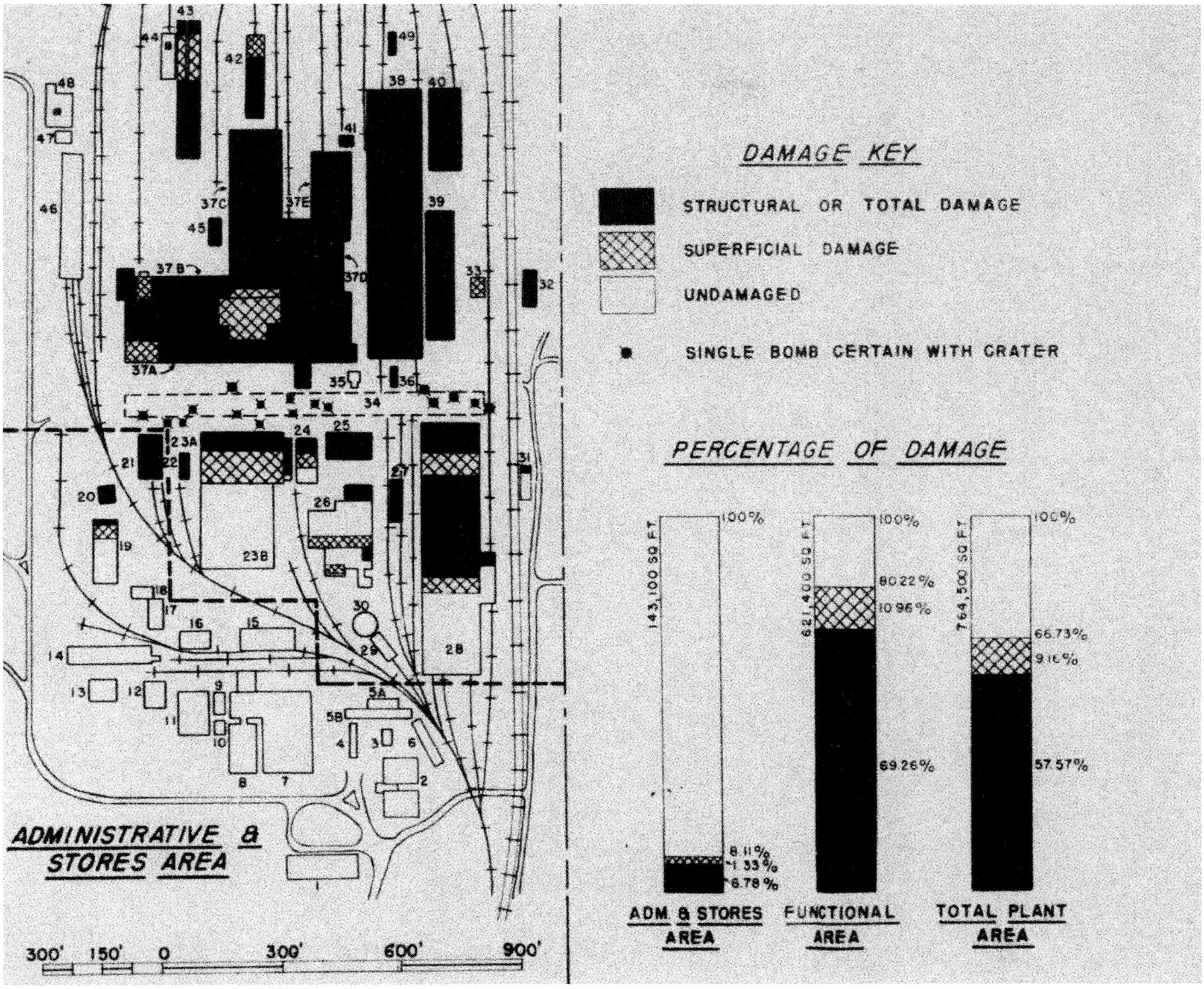

This post-raid drawing shows the extent of the damage to the Central Railroad repair shops in Kuala Lumpur, Malaya, caused by XX BC Mission #37. (*US Air Force*)

The 40th BG's #739 experienced a propeller governor problem and a fuel shortage during Mission #38 to Singapore, forcing an precautionary landing at Cox's Bazar on the return trip. (*40th BG*)

468th BG). Two additional B-29s—one each from the 444th BG (#273 *Big Ain't It?*) and the 468th BG (#663 *Dragon Lady*)—launched late due to mechanical difficulties. Of the grand total of 116 bombers, 106 dropped their ordnance on the primary target, flying in formations ranging from two to ten aircraft. Three B-29s bombed the secondary target and one hit the target of last resort. The planes bombing the secondary target included #668 *The Outlaw* of the 40th BG (fuel transfer problem), #663 *Dragon Lady* of the 468th BG (missed formation due to late take-off), and #424 *Hap's Characters* of the 468th BG (fuel transfer issue). The 444th BG's #580 *Flyin' Jackass* (inoperable fuel transfer system) bombed the target of last resort and returned. Six planes returned early without bombing due to mechanical issues. A total of ten aircraft, including those mentioned above, did not bomb the primary target due to mechanical problems (five for fuel systems; two due to power plants; and two because of propeller governor failure). These three issues continued to be the most common B-29 mechanical problems in the theater. An additional sixteen B-29s landed at airfields other than their home bases due to low fuel or mechanical problems on the return flight. The 462nd BG's #479, piloted by Capt. Ellerbe, ditched in a river near Calcutta, India, due to a lack of fuel. Procedures called for landing at an alternate airfield if the flight engineer calculated the plane would touch down at the home base with less than 400 gallons. The flight engineer on #479 calculated the plane would have 350 gallons, but did not trust the accuracy of his gauges. The pilot opted to attempt a return to their main base when the B-29 exhausted its fuel supply, forcing him to ditch with the loss of three crew members.[36]

Japanese anti-aircraft fire ranged from meager and inaccurate to accurate over Singapore. The B-29 crews bombing the secondary and last resort did not draw any anti-aircraft fire. Some aircraft did encounter meager and inaccurate flak along the flight route. One B-29 crew reported seeing at least nine phosphorous flak bursts. Eleven aircraft noted anti-aircraft fire from ships in the Bay of Bengal and post-mission intelligence recorded these as probably friendly fire from Allied vessels. One B-29 (#538 *Winged Victory* of the 40th BG) flown by Fountain L. Brown returned from Singapore with major flak damage to an engine nacelle, landing flap, and horizontal stabilizer. Additional damage to the fuselage resulted in depressurization, forcing the crew to fly using oxygen masks until they were able to descend.[37] Central fire control (CFC) gunner Robert C. Hall remembered the event:

> We saw no fighters near us before bombs away, but anti-aircraft fire started bursting around us at the time of bombs away. I was sitting in my "swivel chair" in the upper blister, scanning the sky for fighters. After bombs away, as we turned away from the bomb run, there was the "plunk" noise of flak striking us and a strange sensation as the cabin suddenly depressurized. At the time of the sudden noise I was facing to the left of the plane. I spun around trying to see where we were hit, and I saw a gaping hole, perhaps 5 or 6 feet in diameter, like a bite out of the trailing edge of the right wing behind #3 engine nacelle. We had taken a direct hit of an exploding antiaircraft shrapnel shell. Strips of sheet metal from the wing were waving like small flags in the wind, but all propellers were still turning and we were flying straight and level.[38]

Hall's aircraft flew under escort and protection by another bomber. He recalled the presence of the other plane—not from his own 40th BG—helped reassure the crew they were not alone. If forced to ditch or bail out, the other crew could report their position and if fighters attacked, the other bomber offered additional defensive firepower. With one crew member wounded, the men aboard the crippled bomber initiated "field repairs" to their B-29 as it limped home:

> Sometime later, when all engines had kept running and the condition of the plane seemed stable, someone (probably Leonard Morris, the flight engineer) decided that it would help to repair holes in the fuselage so as to get some cabin pressure back....While taking turns on oxygen, we also started plugging dozens of flak holes. Fortunately there was a large supply of chewing gum in the flight lunches, and we used it, together with torn pieces of cabin insulation. We worked hard at it, because restoring cabin pressure would minimize our need for oxygen. We discovered many dozens of holes in the gunnery compartment and the tunnel. I remember taking up floor boards in the gunnery compartment and virtually standing on my head under the floor to plug holes with gum and with insulation that I ripped from the flak-torn fabric. Tepper was doing the same sort of thing. We succeeded in restoring some cabin pressure in this way. Later Tepper, who was an electrical specialist in addition to being left gunner, began repairing wires that were cut by shrapnel where they passed through the tunnel. We discovered many dozens of holes in the gunnery compartment and the tunnel. For a long time Tepper lay on his back in the tunnel with a flashlight trying to locate and read the identification numbers on the wires and twist them back together. He would work for several minutes while I breathed oxygen and watched him to see if he showed signs of hypoxia. Every so often I would pull his foot and get him to come out and put on his oxygen mask for a few minutes. A couple of times he resisted, and we almost got in a fight. I was concerned that he might be intoxicated from hypoxia and unaware of the danger to himself, so I tried to force him to come out for oxygen. He became quite angry and belligerent, probably from shortage of oxygen. In any case, his work paid off handsomely by restoring intercom and some other circuits.[39]

In one coordinated fighter attack during Mission #38, a Japanese Rufe attacked #537 *Male Call* of the 444th BG. The bomber crew returned with holes in the wing, right rudder, and stabilizer from explosive shells. (*Archer via 444th BG*)

Japanese Mitsubishi A6M2 Rufe, a float plane variant of the Mitsubishi Zero fighter. A Japanese pilot flying a Rufe jumped #537 *Male Call* of the 444th BG during Mission #38 to Singapore. (*Lukas*)

Two planes landed with minor flak damage: flak punched a small hole in the 462nd BG's #476, while #538 *Beter 'N' Nutin* of the 444th BG caught a piece that ripped a small hole in its dorsal fin. The latter B-29 added insult to injury when a gunner shot his own vertical stabilizer while defending the bomber due to a failure of the gun synchronizing mechanism. (The full registration of the 40th BG B-29 was #63538 *Winged Victory*—major flak damage—and the 444th BG B-29 was #24538 *Beter 'N' Nutin*—minor flak damage. The XX BC and the groups typically referred to B-29s by their last three registration numbers, and this is a case of two B-29s with the same final three digits.[40])

Japanese fighters intercepted twenty-three of the B-29s during Mission #38. Crews reported attacks by ten fighters over Singapore and seven during the return flight. The planes engaging the bombers during the return flight included two Nates, two Nakajima A6M2 Rufes, two Tojos, and one Val. B-29 crews described fighter opposition as weak, with pilots displaying few aggressive tactics. The Japanese pilots continued to favor frontal attacks from positions above the bombers and opened fire at distances greater than 1,000 yards during 26% of their passes. Intelligence analysts noted this was higher than the average for previous missions and indicated lesser skilled or timid pilots. With the Japanese opening fire at farther distances, B-29 gunners also fired their weapons at ranges over 1,000 yards at a rate higher than average. Some Japanese pilots did press their attacks to within 250 yards and others displayed professional coordination between them during passes. In one coordinated attack, a Rufe approached #537 *Male Call* of the 444th BG from 7 o'clock and commenced firing at 600 yards. The Japanese pilot continued firing until breaking contact at 200 yards, causing major damage to the B-29. The bomber crew returned with holes in the wing, right rudder, and stabilizer from explosive shells. In return, gunners on board the B-29 believed they damaged the Japanese aircraft. Other Japanese pilots displayed skill and prior planning:

> ...two coordinated attacks were rather unusual in their direction of approach. In an attack by two Tojos, one approached from 7 o'clock high and the other from 7 o'clock low. Both opened fire at 1,000 yards and closed to 800 yards, then broke away in split S's. The B-29 also opened fire at 1,000 yards. No damage was inflicted by either side. The gunner thought this was an effective method of attack by the enemy. The other coordinated attack was executed by three Nates against a B-29 flying alone. One Nate approached from 4 o'clock high, while the other two came from 2 o'clock high. All three fighters opened fire and closed to 100 yards, but inflicted no damage to the B-29. The bombardier has a preliminary claim of damage against one of the Nates which approached from 2 o'clock.[41]

Forty-one per cent of the Japanese fighter attacks included the use of aerial bombs:

> Some enemy aircraft made diving attacks while others released their bombs during level flight. Some of the coordinated attacks were executed by fighters flying in trail and others by fighters flying abreast. In one instance, two Tojos flying in trail approached from 8 o'clock high to within 300 feet above the formation. Each released two bombs, then broke away toward 5 o'clock. Another attack was made by two Oscars flying abreast. They approached from 9 o'clock high, and each dropped two bombs as they passed over 500 feet above the formation. One of the coordinated attacks was executed by three Zekes flying in trail, close together. The Zekes approached from 11 o'clock. Each dropped one bomb as they flew 4,000 yards above, and over the B-29 formation. Diving maneuvers were employed by all single enemy aircraft making aerial bombing attacks. In three of these encounters, gunfire was observed as the enemy fighters approached.[42]

Post-mission intelligence analysts estimated the raid destroyed 39% of the buildings and warehouses in the target area, including twenty-one warehouses destroyed, fourteen warehouses partially destroyed, and three large oil tanks severely damaged.

Two days after the mission a B-29 (#804 of the 40th BG) utilized for photographic reconnaissance over Singapore fell victim to a Japanese fighter. The Japanese pilot proved to be aggressive and attacked the B-29's forward section. John Topoloski, the radar operator aboard the bomber, recalled the engagement that wounded the bombardier and downed his plane:

> We opened up on the plane when it came within range in a head-on approach. Nothing happened to the Jap plane and we were incredulous. The Jap plane hit the nose section of our plane with its guns and was successful with its second attack as well. I could hear everything that was said in the plane because I kept my headphones on throughout. While dealing with the fire in the forward compartment and treating Lt. Kintis [bombardier], Sgt. Sandrick [left gunner] reported trouble with the #2 engine. We got orders to jettison everything in the plane. It was hard to see everything we thought valuable a moment ago, being thrown out to try to save the plane. I was one of those who went into the back bomb bay to try to kick out the auxiliary tank that was hanging half in and half out. No chutes. I don't know how we had the daring to do what we did.[43]

Capt. Jim Lyons, the pilot of #804, added more details of the air battle from his perspective:

> We saw a fighter (later identified as a Jack) approaching us from one o'clock high. Bale turned to take him head on, and our forward guns opened up. The fighter was untouched, and to this date I believe those guns were out of sync. On his first pass we received a shell in the nose that started a hydraulic fire and turned Bill Kintis (bombardier) into a human torch and knocked out #2 engine. While Bale and the engineer were feathering the engine, Joe Dimock and I put out the cockpit fire with the extinguisher, dousing Kintis in the process. Dimock shouldn't have been flying as he still had a bullet wound in his arm, received in a previous accident when ammunition exploded on a nearby plane. My hands were burned while I was attempting to pull Bill Kintis out of the flames, but I did not realize this until sometime later. During this time, the Jack made two

> or three more passes, and in so doing, set our bomb bay tank on fire. For some unknown reason, he then broke off the attack and flew away. When the gunners informed us of the fire in the bomb bay, Bales went back to assist and I took over the controls. Teplick and Dimock managed to get the bomb bay doors open, but the bomb bay tank would not release. The gunners stood in the open bomb bay and chopped at the shackles with an ax. It finally came loose, but in falling, struck the doors so that they would not completely close. This negated any thought of ditching at that time.[44]

The situation continued to deteriorate, with Lyons striving to maintain control of the B-29 as other crew members battled to lighten the plane and keep her aloft as long as possible. Lyons recalled:

> I was able to maintain a reasonable altitude and speed, but the cockpit was an utter shambles...maps burned, etc. At this point, the other [B-]29 caught up to us and gave us an accurate position and course home. I thought that, with any luck at all, we would make it home, but two hours or so later, conditions changed radically. We had thrown everything we could overboard and were maintaining altitude when I noticed a small spot on the leading edge of the wing adjacent to the feathered #2 engine. I glanced at it from time to time and suddenly realized it was getting larger and there had to be fire in the wing.[45]

Eventually, the damaged bomber reached its limit and the pilot ordered preparations for bailing out, rather than attempting to ditch the plane. Lyons continued:

> We made preparations to bail out, including rigging a line to Bill's chute. We hoped we could drop him and land close enough to keep him afloat. He was badly burned and had never regained consciousness, but we couldn't bear to leave him behind. We had nearly waited too long, as the plane blew up before I hit the water. I dropped free of my chute much too high and went quite deep. I pulled the cords of my Mae West, only to find there were no cylinders. When I finally surfaced, I managed to partially inflate the vest manually, kick off my shoes, and discard everything on my person.[46]

Topoloski added:

> When we bailed out, I saw all eleven chutes in the air (in addition to my own). We were told to bail out in as rapid succession as we would so we would land as close together as possible. Lt. Bales, who had stayed behind to make sure everyone was out of the plane was the last to have his chute open. He landed some distance away. The instant my chute opened, I saw the plane's left wing break off. When that happened, the body of the plane nosed straight for the water. It hit the water before we did.[47]

A British submarine patrolled the area as part of the Allied air search rescue efforts and its crew moved their vessel to search for the downed B-29 in coordination with Consolidated PBY Catalinas after receiving the bomber's last coordinates. The B-29 crew remained in the water for over twenty-four hours before being rescued. One man spent thirty-six hours in the water before recovery. Lyons experienced a harrowing time with a defective Mae West, awaiting rescue:

> Luckily, four of us landed within shouting distance of each other and eventually managed to get together. We tied ourselves together and for the next twenty-five or so hours, the boys would take turns holding me up out of the water so I could inflate my Mae West. Five of the men were located at daybreak of the second day of the search by captain of [a] Catalina F/O E.A. Lickorish. He spotted a yellow object, circled 50 feet above the waves and discovered it was an injured flier. Within an hour he found four other survivors.[48]

The British submarine rescued the remaining crew members. According to Lyons, the other four men were picked up first by a submarine and then transferred to another Catalina captained by F/Lt. C.R. Bradford, which was just finishing the third day of the search when it had a message from the submarine.[49] Topoloski was the man who spent thirty-six hours awaiting help:

> I know that you can never give up or you're lost, but I was ready to give up when this giant submarine surfaced directly in front of me. The submarine crew threw me a line. I resolved that I was never going to let go of that line. I began swinging around toward the stern of the sub and there was concern that I would be sucked into the propellers. One of the sub crewmen, a champion swimmer, dove in and pulled me away. I can't say enough for the British.[50]

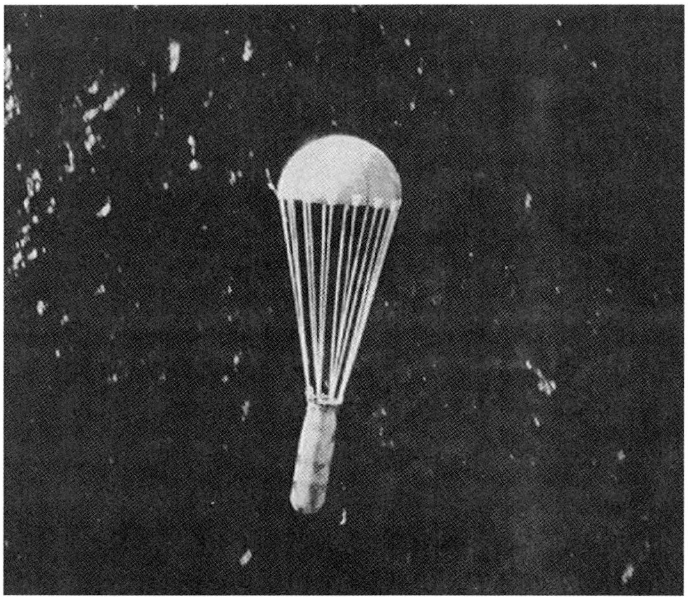

An M-26 sea mine dropped by B-29s. XX BC mined the Johore Strait during Mission #40. (*US Air Force*)

The 444th BG's #538 *Monsoon Goon* (later renamed *Beter 'N' Nutin*). This B-29 completed twenty-five bombing missions with the XX BC (India-China) and XXI BC (Tinian), as well as twenty-four Hump and two mining missions before returning to the United States in 1945 and should not be confused with #891 *Monsoon Goon II*. (*Harper via 444th BG*)

Mission #40: Johore Strait, February 27–28, 1945

The 444th BG launched twelve B-29s in a return to the Singapore area three days after Mission #38. (Note XX BC skips #39 as a mission number and moves to #40 in the official records. Mission #39 was flown on March 4–5, 1945. Mission numbers and chronological dates remain out of sequence in XX BC records until Mission #44 on March 17, 1945.) Mission #40 called for the bombers to mine the Johore Strait, a major approach for Japanese military and civilian vessels sailing to or from Singapore. The secondary mining areas were Penang Harbor, the Pakehan River, and Mergui Harbor. B-29s placed mines around Singapore at the end of January (Mission #31). Post-mission reconnaissance indicated the Japanese placed particular emphasis on reopening the Johore Strait and mine sweepers cleared sufficient channels to reopen the waterway ten to fourteen days after the January mining. The purpose of Mission #40 was to re-sow mines into the strait and continue to hamper Japanese shipping in support of Allied military operations in that area of Asia. The Pakehan River served as a transportation artery for supplies heading to Burma. Large vessels transloaded their cargo to smaller ones at the mouth of the river for continued movement up the waterway. The Japanese utilized Mergui Harbor to offload supplies for overland transportation to their forces in Burma. Earlier mining by Allied forces restricted the port area to small vessels and further mining would continue to hamper full Japanese utilization of the facility.[51]

Each 444th BG bomber carried six M-26 mines, many with delayed action fuses that would arm themselves over varying lengths of time and possibly lull the Japanese into a false sense of security about particular areas of the strait. Ten planes mined the primary target, with one aircraft laying only one mine due to rack problems. The latter bomber's remaining mines were later jettisoned at sea. One B-29 (#273 *Old-Bitch-U-Airy-Bess*) mined Penang Harbor and the twelfth bomber (#277 *Shanghai Lil*) jettisoned its load and returned early due to mechanical problems. The force did not encounter any Japanese anti-aircraft fire or fighters during the mission and all of the B-29s returned safely.[52]

#538 *Beter 'N' Nutin* after its name change from *Monsoon Goon*. (*Harper via 444th BG*)

Chapter 11

March 1945: The Final Missions of the XX Bomber Command within the India-Burma and China Theaters

The [Soviet] Tu-4 was outwardly identical to a B-29 down to the apparently faithful copies of Wright Cyclone engines. These bootlegged Cyclones were in fact, so faithful to the originals that the Soviets had many of the same technical problems that the USAAF faced with the originals early in the B-29 program.

—Gen. Curtis LeMay (former Commander XX Bomber Command)

Fighting ended in Manila, the capital of the Philippines, on the first day of March 1945, but American soldiers maintained their push against Japanese defenders in other areas of Luzon. The XXI Bomber Command (BC) launched the fire bombing of Tokyo on March 9. The first raid destroyed 16½ acres of central Tokyo and killed approximately 100,000 people. The fire raids would continue against Tokyo before shifting to Nagoya, Osaka, and Kobe. United States Marines seized small islands adjacent to Okinawa in late March in preparation for the assault on the latter at the opening of April. On March 26, the last surviving organized Japanese soldiers launched a final suicide charge against the United States Marines on Iwo Jima. In Burma, Allied forces pressed toward Rangoon from the north and west.

The XX BC completed its last month of combat operations from bases in India during March, as elements of the four assigned B-29 groups began transferring to the Marianas for assignment to the XXI BC and their former commander Gen. Curtis LeMay. The XX BC flew ten missions: two of these staged through airfields in China to lay mines in that country's rivers. The XX BC launched missions against Japanese petroleum, shipping, their railroad network, and military supply storage assets in its last month of operations. It is interesting that four of the missions involved aerial mining of Japanese harbors and naval choke points, while three of the remaining seven missions targeted petroleum storage facilities. Thus, all of the March 1945 missions except three targeted Japanese petroleum storage facilities or laid naval mines. The XX BC began its operational history eight months earlier targeting the Japanese steel industry.

Mission #41: Singapore, March 2, 1945

The operations to the Singapore area continued with Mission #41 on March 2, 1945. (Mission numbers do not follow the same order as the chronological dates of the operations until March 17, 1945. This began with Mission #40 flown on February 27–28, 1945, and ends at Mission #42, flown on March 12, 1945.) The warehouses and shops of the Singapore Naval Base were the primary visual target, with the Bukum Island petroleum tank farm as the primary radar target. Pre-mission orders identified the Malayan Collieries as the secondary target and an area of storage huts in Khao Huagang, Thailand, as the target of last resort. Sixty-four B-29s launched for the attack on Singapore (12 from the 40th BG; 20 flying with the 444th BG; 12 from the 462nd BG; and the 468th BG contributed 20).[1]

A near-miss Japanese flak explosion struck the bombs falling from the 40th BG's #846 *Monsoon II* over the

The 468th BG's #678 *Kickapoo Lou* being armed prior to a mission. Japanese flak downed #678 *Kickapoo Lou* during Mission #41 to Singapore. The crew lowered its nose wheel and ten parachutes were observed leaving from the nose wheel door and rear hatch. (*Schutte via 468th BG*)

naval base. The burst forced the bombs to "tumble about" as they fell, but none were seen to detonate prematurely. One B-29 bombed the primary radar target on Bukum Island due to a build-up of ice over its Plexiglass nose that prevented the bombardier from making a visual sighting of the naval base. Ice proved to be a problem for many of the crews and four lead bombers relinquished their positions to other planes due to icing that blocked visual aim of the bombardiers. Three bombers dropped their ordnance on the secondary target and one bombed the target of last resort. Eight planes jettisoned their loads and returned due to various mechanical problems. One of these bombers (#469 *Wham Bam* of the 468th BG) made a bomb run over the primary target, but flak damaged the bomb release mechanism. The pilot diverted after passing over the target and the crew individually toggled each bomb over Khao Huagang. Two B-29s returned with their bomb loads after encountering mechanical issues.[2]

Crews described the Japanese flak as meager but mostly accurate. Thirty-five bombers (59% of the force) received some type of flak damage, including two that crashed as a result of anti-aircraft fire. Several smokeless bright bursts without fragments exploded among the bomber formations. The flight engineer on the 462nd BG's #801 *Phony Express* witnessed one of these bursts near the bomber's engine #4. He noted it appeared so bright he thought the engine was flaming. Much of the accurate flak was credited to Japanese naval vessels firing on the bombers, rather than land-based anti-aircraft guns.[3] One of the bombers downed by flak was #678 *Kickapoo Lou*, piloted by Capt. Millar of the 468th BG:

> Just before releasing bombs A/C #678 was hit by a burst of flak and forced to feather its number 4 engine. The formation split up just after bombs away and A/C #424 (468th) dropped back and escorted #678 for approximately 20 minutes. At about 0322Z A/C #424 left #678 to escort another aircraft in distress [#469 flying in the same formation as #568 and #424]. At about 0331Z, 3 B-29s observed another B-29, presumed to be #678, in a shallow dive with its right wing on fire outboard of #4 engine. The aircraft lowered its nose wheel and 10 parachutes were observed leaving from the nose wheel door and rear hatch. Shortly afterward the right wing came off, the aircraft then disappeared into a low cloud about two miles off the western shore of the Malay peninsula. The crew members of one B-29 definitely saw the crippled B-29 crash in the water at about 0333Z at a position estimated to be 6 miles northwest of Cape Segenting. The crew of one other aircraft which did not see the B-29 after the crew bailed out estimated the crash to be about 9 miles southeast of Cape Segenting. All witnesses agreed the aircraft crashed in the Straits of Malacca about 2 miles from the Malayan coast. None of the witnesses were close enough to the crash to identify the aircraft as #678 but since all other aircraft are accounted for, it is assumed that it was the one crashing.[4]

The 468th BG also lost #469 *Wham Bam*, piloted by Lt. Ellestad, to flak over the primary target:

> A/C #469 was hit by heavy anti-aircraft over the primary target ½ minute before releasing bombs. Fragments of anti-aircraft shells hit number one engine which could not be feathered, damaged the bomb release mechanism making it impossible to salvo bombs, knocked out the pressurization system, tore away number 2 and 3 engine throttle linkage, punctured a hole 1½ feet in diameter in the horizontal stabilizer, punctured the bomb bay tanks, and knocked out the upper front turret, radio compass, drift meter, and engineer's carburetor heat gauges and cylinder temperature gauges as well as the pilot's manifold pressure indicators. After being hit, #469 began to lose 1,500 feet of altitude per minute and airspeed dropped to 170 miles per hour. The crew began to jettison equipment to lighten the aircraft and the bombs were

The 40th BG's #555 *Dark Eyes* returned from Mission #41 with major flak damage to nacelles #1, #2, and #3, as well as the #4 wing tank. Numerous holes perforated the pressurized compartments. (*Changnon via 40th BG*)

Japanese flak punctured the left wing, both horizontal stabilizers, and nacelle #2 of the 40th BG's #233 *Superstitious Aloysious* during Mission #41 to Singapore. (*40th BG*)

#846 *Monsoon II* returned from Mission #41 with flak damage to the right wing tip and the left horizontal stabilizer. (*40th BG*)

> toggled out with a screwdriver. Bomb bay tanks were salvoed but one tank hit the retracting screw on one of the doors making it impossible to close doors and eliminate the possibility of ditching the aircraft. When the aircraft was stripped it was down to 2,000 feet altitude and 150 miles per hour indicated airspeed. The pilot decided to make for Auriel Island and abandon the aircraft there. Auriel Island was reached at 0800Z and the crew bailed out. Crew members landed in the water and were unable to reach the island in spite of life rafts which were dropped by a British Air/Sea Rescue Liberator which was over Auriel Island within 20 minutes after the bail out. All but one [Sgt. Dean Clark, who perished] of the crew members were picked up the following day by a Catalina. The prompt and successful rescue of this crew was accomplished by means of the excellent cooperation of the pilot and Air/Sea Rescue units. As soon as the pilot had ascertained the correct condition of his aircraft and was sure he would not be able to reach a friendly field, he decided on a definite plan of action, notified ground stations and A.S.R. Agencies, and then followed his original plan to the letter enabling rescue units to establish a rendezvous within a few minutes after the aircraft was abandoned.[5]

The seven bombers with major flak damage were the 40th BG's #555 *Dark Eyes* (nacelles #1, #2, and #3, a tank, and forward and rear pressurized compartments), #233 *Superstitious Aloysious* (left wing, right and left horizontal stabilizer, #2 nacelle, and nose wheel door), #718 *Black Magic II* (structural damage to the wings and fuselage and damage to engines #1, #2, and #3); the 444th BG's #732 *Hore-Zontal Dream* (both wings, fuselage, and a fuel cell), and #891 *Monsoon Goon II* (bracing on engine #4, collector ring and pipe torn off); and the 468th BG's #445 *The Craig Comet* (both wings, fuselage, and fuel cell) and #534 *Pioneer III* (wing and fuel cell). Although classified as receiving "minor damage" from flak, the story of #691 *Fast Company* of the 468th BG is worth repeating in brevity. Lt. Clark piloted #691, which sustained flak damage to its electric wires, hydraulic lines, nacelle #2, and landing wheels. Clark made what has been noted

The 468th BG's #691 *Fast Company* following its crash-landing after Mission #41 to Singapore. Lt. Clark piloted #691 *Fast Company*, which sustained flak damage to its electric wires, hydraulic lines, nacelle #2, and landing wheels. (*Schutte via 468th BG*)

A second view of the 468th BG's #691 *Fast Company* after its crash-landing. (*Schutte via 468th BG*)

Looking toward the nose of #691 *Fast Company*. (*Schutte via 468th BG*)

A side view of #691 *Fast Company*. (*Schutte via 468th BG*)

The 40th BG's #795. Japanese flak struck the left wing and fuel cell of #795 over Singapore during Mission #41. (*O'Keefe via 40th BG*)

as an "excellent landing" without the aid of flaps or brakes and with only the nose wheel and one main landing gear extended. Clark's crew included his wounded navigator, Lt. B. Ardman.[6]

The post-mission report described fighter opposition as weak and only one bomber returned with damage attributed to a Japanese pilot. Nearly half of the eighteen fighters engaging the bombers were formidable Nakajima Ki-43 Oscars. Crews described the Japanese aviators as not very aggressive and only 26% of the fifty-six individual and coordinated attacks were pressed within 250 yards of the bombers. Japanese pilots continued to employ both phosphorous and fragmentation aerial bombs, with some aircraft dropping three at one time. One B-29 flew through several phosphorous streamers without harm. The Japanese pilot who damaged a B-29 (#496 *Naughty Nancy* of the 444th BG) during the mission displayed considerable skill. The B-29 crew first spotted him at 2 o'clock high, about two miles from the bomber. As the fighter neared the B-29, the Japanese pilot waggled his wings and moved to attack from 12 o'clock. As the fighter approached to within 1,000 yards, the pilot flipped the aircraft onto its back and made a vertical pursuit curve, opening fire on the B-29 at 500 yards. A 20 mm cannon shell passed through the root of the left wing. The Japanese pilot continued his dive and passed within twenty-five yards of the bomber's tail. The Superfortress crew noted the Japanese pilot almost succeeded in raking the B-29 from nose to tail with 20 mm fire. B-29 gunners claimed one fighter "probably destroyed" and four damaged.[7]

Several warehouses and storage buildings received direct hits. Previous bombings damaged 21.6% of the buildings at the naval base and the March 2 operation left an additional 11.6% of the facility with major or minor damage.

Mission #39: Shanghai, March 4–5, 1945

The 468th BG flew Mission #39 to mine the Yangtze River Harbor area in Shanghai, China, during the night of March 4–5, 1945. Three primary target fields lay in the main channels of the Yangtze in Shanghai and planners identified the secondary target field as a stretch of the river between Hsin-Ti and Yo-Yang Ling. The Japanese utilized Shanghai as a major port facility for military supplies bound for their forces in China and transloaded the material to smaller vessels in the city for transport up the Yangtze River. Mining the river could impede Japanese supplies bound for their front line troops fighting Chinese soldiers. Twelve 468th BG B-29s flew to China for staging prior to the operation. Planners assigned six bombers to mine the first Yangtze primary target field and three planes to each of the other two fields. Five B-29s mined the first field, with the sixth assigned bomber (#530 *Totin-To-Tokyo II*) laying its ordnance in the secondary field area due to carburetor trouble in an engine. The eleven bombers dropped 132 mines in the primary target areas, while the twelfth B-29 placed twelve mines in the secondary stretch of the Yangtze River. Approximately one-third of the mines were set to arm immediately, while the other two-thirds contained delayed arming devices ranging from fifteen to thirty-five days. If not found and retrieved from the murky waters, the mines would continue to be hazards for over a month, as seemingly mine-free areas would become silent obstacles as mines armed.[8]

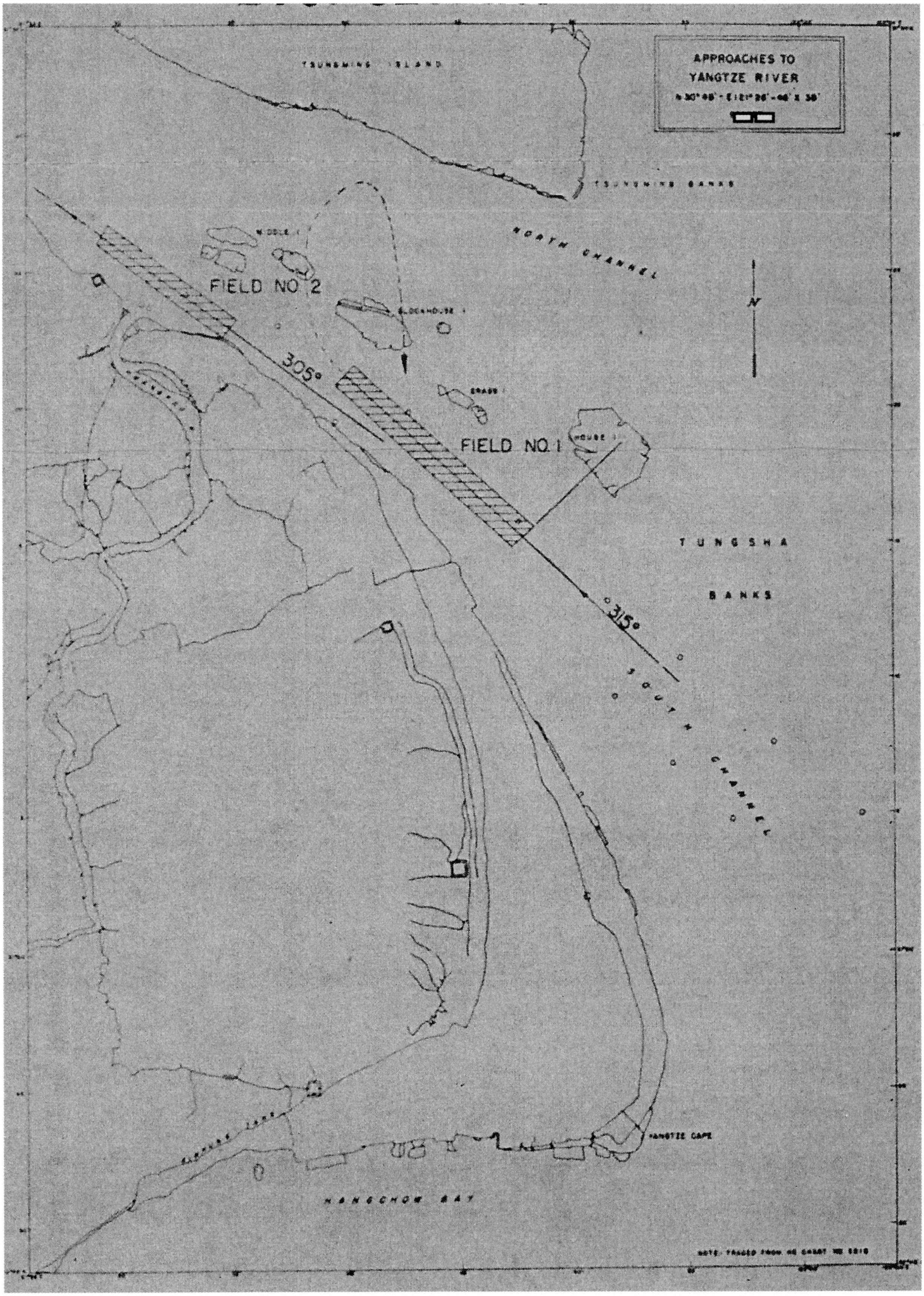

Chart showing the locations for XX BC B-29s to lay mines in the Yangtze River during Mission #39. (*US Air Force*)

The 468th BG's #542 *Lady Hamilton II*. During Mission #43 to Kuala Lumpur, two planes (#542 *Lady Hamilton II* and #272 *Miss Shorty*) reported their visual bomb run obstructed by 10/10 cloud cover. Without alternate radar instructions, the crews diverted and bombed a small vessel at Port Sweetenham Harbor. (*Schutte via 468th BG*)

Only one bomber encountered anti-aircraft fire during the mission. Japanese forces engaged B-29 #663 *Dragon Lady* with meager but accurate 40 mm and machine gun fire as the bomber made its second low pass to lay mines; the plane returned with a small hole in the fuselage. Japanese fighters did not challenge the bombers. Intelligence debriefings after the mission indicated the mines were laid successfully in the primary and secondary fields.[9]

Mission #43: Kuala Lumpur, March 10, 1945

Five days later, the 468th BG flew Mission #43 to the railroad marshalling yards in Kuala Lumpur, Malaya. The field order identified Alor Star airfield as the secondary target and a "hutted area" near Victoria Point in Thailand as the target of last resort. The primary target lay south of Kuala Lumpur and served as an important collection point for coal, tin, and rubber bound for Japanese industry, as well as military supplies and troops traveling to Burma. The yards also performed minor repairs to locomotives. Bombing this target could destroy considerable military supplies and industrial raw materials, as well as obstruct the movement of trains through the area. The secondary target was a small airfield with limited importance, but any strike on the facility could destroy aircraft and equipment. Intelligence identified the target of last resort as a supply storage facility for material awaiting transloading between small vessels and rail cars. Original plans called for the 468th BG to fly this mission on the same day that other XX BC B-29s attacked oil storage facilities in

During Mission #43 to Kuala Lumpur, the crew of #272 *Miss Shorty* of the 468th BG diverted and bombed a small vessel at Port Sweetenham Harbor as a target of opportunity. (*Schutte via 468th BG*)

Singapore (Mission #42). When weather delayed the Singapore operation, the command opted to continue with the Kuala Lumpur mission rather than scrub or move its launch date.[10]

Twenty-nine of the planned thirty bombers took off carrying 500-pound general purpose bombs. Twenty-four of the aloft B-29s bombed the primary target in formations ranging from two to four aircraft, with a single plane making the last pass over the marshalling yards. One of these bombers (#703 *American Beauty*) experienced a rack malfunction and only dropped six bombs on the target. The crew cleared the problem and dropped the remaining ten bombs on the secondary target. Bomber #227 *Lady Be Good* dropped its entire load of sixteen bombs on the last resort target due to an engine problem. Two planes (#542 *Lady Hamilton II* and #272 *Miss Shorty*) reported their visual bomb run obstructed by 10/10 cloud cover. Without alternate radar instructions, the crews diverted and bombed a small vessel at Port Sweetenham Harbor as a target of opportunity. Two aircraft (#279 *My Buddy* and #424 *Hap's Characters*) returned early due to mechanical issues with engines.[11]

Japanese anti-aircraft guns did not engage the bombers over the primary target area, but did with meager and inaccurate fire from two other points along the flying route. Japanese fighters intercepted seventeen of the B-29s over the primary target area without causing any damage to the bombers. As in the previous mission to Kuala

The 468th BG's #534 *Pioneer III* undergoing an engine change. #534 *Pioneer III* flew in the seventh formation over the target during Mission #43 to Kuala Lumpur. (*Schutte via 468th BG*)

Japanese fighters engaged #542 *Lady Hamilton II* the 468th BG during Mission #43 to Kuala Lumpur. A gunner on board the B-29 shot away the plane's own antenna mast during the fighting. (*Schutte via 468th BG*)

Lumpur, most of the fighter attacks originated above and in front of the bombers. Many Japanese pilots flew obsolete aircraft or those not specifically designed for fighter operations. The B-29 crews spotted at least ten Aichi D3A Val carrier-based bombers. Vals were designed as dive bombers rather than fighters and were utilized by the Japanese in the raid against Pearl Harbor in 1941. B-29 crews reported the fighter pilots as not applying aggressive tactics and breaking contact beyond 500 yards. Many ended their attack immediately upon coming under fire from the B-29s. One Japanese pilot seemed more aggressive than his comrades and pressed an attack, passing within an estimated 100 feet of a bomber. The Japanese utilized aerial bombs in many of their attacks, probably as a result of engaging the B-29s with Vals. The post-mission report noted:

> Aerial bombs were encountered in 9 attacks, none however, resulting in damage to B-29s. Most of the bombs were "dropped" from high above formations, rather than "flipped" from close quarters, and some fighters dropped as many as 2 and 3. The "stovepipe" type aerial bomb which, in some slightly different forms, B-29s have seen from time to time, was much in evidence. One such bomb was described as about 8 feet long, and 2 inches by 6 inches in cross-section. Sometimes 2 of these appeared tied together and seemed to revolve around each other. Fragments of all types spilled out of the ends; square silver colored objects, small particles looking like scrap metal; and, in one instance, what appeared to be a chain.[12]

Gunners claimed the destruction of one Val and damage to four other Vals. B-29 #703 *American Beauty* made three passes over the marshalling yards while attempting to clear its bomb rack problems. During these runs, numerous fighters attacked the bomber, and gunners aboard the B-29 expended all of their ammunition in the upper turrets defending the plane. The 468th BG fired 8,230 rounds battling fighters over Kuala Lumpur. B-29 #542 *Lady Hamilton II* shot away its own antenna mast during the fighting, but otherwise did not sustain any damage. The gun systems were designed not to fire when the barrels were pointed at any section of the bomber, but it was evidently possible to hit the antenna, which was not necessarily in the direct line of sight of the fuselage or wings.[13]

Although of poor quality, post-strike photos indicated several buildings in the yards received substantial damage, including the engine roundhouse, passenger car servicing shed, a supply storage warehouse, various workshops, and storage sheds. Six locomotives and eighty-three pieces of rolling stock, along with 3.1 miles of track were destroyed or damaged in the raid.

Mission #42: Singapore, March 12, 1945

The weather over Singapore cleared and XX BC moved the postponed Singapore operation from March 10 to 21, 1945, and labeled Mission #42. Planners called for three groups to fly the mission, each bombing a different primary target: 15 B-29s of the 40th BG targeted the oil storage facility on Samboa Island; 30 bombers from the 444th BG received the oil storage facility on Bukum Island; and 15 462nd BG planes aimed for the oil storage center on Sebarok Island. The Malayan Collieries at Batu Arang were the secondary target, while the XX BC identified a supply transload point at Khao Huagang, Thailand, as the target of last resort. As the Allies squeezed the noose around the Japanese home islands and their sea routes, oil became an increasingly scarce commodity. The oil storage facilities on the three primary target islands could hold a total capacity of 2,800,000 gallons delivered by small vessels from the Palembang oil refineries on Sumatra (struck by the XX BC on August 10–11, 1944) due to shallow water in the area. The oil remained in the storage tanks while awaiting larger tankers bound for Japan. A successful bombing attack could not only destroy the oil, but also the storage tanks and support buildings, helping to decrease the flow of oil to Japan. The Malayan Collieries served as the only source of coal for the Malayan Peninsula and primarily supported the railroad industry and production of electricity. Disruption of the coal production at this site could impact the ability to operate trains carrying military supplies between Singapore and Bangkok. Khao Huagang, the last resort target, lay at the western terminus of the Kra Trans-Isthmus Railroad connecting the Bangkok-Singapore Railroad with shipping facilities on the Pakchan River.[14]

Of the sixty B-29s designated for the raid, only forty-nine made it into the air (12 of the 40th BG, 22 of the 444th BG, and all assigned from the 462nd BG) due to an accident. The 444th BG's #411 *Duchess* developed an engine failure during take off and came to a stop 600 feet from the end of the runway. All of the crew members exited safely, but the disabled bomber blocked the launching of the other aircraft, leaving the raid eleven bombers short of the planned total. Forty-four bombers dumped their

Mission #43's railroad marshalling yard at Kuala Lumpur (now Malaysia). Due to poor post-mission photographs, XX BC added black dots to a pre-mission photograph to show where bombs landed. The rail engine "round house" (with at least eighteen bomb hit markers) is clearly visible in the center. (*US Air Force*)

general purpose and incendiary ordnance on the primary targets after the long flight from India. Three 462nd B-29s (#459, #336 *Assid Test II*, and #503 *Sky Scraper*), along with #738 *Honeywell Honey* of the 40th BG, jettisoned their bombs and returned to India due to mechanical problems. One 444th bomber (#538 *Beter 'N' Nutin*) struck the secondary target due to excessive oil consumption in two engines.[15]

The 40th BG did not encounter any anti-aircraft fire over Samboa Island, and the other groups reported meager and inaccurate flak over Sebarok and Bukum Islands. The Japanese flak proved short in duration and the crews that experienced it noted a time lapse of approximately thirty seconds from the first to the last burst against their formations. Japanese pilots flew more up-to-date models of fighters in the vicinity of Singapore compared to the pilots flying against the 468th BG two days earlier at Kuala Lumpur. Although the Japanese pilots flew Oscars, the bomber crews described them as not aggressive in their attacks and the overall enemy aircraft opposition as much weaker than anticipated. As over Kuala Lumpur and other previous targets, the Japanese fighters tended to attack from above and in front of the B-29s. Despite the lack of aggressive tactics, some of the fighter pilots flew within 250 yards of the bombers before turning and two fighters passed within 100 yards. More of the attacks included Japanese pilots actually firing on the bombers compared to engagements with fighters in other areas.[16] In one action, ten Oscars attacked a formation of four B-29s:

> The formation was on its bomb run when the Oscars were observed about three miles ahead, forming what proved to be a slightly staggered line abreast formation. The attack developed immediately after the Oscars were in position. They approached together from 10 to 1130 o'clock, about 10 degrees high, and each Oscar opened fire at 1,000 yards. As they neared the formation, elements of two and three planes seemed to have singled out individual B-29s in a predetermined order. The attack was not closely pressed, however, the Oscars breaking away on all sides of the formation without coming closer than 200 yards. No hits were scored on any B-29 in the formation. The same attack was repeated with seven Oscars about seven minutes later after bombs away and the formation was on the route home. The Oscars formed behind cloud cover and attacked from the same direction and angle. Again, no hits were scored, and breakaways were at about the same distance.[17]

The 40th BG's #752 *Wichita Witch* flew in the fourth formation over the target during Mission #42 to Singapore. (*40th BG*)

The crew of #738 *Honeywell Honey* of the 40th BG jettisoned their bombs and returned to India due to mechanical problems en route to Singapore on Mission #42. (*40th BG*)

The 462nd BG claimed damage to one Oscar as the Japanese pilot attacked a formation of four B-29s over Sebarok Island. When the fighter swept toward the formation from 11 o'clock high, gunners in all four bombers commenced firing from their upper turrets at 1,000 yards. The Oscar broke off the attack at 400 yards and gunners believed they hit the plane in the process. Fighters did inflict minor damage on two B-29s: the 462nd BG's #711 returned with a small hole in the navigator's station and #336 *Assid Test II* flew home with holes in the cowling of its #1 engine, forcing the pilot to feather the propeller. Gunners of the forty-four B-29s that dropped ordnance on Mission #43 expended 3,710 rounds of ammunition; in comparison, this is slightly less than one-third of the total rounds utilized by gunners aboard half of that number of bombers to defend their aircraft over Kuala Lumpur two days earlier.[18]

During Mission #44 to Rangoon the 444th BG's #202 *Satan's Angel* dropped its ordnance on the Japanese warehouses at Bassein, Burma, after losing an astrodome blister. (*Smith via 444th BG*)

The 444th BG's #537 *Male Call* flew in the sixth formation over the target during Mission #44 to Rangoon. (*Archer via 444th BG*)

The 40th BG's #620 *Sleepy Time Gal* flew in the fifth formation over the target during Mission #45 to Rangoon. (Barg via 40th BG)

Cloud cover prevented post-strike photos of Samboa and Sebarok Islands, while poor quality photos of Bukum Island showed little damage after the raid. Although damage could be seen among the piers and workshops, all of the oil storage tanks remained intact.

Mission #44: Rangoon, March 17, 1945

All four groups targeted Dump Area "B" in Rangoon, Burma, on March 17, 1945. The field order named Dump "B" as the only target for Mission #44. Successful attacks on Japanese shipping and the rail network from Thailand had reduced the amount of supplies reaching Rangoon for onward movement to their hard-pressed forces. Destroying the existing stockpiles of supplies in Rangoon could greatly diminish the fighting ability of Japanese forces and support Allied operations. This was especially true for Dump "B," which held gasoline and ammunition supplies.[19]

Seventy-seven of the planned seventy-eight B-29s launched from India (40th BG: 15 planes; 444th BG: 23 planes; 462nd BG: 15 planes; and the 468th BG: 24 planes). Seventy of the B-29s visually bombed Dump "B" with incendiary and fragmentation ordnance, while two dropped their bombs on targets of opportunity and five returned after jettisoning their load due to mechanical problems. Targets of opportunity included Sagyi Airfield, Burma, and warehouses in Bassein, Burma. Aircraft #424 *Hap's Characters* of the 468th BG bombed the former after suffering a broken oil line and B-29 #202 *Satan's Angel* of the 444th BG dropped its ordnance on the latter after losing an astrodome blister.[20]

The bombing altitude at the primary ranged from 27,000 to 30,000 feet—well above the effective range of most local anti-aircraft guns. Crews reported meager and inaccurate fire from the long-range guns, with two B-29s receiving minor damage (#801 *Phony Express* and #329 *Ding Hao* of the 462nd BG). Japanese aircraft did not challenge the bombers this day. Post-mission photographs and intelligence analysis highlighted the results of a successful mission:

> The main weight of the attack was well concentrated in the central and northern area of the target resulting in the destruction of the majority of the storage units. At least 173 miscellaneous hutments were destroyed and many were undoubtedly damaged. Interpretation

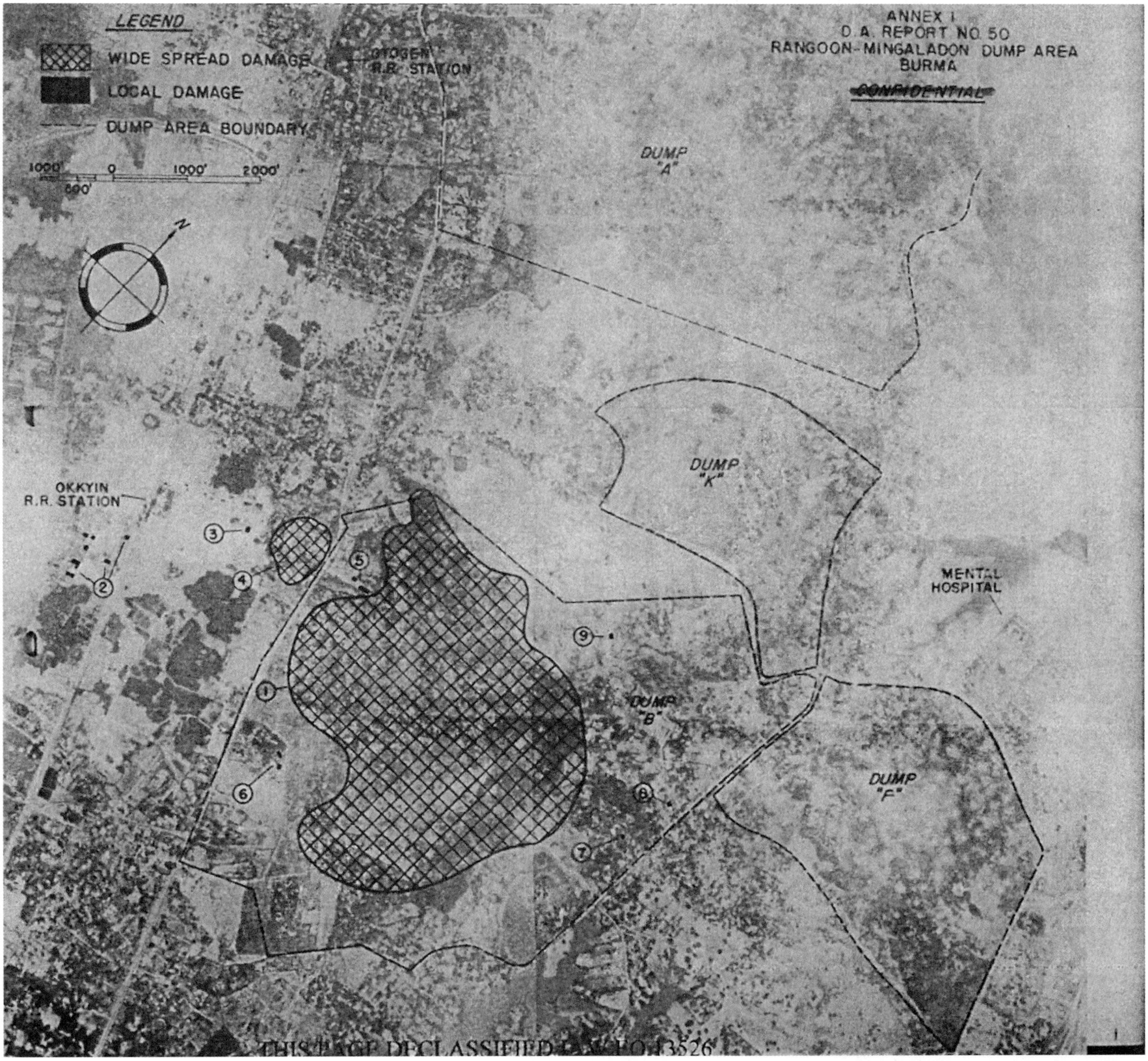

XX BC produced this illustration to show the extent of the damage caused to Japanese Supply Dump "B" (located north of Rangoon, Burma) during Mission #44. (*US Air Force*)

was rendered difficult by the small scale of the photographs, the dense foliage obscuring many of the buildings, and the type of bombs used. Since the majority of the fragmentation bombs fell in the target area, it is reasonable to assume damage to many buildings even though the damage is not readily apparent on the photographs.[21]

The 40th BG's #914 flew with the fifth formation over Rangoon during Mission #45. (*Hougdahl via 40th BG*)

#498 *Lazy Baby* of the 40th BG—also known as *"B" Sweet III*—flew as the lead bomber in the fifth formation over the target during Mission #45 to Rangoon. (*Francklang via 40th BG*)

The 40th BG's #915 *Miss Donna Lee* flew with the second formation during Mission #45.

Mission #45: Rangoon, March 22, 1945

The XX BC returned to Rangoon five days later and again targeted Japanese supply dumps. Plans called for 24 B-29s from the 40th BG, 24 from the 468th BG, 15 from the 444th BG, and 15 from the 462nd BG to simultaneously strike ammunition storage at Rangoon Dump Areas "C" and "E" and the Mingaladon Cantonment area (thirty-nine bombers designated to hit each target). The Mingaladon Cantonment area consisted of quarters and supply storage for Japanese forces manning the Mingaladon airfield. A lack of suitable Japanese facilities along the route from India resulted in a declination to designate any secondary targets for the mission.[22]

All seventy-eight aircraft departed India and headed for Rangoon. Thirty-eight bombers targeted the dumps. Two B-29s deviated from the briefed path for unknown reasons, became disoriented, and returned to India, resulting in only thirty-seven B-29s targeting the Mingaladon Cantonment area. The bombers dropped 244.2 tons of bombs on Dumps "C" and "E" and 272.8 tons on the Cantonment area. All of the B-29s returned safely and post-strike photographs indicated numerous buildings, including barracks, were damaged or destroyed in both target areas.

The 40th BG's #580 taken after March 1945, when the 40th BG flew from the Pacific under the XXI BC. During Mission #45 with the XX BC, #580 bombed Rangoon while flying with the second formation. (*40th BG*)

The 40th BG's #668 *The Outlaw* flew in the second formation during Mission #45 to Rangoon. (*Vacovsky via 40th BG*)

Japanese anti-aircraft fire proved to be fairly inaccurate, although thick in some areas and probably directed by a fighter lingering near the formation's altitude. None of the bombers sustained flak damage during the mission and only one aircraft experienced rocking from a near miss. At least three Japanese fighters flew within sight of the B-29s, but only one, a Kawasaki Ki-45 Nick, made a passing attack on a bomber north of Rangoon. The Nick approached the B-29 between 6 and 7 o'clock at 20,000 feet. The gunners fired upon the fighter at approximately 1,000 yards but did not see any visible hits. The Nick pilot peeled away from the gunfire and did not return.[23]

Mission #46: Yangtze, March 28–29, 1945

The XX BC launched three separate mining missions during the night of March 28–29. The 468th BG laid mines in the Yangtze River Harbor area in Shanghai. Elements of the 468th BG also mined the waters around Saigon/Cam Rahn Bay and the 444th BG laid mines in Singapore.

Planners at XX BC viewed the 468th BG as the best group for the mission to Shanghai due to its experience during Mission #41 earlier in the month. Twelve aircraft, each carrying twelve mines, were selected for the night mission. Six planes targeted one area and six a second area to replenish mines laid during Mission #41. Of the twelve planes, two were not able to take off due to technical difficulties, leaving ten to fly the mission, laying their mines from between 2,000 and 2,100 feet.[24]

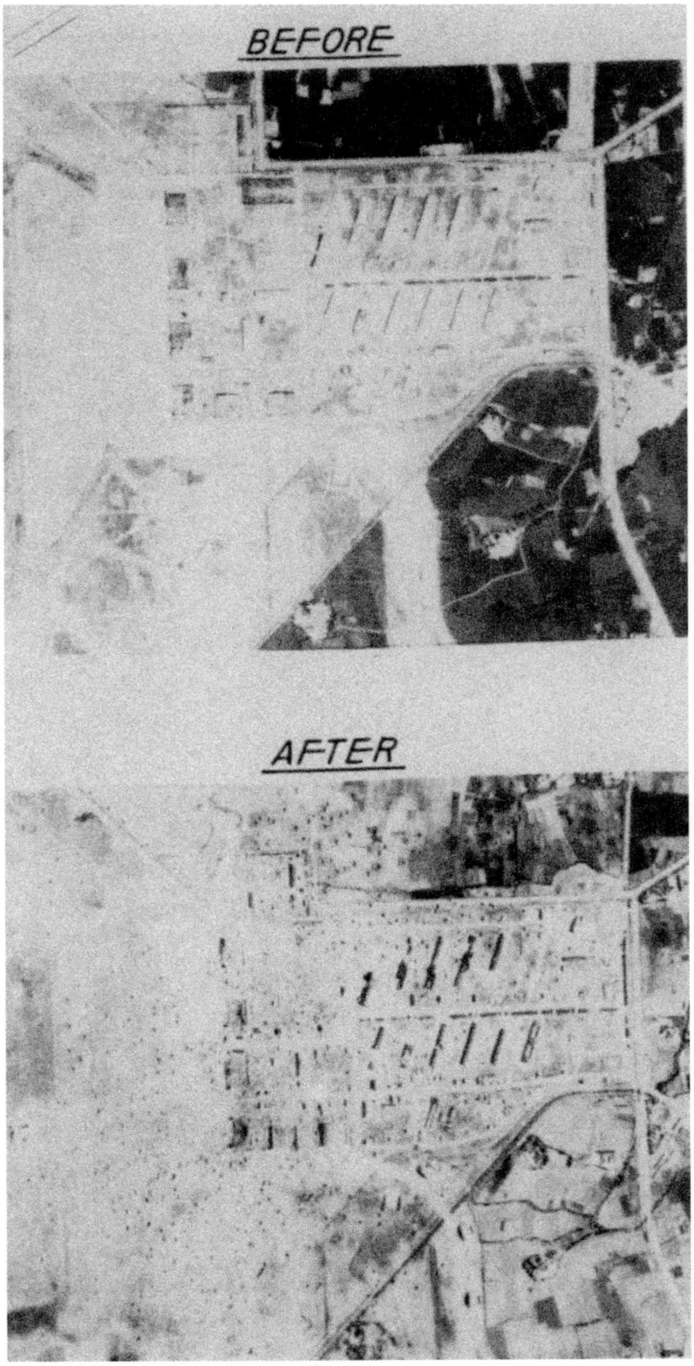

Pre- and post-strike photographs of the Japanese Rangoon supply facility hit by Mission #45. (*US Air Force*)

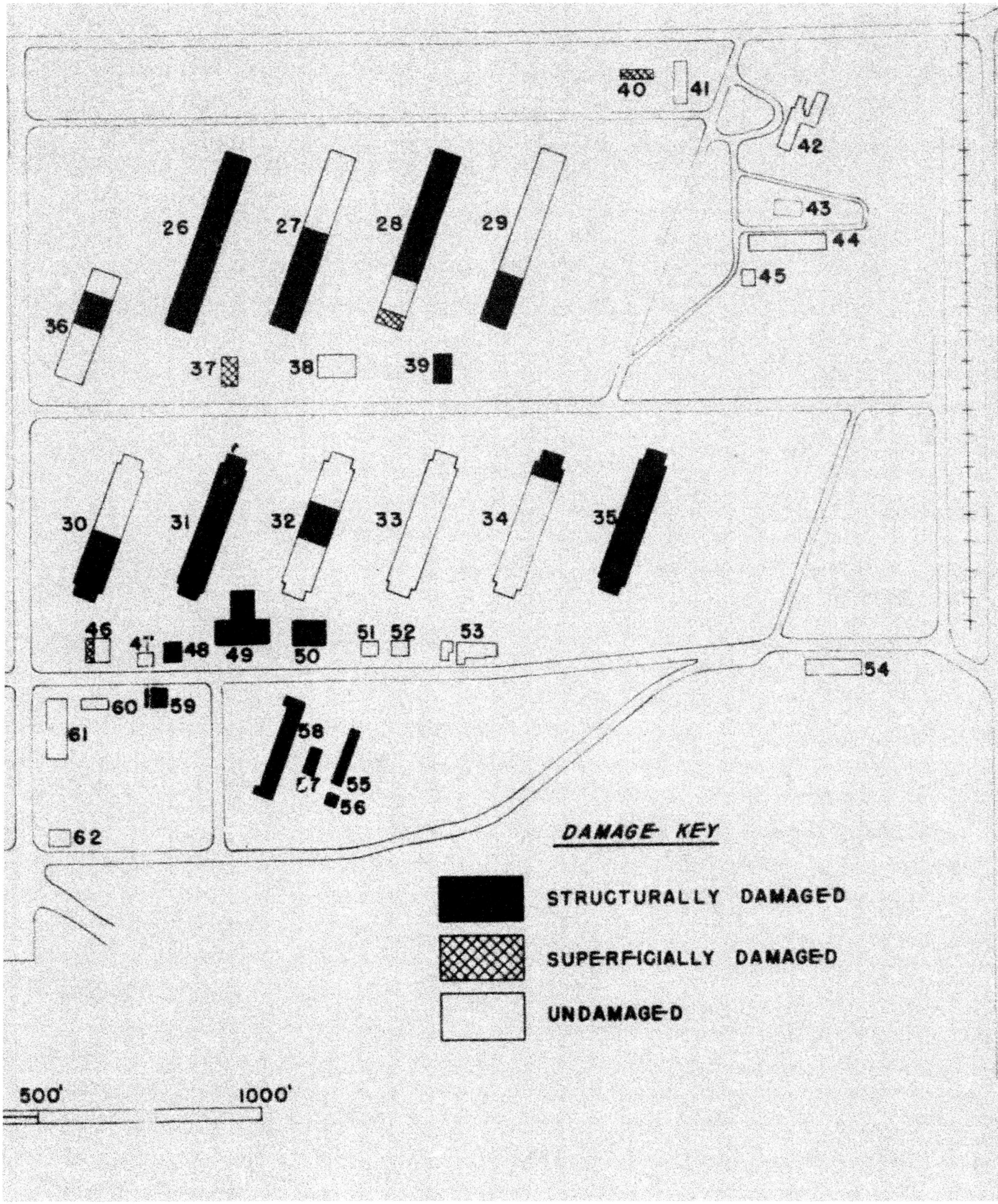

Post-raid visual aid illustrating the damage to the Japanese Rangoon supply facility caused by Mission #45 developed from the post-strike photograph. (*US Air Force*)

The first two B-29s caught the Japanese anti-aircraft gunners by surprise and dropped their mines and depart the target area before the latter could bring their weapons to action. The last eight bombers encountered moderate anti-aircraft fire from light and medium guns. All crews reported tracer fire passing within 150 feet of their aircraft and seeing some of the fire originating from a blacked-out river gunboat. The Japanese did hit one B-29 (#529 *City of Burlington*) in the left wing between the engine and the wing tip, forcing the crew to lay their mines in the area designated for the other group of bombers before making a quick exit. The plane returned safely and without any casualties. The raiding force spotted several Japanese aircraft but none attacked the bombers.[25]

Mission #47: Saigon, March 28–29, 1945

While the mine layers of Mission #46 struck the Shanghai area, the two other missions during the night of March 28–29 targeted French Indo-China (Vietnam) and Singapore. Mission #47 to French Indo-China sent B-29s from the 444th and 468th BG to lay mines in Saigon (Ho Chi Minh City) and Cam Ranh Bay. Secondary mining areas were located at Goh Si Chang harbor and two sections of the Mekong River. Allied offensives in the Philippines and other areas forced Japan to withdraw shipping assets from areas around Malaya and Borneo while increasing the movement of raw materials from these areas to coastal routes along French Indo-China. The purpose of Mission #47 centered on mining the harbor and water routes around Saigon and Cam Ranh Bay (north of Saigon) to impede this new shipping route and disrupt the flow of raw materials to Japan. The Mekong River—the secondary mining area—served as the main transportation route between Saigon and Phnom Penh. Many Japanese personnel and supplies bound for Burma traveled up the Mekong, transloading to Bangkok for onward movement to Rangoon. Goh Si Chang harbor or anchorage lay in the Gulf of Siam (Gulf of Thailand), where large ships could offload to vessels with less draft and move military cargo to shore.[26]

Although the XX BC mined the primary targets on January 25–26, the command believed the Japanese had sufficient time to sweep most of them and produce clear channels for vessels; Mission #47 would re-seed those mines. Saigon and Cam Ranh Bay were also now being utilized as refueling points and harbors of refuge for Japanese vessels avoiding Allied aircraft and submarines. Plans tapped the 468th BG (eighteen B-29s) for this mission: the aircraft would lay the mines from between 2,000 and 4,000 feet. Successful navigation to the area due to excellent radar checkpoints during Mission #30 in January persuaded planners to select the same routes for Mission #47.

Sixteen bombers laid mines in the primary target areas. B-29 #542 *Lady Hamilton II* mined the Mekong River near Phnom Penh following a navigation error, while #445 *The Craig Comet* mined an area just short of its designated target due to excessive consumption of fuel during the inbound flight. The bombers dropped a total of 116 mines in the Saigon and Cam Ranh Bay target areas and ten mines along the Mekong River. One mine detonated on impact with the water and the parachutes failed on approximately twelve more mines.[27]

Anti-aircraft fire in the Saigon and Cam Ranh Bay area proved to be light and crews reported seeing several flashes and tracers associated with the guns. None of the bombers were hit during the operation. The B-29s laying mines in the secondary target areas did not encounter any anti-aircraft fire. One unidentified Japanese fighter made a single attacking pass at a B-29 near the mouth of the Mekong River. The fighter commenced its run from 10 o'clock and pressed the attack until the B-29 opened fire at a range of 600 yards with a total of only fifteen rounds from the upper turret. At this point, the fighter pilot broke contact and disappeared toward 6 o'clock without firing and did not return. The fighter did not appear damaged when it turned away from the bomber and all B-29s safely returned to India.[28]

Mission #48: Singapore, March 28–29, 1945

The third component of the mine laying operation of March 28–29 targeted the waters near Singapore. The secondary targets for this mission flown by the 444th BG were Penang Harbor, Prachuab Songkhla, and Prachuab Kirkikhan. Although mined earlier, planners called for another mission to reseed mines that had been swept by Japanese forces. They selected the Johore Strait, Rhic Strait, and the Inner Middle Channel for mining. The secondary target, Prachuab Songkhla (Songkhla harbor), is on the western Gulf of Thailand and serviced small supply vessels that transloaded their equipment to rail lines. Prachuab Kirkikhan (Kirkikhan harbor) is located just north of Songkhla and provided a similar transload function for the Japanese military.[29]

Thirty-three B-29s targeted the three designated areas: 19 destined for the Johore Strait; nine for the Rhic Strait; and 5 for the Inner Middle Channel. Thirty-two bombers dropped 125 mines at the primary targets. One bomber dropped only one mine on its primary target due to a malfunction. The crew dislodged the remaining mines northeast of the primary target.

B-29 #548 *Maiden USA* suffered a runaway propeller inbound to the target and jettisoned its mines before returning to its base. The 444th BG encountered many light and medium anti-aircraft guns during their flights across the target area, reporting the results as inaccurate, although two B-29s sustained damage. A round ripped a hole in the right horizontal stabilizer of #538 *Beter 'N'Nutin* and #533 *Big Dick* returned with a hole in its right wing. A single-engine Japanese fighter intercepted one of the B-29s at 4,500 feet in the target area. The fighter opened fire at approximately 650 yards from 10 o'clock and tracers streaked past the bomber. The Japanese pilot then banked his aircraft and departed. The incident happened so quickly that the B-29 crew did not return fire. All crewmen returned from the mission without injuries.[30]

Mission #49: Singapore, March 29–30, 1945

Mission #49—the final XX BC operation in the China and Burma-India Theaters—struck Japanese petroleum facilities near Singapore during the night of March 29–30. The Bukum Island petroleum facility served as the primary target for the 40th (14 aircraft) and 462nd BG (15 aircraft), with a secondary target at Alor Star airfield in Malaya and a last resort target at the Khao Huagang railroad jetty in Thailand.[31]

Bukum Island, the primary target, supported forty-five usable oil tanks with a total storage capacity of 1,250,000 barrels. The tank farm normally held and exported petroleum products from the Palembang refineries on Sumatra in the Netherlands East Indies—the target of Mission #5 in August 1944. The Moesi River in Sumatra is too shallow for fully loaded tanker vessels to navigate from the refinery. These vessels departed Palembang with a partial load and then were filled to capacity at Bukum Island, or one of two other islands near Singapore, before sailing for their destinations. Smaller tankers and oil barges transported the petroleum from Palembang to Bukum Island for this process. With American forces cutting the flow of supplies from Southeast Asia to Japan, these petroleum products were destined for Japanese forces still operating to the west and south of the American advance from New Guinea to the Philippines. The destruction of the tanks and their oil would prevent the existing petroleum from aiding the Japanese war effort and reduce the flow of future petroleum supplies. The XX BC selected Alor Star airfield as the secondary target due to its location, rather than any specific strategic value. Damage to the base could include aircraft, hangars, and maintenance facilities. The last resort target lay at the western end of the Bangkok-Singapore rail line and provided access from the railroad to the Bay of Bengal. Military supplies waiting transportation on the rail line were stored in the target area.[32]

Twenty-four of the twenty-nine designated bombers hit the primary target. B-29 #488 of the 462nd BG encountered engine trouble and returned to India. The 462nd BG's #734 switched from radar to visual during the bomb run and then lost sight of the target. Due to a fuel transfer problem, the pilot opted to not return for a second run over the primary target and dropped his load on a target of opportunity (an oil installation on Samboe Island). The other bombers reported various mechanical failures that prevented them from dropping their bombs. The B-29 crews struck the target individually, rather than in formations, and one-third of the Superfortresses encountered meager and inaccurate anti-aircraft fire over both oil installations bombed that night. One single-engine fighter orbited near the primary target but did not engage any of the bombers.

The bombers dropped 260 tons of general purpose and incendiary bombs over the targets. Photographs taken by a reconnaissance B-29 the next day indicated the destruction of seven oil tanks, with three damaged and two possibly still ablaze. Additional damaged or destroyed structures included a warehouse, boiler house, and a loading pier. As the last bomber returned to India from Singapore, the bombing operations of the XX BC and 58th BW from and within the China and India-Burma Theaters ended.[33]

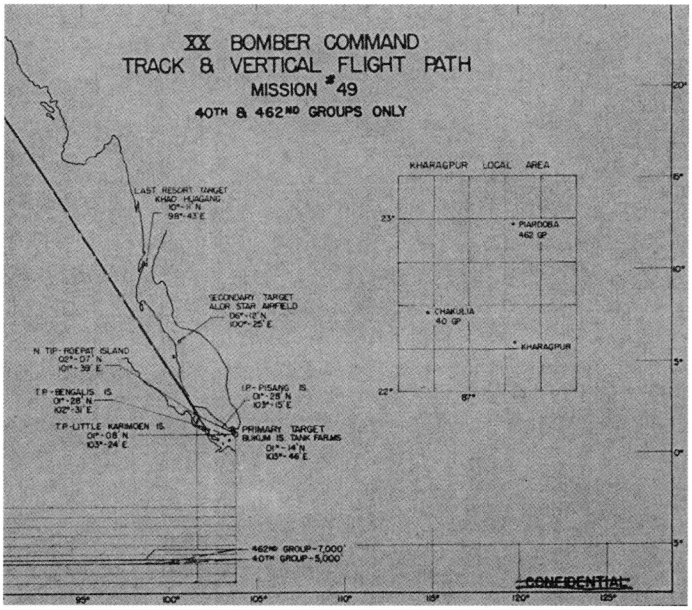

The XX BC map utilized to brief pilots and navigators on the routes to and from Singapore for Mission #49—the final XX BC mission from India and China. (*US Air Force*)

The post-raid damage assessment of the petroleum facilities on Bukum Island after Mission #49. (*US Air Force*)

Epilogue

The XX BC remained in India as a headquarters without operational bomber groups until June 17, 1945. At that point, XX BC transferred to Sakugawa, in Okinawa, on July 7, 1945, where it remained for a week before inactivating and transferring its personnel to the Eighth Air Force headquarters. The planning for the invasion of Japan included reorganizing XX BC and XXI BC and placing their personnel under separate air forces. The Twentieth Air Force—originally built around Gen. Hap Arnold to maintain the independence of XX BC from other military commanders—deployed to the Marianas Islands from Washington, DC, in July 1945. Gen. Curtis LeMay assumed temporary command of the Twentieth Air Force from Arnold on July 16, 1945, and held the position until the arrival of Gen. Nathan Twining on August 2, 1945. Twining served as the first commander of the Thirteenth Air Force, which formed in 1943 to organize the Army Air Force elements at Guadalcanal as the Allies prepared to advance northwest along the Solomon Islands chain. Gen. Twining then commanded the Fifteenth Air Force in the northern Mediterranean from January 1944 until May 1945, when Arnold dispatched him at the end of hostilities in Europe to lead the Twentieth Air Force B-29 campaign against Japan.

With the termination of B-29 operations from India and China and preparations underway for the invasion of Japan, the Twentieth Air Force absorbed XXI BC into its headquarters element and inactivated XX BC. At the same time, the Twentieth Air Force became a subordinate unit of the newly established United States Strategic Air Forces in the Pacific (USASTAF) under the command of Gen. Carl Spaatz, who served as commander of the Eighth Air Force in Europe beginning in May 1942 and commander of the United States Strategic Air Forces in Europe nineteen months later. Gen. LeMay served as Spaatz's chief of staff when XXI BC merged into USASTAF. The Eighth Air Force headquarters moved to Okinawa from Europe without personnel or aircraft. The B-17 and B-24 crews in Europe would transition to B-29s in preparation for the invasion of Japan. Plans also called for the Twentieth Air Force to conduct B-29 operations from the Marianas Islands and the Eighth Air Force—commanded by Gen. Jimmy Doolittle, who led the organization at the end of the conflict in Europe—to fly from Okinawa. The personnel assigned to XX BC transferred to Eighth Air Force headquarters on July 16, when their command inactivated. The utilization of atomic bombs on Hiroshima and Nagasaki ended the war before the Eighth Air Force, with its former XX BC staff, were combat ready.[34]

The 58th BW and its four groups transferred to Tinian, in the Marianas Islands, at the end of March 1945. The wing joined the XXI BC, then under the command of Gen. Curtis LeMay, and flew combat operations against Japan until the end of the war. The 58th BW remained on Tinian until November 15, 1945, after which the headquarters transferred to March Field in California. Gen. Roger Ramey, who assumed command of XX BC (as well as the 58th BW) upon the transfer of Gen. LeMay to XXI BC, moved to command only the 58th BW from April 24, 1945, until November 1, 1946. The four groups assigned to the 58th BW inactivated in 1946: the 40th BG on October 1, 1946; the 444th BG on March 31, 1946; the 462nd BG on March 31, 1946; and the 468th BG on March 31, 1946.

XX BC's three commanders (Wolfe, LeMay, and Ramey) remained in service after World War II. Gen. Kenneth Wolfe assumed command of the Fifth Air Force in October 1945 and then moved to senior procurement and materiel positions, including deputy chief of staff for materiel for the United States Air Force between 1948 and his retirement in 1951. Gen. Curtis LeMay progressed to command the United States Air Forces in Europe. During this assignment LeMay organized the Berlin Airlift of 1948–1949. He commanded the Strategic Air Command between 1948 and 1957, and is credited with building this organization into the nuclear armed bomber force for which it was known throughout the Cold War. In 1961, Gen. LeMay

40th BG prisoners of war released in May 1945. (*Brooks via 40th BG*)

The 40th BG's #738 *Honeywell Honey* at Luliang, China, during the transfer flight to Tinian Island and service under the XXI BC. (*Seith via 40th BG*)

Gen. Curtis LeMay, commander of the XX BC from August 1944 to January 1945, became the chief of staff of the United States Air Force in 1961, and held the position until 1965. He ran as the vice presidential candidate on George Wallace's unsuccessful American Independent Party ticket in 1968. (*US Air Force*)

became the chief of staff of the United States Air Force and held this position during the 1962 Cuban Missile Crisis, when he projected a hard-line position toward the Soviet Union and advocated military action, despite President John F. Kennedy's desire to develop a peaceful solution. LeMay clashed with President Lyndon Johnson's administration over military policy related to the Vietnam War and retired in 1965. Gen. Roger Ramey commanded the Eighth Air Force between 1946 and 1948, and then the Fifth Air Force (Korea and Japan) from 1954 to 1956, before completing his career as the deputy commanding general of the continental air command. He officially retired in January 1957.

Col. William Blanchard, who commanded the 40th BG between August 1944 and February 1945, remained in the military after World War II, attaining the rank of general, and served as the vice chief of staff of the Air Force between 1965 and his untimely death in 1966. Col. James Edmundson, commander of the 468th BG from November 1944 until early 1946, rose to the rank of lieutenant general and capped his career as the deputy commander of US readiness command.

Col. William Blanchard, who commanded the 40th BG between August 1944 and February 1945, remained in the military after World War II, attaining the rank of general, and served as the vice chief of staff of the Air Force between 1965 and his untimely death in 1966. (*US Air Force*)

The Boeing B-29 Superfortress remained the main long-range bomber of the Army Air Force and United States Air Force (after the latter's independence from the United States Army in 1948) until the introduction of the Convair B-36 Peacemaker. During the 1950–1953 Korean War, the United States Air Force utilized the B-29 against targets in North Korea. The bombers conducted daylight raids, leaflet drops, and later shifted to night raids as North Korean air defenses improved with the introduction of Mig-15 fighters. Thirty-four B-29s were lost to combat and operational issues during the war. The United States Air Force reduced the B-29 and its B-50 variant to non-bombing roles after the Korean War and phased the aircraft from inventory in the mid-1960s. The Soviet Tu-4 Bull—the reverse engineered aircraft derived from XX BC B-29s interned in the Soviet Union—served as a bomber for that country throughout the 1950s and was also retired in the early 1960s.[35]

The XX BC faced many challenges as it conducted combat operations from India and China between June 1944 and March 1945. The command and its 58th BW flew a new aircraft that required many technical modifications and was powered by engines that frequently overheated or faced other mechanical failures. The airborne logistical supply line over the Hump between India and China proved dangerous, as crews worked to haul enough fuel and equipment to launch raids against Japan or Manchuria. Yet the problems they faced and solved helped improve the B-29's performance as the XXI BC initiated combat operations from the Marianas Islands. Although the XX BC achieved limited success against its strategic industrial targets, it should be credited for many tactical successes, including damaging the drydock at Singapore; destroying large amounts of military supplies stored near Rangoon, Burma; dropping the Rama VI Bridge at Bangkok, Thailand; and mining Japanese controlled harbors, rivers, and ship channels in several areas. The command served to boost the morale of Americans and Chinese when targeting Japanese targets, especially those on the Japanese home islands, even though it scored limited hits on its targets.

The legacy of 58th BW operations from India and China, as well as Tinian, is preserved at the New England Air

Museum in Connecticut, which houses a memorial to the wing, including a restored B-29. Although constructed in 1945, the bomber (#975) did not see combat service. The New England Air Museum restored the aircraft with an aft fuselage section from #739 and painted the plane to resemble #566 *Jack's Hack*, which flew with the 468th BG from its base on Tinian Island. The museum is also beginning to collect many of the records held by some of the 58th BW groups. The 444th BG selected the planned Bombers in the Prairie Museum in Pratt, Kansas, as the depository for its records and artifacts at the completion of this manuscript. The Pratt Army Airfield Historical Society and the Pratt County Historical Museum have also been supportive of the efforts to preserve the 58th BW's history in Kansas. It is comforting to know the records and artifacts of these four bomb groups will be preserved for future generations with these organizations.

#471 *Ramblin' Reck* of the 40th BG arrived overseas in late August 1944 and returned to the United States as war weary eleven months later after completing sixteen missions from India, three across the Hump, and fifteen operations from Tinian Island with the XXI BC. (*40th BG*)

Opposite: Col. James Edmundson, commander of the 468th BG from November 1944 until early 1946, rose to the rank of lieutenant general and capped his career as the deputy commander of US readiness command. (*US Air Force*)

Endnotes

Chapter 1

1. Establishing direct equivalents of WWII Japanese and American aviation organizations can be challenging. The Japanese *chutai* is approximately equivalent to a small American squadron, with the former authorized around ten aircraft. The Japanese *sentai* is similar to an American group organization, with the former authorized around thirty to thirty-six aircraft. For more information on the 64th *Sentai* see Unmemto Hiroshi, *Saburo Nakamura of the 64th Sentai*. (Dainippon Kaiga, 2010).
2. Carl Berger, *B-29 Superfortress, Ballantine's Illustrated History of World War II, Weapons Book No. 17*. (New York: Ballantine Books, 1970), 61; Koji Takaki and Henry Sakaida, *B-29 Hunters of the JAAF*, Osprey Aviation Elite #5. (Oxford: Osprey Publishing, 2001), 6; Kenn C. Rust, *Twentieth Air Force Story in World War II*. (Terre Haute, IN: Sun Shine House), 7; Gen. Curtis E. LeMay and Bill Yenne, *Superfortress: The Story of the B-29 and American Air Power*. (New York: McGraw-Hill Book Company, 1988), 73; and 444th BG, History, April 1944.
3. Gen. Curtis E. LeMay and Bill Yenne, *Superfortress: The Story of the B-29 and American Air Power*, 73.
4. 444th BG, History, August 31, 1944.
5. For more information on the development and brief combat history of the B-32, see William Wolf, *Consolidated B-32 Dominator: The Ultimate Look from Drawing Board to Scrap Yard*. (Atglen, PA: Schiffer Books, 2006).
6. Carl Berger, *B-29 Superfortress, Ballantine's Illustrated History of World War II, Weapons Book No. 17,* 33.
7. The Columbia University archives hold a 1959 oral interview conducted with Wolfe about his WWII experiences.
8. For more information on the development of the B-29, see William Wolf, *The B-29 Superfortress: The Ultimate Look from Drawing Board to VJ Day*. (Atglen, PA: Schiffer Books, 2006) and Carl Berger, *B-29 Superfortress, Ballantine's Illustrated History of World War II, Weapons Book No. 17*. (New York: Ballantine Books, 1970); Graham M. Simon, *B-29 Superfortress: Giant Bomber of World War Two and Korea*. (Barnsley, UK: Pen and Sword Aviation, 2012); Robert Dorr and Mark Styling, *B-29 Units of World War II, Osprey Combat Aircraft 33*. (Oxford: Osprey Publishing, 2002); David A. Anderson, *B-29 Superfortress at War*. (New York: MacMillan Publishing Company, 1979); Vander M. Jacob, *Building the B-29, Smithsonian History of Aviation and Spaceflight*. (Washington, DC: Smithsonian Institute, 1995); John M. Campbell, *Boeing B-29 Superfortress, Vol. II*. (Atglen, PA: Schiffer Books, 1997).
9. For more information on Claire Chennault, his relationship with Chiang, and the formation of the Flying Tigers, see Daniel Ford, *Flying Tigers: Claire Chennault and his American Volunteers, 1941–1942*. (New York: Smithsonian Books, 2007) and Claire Lee Chennault, *Way of a Fighter: The Memoirs of Claire Lee Chennault*. (New York: G.P. Putnam's Sons, 1949).
10. For more information on the WWII campaigns in Burma, see Louis Allen, *Burma: The Longest War, 1941–1945*. (London: Dent, 1984).
11. For more information on Gen. Stilwell's views on the CBI Theater of Operations, see Barbara W. Tuchman, *Stilwell and the American Experience in China, 1911–1945*. (New York: Macmillan, 1970).
12. For more information on the impact of the Casablanca Conference on the war against Japan, see John Miller, "The Casablanca Conference and Pacific Strategy," *Military Affairs*, Vol. 13, No. 4, 1949, 209–215.
13. Combined Chiefs of Staff Minutes, 68th Meeting, January 22, 1943.
14. For more information on the Cairo and Teheran Conferences, see Keith Sainsbury, *The Turning Point: Roosevelt, Churchill, Stalin, and Chiang-Kai-shek, 1943: The Moscow, Cairo, and Teheran Conferences*. (Oxford: Oxford University Press, 1985).

15. Quoted in Gene Eric Salecker, *Fortress Against the Sun: The B-17 Flying Fortress in the Pacific*. (Cambridge, Massachusetts: Da Capo Press, 2001), 296.
16. Ibid, 295–296; Martin Bowman, *B-17 Flying Fortress Units of the Pacific War, Osprey Combat Aircraft no. 39*. (Oxford: Osprey Publishing, 2003), 80–81.
17. Martin Bowman, *B-17 Flying Fortress Units of the Pacific War, Osprey Combat Aircraft no. 39*, 26–28; Salecker, *Fortress Against the Sun: The B-17 Flying Fortress in the Pacific,* 145–146.
18. John Misterly, Interview with the author, October 15, 2000.
19. B. Vic Dison, Jr., *WWII Memories*, Unpublished memoir, 40th Bomb Group.
20. John Misterly, Jr., *Over and Under: 8 Days in a Dingy in the North Pacific*. (Portland, OR: NTF Publications, 1987), 88–96.
21. Ibid.
22. Dison, *WWII Memories*, Unpublished memoir, 40th Bomb Group.
23. Gen. H. H. Arnold, *Global Missions*. (New York: Harper and Brothers, 1949), 479.
24. 40th Bomb Group, History, April 1 through April 31, 1944, July 14, 1944.
25. J. L. Cate, "Matterhorn Logistics," in W. F. Craven and J. L. Cate, *The Army Air Forces in World War II, Volume V, The Pacific: Matterhorn to Nagasaki June 1944 to August 1945*. (Chicago: University of Chicago Press, 1953), 79.
26. Wilbur H. Morrison, *Point of No Return: The Story of the 20th Air Force,* (New York: Times Books, 1979), 66.
27. Ibid.
28. Misterly, Interview with the author, October 15, 2000.
29. Dr. Yates C. Smith, "From Salina, KS, to Kharagpur, India," New England Air Museum.
30. Morrison, *Point of No Return: The Story of the 20th Air Force,* 67.
31. Ibid, 69.
32. Misterly, Interview with the author, October 15, 2000.
33. Jack R. Millar, Jr., Interview with the author, March 16, 1998.
34. Smith, "From Salina, KS, to Kharagpur, India."
35. Ibid.
36. Morton Roth, "Going Overseas," *40th Bomb Group Association Memories, Vol. 22*, July 1988, 1–4.
37. Ibid.
38. Ed Vickery, A Personal Recollection of the Trip to India, unpublished memoir, 40th Bomb Group.
39. Ibid.
40. George W. Steinman, "Diary," *40th Bomb Group Association Memories, Vol. 22*, July 1988, 6–8.
41. Willard W. Holderby, "Diary," New England Air Museum.
42. Cate, "Matterhorn Logistics," 65.
43. Ibid, 78–79.
44. Holderby, "Diary."
45. Misterly, *Over and Under: 8 Days in a Dingy in the North Pacific*, 120.
46. Morrison, *Point of No Return: The Story of the 20th Air Force*, 69.
47. Robert Schumacher, Interview with the author, September 22, 2000.
48. Gen. Curtis E. LeMay and Bill Yenne, *Superfortress: The Story of the B-29 and American Air Power,* 72.
49. Cate, "Matterhorn Logistics," 65–80.

Chapter 2

1. For more information on Operation *Ichi-Go*, see Dick Wilson, *When Tigers Fight: The Story of the Sino–Japanese War, 1937–1945*. (New York: Viking Press, 1982).
2. 768th Bomb Squadron, "History of the 768th Bomb Squadron, 1 May–31 May 1944," No date.
3. Ibid.
4. 40th Bomb Group, "History 1 June through 30 June 1944," 4 July 1944.
5. Ibid.
6. Cal Brown, "I Shot Out Our Own Engine," unpublished memoir, 40th BG Association.
7. 40th Bomb Group, "Narrative of Ditching by Crew of A/C #282," June 8, 1944.
8. 768th Bomb Squadron, "History of the 768th Bombardment Squadron (VH), 1 June 1944 – 30 June 1944," July 1944.
9. XX Bomber Command, "Tactical Mission Report, Field Order No.1, Mission No. 1, June 26, 1944.
10. Ibid.
11. Ibid.
12. Ibid.
13. 40th Bomb Group, "History 1 June through 30 June 1944," July 4, 1944.
14. 40th Bomb Group, "Narrative of Ditching by Crew of A/C #282," June 8, 1944.
15. Ibid.
16. 40th Bomb Group, "History 1 June through 30 June 1944," July 4, 1944.

17. Wayne Wiseman, "Ditching –The First B-29 Combat Mission," *40th Bomb Group Association Memories*, #3.
18. Ibid.
19. Ibid.
20. 444th Bomb Group, "History," June 1944.
21. 771st Bomb Squadron, "Historical Data 1 June through 30 June 44," July 4, 1944.
22. 468th Bomb Group, "History of the 468th Bomb Group, Advanced Echelon at A-7," July 1944.
23. Robert Schumacher, Interview with the author, September 22, 2000.
24. 13th Bomb Maintenance Squadron, "History of the 13th Bombardment Maintenance Squadron June 1944," June 30, 1944.
25. Jerry Noble, "Comments," in "Yawata: First land-bombing of Japan," *40th Bomb Group Association Memories*, No. 40, October 1991.
26. Robert Hall, "Memories," in "Yawata: First land-bombing of Japan," *40th Bomb Group Association Memories*, No. 40, October 1991.
27. 793rd Bomb Squadron, "Squadron History for the Month of June 1944," June 30, 1944.
28. Ibid.
29. Jack Millar, Interview with the Author, September 4, 2000.
30. Ibid.
31. Ibid.
32. Ferris Albers, "Memories," in "Yawata: First land-bombing of Japan," *40th Bomb Group Association Memories*, No. 40, October 1991.
33. Ibid.
34. Jerry Noble, "Comments".
35. Ferris Albers, "Memories."
36. Kenneth P. Werrell, *Archie, Flak, AAA, and SAM: A Short Operational History of Ground-Based Air Defense*. (Maxwell Air Force Base, Alabama: Air University Press, 1988), 153–157.
37. John Misterly, Jr., *Over and Under: 8 Days in a Dingy in the North Pacific*. (Portland, OR: NTF Publications, 1987), 141; Interview with John Misterly, October 2000.
38. Robert Schumacher, Interview with the author.
39. Jack Millar, Interview with the Author.
40. Ferris Albers, "Memories."
41. Lou Stoumen, "A YANK Reporter Describes Trip to Nippon's Pittsburgh in a Superfortress of the New Twentieth Air Force," *YANK: The Army Weekly*, Vol. 2, No. 9, August 3, 1944, 2–4.
42. Tillman Durdin, "B-29 Bombing Trip to Japan is Described by Eyewitness," *New York Times*, June 17, 1944, 1.
43. Clay Gowran, "Tribune Man Sees B-29s Bomb Japan," *Chicago Daily Tribune*, June 17, 1944, 1.
44. Steven Zaloga, *Defense of Japan 1945, Osprey Fortress Series No. 99*. (Oxford: Osprey Publishing, 2010), 51.
45. Koji Takaki and Henry Sakaida, *B-29 Hunters of the JAAF, Osprey Aviation Elite No. 5*. (Oxford: Osprey Publishing, 2001), 7–9.
46. Tillman Durdin, "B-29 Bombing Trip to Japan is Described by Eyewitness."
47. Lou Stoumen, "A YANK Reporter Describes Trip to Nippon's Pittsburgh in a Superfortress of the New Twentieth Air Force."
48. Quoted in Koji Takaki and Henry Sakaida, *B-29 Hunters of the JAAF, Osprey Aviation Elite No. 5*. (Oxford: Osprey Publishing, 2001), 9.
49. Ibid.
50. Ibid.
51. United Press, "Tokyo Tries to Belittle Raid; Claims Two Superfortresses," *New York Times*, June 16, 1944, 1.
52. Quoted in Gen. Curtis E. LeMay and Bill Yenne, *Superfortress: The Story of the B-29 and American Air Power*. (New York: McGraw-Hil Book Company, 1988), 77.
53. Jerry Noble, "Comments."
54. Ferris Albers, "Memories."
55. 9th Bombardment Maintenance Squadron, "History of the 9th Bombardment Maintenance Squadron (VH), 1 June – 30 June 1944," July 1944.
56. XX Bomber Command.
57. Jack Millar, Interview with the Author.
58. 768th Bomb Squadron, "History of the 768th Bombardment Squadron (VH), 1 June 1944 – 30 June 1944," July 1944.
59. James Lea Cate, "XX Bomber Command Against Japan," in W. F. Craven and J. L. Cate, *The Army Air Forces in World War II, Volume V, The Pacific: Matterhorn to Nagasaki June 1944 to August 1945* (Chicago: University of Chicago Press, 1953), 101; and United Press, "Tokyo Tries to Belittle Raid; Claims Two Superfortresses," *New York Times*, June 16, 1944, 1.
60. William Hunter, "From the Diary of William Hunter," in "Yawata: First land-bombing of Japan," *40th Bomb Group Association Memories*, No. 40, October 1991.
61. Jack Millar, Interview with the Author.
62. Lou Stoumen, "A YANK Reporter Describes Trip to Nippon's Pittsburgh in a Superfortress of the New Twentieth Air Force."

63. Tillman Durdin, "B-29 Bombing Trip to Japan is Described by Eyewitness."
64. Jack Millar, Interview with the Author.
65. Lou Stoumen, "A YANK Reporter Describes Trip to Nippon's Pittsburgh in a Superfortress of the New Twentieth Air Force."
66. "B-29 Superforts Bomb Japanese Mainland," *Life*, July 10, 1944, 80.
67. Ferris Albers, "Memories."
68. Jack Millar, Interview with the Author.
69. "Tokyo Falsehood Proved," *New York Times*, July 8, 1944, 3.
70. John Misterly, Interview with the author, October 15, 2000.

Chapter 3

1. James Lea Cate, "XX Bomber Command Against Japan," in W. F. Craven and J. L. Cate, *The Army Air Forces in World War II, Volume V, The Pacific: Matterhorn to Nagasaki June 1944 to August 1945*. (Chicago: University of Chicago Press, 1953), 103–105.
2. XX Bomber Command, "Tactical Mission Report, Field Order No.3, Mission No. 3," August 7, 1944.
3. Ferris Albers, "Memories," in "Yawata: First land-bombing of Japan," *40th Bomb Group Association Memories*, No. 40, October 1991.
4. XX Bomber Command, 7 August 1944; 792nd Bomb Squadron, "792nd Bomb Squadron History, July 1944," August 1944.
5. XX Bomber Command, 7
6. 40th Bomb Group, "1 July Through 31 July 1944," No published date.
7. XX Bomber Command, "Tactical Mission Report, Field Order No. 4, Mission No. 4," September 13, 1944.
8. "Alvin Hills #291 Crash," 40th BG Association records; 40th Bomb Group, "1 July Through 31 July 1944," No published date.
9. 10th Bomb Maintenance Squadron, "10th History for July," August 1944.
10. XX Bomber Command, September 13, 1944.
11. Ibid.
12. 40th Bomb Group, "1 July Through 31 July 1944," No published date; XX Bomber Command, September 13, 1944.
13. 768th Bomb Squadron, "History of the 768th Bomb Squadron, 1 August to 31 August 1944," No date.
14. Gen. Curtis E. LeMay and Bill Yenne, *Superfortress: The Story of the B-29 and American Air Power*. (New York: McGraw-Hill Book Company, 1988), 86–87. For more information on the Soviet development of the Tu-4 Bull from the B-29, see Gordon, Yefim and Vladimir Rigmant. *Tupolev Tu-4: Soviet Superfortress*. (Hinckley, Leicestershire: Midland Counties Publications Ltd., 2002).
15. XX Bomber Command, September 13, 1944.
16. 40th Bomb Group, "1 July Through 31 July 1944," No published date.
17. 795th Bomb Squadron, "Squadron History," September 1944; Wilbur H. Morrison, *Point of No Return: The Story of the 20th Air Force*. (New York: Times Books, 1979), 97; Carl Berger, *B-29 Superfortress, Ballantine's Illustrated History of World War II, Weapons Book No. 17*. (New York: Ballantine Books, 1970), 78.
18. 40th Bomb Group, "1 July Through 31 July 1944," No published date; XX Bomber Command, September 13, 1944.
19. For further information on ATC supply flights across the Hump, see: John D. Plating, *The Hump: America's Strategy for Keeping China in World War II*. Williams-Ford Texas A&M Military History Series. (College Station, TX: Texas A&M University Press, 2011); Thorne Bliss, *The Hump: The Great Military Airlift of World War II*. (Philadelphia: Lippincott, 1965); Otha C. Spencer, *Flying the Hump: Memories of an Air War*. Williams-Ford Texas A&M Military History Series. (College Station, TX: Texas A&M University Press, 1994); William J. Koenig, *Over the Hump: Airlift to China, Ballantine's Illustrated History of the Violent Century, Campaign Book No. 23*. (New York: Ballantine, 1972).
20. Curtis LeMay and Bill Yenne, *Superfortress: The Story of the B-29 and American Air Power*. (New York: The McGraw-Hill Book Company, 1988), 83.
21. "Gasoline Pumped from Cargo Keeps Plane Aloft 15 Hours," *The Hump Express*, Vol. 1, No. 5, January 15, 1945, www.cbi-theater-10.comcast.net, accessed July 3, 2011.
22. George Lowery, "The Hump – Rocks in those Clouds," *40th Bomb Group Association Memories*, Issue #12, November 1986, 1.
23. Willard Holderby, "Diary," New England Air Museum.
24. The Hump Express, Vol. 1, No. 2, January 25, 1945, www.cbi-theater-10.comcast.net, accessed July 3, 2011.
25. "Violent Weather – No B-29 Had It Worse Than On This Hump Flight," *40th Bomb Group Association Memories*, Issue #34, August 1990, 1.
26. Ibid.

27. Ibid.
28. Ibid.
29. "468th Bomb Group China–Burma–India Losses," 468th Bomb Group Association.
30. Ibid.
31. Ibid.
32. Wilbur H. Morrison, *Point of No Return: The Story of the 20th Air Force*, NY: Times Books, 1979, 84–88; and Keith Wheeler, *Bombers Over Japan*. (NY: Time Life Books, 1982), 54–56.
33. "Forced Landing at the Turning Point," *40th Bomb Group Association Memories*, Issue #16, July 1987, 2.
34. Ibid.
35. Ibid., 3.
36. Ibid., 4.
37. Ibid.
38. John Misterly, Jr., *Over and Under: 8 Days in a Dingy in the North Pacific*. (Portland, OR: NTF Publications, 1987), 148–157 and Interview with John Misterly September 18, 2000.
39. William H. Tunner, *Over the Hump*. (Washington, DC: Office of Air Force History, 1985), 82.
40. Ibid.

Chapter 4

1. XX Bomber Command, "Tactical Mission Report, Field Order No.5," Mission No. 5, September 22, 1944.
2. 462nd Bomb Group, "Historical Data," September 1, 1944; 768th Bomb Squadron, "1 August to 31 August," No publication date.
3. Wilbur H. Morrison, *Point of No Return: The Story of the 20th Air Force*. (New York: Times Books, 1979), 101–104.
4. XX Bomber Command, Mission No. 5, September 22, 1944; 468th Bomb Group, "Headquarters 468th Bombardment – August 1944," No publication date.
5. Morrison, *Point of No Return: The Story of the 20th Air Force,* 110.
6. John Misterly, Jr., *Over and Under: 8 Days in a Dingy in the North Pacific*. (Portland, OR: NTF Publications, 1987), 171–172.
7. 444th Bomb Group, "History August 1944," September 1, 1944.
8. Misterly, *Over and Under: 8 Days in a Dingy in the North Pacific*, 172.
9. XX Bomber Command, September 22, 1944.
10. Morrison, *Point of No Return: The Story of the 20th Air Force,* 110.
11. Ira Matthews, "Tribute to a Combat Crew," 40th BG Association.
12. Ibid.
13. Ibid.
14. 444th Bomb Group, September 1, 1944.
15. Matthews.
16. XX Bomber Command, "Tactical Mission Report, Field Order No. 6, Mission No. 6," September 26, 1944.
17. XX Bomber Command, September 26, 1944.
18. XX Bomber Command, September 26, 1944; 468th Bomb Group, "Headquarters 468th Bombardment – August 1944," No publication date.
19. XX Bomber Command, September 26, 1944.
20. Ibid.
21. Morrison, *Point of No Return: The Story of the 20th Air Force*; 462nd Bomb Group, "Historical Data August 1944," September 1, 1944.
22. 468th Bomb Group, "Headquarters 468th Bombardment – August 1944," No publication date.
23. XX Bomber Command, "Tactical Mission Report, Field Order No. 7, Mission No. 7," September 28, 1944.
24. Ibid.
25. 40th Bomb Group, "Group History, 1 August 1944 through 31 August 1944," No publication date.
26. 462nd Bomb Group, "Historical Data August 1944," September 1, 1944.
27. XX Bomber Command, September 26, 1944; 444th Bomb Group, "History August 1944," September 1, 1944; 462nd Bomb Group, "Historical Data August 1944," September 1, 1944; 468th Bomb Group, "Headquarters 468th Bombardment – August 1944," No publication date.
28. XX Bomber Command, September 26, 1944; 468th Bomb Group, "Headquarters 468th Bombardment – August 1944," No publication date.
29. Misterly, *Over and Under: 8 Days in a Dingy in the North Pacific*, 175.
30. XX Bomber Command, September 28, 1944; 40th Bomb Group, "History 1 August through 31 August 1944," No final publication date.
31. 768th Bomb Squadron, "History of the 768th Bomb Squadron, 1 August to 31 August 1944," No Date.
32. 468th Bomb Group, "Headquarters 468th Bombardment – August 1944," No publication date.
33. Koji Takaki and Henry Sakaida, *B-29 Hunters of the JAAF, Osprey Aviation Elite #5* (Oxford: Osprey Publishing, 2001), 14–18.

34. Misterly, *Over and Under: 8 Days in a Dingy in the North Pacific*, 175–176.
35. Takaki and Sakaida, *B-29 Hunters of the JAAF, Osprey Aviation Elite #5*, 17–18; Morrison, *Point of No Return: The Story of the 20th Air Force*.
36. Misterly, *Over and Under: 8 Days in a Dingy in the North Pacific*, 176.
37. Takaki and Sakaida, *B-29 Hunters of the JAAF, Osprey Aviation Elite #5*, 17–18.
38. Walter J. Boyne, "Carbon Copy Bomber," *Air Force Magazine*, Vol. 92, No. 6, June 2009; 40th Bomb Group, "Group History, 1 August 1944 through 31 August 1944," No final publication date.
39. B-29-5-BW "Praying Mantis" Serial Number 42-6286. www.Pacificwrecks.com, July 26, 2011. Accessed February 24, 2012.
40. 40th Bomb Group, "Group History, 1 August 1944 through 31 August 1944," No final publication date; 444th Bomb Group, "History August 1944," September 1, 1944; 462nd Bomb Group, "Historical Data August 1944," September 1, 1944.
41. XX Bomber Command, September 28, 1944.

Chapter 5

1. 768th Bomb Squadron, "History of the 768th Bomb Squadron, 1 September to 30 September 1944," No publication Date.
2. Curtis LeMay and Bill Yenne, *Superfortress: The Story of the B-29 and American Air Power.* (New York: McGraw-Hill Book Company, 1988), 88.
3. XX Bomber Command, "Tactical Mission Report, Field Order No. 8, Mission No. 8," October 1, 1944.
4. James Ira Cornett, "LeMay Flies to Anshan with Cornett," *40th Bomb Group Association Memories*, May 1984.
5. XX Bomber Command, October 1, 1944.
6. Eric Hammel, *Air War Pacific Chronology: America's Air War Against Japan in East Asia and the Pacific 1941–1945.* (Pacifica, CA: Pacifica Press, 1988).
7. Ibid.
8. Ibid.
9. 468th Bomb Group, "Headquarters 468th Bombardment Group September 1944," No publication date.
10. John Misterly, Interview with the author; John Misterly, Jr., *Over and Under: 8 Days in a Dingy in the North Pacific*. (Portland, OR: NTF Publications, 1987), 178.
11. "History for the Month of 793rd Bomb Squadron September 1944," No publication date.
12. 444th BG History, "September 1944," October 8, 1944.
13. 444th Bomb Group, "History," February 9, 1945.
14. XX Bomber Command, October 1, 1944.
15. Cornett, "LeMay Flies to Anshan with Cornett."
16. 444th Bomb Group, October 8, 1944.
17. Ibid.
18. LeMay and Yenne, *Superfortress: The Story of the B-29 and American Air Power,* 78–84.
19. Ibid, 81.
20. Ibid, 82.
21. 444th Bomb Group, October 8, 1944.
22. 3. XX Bomber Command, "Tactical Mission Report, Field Order No.9, Mission No. 9," October 13, 1944.
23. Ibid.
24. Ibid.
25. Ibid.
26. XX Bomber Command, October 13, 1944; 40th Bomb Group, "Group History, 1 September 1944 through 31 September 1944," November 20, 1944; 444th Bomb Group, October 8, 1944; 462nd Bomb Group, "Historical Data September," October 10, 1944; 468th Bomb Group, "Headquarters 468th Bombardment Group September 1944," No publication date.
27. Willard Holderby, "Diary," New England Air Museum
28. Robert Schumacher, Interview with the author, September 15, 2000.
29. B. Vic Dison, Jr., *WWII Memories*, Unpublished memoir, 40th Bomb Group.
30. "Most of Them Jump Into Trenches; He Jumps Out," *The Hump Express*, Vol. 1, No. 5., February 15, 1945, www.cbi-theater-10.comcast.net, accessed July 3, 2011.
31. Holderby, "Diary."
32. LeMay and Yenne, *Superfortress: The Story of the B-29 and American Air Power,* 89.
33. Ibid.
34. 40th Bomb Group, "Group History, 1 September 1944 through 31 September 1944," November 20, 1944.
35. 40th Bomb Group Forward Detachment, "Forward Base Detachment History, 1 September 1944 to 30 September 1944," October 28, 1944.
36. For more information on the Northrop P–61 Black Widow, see Garry R. Pape and Ronald C. Harrison, *Queen of the Midnight Skies: The Story of America's Air Force Night Fighters.* (West Chester, PA: Schiffer Military History, 1992); Jeff Kolln, *Northrop's Night Hunter: P-61 Black Widow.* (North Branch, MN: Specialty Press, 2008).
37. 426th NFS, "Historical Report," October 1944.

38. William C. Odell, Personal Interview with the Author, July 2001. Odell served as the Commander of the 547th NFS.
39. 426th NFS, October 1944.

Chapter 6

1. XX Bomber Command, "Tactical Mission Report, Field Order No.10, Mission No. 10," October 26, 1944.
2. Ibid.
3. XX Bomber Command, October 26, 1944; 40th Bomb Group, "1 October Through 31 October 1944," November 20, 1944; 444th Bomb Group, "History October 1944," November 9, 1944.
4. XX Bomber Command, October 26, 1944.
5. XX Bomber Command, "Tactical Mission Report, Field Order No. 11, Mission No. 11," October 28, 1944.
6. XX Bomber Command, October 28, 1944; 444th Bomb Group, "History October 1944," November 9, 1944.
7. 462nd Bomb Group, "Historical Data October 1944," November 5, 1944.
8. 101. 768th Bomb Squadron, "History of the 768th Bomb Squadron, 1 October to 31 October 1944," No publication Date.
9. XX Bomber Command, October 28, 1944.
10. Ibid.
11. Ibid.
12. XX Bomber Command, "Tactical Mission Report, Field Order No.12, Mission No. 12," October 28, 1944.
13. 40th Bomb Group, November 20, 1944.
14. XX Bomber Command, "Tactical Mission Report, Field Order No.12, Mission No. 12," October 28, 1944.
15. Carter McGregor, Ralph Weinberg, Robert Moss, Joe Duemig, Ed Haggerty, and Fritz Kulicka, "Tragic Loss of Ed Hornyia Over Formosa (Taiwan)," *40th Bomb Group Association Memories*, Issue #54, January 1995.
16. Ibid.
17. Ibid.
18. Brown, "I Shot Out Our Own Engine."
19. Ted Urban, Unpublished Memoir, March 2004.
20. Brown, "I Shot Out Our Own Engine."
21. XX Bomber Command, "Tactical Mission Report, Field Order No. 13, Mission No. 13," November 4, 1944.
22. Ibid.
23. XX Bomber Command, "Tactical Mission Report, Field Order No. 13, Mission No. 13," November 4, 1944; 768th Bomb Squadron.
24. XX Bomber Command, "Tactical Mission Report, Field Order No. 13, Mission No. 13," November 4, 1944.
25. Ibid.
26. Harry Changnon, Russell Elwell, Bill Gardner, Jack Halpern, Jack Ledford, Duoyne McCullough, Howard Oblender, and Gilbert Rodencal, "Ledford Crew Makes it Back from Omura," *40th Bomb Group Association Memories*, Issue #62, July 1997.
27. Ibid.
28. Ibid.
29. Ibid.
30. Ibid.
31. Ibid.
32. Ibid.
33. Ibid.
34. Ibid.
35. Ibid.
36. John K. Jensen, "Gun Battle Over Japan," *40th Bomb Group Association Memories*, Issue #10, July 1986.
37. Ibid.
38. XX Bomber Command, "Gen. Orders Number 84," December 15, 1944.

Chapter 7

1. XX Bomber Command, "Tactical Mission Report, Field Order No. 14, Mission No. 14," November 13, 1944.
2. Ibid.
3. Ibid; 468th Bomb Group, "Headquarters 468th Bombardment Group History November 1944," No publication date.
4. XX Bomber Command, 13 November 1944; 40th Bomb Group, "Group History, 1 November 1944 through 30 November 1944," January 29, 1945.
5. Ibid.
6. XX Bomber Command, November 13, 1944.
7. Ibid.
8. XX Bomber Command, November 13, 1944; 40th Bomb Group, "Group History, 1 November 1944 through 30 November 1944," January 29, 1945.
9. XX Bomber Command, "Tactical Mission Report, Field Order No. 15, Mission No. 15," November 15, 1944.
10. 462nd Bomb Group, "Historical Data November," December 15, 1944.
11. XX Bomber Command, November 15, 1944.

12. XX Bomber Command, "Tactical Mission Report, Field Order No. 16," Mission No. 16, November 21, 1944.
13. Ibid.
14. Francis Morgan, Carl Rieger, Watson Lankford, Dwight Collins, Thomas Carroll, and Harry Changnon, "Richard Vickery's Crew and the Nanking," *40th Bomb Group Association Memories*, Issue #43, April 1992.
15. XX Bomber Command, November 21, 1944.
16. Ibid.
17. XX Bomber Command, November 21, 1944; 468th Bomb Group, "Headquarters 468th Bombardment Group History November 1944," No publication date.
18. 444th Bomb Group, "History November 1944," December 13, 1944.
19. Francis Morgan, Carl Rieger, Watson Lankford, Dwight Collins, Thomas Carroll, and Harry Changnon.
20. Ibid.
21. Ibid.
22. Ibid.
23. Ibid.
24. Ibid.
25. Ibid.
26. XX Bomber Command, "Tactical Mission Report, Field Order No. 17, Mission No. 17," December 1, 1944.
27. 40th Bomb Group, "Group History, 1 November 1944 through 30 November 1944," January 29, 1945; 468th Bomb Group, "Headquarters 468th Bombardment Group History November 1944," No publication date.
28. XX Bomber Command, December 1, 1944.
29. 462nd Bomb Group, "Historical Data November," December 15, 1944.
30. Leland Jones, Dick Steiner, James Cowden, Harry Changnon, Howard Anderson, and Leonard Koenig, "To Omura and Return!" *40th Bomb Group Association Memories*, Issue #15, May 1987.
31. Ibid.
32. Ibid.
33. Ibid.
34. Ibid.
35. Ibid.
36. Ibid.
37. XX Bomber Command, December 1, 1944; 40th Bomb Group, "Group History, 1 November 1944 through 30 November 1944," January 29, 1945; 444th Bomb Group, "History November 1944," December 13, 1944.
38. 444th Bomb Group, "History November 1944," December 13, 1944.
39. Ibid.
40. 468th Bomb Group, "Headquarters 468th Bombardment Group History November 1944," No publication date.
41. Leland Jones, Dick Steiner, James Cowden, Harry Changnon, Howard Anderson, and Leonard Koenig.
42. Ibid.
43. XX Bomber Command, December 1, 1944.
44. XX Bomber Command, "Tactical Mission Report, Field Order No. 18, Mission No. 18," December 7, 1944.
45. Ibid.
46. XX Bomber Command, December 7, 1944; 40th Bomb Group, "Group History, 1 November 1944 through 30 November 1944," January 29, 1945.

Chapter 8

1. For more information on Wedemeyer's military service in World War II, see: Albert C. Wedemeyer, *Wedemeyer Reports*. (New York: Henry Holt and Company, 1958).
2. XX Bomber Command, "Tactical Mission Report, Field Order No. 19, Mission No. 19," December 19, 1944.
3. 468th Bomb Group, "Headquarters 468th Bombardment Group History December 1944," No publication date.
4. XX Bomber Command, December 19, 1944; 40th Bomb Group, "Group History, 1 December 1944 through 31 December 1944," January 23, 1945; 444th Bomb Group, "History December 1944," January 5, 1945.
5. 40th Bomb Group, "Group History, 1 December 1944 through 31 December 1944," January 23, 1945.
6. For more information on the Manchurian Air Force, see: Philipp Jowett, *Rays of the Rising Sun, Vol. 1: Japan's Asian Allies 1931–1945, China and Manchukuo*. (Solihull, UK: Helgon and Co., 2005).
7. XX Bomber Command, December 19, 1944.
8. Ibid.
9. Ibid.
10. Ibid.
11. Koji Takaki and Henry Sakaida, *B-29 Hunters of the JAAF, Osprey Aviation Elite #5*. (Oxford: Osprey Publishing Ltd, 2001), 19–22.
12. 444th Bomb Group, "History December 1944," January 5, 1945.
13. 462nd Bomb Group, "Historical Date December 1944," January 5, 1945; 468th Bomb Group, "Headquarters 468th Bombardment Group History December 1944," No publication date.
14. Harry Changnon, ed. "Editor's Introduction," *40th Bomb Group Association Memories*, Issue #6, No date.

15. Louis Jones,"The 'Dixie Mission' to the Communist Chinese," *40th Bomb Group Association Memories*, Issue #14, March 1987. For more information on the Dixie Mission to the Chinese Communists, see: David D. Barrett, *Dixie Mission: The United States Army Observer Group in Yenan 1944.* (Berkeley: Center for Chinese Studies, University of California, 1970).
16. 40th Bomb Group, "Group History 1 February thru 28 February 1945," March 8, 1945.
17. Jones, "The 'Dixie Mission' to the Communist Chinese"
18. Takaki and Sakaida, *B-29 Hunters of the JAAF, Osprey Aviation Elite #5,* 22.
19. XX Bomber Command, "Tactical Mission Report, Field Order No.20," Mission No. 20," December 26, 1944.
20. Changnon, "Editor's Introduction."
21. 40th Bomb Group, "Group History, 1 December 1944 through 31 December 1944," January 23, 1945.
22. G. M. Etherington, "Disaster and Capture," *40th Bomb Group Association Memories*, Issue #6, No date.
23. Julian Cochran, "Memories of Julian Cochran," *40th Bomb Group Association Memories*, Issue #6, No date.
24. Etherington, "Disaster and Capture."
25. Cochran, "Memories of Julian Cochran."
26. Ibid. For more information on Allied POWs held in Rangoon see: Jean Newland, *Guests of the Emperor: Allied POWs of WWII in Rangoon, Burma.* (Bloomington, IN: AuthorHouse, 2012).
27. Norman Larsen, "The Fate of POW 1117 in the Rangoon Air Disaster," *40th Bomb Group Association Memories*, Issue #32, April 1990.
28. Ibid.
29. Wilbur H. Morrison, *Point of No Return: The Story of the 20th Air Force,* (New York: Times Books, 1979), 153.
30. Gen. Curtis LeMay and Bill Yenne, *Superfortress: The Story of the B-29 and American Air Power.* (New York: McGraw-Hill Book Company, 1988), 91.
31. XX Bomber Command, "Tactical Mission Report, Field Order No. 21," Mission No. 21," January 4, 1945.
32. Ibid.
33. Ibid.
34. XX Bomber Command, January 4, 1945; 444th Bomb Group, "History December 1944," January 5, 1945.
35. XX Bomber Command, January 4, 1945.
36. LeMay and Yenne, *Superfortress: The Story of the B-29 and American Air Power*, 91.
37. XX Bomber Command, "Tactical Mission Report, Field Order No. 22, Mission No. 22," January 9, 1945.
38. Ibid.
39. Ibid.
40. Ibid.
41. Ibid.
42. Ibid.
43. 40th Bomb Group, "Group History, 1 December 1944 to 30 December 1944," January 23, 1945.
44. 462nd Bomb Group, "Historical Data, December 1944," January 5, 1945.
45. John Elliott and others, "Beaufighter Shoots Down B-29 #331 over Burma," *40th Bomb Group Association Memories*, Issue #57, December 1995.
46. Ibid.
47. 444th Bomb Group, "History," September 30, 1944.
48. XX Bomber Command, "Tactical Mission Report, Field Order No. 23, Mission No. 23," January 11, 1945.
49. Ibid.
50. Ibid.
51. 40th Bomb Group, "Group History, 1 December 1944 to 30 December 1944," January 23, 1945.
52. XX Bomber Command, "Tactical Mission Report, Field Order No. 23, Mission No. 23," January 11, 1945.
53. Ibid.
54. United States Army Air Force. Missing Air Crew Report #10592, December 23, 1944, with attachment dated October 8, 1945.
55. Takaki and Sakaida, *B-29 Hunters of the JAAF, Osprey Aviation Elite #5*, p. 23.

Chapter 9

1. J. L. Cate, "Exit Matterhorn," in W. F. Craven and J. L. Cate, *The Army Air Forces in World War II, Volume V, The Pacific: Matterhorn to Nagasaki June 1944 to August 1945.* (Chicago: University of Chicago Press, 1953), 156–158.
2. XX Bomber Command, "Tactical Mission Report, Field Order No. 24," Mission No. 24, January 12, 1945.
3. XX Bomber Command, January 12, 1945; 40th Bomb Group, "Group History, 1 January through 31 January 1945," February 3, 1945; 462nd Bomb Group, "Historical Data January 1945," February 5, 1945.
4. XX Bomber Command, January 12, 1945.
5. XX Bomber Command, "Tactical Mission Report, Field Order No. 25, Mission No. 25," January 26, 1945.

6. XX Bomber Command, January 26, 1945; 468th Bomb Group, "Headquarters 468th Bombardment Group January 1945," No publication date.
7. XX Bomber Command, January 26, 1945; 40th Bomb Group, "Group History, 1 January through 31 January 1945," February 3, 1945; 462nd Bomb Group, "Historical Data January 1945," February 5, 1945; 468th Bomb Group, "Headquarters 468th Bombardment Group January 1945," No publication date.
8. XX Bomber Command, January 26, 1945.
9. XX Bomber Command, "Tactical Mission Report, Field Order No. 26, Mission No. 26," January 28, 1945.
10. Ibid.
11. Ibid.
12. XX Bomber Command, "Tactical Mission Report, Field Order No. 27, Mission No. 27," February 2, 1945.
13. Ibid.
14. XX Bomber Command, February 2, 1945; 444th Bomb Group, "History January 1945," February 6, 1945; 462nd Bomb Group, "Historical Data January 1945," February 5, 1945.
15. XX Bomber Command, February 2, 1945.
16. Ibid.
17. Ibid.
18. Ibid.
19. XX Bomber Command, February 2, 1945; 40th Bomb Group, "Group History, 1 January through 31 January 1945," February 3, 1945; 444th Bomb Group, "History January 1945," February 6, 1945; 462nd Bomb Group, "Historical Data January 1945," February 5, 1945; 468th Bomb Group, "Headquarters 468th Bombardment Group January 1945," No publication date.
20. XX Bomber Command, February 2, 1945.
21. Ibid.
22. United States Army Air Force, "Missing Air Crew Report #10879," January 29, 1945, with attachments.
23. XX Bomber Command, February 2, 1945; 468th Bomb Group, "Headquarters 468th Bombardment Group January 1945," No publication date.
24. XX Bomber Command, February 2, 1945.
25. 40th Bomb Group, "Group History, 1 January through 31 January 1945," February 3, 1945.
26. XX Bomber Command, "Tactical Mission Report, Field Order No.28, Mission No. 28, February 6, 1945.
27. Ibid.
28. Ibid.
29. XX Bomber Command, "Tactical Mission Report, Field Order No. 29, Mission No. 29," February 9, 1945.
30. XX Bomber Command, February 9, 1945; 40th Bomb Group, "Group History, 1 January through 31 January 1945," February 3, 1945; 444th Bomb Group, "History January 1945," February 6, 1945; 462nd Bomb Group, "Historical Data January 1945," February 5, 1945; 468th Bomb Group, "Headquarters 468th Bombardment Group January 1945," No publication date.
31. XX Bomber Command, February 9, 1945.
32. Ibid.
33. XX Bomber Command, February 9, 1945; 40th Bomb Group, "Group History, 1 January through 31 January 1945," February 3, 1945; 468th Bomb Group, "Headquarters 468th Bombardment Group January 1945," No publication date.
34. XX Bomber Command, "Tactical Mission Report, Field Order No. 30 and 31, Missions No. 30 and 31," February 16, 1945.
35. XX Bomber Command, February 16, 1945; 462nd Bomb Group, "Historical Data January 1945," February 5, 1945.
36. XX Bomber Command, February 16, 1945.
37. Ibid.
38. For more information on the German submarines based at Penang, see: Lawrence Paterson, *Hitler's Grey Wolves: U–Boats in the Indian Ocean.* (Greenhill Books, 2006).
39. XX Bomber Command, February 16, 1945; 444th Bomb Group, "History January 1945," February 6, 1945.
40. Ibid.
41. XX Bomber Command, "Tactical Mission Report, Field Order No. 32, Mission No. 32," February 20, 1945.
42. XX Bomber Command, February 20, 1945; 40th Bomb Group, "Group History, 1 January through 31 January 1945," February 3, 1945.
43. XX Bomber Command, February 20, 1945.

Chapter 10

1. XX Bomber Command, "Tactical Mission Report, Field Order No. 33," Mission No. 33, February 24, 1945.
2. Ibid.
3. Ibid.
4. XX Bomber Command, February 24, 1945; 444th Bomb Group, "History February 1945," March 5, 1945.
5. 444th Bomb Group, "History February 1945," March 5, 1945.
6. XX Bomber Command, February 24, 1945; 444th Bomb Group, "History February 1945," March 5, 1945.

7. XX Bomber Command, February 24, 1945; 40th Bomb Group, "1 February 1945 through 28 February 1945," March 4, 1945.
8. XX Bomber Command, February 24, 1945.
9. Ibid.
10. Ibid.
11. XX Bomber Command, "Tactical Mission Report, Field Order No. 34," Mission No. 34, March 1, 1945.
12. XX Bomber Command, March 1, 1945; 462nd Bomb Group, "Historical Data February 1945," March 5, 1945.
13. XX Bomber Command, March 1, 1945; 444th Bomb Group, "History February 1945," March 5, 1945.
14. XX Bomber Command, March 1, 1945; 462nd Bomb Group, "Historical Data February 1945," March 5, 1945.
15. Ibid.
16. XX Bomber Command, March 1, 1945.
17. XX Bomber Command, "Tactical Mission Report, Field Order No.35," Mission No. 35, March 3, 1945.
18. Ibid.
19. XX Bomber Command, March 3, 1945; 468th Bomb Group, "Headquarters 468th Bombardment Group February 1945," No publication date.
20. XX Bomber Command, March 3, 1945.
21. Ibid.
22. Ira Matthews, "The Rama VI Bridge," *Eighty-One War Stories*. 40th Bomb Group Association.
23. XX Bomber Command, "Tactical Mission Report, Field Order No. 36," Mission No. 36, March 8, 1945.
24. Ibid.
25. Ibid.
26. XX Bomber Command, March 8, 1945; 462nd Bomb Group, "Historical Data February 1945," March 5, 1945.
27. XX Bomber Command, March 8, 1945.
28. Ibid.
29. XX Bomber Command, March 8, 1945; 462nd Bomb Group, "Historical Data February 1945," March 5, 1945.
30. XX Bomber Command, March 8, 1945.
31. XX Bomber Command, "Tactical Mission Report, Field Order No. 37," Mission No. 37, March 10, 1945.
32. XX Bomber Command, March 10, 1945; 444th Bomb Group, "History February 1945," March 5, 1945.
33. XX Bomber Command, March 10, 1945.
34. Ibid.
35. XX Bomber Command, "Tactical Mission Report, Field Order No. 38," Mission No. 38, March 13, 1945.
36. XX Bomber Command, March 13, 1945; 40th Bomb Group, "1 February 1945 through 28 February 1945," March 4, 1945; 444th Bomb Group, "History February 1945," March 5, 1945; 462nd Bomb Group, "Historical Data February 1945," March 5, 1945; 468th Bomb Group, "Headquarters 468th Bombardment Group February 1945," No publication date.
37. XX Bomber Command, March 13, 1945; 40th Bomb Group, "1 February 1945 through 28 February 1945," March 4, 1945.
38. Robert Hall, "Battle Damage over Singapore," *40th Bomb Group Association Memories*, Issue #2, No publication date.
39. Ibid.
40. XX Bomber Command, March 13, 1945; 40th Bomb Group, "1 February 1945 through 28 February 1945," March 4, 1945; 444th Bomb Group, "History February 1945," March 5, 1945; 462nd Bomb Group, "Historical Data February 1945," March 5, 1945; 468th Bomb Group, "Headquarters 468th Bombardment Group February 1945," No publication date.
41. XX Bomber Command, March 13, 1945.
42. Ibid.
43. Jim Lyons, John Topolski, Anthony P. Peleckis, Louis Sandrick, and Larry Dover, "Bail Out and Rescue of Jim Lyons' Crew in #804," *40th Bomb Group Association Memories*, Issue #21, May 1988.
44. Ibid.
45. Ibid.
46. Ibid.
47. Ibid.
48. Ibid.
49. Ibid.
50. Ibid; 444th Bomb Group, "History February 1945," March 5, 1945.
51. XX Bomber Command, "Tactical Mission Report, Field Order No. 40," Mission No. 40, March 19, 1945.
52. Ibid.

Chapter 11

1. XX Bomber Command, "Tactical Mission Report, Field Order No. 41," Mission No. 41. March 23, 1945.
2. XX Bomber Command, March 23, 1945; 40th Bomb Group, "1 March 1945 through 31 March 1945," April 3, 1945; 468th Bomb Group, "Headquarters 468th Bombardment Group March 1945," No publication date.
3. XX Bomber Command, March 23, 1945; 462nd Bomb Group, "Historical Data March 1945," April 5, 1945.
4. XX Bomber Command, March 23, 1945.

5. Ibid.
6. Ibid.
7. XX Bomber Command, March 23, 1945; 444th Bomb Group, "History March 1945," April 15, 1945.
8. XX Bomber Command, "Tactical Mission Report, Field Order No. 39," Mission No. 39. March 18, 1945.
9. Ibid.
10. XX Bomber Command, "Tactical Mission Report, Field Order No. 43," Mission No. 43. March 31, 1945.
11. XX Bomber Command, March 31, 1945; 468th Bomb Group, "Headquarters 468th Bombardment Group March 1945," No publication date.
12. XX Bomber Command, March 31, 1945.
13. XX Bomber Command, March 31, 1945; 468th Bomb Group, "Headquarters 468th Bombardment Group March 1945," No publication date.
14. XX Bomber Command, "Tactical Mission Report, Field Order No. 42," Mission No. 42. March 29, 1945.
15. XX Bomber Command, March 29, 1945; 444th Bomb Group, "History March 1945," April 15, 1945; 462nd Bomb Group, "Historical Data March 1945," April 5, 1945.
16. XX Bomber Command, March 29, 1945; 40th Bomb Group, "1 March 1945 through 31 March 1945," April 3, 1945.
17. XX Bomber Command, March 29, 1945.
18. XX Bomber Command, March 29, 1945; 462nd Bomb Group, "Historical Data March 1945," April 5, 1945.
19. XX Bomber Command, "Tactical Mission Report, Field Order No. 44," Mission No. 44. March 17, 1945.
20. Ibid.
21. Ibid.
22. XX Bomber Command, "Tactical Mission Report, Field Order No. 45," Mission No. 45. April 8, 1945.
23. Ibid.
24. XX Bomber Command, "Tactical Mission Report, Field Order No. 46," Mission No. 46. April 15, 1945.
25. Ibid.
26. XX Bomber Command, "Tactical Mission Report, Field Order No. 47," Mission No. 47. April 18, 1945.
27. XX Bomber Command, April 18, 1945; 468th Bomb Group, "Headquarters 468th Bombardment Group March 1945," No publication date.
28. XX Bomber Command, April 18, 1945.
29. XX Bomber Command, "Tactical Mission Report, Field Order No. 48," Mission No. 48. April 18, 1945.
30. XX Bomber Command, April 18, 1945; 444th Bomb Group, "History March 1945," April 15, 1945.
31. XX Bomber Command, "Tactical Mission Report, Field Order No.49," Mission No. 49. April 13, 1945.
32. Ibid.
33. Ibid.
34. For a brief review of the politics and inter- and intra-service rivalries behind the establishment and command selection of USASTAF, see: Frank Futrell and James Taylor, "Reorganization for Victory," in W. F. Craven and J. L. Cate, *The Army Air Forces in World War II, Volume V, The Pacific: Matterhorn to Nagasaki June 1944 to August 1945.* (Chicago: University of Chicago Press, 1953), 676–702.
35. For more information on the post-World War II operations of the B-29, see Graham M. Simon, *B-29 Superfortress: Giant Bomber of World War Two and Korea.* (Barnsley, UK: Pen and Sword Aviation, 2012).

INDEX